Introduction to United States International Taxation

Introduction to United States International Taxation

Seventh Edition

James R. Repetti
Diane M. Ring
Stephen E. Shay

Wolters Kluwer

Published by:
Kluwer Law International B.V.
PO Box 316
2400 AH Alphen aan den Rijn
The Netherlands
E-mail: international-sales@wolterskluwer.com
Website: lrus.wolterskluwer.com

Sold and distributed by:
Wolters Kluwer Legal & Regulatory U.S.
7201 McKinney Circle
Frederick, MD 21704
United States of America
E-mail: customer.service@wolterskluwer.com

ISBN 978-94-035-2385-9

e-Book: ISBN 978-94-035-2390-3
web-PDF: ISBN 978-94-035-2391-0

About the Authors

Professor James R. Repetti is the inaugural holder of the William J. Kenealy, S.J. Chair at Boston College Law School. He is an author of the texts, *Partnership Income Taxation, Introduction to United States International Taxation, Federal Wealth Transfer Taxation, Problems in Federal Wealth Transfer Taxation,* and *Tax Aspects of Organizing and Operating a Business.* He has acted as a consultant to the US Senate, Internal Revenue Service, and Justice Department, and has appeared as a commentator in publications such as the *Washington Post, Wall Street Journal, Bloomberg, Marketplace, Boston Globe, Christian Science Monitor, and Forbes Magazine.* He holds an A.B. from Harvard University and a J.D. and M.B.A. from Boston College.

Diane M. Ring currently serves as the Associate Dean of Faculty, Professor of Law, and the Dr. Thomas F. Carney Distinguished Scholar at Boston College Law. She researches and writes primarily in the fields of international taxation, corporate taxation, labor and taxation, and ethical issues in tax practice. Her recent work addresses issues including information exchange, tax leaks, international tax relations, regulation in the pandemic, sharing economy and human equity transactions, and ethics in international tax. Diane was a consultant for the United Nation's 2014 project on tax base protection for developing countries, and the U.N.'s 2013 project on treaty administration for developing countries. She is currently Special Advisor to VIRTEU (VAT fraud: Interdisciplinary Research on Tax Crimes), a 2020-2021 research project funded by the European Union under the HERCULE III programme targeting the relationship between corruption and tax fraud. She is also the co-author in three casebooks in taxation—one on international taxation, one on corporate taxation, and one on ethical problems in federal tax practice. Diane was the IBFD 2019 Professor in Residence in Amsterdam.

Prior to joining Boston College Law School, Diane was an Associate Professor of Law at the University of Florida Levin College of Law, and an Assistant Professor at Harvard Law School. Before entering academia, she practiced in Washington, D.C., and clerked for Judge Jon O. Newman of the Second Circuit Court of Appeals. She received her A.B. and J.D. from Harvard University.

Stephen E. Shay is the Paulus Endowment Senior Tax Fellow at Boston College Law School. Mr. Shay previously has served as Deputy Assistant Secretary for International Tax Affairs in the United States Department of the Treasury in the Obama Administration and was in private practice as a tax partner with Ropes & Gray, LLP. He has been a Professor of Practice at Harvard Law School and a Lecturer at Yale Law School, University of Oxford, and the Leiden International Tax Institute. Mr. Shay consults for international organizations and private parties and has testified numerous times before Congress. He is a 1972 graduate of Wesleyan University, and he earned his J.D. and his M.B.A. from Columbia University in 1976.

Table of Contents

About the Authors v

Preface xvii

CHAPTER 1
Introduction 1

CHAPTER 2
The United States Income Tax System: General Description 5

2.1 Introduction 5

2.1.1 Scope 5

2.1.2 Classification Issues 5

2.2 The Corporation Income Tax 7

2.2.1 Tax Rates 7

2.2.2 The Tax Base 7

2.2.2.1 Gross Income 7

2.2.2.2 Deductible Expenditures 8

2.2.2.3 Expenditures Not Deductible 10

2.2.2.4 Special Limitations on Tax Shelter Losses 11

2.2.2.5 Special Limitations on Deductibility of Corporate Interest Expense 11

2.2.2.6 Net Operating Loss Carryforward and Carryback 11

2.2.3 Capital Gains and Losses 12

2.2.4 Credits Against Tax 13

2.2.5 Transactions Between Corporations and Shareholders 14

2.2.6 Penalty Taxes 17

2.2.6.1 Accumulated Earnings Tax 17

2.2.6.2 Personal Holding Company Tax 17

2.3 The Individual Income Tax 18

2.3.1 Tax Rates 18

2.3.2 The Tax Base 18
2.3.2.1 Gross Income 18
2.3.2.2 Dividends and Capital Gains and Losses 19
2.3.2.3 Deductible Expenditures: Business and Investment 20
2.3.2.4 Expenditures Not Deductible 21
2.3.2.5 Special Limitations on Tax Shelter Losses, Interest Deductions, and Trade or Business Expenses 21
2.3.2.5.1 Limitation of Deductions to Amount at Risk 21
2.3.2.5.2 Limitations on the Deduction for Interest Expense 22
2.3.2.5.3 Limitations on the Deduction of Passive Activity Losses 24
2.3.2.5.4 Limitations on Deductibility of Trade or Business Expenses 25
2.3.2.6 Deductible Expenditures: Personal and Mixed Business-Personal 25
2.3.3 Credits Against Tax 26
2.3.4 Alternative Minimum Tax: Individuals 26
2.4 Trusts 27
2.5 Partnerships 27
2.6 S Corporations 29
2.7 Other Flow Through Entities 29
2.7.1 Regulated Investment Company (RIC) 29
2.7.2 Real Estate Investment Trust (REIT) 30
2.7.3 Real Estate Mortgage Investment Conduit (REMIC) 30
2.8 Accounting Aspects 30
2.9 Statute of Limitations, Information Reporting, and Penalties 32

CHAPTER 3
Jurisdictional Principles 35

CHAPTER 4
Source Rules 41
4.1 General 41
4.2 Application of Source Rules to Specific Items of Gross Income 42
4.2.1 Interest 43
4.2.2 Dividends 44
4.2.3 Personal Services Income 44
4.2.4 Rents and Royalties 45
4.2.5 Gains from Disposition of Real Property 46
4.2.6 Gains from Sale of Personal Property 46
4.2.7 Insurance Underwriting Income 48

4.3 Application of Source Rules to Other Items of Income 48
4.4 Allocation of Deductions to Arrive at Taxable Income 50
4.4.1 Background 50
4.4.2 General Rules 50
4.4.3 Special Rules 52
4.4.3.1 Interest 52
4.4.3.1.1 General 52
4.4.3.1.2 Elective Worldwide Allocation 53
4.4.3.1.3 Foreign Taxpayers 54
4.4.3.1.4 Anti-abuse 55
4.4.3.1.5 Partnerships 56
4.4.3.2 Research and Experimentation Expenses 56
4.4.3.3 Stewardship and Other Expenses 58

CHAPTER 5
Income Taxation of Nonresident Aliens and Foreign Corporations 61
5.1 Introduction 61
5.2 The "Trade or Business" Concept 62
5.2.1 Background 62
5.2.2 The Existence of a Trade or Business 63
5.2.3 The Location of a Trade or Business in the United States 65
5.2.4 Impact of Treaties on US Trade or Business 66
5.3 The "Effectively Connected" Concept 67
5.3.1 General 67
5.3.2 Capital Gains and Fixed or Determinable Income 69
5.3.2.1 The "Asset Use" Test 69
5.3.2.2 The "Business Activities" Test 70
5.3.2.3 Other Income 70
5.3.2.4 Foreign Source Income Effectively Connected with a US Business 71
5.4 Gains from the Disposition of Real Property interests 73
5.5 Taxation of Nonresident Aliens 75
5.5.1 General 75
5.5.2 Determination of Status as Resident or Nonresident 75
5.5.2.1 The Permanent Residence Test 76
5.5.2.2 The Substantial Presence Test 76
5.5.2.3 The First Year Election 77
5.5.3 Income Taxed at 30% Rate 78
5.5.4 Income Taxed at Full US Progressive Tax Rates 79
5.5.5 Exempt Income 79
5.5.5.1 Bank Deposits 80
5.5.5.2 Dividends from Foreign Business Income 80
5.5.5.3 Portfolio Interest 80
5.5.5.4 Capital Gains 81
5.5.6 Treaties 81

5.5.7 Taxation of Nonresident Aliens Who Are Former US Citizens or Legal Permanent Residents 81
5.5.7.1 Covered Expatriates: Former US Citizens 82
5.5.7.2 Covered Expatriates: Former US Residents 82
5.5.7.3 Deferral of Payment 82
5.6 Taxation of Foreign Corporations 83
5.6.1 General 83
5.6.2 Income of Foreign Corporations Taxed at 30% Rate 83
5.6.3 Income of Foreign Corporations Taxed at Normal Corporation Tax Rates 83
5.6.4 Exempt Income 84
5.6.5 Branch Profits Tax 84
5.6.5.1 Background 84
5.6.5.2 Structure of the Branch Profits Tax 84
5.6.5.3 Treaty Aspects 86
5.6.6 Branch Interest Tax 87
5.6.6.1 General 87
5.6.6.2 Treaty Aspects 88
5.6.7 Penalty Taxes Applicable to Foreign Corporations and Domestic Corporations with Foreign Shareholders 88
5.6.7.1 Accumulated Earnings Tax 88
5.6.7.1.1 Foreign Corporations with US Income 88
5.6.7.1.2 Foreign Shareholders in Domestic Corporations 89
5.6.7.2 Personal Holding Company Tax 89
5.6.8 Comparison of Branch and Subsidiary Operations 89
5.7 Taxation of Foreign Partnerships and Foreign Partners 90
5.7.1 Foreign Partnerships 90
5.7.2 Foreign Partners in a US or Foreign Partnership 90
5.8 Taxation of Foreign Trusts and Foreign Beneficiaries 91
5.8.1 Foreign Trusts 91
5.8.1.1 Classification Issues 91
5.8.1.2 Taxation of Foreign Trusts 92
5.8.2 Taxation of Foreign Beneficiaries 93
5.8.3 Foreign Grantor Trusts 93
5.9 Procedural Aspects 94
5.9.1 Return and Disclosure Requirements 94
5.9.2 Withholding at Source 95
5.9.2.1 Fixed or Determinable Income 95
5.9.2.2 Disposition of US Real Property Interests 96
5.9.2.3 Withholding on Foreign Partners 97
5.10 Base Erosion Anti-Abuse Tax ("BEAT") 97
5.11 Foreign Account Tax Compliance Act ("FATCA") 98

CHAPTER 6
Treatment of Foreign Business Operations and Investments by US Persons 101
6.1 Introduction 101
6.2 Reasons for the Partial Shift from Deferral to Current Taxation and Dividend Exemption 103
6.2.1 Brief Overview of How GILTI Applies to Controlled Foreign Corporations 106
6.2.2 Non-controlled Foreign Corporations 109
6.2.3 Summary 109
6.3 Business Operations Through Foreign Corporations Controlled by US Persons: Subpart F 109
6.3.1 The Structure of Subpart F 109
6.3.2 Tax Treatment of US Shareholders 110
6.3.3 Definition of a CFC 111
6.3.4 Income Taxable to US Shareholders 112
6.3.4.1 Subpart F Income 112
6.3.4.2 Earnings Invested in US Property 116
6.3.5 Foreign Tax Credit 118
6.3.6 Distributions and Adjustments to Basis 118
6.3.7 Denial of Deferral Benefits for Boycott Income and Foreign Bribes and to Achieve Other US Foreign Policy Objectives 118
6.3.8 Disposition of Stock in a Controlled Foreign Corporation: Section 1248 119
6.3.8.1 Background 119
6.3.8.2 Scope of Coverage 119
6.3.8.3 Calculation of Tax 120
6.3.9 Deemed Repatriation Tax on Deferred Earnings 120
6.4 Global Intangible Low-Taxed Income (GILTI) 122
6.4.1 Background 122
6.4.2 Shareholder Level Determination of GILTI 123
6.4.3 Shareholder Level Taxation of GILTI 124
6.4.3.1 Corporate US Shareholder 124
6.4.3.2 Individual US Shareholder 125
6.5 Foreign Dividend Exemption 125
6.5.1 Corporate US Shareholder's Section 245A DRD 125
6.5.2 Dividends from Controlled Foreign Corporations 126
6.5.3 Effective Date and Extraordinary Transactions 126

CHAPTER 7
Formation, Reorganization, and Liquidation of Foreign Corporations: Section 367 129
7.1 Background 129
7.1.1 Section 351: Formation of Corporation and Transfers of Stock to Controlling Stockholders in Exchange for Property 130
7.1.2 Reorganizations 130

7.1.3 Liquidations 132
7.2 Application of Section 367(a) 132
7.2.1 General 132
7.2.2 "Outbound" Transfers 132
7.2.3 Transfers of Assets Other than Intangibles or Stock and the Branch Loss Recapture Rule 133
7.2.4 Transfers of Intangibles 135
7.2.5 Transfers of Stock 136
7.2.6 Spin-Offs 137
7.2.7 Liquidations 138
7.3 Section 367(b) and the Repatriation of Earnings and Profits 138
7.3.1 Outbound Transfers to Other Entities 140
7.4 Section 1248 and Section 367(b) 141
7.5 Inversions 142

CHAPTER 8
Foreign Investment Activities by US Persons Utilizing Foreign Corporations 145
8.1 Background 145
8.2 Passive Foreign Investment Companies 146
8.2.1 Definition of Passive Foreign Investment Company (PFIC) 146
8.2.2 Imposition of an "Interest Charge" on US Shareholders 147
8.2.3 Qualified Electing Funds 148
8.2.4 Mark-to-Market Election 149
8.2.5 Relation Between PFIC and Subpart F 150
8.3 Investment Through Foreign Trusts 150
8.3.1 Background 150
8.3.2 Foreign Grantor Trusts 150
8.3.3 Transfers to and Distributions from Non-grantor Trusts 151
8.3.4 Procedural Aspects 152

CHAPTER 9
Taxation of Foreign Source Income of US Persons: The Foreign Tax Credit 153
9.1 General 153
9.2 Treatment of Foreign Taxes in General 153
9.3 Objectives of the Foreign Tax Credit 154
9.4 The Direct Foreign Tax Credit 157
9.4.1 Eligibility for Tax Credit 157
9.4.1.1 Persons Eligible 157
9.4.1.2 Taxes Eligible 157
9.4.2 In Lieu of Taxes 160
9.4.3 Time and Manner of Claiming Credit 160
9.4.4 Nonresident Aliens and Foreign Corporations 161
9.5 The Indirect Foreign Tax Credit 161
9.5.1 Corporate US Shareholders 161

9.5.2 Individual US Shareholders 164
9.6 Responses to Foreign Tax Credit Abuse 165
9.6.1 Dividend Sale Transactions 165
9.6.2 Foreign Tax Credit Generator Transactions 166
9.6.3 Additional Anti-abuse Provisions 166
9.6.3.1 The Problem 166
9.6.3.2 Section 909 Foreign Tax Credit Splitter Rules and Technical Taxpayer Regulations 167
9.6.4 Covered Asset Acquisition 168

CHAPTER 10
Limitations on the Foreign Tax Credit 171
10.1 Historical Background 171
10.1.1 Limitations on the Foreign Tax Credit: Introduction of Baskets 171
10.1.2 The Passive Category Income and General Category Income Baskets 175
10.2 The Two New Post-2017 Limitation Categories 178
10.2.1 The GILTI Category 179
10.2.2 The Foreign Branch Category 180
10.2.3 Carryback and Carryover of Excess Credits 180
10.2.4 Income that Would Previously Have Been Placed in a Different Basket 181
10.3 The Look-Through Rules 181
10.3.1 Dividends, Interest, Rents, and Royalties from Controlled Foreign Corporations 181
10.3.2 Dividends from Noncontrolled Section 902 Corporations 182
10.4 The Treatment of Losses 182
10.4.1 Foreign Losses 182
10.4.2 US Losses 184
10.5 Special Limitations on the Foreign Tax Credit 185
10.6 Relief for Small Investors 185
10.7 Foreign Tax Credits and Treaties 185
10.8 Summary Perspectives on the Foreign Tax Credit Mechanism 186

CHAPTER 11
Special Treatment of Foreign Income 189
11.1 General 189
11.2 Incentives to Increase US Exports 189
11.2.1 Background 189
11.2.2 A New Export Subsidy: The Deduction for Foreign Derived Intangible Income (FDII) 191
11.2.2.1 Background 191
11.2.2.2 The FDII Deduction 191
11.2.2.3 FDII and Treaties 194

11.2.3 Treatment of Income Earned Abroad 194
11.2.3.1 General 194
11.2.3.2 Eligibility for the Exclusion 195
11.2.3.3 The Foreign Earned Income Component 196
11.2.3.4 The Housing Cost Component 197
11.2.3.5 Election of Section 911 Benefits 198

CHAPTER 12
Transfer Pricing 199
12.1 Background 199
12.2 Scope of Coverage 201
12.3 General Approach 202
12.3.1 Determining Comparability 202
12.3.2 Arm's Length Ranges 204
12.3.3 Determining "the Transaction" 204
12.4 Specific Transactions 205
12.4.1 Sales of Goods 205
12.4.1.1 Comparable Uncontrolled Price Method 206
12.4.1.2 Resale Price Method 206
12.4.1.3 Cost Plus Method 207
12.4.1.4 Comparable Profits Method 208
12.4.1.4.1 Profit Level Indicators 208
12.4.1.4.2 Calculating Operating Profit 208
12.4.1.5 Profit Split 209
12.4.2 Intangibles 210
12.4.2.1 Comparable Uncontrolled Transaction 211
12.4.2.2 Cost Sharing Agreements 212
12.4.3 Services 215
12.4.4 Loans 216
12.5 Other Aspects of Section 482 Allocations 217
12.5.1 Set Offs 217
12.5.2 Correlative Adjustments 218
12.5.3 Adjustments of Accounts after Section 482 Allocation 218
12.6 International Aspects 219
12.6.1 Treaties 219
12.6.2 Foreign Tax Credit 219
12.6.3 Blocked Income 220
12.7 Advance Pricing Agreements 221
12.8 Accuracy-Related Penalties 223

CHAPTER 13
Foreign Currency Issues 225
13.1 Background 225
13.2 Basic Concepts 227
13.2.1 Functional Currency and Qualified Business Unit 227

13.2.2 Translation of Foreign Currency Income and Foreign Taxes into Dollars 228
13.2.2.1 Translation of Branch Operations 228
13.2.2.2 Translation of Corporate Earnings and Profits 231
13.2.2.3 Translation of Foreign Taxes 232
13.3 Transactions in a Nonfunctional Currency 232
13.3.1 "Section 988 Transactions" 233
13.3.2 Foreign Exchange Futures Contracts, Hedges, and Other Financial Transactions 234
13.3.3 Other Transactions 235

CHAPTER 14
Income Tax Treaties 237
14.1 Background 237
14.2 Treaty Objectives and Techniques 238
14.3 Status of Treaties 241
14.4 Qualification for Treaty Benefits 242
14.4.1 Persons Covered 242
14.4.1.1 "Tiebreaker" Clause 242
14.4.1.2 "Hybrid" Entities 243
14.4.1.3 "Saving Clause" 245
14.4.2 Disclosure Requirements 245
14.4.3 Limitation on Treaty Benefits 246
14.4.3.1 Background 246
14.4.3.2 Structure of Limitation on Benefits Article 247
14.4.4 Overall Evaluation of Limitation on Benefits Provisions 248
14.4.5 New "Special Tax Regime" Rule 249
14.4.6 Taxes Covered 250
14.5 Treatment of Business Income 250
14.5.1 In General 250
14.5.2 Permanent Establishment 251
14.5.3 Business Profits 253
14.5.4 "Attributable To" 253
14.6 Treatment of Investment Income 255
14.6.1 In General 255
14.6.2 Classification Issues 255
14.7 Real Property 256
14.8 Gains from the Disposition of Property 256
14.9 Treatment of Personal Services Income 256
14.9.1 Employees 256
14.9.2 Independent Personal Services 257
14.10 Foreign Tax Credit Aspects 258
14.11 Nondiscrimination 259
14.12 Administrative Provisions 261
14.12.1 Competent Authority Provisions 261

14.12.2 Mandatory Arbitration 262
14.12.3 Exchange of Information 262

CHAPTER 15
Wealth Transfer Taxation 265
15.1 The US Wealth Transfer Tax System: General Description 265
15.1.1 Background 265
15.1.2 The Estate Tax on US Citizens and Residents 266
15.1.3 The Gift Tax on US Citizens and Residents 268
15.1.4 The Generation-Skipping Tax 269
15.2 Jurisdictional Principles 270
15.3 Estate Tax: International Aspects 271
15.3.1 Situs Rules 271
15.3.1.1 Property Situated Within the United States 271
15.3.1.2 Property Situated Outside the United States 272
15.3.2 US Taxation of Citizens and Resident Aliens: The Foreign Tax Credit 273
15.3.3 Estate Taxation of Nonresident Aliens 274
15.4 Gift Tax: International Aspects 275
15.4.1 Gift Taxation of US Citizens and Resident Aliens 275
15.4.2 Gift Taxation of Nonresident Aliens 275
15.5 The Generation-Skipping Tax: International Aspects 275
15.6 Expatriation to Avoid Transfer Taxes 276
15.6.1 Estate Tax for Taxpayers Who Expatriated Before June 17, 2008 276
15.6.2 Gift Tax for Taxpayers Who Expatriated Before June 17, 2008 277
15.6.3 Estate and Gift Tax for Taxpayers Who Expatriated on or after June 17, 2008 277
15.7 Wealth Transfer Tax Treaties 278
15.7.1 Background 278
15.7.2 Domicile 278
15.7.3 Rules for Taxation 279
15.7.3.1 Real Property 279
15.7.3.2 Business Property 279
15.7.3.3 Other Property 279
15.7.4 Deductions and Exemptions 280
15.7.5 Relief from Double Taxation 280

Index 281

Preface

The 2021 edition of Introduction to United States International Taxation, as did its predecessor editions, presents the basic principles and rules of the US international tax system in a relatively brief and manageable form. We emphasize the word "Introduction" in the title. The book is not intended to serve as an exhaustive treatise that discusses in depth the wealth of technical detail involved in applying US tax rules in an international context. Instead, the purpose is to provide an overview of the principles adopted by the US in taxing US or foreign individuals and corporations as they invest, work, or carry on a trade or business in the US or abroad.

This book seeks to accomplish two objectives. First, we provide a structural framework for analyzing a US tax problem. As a general matter, tax practitioners outside the US whose clients have activities in the US will rely on their US tax advisors for technical advice on the US tax aspects of their clients' transactions. This book is intended to enable the foreign tax advisor to place the material received from US advisors in the context of the overall structure of the US international tax system and thus be able to evaluate the advice received and to relate it to her own tax system.

The second objective is to help professors and students within and outside the US to obtain a grasp of the fundamentals of US international tax principles and rules. This book can serve as a text or supplement to courses that deal in whole or in part with the US tax system.

In line with these objectives, we have included references to the Internal Revenue Code provisions under discussion and to the more important Treasury Regulations that are issued interpreting the statutory rules. In addition, we have also included significant administrative announcements of the Internal Revenue Service (Revenue Rulings and Revenue Procedures) as well as references to important cases that have arisen. Many of these materials should be available through government websites, including the Internal Revenue Service (IRS) website. But we have attempted to insure that the text discussion of a provision is self-contained so that the reader will be able to obtain a general understanding of the matter under discussion without needing to resort to the footnote references. However, we did feel it important to provide sufficient reference materials so that the tax practitioner, professor, or student would have a starting point to examine in greater technical detail the explanation offered in the text. The footnote references are by no means exhaustive.

The statutory references throughout this book are to the Internal Revenue Code of 1986, as amended, and are given without further explanation as, for example, "Section 954." References to particular revenue legislation are made by the year of enactment and typically do not include the full name of the legislation. Thus, for example, the Tax Reform Act of 1986 is referred to as the "1986 Act" and the American Taxpayer Relief Act of 2012 as the "2012 Act." The rapid acceleration of tax legislative change in the US has required the use of numerous and highly important transition rules. As a general matter, transition rules are not discussed. Regulations issued by the Treasury Department in final form are cited, for example, "Treas. Reg. Sec. 1.954-1." Temporary Treasury Regulations, which are binding on taxpayers and tax administrators while in force, are cited, for example, "Temp. Treas. Reg. Sec. 1.861-12T." Proposed Regulations, which may not be relied upon until made final, are cited, for example, "Prop. Treas. Reg. Sec. 1.1411-3." Citations to the Internal Revenue Code and to the Treasury Regulations issued thereunder are current as of January 1, 2021.

We are greatly indebted to the two original authors of this book. Paul R. McDaniel passed away on July 16, 2010. We will miss greatly Paul's intellect, personal warmth, good humor. and guiding hand. We also thank Hugh J. Ault, who along with Paul, made this book what it is today. Hugh's encyclopedic knowledge and intellect shaped prior editions of this book in many ways and we miss his contributions. Lastly, we thank Reid Diaz, a student at Boston College Law School, for research assistance.

CHAPTER 1

Introduction

This book is intended to provide an introduction to the application of the US income and wealth transfer tax systems to taxpayers investing or transacting business in the US and other countries. The bulk of the materials deal with the income tax since this is the tax that affects most directly the day-to-day conduct of business and investment affairs by individuals and corporations. The wealth transfer tax system is dealt with in less detail, because within the US context it is a less fully developed tax than the income tax and is more limited in its application to international transactions. Other US taxes, such as the social security tax, the unemployment tax, various excise taxes, tariff duties, and state taxes are not considered in this book although, of course, it is possible for a particular taxpayer engaged in international transactions to encounter these taxes.

A grasp of the basic structure of the US income tax system as it is applied in its purely domestic context is essential to an understanding of the US international income tax system. These basic rules are always applied to US citizens and corporations in their international transactions and to foreign individuals or corporations engaged in a trade or business or investing in the US. Accordingly, Chapter 2 provides an overview of the US income tax system, briefly describing the corporation income tax, the individual income tax, the income tax treatment of partnerships and trusts, and accounting aspects of the US income tax. The purpose of the general description is to provide a structural framework against which the international tax rules may be considered. Where particular provisions have special significance in the international context, they are only cursorily considered in Chapter 2, with more detailed analysis deferred until subsequent chapters. This approach is adopted, for example, in the case of the provisions dealing with the various forms of tax-free corporate reorganizations (considered in Chapter 7).

The basic jurisdictional principles adopted by the US with respect to application of its income tax to international investment and business transactions are considered in Chapters 3 and 4. These provisions are fundamental and cut across all the situations dealt with in subsequent chapters. That is, the basic provisions governing jurisdiction and the source of income and deductions are applied alike to US taxpayers investing, working, or carrying on a trade or business abroad and to foreign individuals and corporations investing, earning income, or carrying on a trade or business in the US.

Chapter 5 then turns to the specific application of the income tax to foreign corporations and nonresident alien individuals. The material in this chapter examines the US rules for taxing foreign corporations, foreign partnerships, foreign trusts, and nonresident aliens on their business and investment income derived from US sources. Procedural aspects in the application of the tax are also considered.

Historically, one of the most controversial aspects of the US international tax structure has been the income tax treatment of foreign corporations controlled by US shareholders. Until the 2017 Tax Act, the US generally deferred taxes on the income of US controlled foreign corporations ("CFCs") until such income was distributed to US shareholders. The "subpart F" provisions sought to limit deferral to legitimate business income earned by CFCs. The 2017 Tax Act, while retaining subpart F, has significantly changed the US scheme of taxation. A new "GILTI" regime now allows a certain amount of a CFC's earnings to be exempt from US taxation entirely—both as the CFC earns it and, later, when it is distributed to US *corporate* shareholders as a dividend. (*Individual* US shareholders continue to have US tax deferred on this amount as it is earned by the CFC, but it becomes taxable when the CFC distributes it to them.) At the same time, the GILTI regime now taxes US shareholders currently on amounts of income earned by the CFC that exceed the amounts that are tax-free regardless of whether such income is distributed. It reduces the effective US tax on such income, however, from 21% to 10.5% (before taking account of certain deductions and foreign taxes) for US corporate shareholders. The operation of GILTI and subpart F and the roles they play in the overall US international income tax structure are examined in Chapter 6.

Chapter 7 discusses tax-free corporate reorganizations, which are often employed to achieve tax-free mergers and acquisitions. Chapter 7 then describes the ways in which these transactions may become taxable in situations involving transfers to or from foreign corporations.

Chapter 8 reviews the taxation of passive foreign investments by US persons utilizing foreign corporations not controlled by US persons.

The basic mechanism adopted by the US to alleviate international double taxation on foreign source income derived by US persons is the foreign tax credit. Chapter 9 discusses the credit, and Chapter 10 explains the limitations that apply to the credit. The 2017 Tax Act adds new foreign tax credit limits for foreign taxes on GILTI and also on foreign branch income. Chapter 10 describes the complex interaction of these new limitation categories with the exemption of foreign dividends (for which foreign tax credits are not allowed).

Chapter 11 explores the rules adopted starting in the 1970s to provide incentives for increased US exports (each was found to violate an international trade agreement and repealed) including the most recent attempt in the form of the "FDII" rules. FDII reduces from 21% to 13.125% the effective US tax on income of a US corporation arising from foreign sales and services according to a formula that seeks to apply the reduced tax rate to the US corporation's foreign income that is attributable to its intangible property. To that end, the formula treats income exceeding 10% of the corporation's domestic tangible assets as if attributable to intangible property. Then, the formula estimates the portion of this income due to intangible property that should be treated as foreign and secure the benefit of lower taxation. This amount is the same portion of total income from intangible property (calculated per the formula) as the corporation's foreign income from sales and services provided to foreign persons for foreign use bears to the corporation's total income. The reduced tax on profits in excess of 10% of domestic tangible assets is intended to encourage US corporations to not transfer intangible property overseas. The incentive instead is intended to encourage US corporations to retain intangible property in the US and license such property overseas. In addition to FDII, Chapter 11 also discusses tax incentives to encourage US individuals to work abroad.

The general inter-company pricing rules of Section 482 and special transfer pricing rules applicable to particular transactions, which are of importance to multinational corporations, are discussed in Chapter 12.

The US has adopted a comprehensive set of rules for the treatment of transactions involving currencies other than the US dollar (USD). Those provisions are described in Chapter 13.

Chapter 14 then turns to a consideration of the income tax treaties entered into by the United States. These bilateral treaties address the application of the signatories' own tax systems to particular transactions, types of income, and categories of taxpayers. The basic approach of the US in its income tax treaties is considered. Particular emphasis is placed on typical treaty provisions, especially those contained in the US Model Treaty, that deal with the matters considered in Chapters 3-13 and on the scope of and limitations on treaty benefits. The purpose of this discussion is to examine those situations in which US income tax treaty provisions modify the basic rules discussed in the preceding chapters and to identify major treaty provisions in flux.

Chapter 15 deals with the US wealth transfer tax system. As in the case of the income tax, a very general description is provided of the US wealth transfer tax system. The jurisdictional bases of the tax are considered. Then the three separate transfer taxes: estate tax, gift tax, and generation-skipping tax are examined in their application to transfers of property owned abroad by US citizens and property owned in the US by nonresident alien individuals. Estate and gift tax treaties entered into by the US are also discussed, again with the focus centering on the situations in which the treaty provisions modify the otherwise applicable wealth transfer tax rules.

CHAPTER 2

The United States Income Tax System: General Description

2.1 INTRODUCTION

2.1.1 Scope

This chapter describes the basic principles of US income taxation. The discussion in this section 2.1 focuses on the rules used by the US to classify an entity, whether foreign or domestic, as a corporation, partnership, or trust. Sections 2.2-2.6 then describe the US tax rules applicable to corporations, individuals, partnerships, and trusts. Relevant portions of subsequent chapters discuss the tests for determining when an entity or individual will be classified as foreign or domestic.

2.1.2 Classification Issues

An important initial determination is the proper classification of an entity for income tax purposes as a corporation, partnership, or trust. In general, US tax rules treat a corporation as a taxable entity that is separate from its owners. As a result, the corporation pays taxes on its income and its stockholders are taxed again on any earnings that the corporation may subsequently distribute to them. In contrast, a partnership is generally treated as a conduit, which does not pay taxes on its income. Rather the partnership's income and expenses are reported by the partners on their individual tax returns. A trust, in general, is treated as a separate taxable entity, if it has the ability to accumulate its income, or as a conduit, if it does not.

Detailed Treasury Regulations issued in 1996 (the so-called check-the-box regulations) provide extensive rules for classifying entities.[1] The term "check-the-box" refers to the ability of entity owners in some circumstances to select the tax classification of an entity. Under the Regulations, an entity that carries on a trade or business is classified as a corporation or a partnership.[2] In contrast, an entity that is protecting or conserving property and is not carrying on a trade or business is classified as a trust.

Certain entities are always classified as "corporations." The owners of these "per se" corporations are not allowed to select a different classification. In the domestic context the per se corporations include, among others, entities incorporated under US federal law or state corporate law, and insurance companies.[3] In the foreign context, certain entities such as the *Aktiengesellschaft* in Germany and the *Société Anonyme* in France are also classified as per se corporations.[4]

If a domestic entity is not classified as a per se corporation under the above rules, it is treated by default as a partnership if it has two or more owners or is disregarded as a separate entity from its owner if it has one owner.[5] The owner(s), however, may elect to have the entity treated as a corporation.[6] If a foreign entity is not classified as a per se corporation under the above rules, it is classified pursuant to default rules as a partnership if it has two or more owners and at least one of them does not have limited liability or as a corporation if all of its owners have limited liability.[7] Again, however, the owners of such foreign entity that is not a per se corporation may elect an alternative classification if they desire a classification other than that provided by the default rules. For example, if the default rules classify the entity as a corporation but the owner(s) desires to have it classified as a partnership or to be disregarded, the owners may elect such classification. One result of this elective regime is an increased number of situations in which the US classifies an entity as a partnership or a branch[8] and another country classifies it as a corporation, or vice versa, so-called hybrid entities. Hybrid entities are discussed at Chapter 14 section 14.4.1.2.

1. Treas. Reg. Sec. 301.7701-2(b). The regulations were generally effective in 1997. Prior to 1997, the regulations used a six-part test to determine whether an entity should be classified as an association taxable as a corporation, a partnership or a trust: (1) the existence of associates; (2) an object to carry on a business for profit; (3) continuity of life; (4) centralization of management; (5) limited liability; and (6) free transferability of interests. The first two factors were always possessed by a corporation and a partnership. Thus, the remaining four characteristics effectively functioned as the test to distinguish corporations from partnerships. An entity possessing three or more would be characterized as a corporation. *See* New York State Bar Association Tax Section, "Report on 'Check the Box' Entity Classification System proposed in Notice 95-14," Part II.A.1 (Aug. 30, 1995), available at 95 TNT 173-64 (Aug. 31, 1995).
2. Treas. Reg. Sec. 301.7701-2(a), 301.7701-4(a), and (b).
3. Treas. Reg. Sec. 301.7701-2(b)(1)-(7). Per se corporations also include business entities that are taxable as a corporation under specific code provisions such as those that apply to a publicly-traded partnership (Sec. 7704), a regulated investment company (Sec. 851) and a real estate investment trust (Sec. 857(b)(1)).
4. The entire list is set forth in Treas. Reg. Sec. 301.7701-2(b)(8)(i).
5. Treas. Reg. Sec. 301.7701-3(a) and (b).
6. Treas. Reg. Sec. 301.7701-3(a) and (b)(1).
7. Treas. Reg. Sec. 301.7701-3(b)(2). The determination whether an owner has limited liability is made by reference to the law of the country under which the entity is organized.
8. A disregarded entity will be a branch if it carries on business.

Under US tax law, a trust is generally an entity "created either by a will or by an inter vivos declaration whereby trustees take title to property for the purpose of protecting or conserving it for the beneficiaries under the ordinary rules applied in chancery or probate courts."[9] The key feature that distinguishes a trust from a corporation or a partnership is that the trust is preserving property and not carrying on a business. Treasury Regulations explain, "Generally speaking, an arrangement will be treated as a trust under the Internal Revenue Code if it can be shown that the purpose of the arrangement is to vest in trustees responsibility for the protection and conservation of property for beneficiaries who cannot share in the discharge of this responsibility and, therefore, are not associates in a joint enterprise for the conduct of business for profit."[10] A trust that is carrying on a business, such as a type of trust often referred to as a "business trust," is not classified as a trust for US tax purposes, but rather will be treated as a corporation or a partnership under the rules described above.[11]

2.2 THE CORPORATION INCOME TAX

2.2.1 Tax Rates

Corporations are subject to a flat tax of 21% on taxable income.[12]

2.2.2 The Tax Base

The corporate tax rates are applied to *taxable income*. The starting point in computing taxable income is *gross income* (gross receipts minus the cost of goods sold). Unlike many European systems, no distinction is made in general between sources or categories of income. From this figure are subtracted the allowable *deductions*. The difference is taxable income.[13]

2.2.2.1 Gross Income

Most receipts constitute gross income to a corporation. The notable exceptions are interest from state and local bonds,[14] life insurance proceeds,[15] stockholder contributions to the corporation's capital,[16] certain non-stockholder contributions to the

9. Treas. Reg. Sec. 301.7701-4(a).
10. *Id.*
11. Treas. Reg. Sec. 301.7701-4(b).
12. Sec. 11(b).
13. Secs. 61 and 63(a).
14. Sec. 103.
15. Sec. 101.
16. Sec. 118(a).

corporation's capital,[17] cancellation of indebtedness income under certain circumstances,[18] and gifts or bequests.[19]

2.2.2.2 *Deductible Expenditures*

The deductions allowed in arriving at taxable income fall into two broad categories:

(1) Those deductions that constitute costs of producing income for the year in question, with accounting and economic principles providing the norms for determining the proper amount.
(2) Special deductions that are permitted to be taken in amounts in excess of or in addition to those otherwise allowable for the year under the principles developed in the first category, above.

In the first category, the principal deductions are for the ordinary and necessary expenses incurred in a trade or business (wages, overhead, advertising, etc.), contributions to employee retirement plans, interest incurred for a trade or business, taxes, and depreciation (declining balance method for machinery and equipment; straight-line method for improved real estate).[20] Losses on business assets are deductible when the asset is disposed of or becomes totally worthless.[21] Similar rules apply to bad debts.[22] In the case of inventory a loss may be deducted for a decline in value.[23] Capital expenditures—in general outlays for the acquisition or improvement of property[24]—must be added to the cost basis[25] of the asset to which they relate and recovered over the prescribed period for the asset either through annual depreciation (or amortization) deductions or, in the case of certain non-depreciable assets, upon

17. Not all non-stockholder contributions to capital are tax-free. Contributions to aid construction, contributions by customers or potential customer of the corporation, and contributions by governmental entities or civic groups are taxable to the corporation. Sec. 118(b). To the extent the corporation receives contributions to capital from non-stockholders that are tax-free, it is required to reduce its tax basis (*see infra* note 25 for a discussion of tax basis) in its assets. Sec. 362(c). Stockholder contributions of property to the capital of the corporation, generally take a carry-over basis. That is, the corporation generally takes as its basis the basis that the contributor had (*see infra* note 68 for an exception involving contributions of property with a value less than their tax bases).
18. Income from the cancellation of debt is exempt if the taxpayer is in a bankruptcy proceeding or is insolvent. Sec. 108(a). The exemption is coupled with a reduction in specified tax attributes such as net operating loss carryovers and basis. Secs. 108(b) and 1017.
19. Sec. 102.
20. *See* in general Secs. 162-168 and 401-415. Alternative (generally slower) depreciation rules apply to property used predominantly outside of the United States. Sec. 168(g).
21. Sec. 165.
22. Sec. 166. In some cases, a deduction for partial worthlessness is allowed.
23. Treas. Reg. Sec. 1.471-2.
24. Treas. Reg. Secs. 1-263(a)-1 et seq.
25. "Cost basis," as the name implies, is the original cost of the asset. Sec. 1012. This figure is adjusted for various items during the time the asset is held, e.g., the cost basis is reduced by depreciation or increased by capital improvements. Sec. 1016. The resulting "adjusted basis" (often referred to as "tax basis") is in effect a running balance of the tax attributes of an asset. Basis is not adjusted for inflation.

ultimate sale of the asset (through decreased taxable gain or increased deductible loss).[26]

In the second category are a large number of provisions that permit certain capital expenditures to be recovered for tax purposes more rapidly than would be allowed under the principles applicable to items in classification one. The total amount deductible is not changed, but the timing of the deductions is altered. Various techniques are employed to accelerate the deductions.

In some cases, the entire capital cost may be deducted in the year paid or incurred. Principal examples of such items are intangible drilling and development costs incurred by companies involved in oil and gas drilling and development; research and development expenditures incurred before January 1, 2022; circulation costs incurred by newspapers or other periodicals; and certain expenditures to remove architectural barriers to the handicapped and the elderly.[27] Also, in certain circumstances purchases of tangible personal property, certain software, and certain real estate may be immediately expensed.[28]

In other situations, capital expenditures are permitted to be amortized and deducted over an arbitrary period—usually fifteen years—even though the useful life of the asset to which the expenditure relates is longer (or indeterminate). For example, taxpayers who incur costs for starting a new trade or business, or forming a corporation or partnership generally amortize such costs over a fifteen-year period.[29] The costs of purchased intangible assets such as goodwill are also amortized over a fifteen-year period.[30] The costs of constructing pollution control facilities are amortized over five years.[31]

Other techniques adopted by the US to permit more rapid recovery of asset costs than would be available under normal depreciation rules are to provide accelerated rates of depreciation for certain assets or to provide time periods over which depreciation may be taken which are shorter than the economic useful life of the property. Thus, tangible personal property, i.e., machinery, equipment, etc. is depreciated at a rate not in excess of 200% of the rate that would have been used had the depreciation deduction been computed under the straight-line method.[32] Some acceleration of

26. Sec. 263(a). Section 263A provides detailed rules for the capitalization of costs, including interest expense, to self-produced or constructed assets and inventory.
27. *See*, respectively, Secs. 263(c), 174, 173, and 190. In addition, annual expenditures of up to USD 1,000,000 (adjusted for inflation after 2017) for purchases of tangible personal property, certain software and certain real estate may be immediately expensed. Sec. 179(a), (b)(1), and (6). The amount deductible begins to phase out for any given year after expenditures exceeding USD 2,500,000 have been made for that year. Sec. 179.
28. Secs. 179 and 168(k).
29. *See*, respectively, Secs. 195, 248, and 709. The taxpayer is permitted to deduct immediately USD 5,000 of the start-up or organization cost in the first year of business and amortize the remaining cost over a fifteen-year period. The USD 5,000 immediate deduction is reduced, however, to the extent the start-up or organization costs exceed USD 50,000. Thus, taxpayers who incur such costs in excess of USD 55,000 must amortize the entire cost over fifteen years.
30. Sec. 197.
31. *See* Sec. 169.
32. Sec. 168(a) and (b). These generous provisions do not apply to tangible personal property used predominately outside the US. Sec. 168(g)(1)(A).

depreciation deductions for commercial real estate and residential rental property is provided by permitting the costs of such property to be depreciated over 39 and 27.5 years, respectively, rather than over the useful life of the property. Shorter depreciation time periods are also provided for tangible personal property. In addition, the taxpayer may elect to expense a portion of the cost of certain capital expenditures in the year of acquisition.[33]

Another important deduction concerns intercorporate dividends. Dividends received by a corporation on stock of another corporation are includible in the payee's income and are not deductible by the payer corporation. If the dividend is from a US corporation, a "dividends received deduction" ("DRD") is then granted to the payee corporation, in effecting exempting a portion or the entire dividend from the payee's income. The deduction is equal to 50% of the dividend received if the payee corporation owns less than 20% of the stock of the payer corporation, 65% of the dividend received if the payee corporation owns 20% but less than 80% of the stock of the payer corporation, and 100% of the dividend received if the payer and payee corporations are members of an affiliated group, i.e., subject to 80% common control.[34] Similar deductions are allowed under Section 245 when a US corporation receives a dividend from a foreign corporation (other than a passive foreign investment company, Chapter 8 section 8.2) in which it owns 10% or more of the stock to the extent the foreign corporation's income is derived from US sources.

2.2.2.3 *Expenditures Not Deductible*

A few expenditures are disallowed as deductions. In some cases, a deduction is not permitted because the expenditure incurred often may constitute a disguised dividend. Principal examples include amounts paid as "excessive compensation"; premiums for life insurance on the life of any officer or shareholder of the corporation if the corporation is the beneficiary under the policy; certain travel and entertainment costs; nonemployee corporate gifts in excess of USD 25 per donee; and 50% of certain costs involving meals or entertainment.[35] In addition, losses incurred in sales or exchanges between related taxpayers, such as a corporation and a shareholder owning 50% or more of the stock of the corporation (or between two corporations owned by such a shareholder), are not deductible.[36]

Deductions are also disallowed where the expenditures constitute a cost of producing tax-exempt income (including interest incurred to purchase or carry tax-exempt state and local bonds).[37] In this category too may be placed the limitation on

33. Sec. 179. Up to USD 1,000,000 of the cost may be expensed, though the deduction is reduced if the taxpayer's total expenditures exceed USD 2,500,000. Section 179 does not apply to property used predominately outside the US. Secs. 179(d)(1) and 50(b).
34. Sec. 243(a)-(b)(2)(A). As discussed in the text, these deductions are only available if the payer corporation is a US corporation. Separate rules, which are discussed in Chapter 6 section 6.5.1, apply to dividend payments from certain foreign corporations.
35. *See*, respectively, Secs. 162(a)(1), 264, 274(a), and (n).
36. Sec. 267.
37. Sec. 265.

the deductibility of interest incurred in making certain acquisitions of the stock or assets of another corporation (dividends from the acquired corporation being in general nontaxable).[38]

In other instances, deductions are disallowed for nontax policy reasons. Examples include the limitation on deductible charitable contributions to 10% of taxable income; limitations imposed on costs of lobbying; the denial of deductions for certain illegal payments; the denial of a deduction for "excess golden parachute" payments made to executives and other costs of a target corporation in corporate takeover situations; and the denial of a deduction for most types of executive compensation in excess of USD 1 million per year paid by publicly held corporations.[39]

2.2.2.4 Special Limitations on Tax Shelter Losses

Limitations are imposed on the deductibility of losses from activities in which the taxpayer is a passive investor. These rules are intended to limit the benefits of "tax shelter" transactions. Although the rules apply to closely held corporations and personal service corporations, their primary impact is on individuals, and they are discussed in section 2.3.2.5.3.

2.2.2.5 Special Limitations on Deductibility of Corporate Interest Expense

Corporations that have gross receipts from a trade or business in excess of USD 25 million cannot deduct interest expenses attributable to a trade or business to the extent such expenses exceed 30% of the corporation's "adjusted taxable income."[40] In general, "adjusted taxable income" is defined as taxable income attributable to a trade or business without deductions for net operating losses, business interest expenses, and depreciation expenses.[41] There are other limitations imposed on the deductibility of interest expense that are aimed primarily at individual taxpayers and considered in section 2.3.2.5.2.

2.2.2.6 Net Operating Loss Carryforward and Carryback

If the corporation's deductions for the year exceed its income, the resulting "net operating loss" ("NOL") can be carried forward for an unlimited number of years and used as a deduction to reduce future taxable income.[42] The amount of income reduced

38. Sec. 279. The acquisition must involve the acquirer issuing convertible securities.
39. *See,* respectively, Secs. 170(b)(2), 162(e), 162(c), 280G, and 162(m).
40. Sec. 163(j). As discussed in section 2.3.2.5.2, this restriction also applies to individuals and partnerships. The Coronavirus Aid, Relief, and Economic Security (CARES) Act increased the 30% limit to 50% for the years 2019 and 2020 to help soften the economic downturn triggered by COVID-19. Sec. 163(j)(10).
41. Sec. 163(j)(8). Depreciation expenses, however, will reduce adjusted taxable income for taxable years beginning on or after Jan. 1, 2022. Sec. 163(j)(8)(A)(v).
42. Sec. 172(b)(1)(A). Special rules apply for NOLs incurred in the years 2018-2020. Section 2303 of the Coronavirus Aid, Relief, and Economic Security Act (CARES Act) allows taxpayers to carry

in the carryover year, however, cannot exceed 80% of the taxpayer's taxable income in that year.[43]

2.2.3 Capital Gains and Losses

Unlike individuals, gain from the sale or exchange of "capital assets" by corporations do not qualify for a special tax rate. Capital gains realized by corporations are subject to the general 21% rate. However, capital gain or loss classification can be important for purposes of recovering basis in certain taxable transactions and for imposing limitations on the deductibility of capital losses.[44] Capital losses may be deducted only against capital gains.[45] If capital losses exceed capital gains, in general, the excess can be carried back three years and forward five years.[46]

"Capital assets" include tangible and intangible assets owned by a corporation other than: (1) inventory, (2) property held primarily for sale to customers in the ordinary course of business, (3) patents and copyrights, and (4) accounts receivable.[47]

Depreciable property is not a capital asset under the basic definition. Section 1231, however, provides that if there is a net gain from the sales of depreciable property during the taxable year, such net gain is generally treated as capital gain. If instead a net loss occurs, such loss is deductible as an ordinary loss.

Gain that would otherwise qualify as capital gain under Section 1231 may be treated as ordinary income if one of the various "recapture" provisions is applicable. Thus, under Section 1245, the gain on the sale of depreciable personal property (e.g., machinery and equipment) is taxed as ordinary income to the extent of depreciation previously taken with respect to the property. That is, despite Section 1231, the prior depreciation deductions are recognized as ordinary income upon sale at a gain. The reason for ordinary income classification is that the sale at a gain has demonstrated that the taxpayer's prior depreciation deductions exceeded economic depreciation. Similar recapture rules apply to gain on the sale of certain other assets.[48] Given that no preferential tax rate is provided for capital gains realized by corporations, the only significance of the recapture provisions is that capital losses cannot be deducted against recapture income and, in some cases, characterization of gain as recapture income can accelerate the timing of gain recognition.

Certain sales or exchanges of capital assets are tax-free. For example, no tax is imposed on gain realized on exchanges of real property used in a trade or business or

---

back NOLs for 5 years during the years 2018-2020. *See* Sec. 172(b)(1)(D)(i). The purpose for this rule was to allow companies incurring losses during the COVID-19 pandemic to obtain immediate refunds by carrying back such losses to prior years when they may have incurred tax liabilities.

43. Sec. 172(a).
44. Generally, capital gains and losses arise in transactions that constitute a "sale or exchange." Sec. 1222. But Congress increasingly has subjected sophisticated financial transactions and dealers in stocks to constructive realization regimes. *See, e.g.,* Secs. 1256 and 1259.
45. Sec. 1211(a).
46. Sec. 1212.
47. Sec. 1221.
48. Secs. 1250, 1254, 1252, and 1255.

held for investment or on gain realized on an involuntary conversion of property (e.g., through condemnation by the government, fire) if the proceeds received are reinvested in similar property.[49] In each case, the corollary of nonrecognition of gain is that the property acquired takes the same tax basis as that of the property transferred (the so-called exchanged basis rule). As a result, the "tax-free" exchanges are actually tax-deferred exchanges, since the gain will be recognized on the ultimate sale or exchange of the property acquired.

2.2.4 Credits Against Tax

A flat tax rate of 21%, as prescribed in Section 11, is applied to taxable income determined under the foregoing rules. Against the resulting tax liability, however, certain credits are allowed. Again, the credits are of two types.

The first group of tax credits includes those that are structural in nature. Included are the credits for taxes paid to other countries and for withheld taxes paid to the US on amounts paid to nonresident aliens or foreign corporations.[50]

In the second group are credits provided to encourage or subsidize particular activities. The most important of these for corporations is the general business tax credit. This credit in turn is the sum of a number of separate tax credits, each of which provides a tax credit equal to a specific percentage of qualifying costs.[51] The amount of the allowable credit is limited to the greater of the corporation's minimum tax liability (applicable to years prior to 2018) or 25% of the corporation's regular income tax liability in excess of USD 25,000.[52] Allowable credits in excess of the limits may be carried back one year and forward twenty years.[53]

Several tax credits make up the general business credit, and include:

(1) credits for certain investments in qualified energy conservation or conversion property or in qualified alternative energy property, such as solar or wind energy devices;[54]
(2) a credit for the cost of producing alcohol-based fuel;[55] and
(3) a credit for investment in low-income housing projects.[56]

A tax credit also is provided for incrementally increasing costs for qualified research activity.[57]

49. Secs. 1031 and 1033.
50. Secs. 27, 901, 33, and 1462.
51. Sec. 38(a) and (b).
52. Sec. 38(c).
53. Sec. 39.
54. Secs. 46 and 48.
55. Sec. 40. The amount of this credit is directly included in gross income. Sec. 87.
56. Sec. 42.
57. Sec. 41.

2.2.5 Transactions Between Corporations and Shareholders

Under US tax rules, a corporation is an entity separate and distinct from its shareholders. As a result, corporate earnings are taxed to the corporation and distributions from the corporation to its stockholders are taxed to the individual shareholders, although at a reduced rate (section 2.3.2.2).

The *formation* of a corporation is generally accomplished tax-free. That is, the transfer of property to a corporation results in no current tax to the shareholders if the transferor-shareholders are in control (80%) of the corporation immediately after the transfer. The corporation realizes no gain on the issuance of its stock. The shareholders have a tax basis in their stock equal to the aggregate bases of the property transferred to the corporation.[58]

Distributions of cash or property by a corporation to its shareholders constitute taxable dividends to the shareholders to the extent of the corporation's earnings and profits (current and accumulated).[59] In general terms, "earnings and profits" (a technical tax concept) correspond closely to the accounting concept of "earned surplus" of a corporation.[60] If the corporation distributes property with a fair market value in excess of basis, the corporation must recognize gain as if it had sold the property to the distributee. As a result, taxable income is realized at both the corporate level and the shareholder level in such transactions.[61]

For both individual and corporate shareholders, the amount of the distribution equals the fair market value of the property and the quantity of cash distributed. If the distribution is not out of earnings and profits, the shareholder reduces basis in the stock by the amount of the distribution and, if the distribution is in excess of that basis, such excess is taxed as a capital gain. Corporate shareholders receiving a distribution that qualifies as a dividend (i.e., a distribution out of earnings and profits) is allowed a DRD, as noted in section 2.2.2.2.[62] Distributions to individuals that qualify as dividends generally are taxed at a preferential rate that may not exceed 20% (section 2.3.2.2).

58. Secs. 351, 358, 362, and 1032. Property (other than stock) and certain types of preferred stock (so-called boot) received by the transferor-shareholder do not qualify for tax-free treatment, and the value of such property or preferred stock is immediately taxable to the recipient shareholder. Secs. 351(b), (g), 356(a), and (e). The corporation's tax basis in the property transferred to it by a shareholder generally equals the shareholder's basis. Sec. 362(a). However, if the transferred property in the aggregate has a fair market value less than its tax basis, the corporation's tax basis in the property is decreased. Sec. 362(e).
59. Sec. 316. Dividends paid are not deductible by the corporation, but interest paid on corporate debt is deductible subject to the limitations discussed in section 2.2.2.5. This distinction places enormous pressure on classifying sophisticated securities as debt or equity. The resolution of the issue is a factual matter ultimately resolved by the courts. In some instances, Congress has provided statutory rules, or authorization for Treasury Regulations, to limit the deductibility of "interest" where the security involved and/or characteristics of the corporation cause the security to appear more like equity than debt. *See* Secs. 385, 163(e), (j), and (l). The debt-equity problem is intractable in a classical (non-integrated) corporate/shareholder tax regime such as that employed by the US where the corporation is treated as a taxable entity separate from its shareholders.
60. Sec. 312.
61. Sec. 311(b).
62. Secs. 301(b)-(c) and 243.

This preferential treatment of dividend distributions may be viewed as a form of partial integration of corporate and shareholder taxes.

In general, a distribution of the corporation's own stock (a "stock dividend") is nontaxable to the stockholder. However, situations that involve a change in the proportionate interest of a stockholder in the corporation can result in income to the stockholder.[63]

Dividend distributions to individuals were historically taxed at higher rates than an individual's gain in the sale of her stock. As a result, a substantial portion of the corporate tax rules are aimed at preventing stockholders from "bailing out" corporate earnings at capital gain rates. Because dividends to individuals are now generally taxed at the same 20% rate as capital gains (section 2.3.2.2), the importance of the "bail-out" rules has diminished. Individuals will still have an incentive, however, to "bail out" corporate earnings as capital gains, if they have a high basis in their stock or have capital losses to offset their capital gains.

A *redemption* of stock (i.e., a purchase by the corporation of its own stock from a stockholder) results in capital gain to the redeemed stockholder provided that the distribution by the corporation significantly reduces the stockholder's ownership in the corporation. Rules are provided for determining whether a particular distribution falls on the ordinary dividend or on the capital gain side of the line.[64] As in the case of a dividend distribution, the transfer of appreciated property by a corporation to redeem its own stock will give rise to recognition of gain by the distributing corporation.[65]

Distributions *in partial* or *complete liquidation* of a corporation also are treated as *exchanges* which qualify for capital gain treatment to individual shareholders. Again, the corporation recognizes gain on the distribution of appreciated property in liquidation.[66] The liquidation of an 80% owned subsidiary, however, is tax-free to both the corporate parent and the subsidiary; correspondingly, the parent takes a transferred basis in the assets acquired in the liquidation.[67]

The Code permits a variety of corporate *reorganizations* to be effected on a tax-free basis. In general, these provisions are designed to permit business transactions involving certain corporate readjustments to be consummated without a tax being incurred by the participating corporations or their shareholders at the time of the transaction. The theory of these provisions is that the readjustments, while they may produce changes in the structure of a business enterprise, do not involve such fundamental changes in the nature or character of the relation of the owners of the enterprise to the assets of the enterprise as to warrant a tax on the accrued gain or allowance of a loss deduction. The nonrecognition provisions cover a wide spectrum of transactions ranging from statutory mergers to exchanges of stock for stock, stock for

63. Sec. 305. *See also* Sec. 306 as to the treatment of preferred stock distributed by a corporation.
64. Sec. 302(b).
65. Secs. 302 and 311(b). *See also* Sec. 304, which treats amounts paid by one corporation for the purchase of stock of a second corporation as dividends where the same shareholders control both corporations.
66. Secs. 302(b)(4), 311, 331, and 336.
67. Secs. 332, 337, and 334(b)(1).

assets, recapitalizations of a single corporation, or a mere change in the form or name of the corporation.

In a qualifying reorganization, neither the stockholders of the corporations involved nor the corporations themselves recognize any gain or loss. As a corollary, special basis rules are required to reflect the nonrecognition of gain. In general, the shareholders substitute the basis in their old stock as the basis in the new stock. At the corporation level, assets acquired in a reorganization generally carryover the same basis to the acquiring corporation as they had in the hands of the transferring corporation.[68] In certain types of reorganizations, the receipt of cash or other property is permitted in addition to the receipt of stock in the acquiring corporation. In such cases, the cash or value of other property is taxed at the time of the reorganization, the gain generally being classified as capital gain.[69]

Special rules are also provided to permit certain tax-free divisions of existing corporations. These rules are quite restrictive since corporate divisions had earlier presented the possibility of "bailing out" cash and other liquid assets as capital gains rather than as dividend income.[70] As discussed above, application of the same preferential tax rate to both dividend income and capital gains has reduced some of the incentive to bail out earnings as capital gains.

In qualifying acquisitive reorganizations, special rules are provided to carryover the corporate attributes of the transferring corporation to the acquiring corporation, such as its earnings and profits account and net operating loss carryovers.[71]

The reorganization provisions are discussed in greater detail in Chapter 7 section 7.1.2 where reorganizations involving US and foreign corporations are considered.

Consolidated returns may be filed by corporate groups where the parent corporation owns at least 80% of the stock of its subsidiary corporations. Under the consolidated return rules, income and deductions of the various members of the group are consolidated and the net income of the group is subject to tax. Dividends within the corporate group are not taxable. Regulations provide detailed rules for the tax treatment of inter-company transactions.[72] A foreign corporation in general may not be a member of a consolidated return group and, therefore, the significance of the consolidated return rules is limited to domestic corporate groups.[73]

68. Sec. 362(b). However, if the transferred property in the aggregate has a fair market value less than its tax basis, the acquiring corporation's aggregate tax basis in the property cannot exceed the fair market value. Sec. 362(e).
69. *See* Secs. 354, 356-358, and 361-362.
70. Secs. 368(a)(1)(D) and 355.
71. Sec. 381. Strict limitations are imposed on the deductibility of net operating loss carryovers by an acquiring corporation, whether in a taxable or tax-free acquisition, by Sections 382-384 and 269.
72. The consolidated return rules are contained almost entirely in Treasury Regulations which have nearly the same authority as a Code provision. *See* Treas. Reg. Sec. 1.1502-1 and following for the highly complex rules governing consolidated returns.
73. However, a foreign taxpayer may own the stock of a US parent which in turn has US subsidiaries and the US group may file a consolidated return.

2.2.6 Penalty Taxes

2.2.6.1 Accumulated Earnings Tax

During most of US tax history, the top corporate rate has been lower than the top individual rate. For example, in 2021, the corporate rate is 21% on ordinary income and capital gain and the top individual rate is 37% on ordinary income. As a result, the total tax burden on the corporation and its shareholders could be minimized in some situations by retaining profits in the corporation to be reinvested for as long as possible. In order to discourage such accumulations, Sections 531-537 were adopted, and these impose an "accumulated earnings tax" of 20% on certain corporate earnings retentions. The 20% accumulated earnings tax in effect represents the tax that would have been applied to dividend distributions had the corporation actually distributed its earnings to stockholders.

The tax is applied to every corporation "formed or availed of for the purpose of avoiding the income tax with respect to its shareholders ... by permitting earnings and profits to accumulate [beyond the reasonable needs of the business] instead of being divided or distributed." The determination of the reasonable needs of the business involves a complex factual inquiry into all aspects of the corporation's business.[74] US corporations with foreign shareholders and foreign corporations with US shareholders are subject to the tax, although in the latter case only with respect to the corporation's US source income. Foreign corporations doing business in the US that have only foreign shareholders generally are not subject to the tax (*see* Chapter 5 section 5.6.7.1).

2.2.6.2 Personal Holding Company Tax

Under the personal holding company tax provisions,[75] a penalty tax of 20% is imposed on the "undistributed personal holding company income" of a corporation which qualifies as a personal holding company. Personal holding company income in general consists of dividends, interest, royalties, annuities, and certain rents. The personal holding company provisions are directed at closely held corporations in which five or fewer individuals own (directly or by attribution) more than 50% of the stock of the corporation. Corporations which run afoul of the personal holding company tax can avoid the tax by payment of a so-called deficiency dividend. The deficiency dividend can be deducted in determining the corporation's undistributed holding company income and hence eliminates the personal holding company penalty tax liability.[76] The shareholders correspondingly include the deficiency dividend in income.

74. *See, e.g., Bardahl Mfg. Corp. v. Commissioner,* TC Memo 1965-200.
75. The personal holding company tax rules are contained in Sections 541-547. A corporation can be used as an investment vehicle and avoid any problems under the personal holding company tax if the corporation is subject to single level taxation under Subchapter S of the Tax Code. *See* section 2.5.
76. Secs. 545(a) and 561.

The personal holding company tax can apply to any US corporation regardless of the source of its income and regardless of whether a significant part or all of its shareholders are foreign.

2.3 THE INDIVIDUAL INCOME TAX

2.3.1 Tax Rates

Individuals are in general subject to marginal tax rates ranging from 10% to 37%. Separate rate schedules are provided for married couples filing joint returns, married couples filing separate returns, heads of households, and single persons. The rate brackets for heads of household (generally involved where a single parent maintains a household with dependent children) are about halfway between those for joint returns and single persons. The rate brackets are adjusted annually for inflation.[77] A special reduced rate applies to capital gains and dividend distributions. An additional tax of 3.8% is added to net investment income for high-income taxpayers.[78] Net investment income includes dividends and capital gains, which are subject to preferential rates and discussed in section 2.3.2.2. It also includes rents, royalties, and interest income, items that do not normally qualify for reduced rates. As a result, it is possible that an individual will find that her highest marginal rate will be 40.8% (the sum of 37.0% and 3.8%) on income such as rents, royalties, and interest.

2.3.2 The Tax Base

The individual tax rates are applied to *taxable income*. The starting point in computing taxable income is *gross income* (gross receipts minus the cost of goods sold). From this figure are first subtracted allowable *business deductions* and certain *adjustments* to arrive at *adjusted gross income*. From adjusted gross income are then subtracted certain *personal deductions*. The taxpayer used to be allowed a deduction for *personal exemptions* to arrive at the final figure for taxable income, but this deduction is not allowed through the year 2025.[79]

2.3.2.1 Gross Income

Gross income includes income "from whatever source derived."[80] However, as discussed in section 2.2.2.1, certain statutory exceptions are provided. The principal exclusions are interest on state and local bonds; contributions to and income earned by qualified employee retirement plans and the value of certain other fringe benefits of

77. Sec. 1(a)-(c) and (f).
78. Sec. 1411(a). Taxpayers who file their tax returns as individuals and have modified adjusted gross income in excess of USD 200,000 and taxpayers who are married and file joint returns with modified adjusted gross income over USD 250,000 are subject to this tax. Sec. 1411(b) and (d).
79. Sec. 151(d)(5).
80. Sec. 61.

employees; the accrued gain in property transferred by gift or bequest; receipts of gifts, bequests and proceeds of life insurance; compensation for physical injuries; certain scholarships and fellowship grants; and all or part of the gain on the sale or exchange of residences.[81] By administrative action, benefits paid under certain programs to further social welfare objectives of the government are also excluded from gross income.

2.3.2.2 *Dividends and Capital Gains and Losses*

Dividends received by an individual from a US corporation or a qualified foreign corporation are taxed at a maximum rate of 20%.[82] Qualified foreign corporations include foreign corporations whose stock is traded on an established US securities market or foreign corporations eligible for benefits under a comprehensive income tax treaty that includes an adequate exchange of information program.[83] Dividend income of high-income individuals will also be subject to the 3.8% add-on tax of Section 1411 (section 2.3.1) with the result that such individuals will pay a maximum tax of 23.8% on qualified dividends.

A maze of rates and rules apply to gains realized on the sale or exchange of a "capital asset" by an individual.[84]

In simplified form, the preferential capital gain regime is as follows:[85]

(1) The general rule is that gain realized on the sale of a capital asset held for more than twelve months is taxed at a maximum 20% rate. This rate is reduced for lower income taxpayers. For example, the 20% rate applies in 2021 to unmarried taxpayers with income over USD 445,850.[86] A capital gains tax rate of 15% applies to unmarried taxpayers with taxable income between USD 40,000 and USD 445,850 in 2021.[87] A 0% tax rate applies in 2021 to long-term capital gains of unmarried taxpayers with taxable income of USD 40,000 or less.[88] The various break points for the 0%, 15%, and 20% rates are adjusted annually for inflation.

---

81. The provisions excluding receipts from gross income appear generally in Sections 101 and following.
82. Sec. 1(h)(11).
83. Notice 2011-64, 2011-2 C.B. 231, lists treaties that Treasury has determined provide for adequate exchanges of information. Notice 2003-71, 2003-2 C.B. 922, provides additional guidance about when securities of a foreign corporation will be considered to be traded on an established US securities market.
84. Such capital gain will also constitute net investment income and be subject to the additional 3.8% tax (section 2.3.1) for high-income individuals under Section 1411.
85. Section 1(h) sets forth rules for capital gains. The text summary masks the extraordinary complexity of the calculation required under Section 1(h).
86. *Id.*
87. *Id.*
88. Rev. Proc. 2019-44 Sec. 3.03, 2019-47 IRB 1093 (2019).

(2) "Collectibles" (e.g., stamp collections, rare coins) are subject to a maximum rate of 28% (thus benefiting only taxpayers whose ordinary income is taxed at rates higher than 28%).
(3) Gain on the sale of depreciable real estate is taxed at a 25% rate to the extent that gain is attributable to prior depreciation deductions which reduced basis and at regular capital gain rates on the balance of any gain.
(4) Gain realized on the sale of qualified "small business stock" acquired on or after Sept. 28, 2010 and held for more than five years is excluded from income.[89]
(5) If the asset sold is the taxpayer's principal residence, then gain up to USD 250,000 (USD 500,000 for married taxpayers) is excluded from income if specified conditions are met.[90]
(6) If the asset sold has been held for twelve months or less, the gain is taxed at the taxpayer's ordinary income tax rates.

The items subject to the rates discussed above will usually constitute net investment income under Section 1411 for high-income individuals. As a result, high-income taxpayers will pay a rate on their capital gains that is equal to the rates described above plus an additional 3.8%. The other capital gain rules described in section 2.2.3 generally apply to individuals, except that capital losses in excess of capital gains may not be carried back, but may be carried forward indefinitely.

Arguments for preferential treatment of capital gains on tax policy grounds generally are unconvincing, and there is no discernible rationale at all for the preferential scheme described above. One clear result, however, is the addition of inordinate complexity in the Code.

2.3.2.3 *Deductible Expenditures: Business and Investment*

For an individual, the deductions allowed from gross income in arriving at adjusted gross income generally are the same as those allowed to corporations described in section 2.2.2.2.

In addition to the ordinary and necessary expenses of a trade or business, an individual was historically allowed to deduct all ordinary and necessary expenses paid or incurred for the production or collection of income, and for the management, conservation, or maintenance of property held for the production of income.[91] However, as discussed in section 2.3.2.6, expenditures incurred for the production of income in an activity that is not a trade or business are not deductible during the period 2018-2025 unless related to the production of rental or royalty income.

89. Sec. 1202(a)(4).
90. Sec. 121.
91. Sec. 212. Such costs, although costs of producing income, are usually deducted from adjusted gross income and then only to the extent they exceed 2% of the taxpayer's adjusted gross income. Sec. 67.

The 2017 Act[92] added a new 20% deduction for trade or business income from certain "qualified trades or businesses" that are earned by individuals either directly or as partners in partnerships.[93] The result is that the maximum tax rate that can apply to qualified trades or businesses is 29.6%. In general, qualified trades or businesses do *not* include performance of services in the fields of health, law, accounting, actuarial science, performing arts, consulting, athletics, financial services, investing, investment management, trading, and dealing in certain assets.[94]

2.3.2.4 *Expenditures Not Deductible*

Many of the expenditures that are disallowed as deductions for corporations, described in section 2.2.2.3 above, are in general also disallowed as to individuals. Thus, for example, charitable deductions by individuals are limited and losses on sales to related individuals are restricted.[95] Individuals are also denied deductions for personal, living, or family expenses except as provided in section 2.3.2.6 below.[96]

Prior to the enactment of the 2017 Act, special rules permitted limited deductions for a category of "mixed" business-personal expenditures. These expenditures involved activities in which there was a significant personal element, but as to which there was also a profit-seeking or investment element. Examples of mixed business-personal expenditures included moving expenses and so-called hobby situations where it was unclear whether the taxpayer actually engaged in the activity to make a profit.[97] In addition, expenses in an activity that the taxpayer engaged in for profit, but that did not rise to the level of a trade or business, were also deductible.[98] The 2017 Act has suspended the deductibility of many of these expenses, referred to as "miscellaneous itemized deductions," for the period 2018-2025.[99]

2.3.2.5 *Special Limitations on Tax Shelter Losses, Interest Deductions, and Trade or Business Expenses*

2.3.2.5.1 *Limitation of Deductions to Amount at Risk*

US tax law permits individuals to deduct currently the costs incurred in engaging in a trade or business or activity producing rents or royalties even if borrowing represented the source of the invested funds. At one time, this deductibility resulted even if the

92. P.L. 115-97 (2017).
93. Sec. 199A. The 20% deduction is also available to individual S corporation stockholders for the S corporation's income from "qualified trades or businesses." S corporations are discussed in section 2.6. The deduction is not available to employees.
94. Sec. 199A(d).
95. Secs. 170(b), (e), (g), and 267.
96. Sec. 262.
97. *See* Secs. 217 and 183.
98. Sec. 212. A taxpayer must engage in a profit-making activity with "continuity and regularity" for it to qualify as a trade or business. *Comm. v. Groetzinger*, 480 U.S. 23 (1987).
99. *See* Sec. 217(g) for the suspension of the deduction for moving expenses and Sec. 67(b) and (g) for the definition of miscellaneous itemized deductions and the suspension of their deductibility.

borrowing was "nonrecourse," i.e., the lender agreed to look for repayment of the loan only from the property securing the loan and not from other assets of the borrower. Thus, for example, an individual who purchased a building entirely with borrowed funds that he had no obligation to repay personally could begin taking depreciation deductions before making any principal payments on the loan. This mismatch between investment and deductions was one of the foundations upon which "tax shelters" were created, especially when accelerated deductions were involved.

To deal with the above situation, "at risk" rules, in general, limit a taxpayer's current deductions from an activity to the amount by which the taxpayer's personal assets are at risk with respect to the activity. A taxpayer is at risk to the extent she has made an actual investment of cash or property or has borrowed on the basis of personal liability to invest in an activity. If the deductions from an activity for a current year exceed the taxpayer's at risk amount for that year, the excess cannot be deducted but must be deferred until future years when the taxpayer has increased her at risk amount (which can also be produced by the realization of net taxable income from the activity). As a result, deductions attributable to nonrecourse borrowing cannot, in general, be taken until principal payments are made on a nonrecourse loan. An important exception to the general rule is permitted in the case of real estate where nonrecourse borrowing from third party lending institutions is treated as at risk.

Although the at-risk rules were developed in the context where current *accelerated* deductions were being generated by nonrecourse borrowing, the rules also apply to deny current deductions for the ordinary and necessary expenses of a trade or business to the extent the taxpayer is not at risk.[100]

2.3.2.5.2 Limitations on the Deduction for Interest Expense

Congress has imposed increasingly stringent limitations on the deductibility of interest expense. The limiting rules require allocation of interest expense to particular categories of income or activities and several different allocation methods are employed. The result is a set of rules which are based on no discernible rational principle for treating interest expenses in an income tax system.

The following discussion summarizes briefly the existing limitations:

(1) *Trade or business interest* expense is deductible without regard to any of the limitations on interest expense if the individual taxpayer's gross receipts from a trade or business do not exceed USD 25 million.[101] Similar to the treatment of corporations,[102] individuals who have gross receipts in excess of USD 25 million can only deduct interest expenses attributable to a trade or business to

The nondeductible miscellaneous itemized deductions include "hobby" expenses and profit-seeking expenses in an activity that does not rise to the level of a trade or business and that is not attributable to rents or royalties. Sec. 67(b). *See supra* note 98, above, for the distinction between a profit-making activity and a trade or business.

100. Sec. 465. Similar at-risk rules limit the current utilization of certain business tax credits. Sec. 49.
101. Secs. 163(a), (h)(2)(A), (j), and 448(c).
102. *See* section 2.2.2.5.

the extent such expenses do not exceed 30% (50% in 2020)[103] of their "adjusted taxable income."[104] In general, adjusted taxable income is defined as taxable income attributable to its trades or businesses without deductions for net operating losses, business interest expenses, and depreciation expenses.[105]

(2) *Investment interest* expense can be deducted only to the extent of investment income for the taxable year; any excess is carried forward to future years when the taxpayer has investment income.[106]

(3) *Passive activity interest* expense is limited by the rules discussed in section 2.3.2.5.3.

(4) *Qualified residence interest* incurred on debt to acquire the taxpayer's principal residence and on one secondary residence qualifies for full deductibility to the extent the total debt does not exceed USD 750,000.[107]

(5) *Personal interest* is interest other than that described in categories 1-4, above, and is nondeductible in its entirety.[108] Thus, interest incurred to purchase consumer durables, on income tax deficiencies, or to finance vacations is all nondeductible.

As a general rule, interest expense is placed in one of the above categories by *tracing* the borrowed funds. Thus, investment interest is determined by tracing borrowed funds into properties that generate investment income, for example, dividends, interest, rents, and capital gains. Since money is fungible, the tracing approach to classification of interest expense requires a suspension of belief in economic reality as well as the imposition of complex administrative and record-keeping burdens on taxpayers and tax administrators.[109]

Other provisions impose separate limitations on different categories of interest expense. Thus, for example, Section 263A(f) requires that interest expense incurred during the production period of property (such as a building) be capitalized and added to the basis of the property. Under this provision, interest is allocated to the appropriate property under both a *tracing* and a *stacking* procedure. Debt that can be specifically traced to a particular activity must be allocated to it (e.g., a loan obtained to construct a building). If production expenditures exceed that amount of debt, then other debt of the taxpayer is allocated to the property (and interest thereon is required to be

---

103. The Coronavirus Aid, Relief, and Economic Security (CARES) Act increased the limit to 50% for the years 2019 and 2020 to help soften the economic downturn triggered by COVID-19. Sec. 163(j)(10).
104. Sec. 163(j).
105. Sec. 163(j)(8). Depreciation expenses, however, will reduce adjusted taxable income for taxable years beginning on or after Jan. 1, 2022. Sec. 163(j)(8)(A)(v).
106. Sec. 163(d).
107. Sec. 163(h)(2)(D) and (3).
108. Sec. 163(h)(1)-(2). A limited deduction is allowed for interest expense on debt incurred to finance qualified higher education costs, an item that normally would be classified as personal interest. Sec. 221.
109. Temp. Treas. Reg. Sec. 1.163-8T, -9T and -10T provides rules for placing interest expense in the above categories and some simplifying procedures to ease administrative problems involved in the tracing approach.

capitalized in that property). In other words, where a taxpayer is engaged in the production of long-lived properties, such as buildings, all debt of the taxpayer must first be stacked against the costs of producing that building to the extent of those costs.[110]

In other situations, important in the international context, interest expense is allocated on the theory that money is fungible and still different allocation rules are employed (*see* Chapter 4 section 4.4.3.1).

The above tabulation does not exhaust—although it may have exhausted the reader—the list of rules applicable to the treatment of interest expense. For example, complex rules are also employed to determine the amount of interest currently deductible with respect to debt obligations that are issued or purchased at a discount (*see* section 2.8).

2.3.2.5.3 Limitations on the Deduction of Passive Activity Losses

Despite the at-risk rules, the limitations on investment interest, and the alternative minimum tax (discussed in section 2.3.4 below), yet another set of rules impose further limitations on "tax shelters." These rules are contained in the provisions limiting the current deduction from passive activities to the amount of the taxpayer's passive activity income. In other words, deductions generated by passive activities cannot be used to "shelter" personal service, active trade or business, or portfolio investment income.[111] Any excess passive loss is carried over to be deducted in a subsequent year in which the taxpayer has passive income or terminates her interest in the passive activity.

An "activity" is "passive" with respect to a taxpayer if it involves the rental of property or if it is a trade or business in which the taxpayer does not "materially participate." The quoted terms are defined in torturous detail in the Code and Regulations.[112]

There are several noteworthy aspects to the passive activity loss regime. First, it requires allocation of deductions among several classifications of income. When coupled with the interest expense deduction rules discussed above, it can be seen that the US has overlaid its "global" system of income taxation with very substantial elements of a schedular system. This overlay has produced an extreme level of complexity in the US income tax system. Second, as in the case of the at-risk rules, the passive activity loss rules deny deduction of economic costs currently incurred to produce income—a result incompatible with a global income tax regime. Finally, in a truly remarkable turn in US tax legislation, Congress required that the Treasury issue regulations producing the opposite result from that of the general statutory rules where

110. *See* Treas. Reg. Sec. 1.263A-8 for the rules implementing the capitalization of interest requirements of Sec. 263A.
111. Sec. 469. Similar limitations apply to tax credits generated by passive activities.
112. *See* Treas. Reg. Sec. 1.469-0 to -11.

"necessary or appropriate" to carry out the purposes of the passive activity loss rules.[113]

2.3.2.5.4 *Limitations on Deductibility of Trade or Business Expenses*

Section 461(l) limits the ability of individual taxpayers to deduct trade or business expenses from nonbusiness income. Beginning in 2021, individuals cannot use more than USD 250,000 (USD 500,000 for married individuals filing jointly) of business losses to offset nonbusiness income.[114]

2.3.2.6 *Deductible Expenditures: Personal and Mixed Business-Personal*

Certain deductions are permitted even though they often do not represent costs of producing income. These expenses, so-called itemized deductions include interest on qualified personal residences (discussed in section 2.3.2.5.2 above), certain state, local, and foreign taxes, casualty losses, charitable contributions, and medical expenses. In several instances, limitations are imposed on the deductible amounts.[115] The amounts that are allowed as deductions under these rules generally are subtracted from adjusted gross income to arrive at taxable income.[116]

Most taxpayers do not claim the above-itemized deductions in calculating taxable income because a generous "standard deduction" may be claimed in lieu of the itemized deductions. The standard deduction for taxpayers who are not married is USD 12,000, adjusted for inflation after 2018.[117] The standard deduction for married individuals filing a joint return is USD 24,000, also adjusted for inflation after 2018. An individual may claim the standard deduction regardless of whether she has any itemized deductions. The large standard deduction helps to insure that persons with low incomes will not incur any income tax liability and to reduce record keeping that would be required to authenticate itemized deductions.

Prior to the enactment of the 2017 Act, special rules also permitted limited deductions for a category of "mixed" business-personal expenditures. As discussed in section 2.3.2.4, the 2017 Act has suspended the deductibility of many of these expenses, referred to as "miscellaneous itemized deductions," for the period 2018-2025.[118]

---

113. Sec. 469(l). *See* Temp. Treas. Reg. Sec. 1.469-2T(f)(1).
114. The limitation was supposed to take effect in 2018, but the Coronavirus Aid, Relief, and Economic Security (CARES) Act delayed the effective date until 2021. Sec. 461(l)(1)(B).
115. *See* Secs. 164(b)(6), 165(c), 170(b), (e), and 213(a).
116. Sec. 63.
117. Sec. 63(c).
118. *See* Sec. 217(g) for the suspension of the deduction for moving expenses and Section 67(b) and (g) for the definition of miscellaneous itemized deductions and the suspension of their deductibility. The non-deductible miscellaneous itemized deductions include "hobby" expenses and non-trade or business expenses to produce income that is not attributable to rents or royalties. Sec. 67(b).

2.3.3 Credits Against Tax

The tax rates described in Section 1 of the Code apply to taxable income determined under the foregoing rules. Against the resulting tax liability, however, certain credits against tax are allowed. As in the case of corporations, the credits are of two types.

The first group of tax credits is structural in nature and includes the credits for taxes withheld by the individual's employer, estimated taxes previously paid, and income taxes paid to other countries.[119]

In the second group consists of credits provided to encourage or subsidize particular persons or activities. These include, for example, the general business credit discussed in section 2.2.4 above, a tax credit for costs of childcare incurred to enable the taxpayer to work outside the home, a refundable earned income credit, a tax credit for the elderly, a USD 1,000 tax credit per each child of the taxpayer under age 17, and tax credits for costs of higher education.[120]

2.3.4 Alternative Minimum Tax: Individuals

Individuals are required to pay an Alternative Minimum Tax (AMT) if the AMT liability exceeds their regular tax liability. The starting point is to calculate Alternative Minimum Taxable Income (AMTI) by increasing their taxable income to reflect certain "adjustments" and "preferences." The "adjustments" include reduced depreciation rates, elimination of the standard deduction, and the addition of income from the exercise of certain stock options that the taxpayer was allowed to exclude in calculating taxable income.[121] "Preferences" include certain tax-exempt interest and depletion allowances that are added back to the taxpayer's taxable income to calculate AMTI.[122] The AMTI is then reduced by an exemption amount equal to USD 109,400 for married taxpayers, adjusted for inflation after 2018, to calculate the "taxable excess."[123] Finally, the AMTI is calculated by applying a rate of 26% to the first USD 175,000 (adjusted for inflation after 2011) of the taxable excess and a rate of 28% to the remainder.[124] The special lower rates described in section 2.3.2.2 apply to capital gains, however.[125]

119. Secs. 31, 6315, 27, and 901.
120. Secs. 21, 32, 22, 24, and 25A. The maximum possible childcare credit under Section 21 is USD 2,100 (lower credit amounts are available for taxpayers with only one dependent and/or with higher adjusted gross income). Thus, the credit is inadequate to cover the actual costs of securing childcare while the taxpayer is working.
121. Sec. 56(b).
122. Sec. 57(a).
123. Sec. 55(b). This exemption is phased-out above specified income levels (e.g., married taxpayers with over USD 1 million of income, adjusted for inflation after 2018). Sec. 55(b)(1)(A) and (3), (d)(1), (3), and (4).
124. Sec. 55(b)(1) and (d)(3).
125. Sec. 55(b)(3).

2.4 TRUSTS

The tax treatment of trusts is complicated. In general, tax treatment depends on whether the trust is allowed to accumulate income. In the case of a so-called simple trust, which must distribute all of its ordinary income currently, the trust pays no income tax and the beneficiaries include the distributed amounts in their own income. In effect, the trust is treated as a conduit. This is accomplished by requiring the trust to report the taxable income it receives, but then allowing it to deduct the income that is distributed to the beneficiaries for that year.[126] The beneficiary reports the income on her individual tax return with the same character as that income had in the hands of the trust.[127]

In more complicated trusts (so-called complex trusts), which are permitted to accumulate all or part of the trust's ordinary income, the trust itself pays tax on income in the year that it is recognized and accumulated.[128] That income is generally not taxable to the recipient when subsequently distributed in later years.[129] If the complex trust distributes its income in the same year it receives it, the treatment is the same as for the simple trust—the trust recognizes taxable income, but is then allowed to deduct the distribution.

In some cases, the grantor of a trust retains such extensive controls or powers over the trust that she is considered to remain the owner of the trust property for income tax purposes. Under the "grantor trust" rules, the creator of the trust is taxable on the trust income each year and, in effect, makes a gift of the trust income to the beneficiary who in fact receives it.[130]

The treatment of foreign trusts and foreign beneficiaries is discussed at Chapter 5 section 5.8.

2.5 PARTNERSHIPS

Under US tax principles, a partnership is not treated as a separate taxpaying entity. Partnership income and deductions "flow through" to the individual partners, whether natural persons or juridical entities, and are taxed to them in accordance with the principles outlined in the preceding sections. The partnership itself is treated as an accounting entity for purposes of computing the partnership's net income or loss which is then apportioned to its partners. Accordingly, the partnership must file a tax return which fundamentally operates as an information return with respect to the items of partnership income and deduction.[131] The partnership's method of accounting, i.e.,

126. Secs. 641 and 651.
127. Sec. 652.
128. Sec. 641.
129. *See* Sec. 662(a). All the rules pertaining to the taxation of simple and complex trusts are contained in Sections 641-667 of the Code.
130. *See* Secs. 671-677.
131. Rules governing partnerships are set forth in Sections 701-761. Virtually all states have enacted legislation establishing "limited liability companies" (LLCs). An LLC has the corporate characteristic of limited liability but for tax purposes may be treated as either a partnership or

accrual or cash, generally determines when the partners recognize the partnership's income and expenses.[132]

In general, income and deductions realized at the partnership level retain their tax character when passed through to the partners.[133] Thus, for example, if the partnership realizes an item of tax-exempt income, that income remains tax-exempt in the hands of the partner to whom the income is allocated. Since the partnership earnings are taxed to the partners whether distributed or not, a partnership distribution to a partner ordinarily does not generate any further tax to the partner when received.[134]

The US tax rules applicable to partnerships treat the partnership in some cases as simply an aggregate of the individual partners, while for other purposes treat the partnership as a separate entity, independent of its individual members. For example, certain tax elections are made by the partnership as an entity rather than by the individual partners.[135] On the other hand, some limitations on deductions are applied to the individual partners rather than to the partnership itself, treating the partnership as an aggregate of the partners involved.[136]

The partnership is a popular form for conducting business and carrying on investment activities, for US persons and foreigners alike. Regulations provide great flexibility in allocating items of income, gain, deductions, and credit among the partners.[137] These rules permit the partners to control the timing and allocation of income and deductions to a degree that is not possible with an entity taxed as a corporation. Moreover, unlike a corporation, a partnership generally can be liquidated without current income tax consequences,[138] again in marked contrast to a corporate liquidation which normally produces two levels of tax.[139]

The reduction of the maximum corporate tax rate to 21% may reduce the popularity of partnerships, however, in situations where the business entity will retain its earnings for a significant period of time.[140]

---

a corporation. The text discussion of partnerships applies equally to an LLC which is taxed as a partnership. It applies also to any entity that has elected to be taxed as a partnership pursuant to the rules described in section 2.1.2.

132. Sec. 706(a).

133. Sec. 702(b).

134. This is not true if the total of partnership cash distributions to the partner exceed the partner's share of undistributed partnership income and the partner's original investment in the partnership. In that case, the partner will recognize gain.

135. *See* Sec. 703(b).

136. *See* Treas. Reg. Sec. 1.702-1(a)(8)(iii).

137. Treas. Reg. Sec. 1.704-1(b)(2).

138. Secs. 731-735.

139. To offset in part the tax advantages of the partnership form, a category of "publicly traded partnerships" was created that are taxable as corporations. Sec. 7704. Taxation as a corporation under these rules is not difficult to avoid, especially for passive investment partnerships.

140. *See* James R. Repetti, *The Impact of the 2017 Act's Tax Rate Changes on Choice of Entity*, 21 FLA. TAX REV. 687 (2018).

2.6 S CORPORATIONS

Another entity is the so-called S Corporation[141] in which all items of income, deduction, and credit are taken into account by the shareholders in proportion to their stock ownership. This is in contrast to partnerships, which as described in section 2.5, above, have great flexibility in allocating such items among partners.

The S corporation regime was originally developed for small business corporations. Accordingly, several eligibility requirements are imposed which are not applicable to partnerships. The S corporation: (i) can have no more than 100 shareholders, (family members count as a single shareholder), all of whom must be individual US citizens or residents (or certain qualified trusts and tax-exempt organizations), and (ii) can have only one class of stock. An S corporation which has a 100% owned subsidiary must treat all tax attributes of the subsidiary as its own.[142]

While an S corporation is often referred to as a corporation taxed like a partnership, such a statement is misleading. First, unlike a partnership, an S corporation realizes gain on all distributions of appreciated property, just as does a C corporation.[143] Second, all the rules applicable to C corporations (not the partnership rules) apply to S corporations in situations not dealt with by specific S corporation rules. Third, unlike a partnership, an S corporation cannot make special allocations of tax items among owners. Instead, each S corporation shareholder includes her share of income and expenses in proportion to her relative stock ownership.

An S corporation can be a vehicle through which US investors carry on transactions abroad. The form is of no utility to a foreign corporation or a nonresident alien individual since neither can be a shareholder in an S corporation.

2.7 OTHER FLOW THROUGH ENTITIES

2.7.1 Regulated Investment Company (RIC)

Certain types of investment companies, including mutual funds, may elect to be taxed on a flow through basis even though they otherwise are classified as corporations. All distributed income of the corporation is taxed only to the shareholders; the RIC is subject to taxation only on undistributed income. A qualifying RIC must maintain a diversified portfolio, and 90% of its gross income must be derived from dividends,

141. Corporations subject to the corporate tax regime described in section 2.2 are referred to as "C" corporations. The rules governing S corporations are set forth in Sections 1361-1378.
142. Sec. 1361. There is no limit on the size of an S corporation, whether measured in terms of income or assets.
143. The effect of this rule for an S corporation, however, is generally to accelerate the tax on the gain. Two levels of tax are usually avoided because the shareholders' basis in their stock is stepped up by the corporate level gain recognition and then reduced by the amount of the distribution. In some situations, however, corporate and shareholder level tax can both be incurred.

interest, and gains from the sale of stock or securities.[144] The governing provisions spell out in great detail other requirements that must be satisfied by the RIC.[145]

2.7.2 Real Estate Investment Trust (REIT)

A REIT is treated as a flow through entity if the detailed requirements of Sections 856-860 are satisfied. The most important of the requirements are that 75% of the REIT's gross income must be derived from passive real estate activities (the balance can only be from other passive investments such as stocks and bonds), the ownership interests must be widely held, and 90% of the REIT's taxable income must be distributed as dividends.[146] If the statutory requirements are met, distributions from the REIT are taxed only to the owners of the interests in the REIT.

2.7.3 Real Estate Mortgage Investment Conduit (REMIC)

A REMIC itself is not subject to tax; the holder of an interest in the REMIC is taxed directly on the REMIC income, whether distributed or not. The REMIC provisions (contained in Sections 860A-860E) were enacted to facilitate the pooling of real estate mortgages in an entity which could issue more than one class of ownership interest.

2.8 ACCOUNTING ASPECTS

Income and deductions are accounted for in the US tax system under a special set of a tax accounting rules. While there are many instances in which tax and financial accounting methods correspond, the tax accounting principles nonetheless represent a separate body of rules. There is no general requirement of conformity between tax and book accounting.

There are two general methods of accounting for income and deductions: the cash method and the accrual method. Under the *cash method* an income item is recognized in the year in which cash (or its equivalent) is received and an expense item is deductible in the year in which it is paid. (The expense must constitute a currently deductible expense rather than a capital expenditure.) Under the *accrual method* of accounting, the taxpayer includes items of income in the year in which a right to the payment arises and subtracts deductions in the year in which an expense is incurred. The accrual method of accounting is used by most business operations and is required for C corporations with gross receipts over USD 25 million and, in general, other businesses that operate with an inventory.[147] While the tax accrual method corresponds in general outline to financial accounting there are important differences. An

144. Sec. 851(b).
145. The RIC provisions are contained in Sections 851-855 and 860.
146. Sec. 856(c).
147. Sec. 448(c).

overriding principle in the tax accounting area is that the accounting method chosen must "clearly reflect income."[148]

Whatever the general accounting method of a taxpayer, there are a number of rules covering specific situations. For example, whether on the cash or accrual method, the taxpayer may account for certain sales of assets under the so-called installment sale method whereby the purchase payment received each year on the sale of an asset is treated in part as return of investment and in part as income.[149] Moreover, accrual method taxpayers that prepare financial statements must recognize income on their tax returns when they report such amounts as income on their financial statements even though such amounts have not yet accrued as income for tax purposes.[150]

The US has extensively developed rules relating to the "time value of money." The general effect of these provisions, where applicable, is to place both parties to a transaction on an accrual basis (even if one or both otherwise is entitled to use the cash method of accounting) or both parties on a cash basis (even if one or both otherwise would be on an accrual basis). The most important of the time value of money provisions are those dealing with "original issue discount."[151] In its simplest form, original issue discount arises, for example, where a corporation issues a ten-year bond with a face amount of USD 1,000 but, because it carries a below-market nominal interest rate, an investor will pay only USD 900 for the bond. The USD 100 differential is in fact interest, and both issuer and investor are required to account for that interest on an accrual basis. Thus, the borrower is entitled to deduct the interest on an accrual method over the ten-year period of the bond and the investor must include the same amount in income each year, even though no interest payment reflecting the discount is made until year ten. The original issue discount rules apply to a wide variety of situations involving financial instruments and must be considered in virtually every transaction involving the issuance of debt.[152]

Similar time value of money rules apply in the case of leases of property and special situations such as nuclear decommissioning costs.[153]

Income must be accounted for on an annual basis, usually the calendar year, though the corporate taxpayer is generally free to choose a fiscal year differing from the calendar year.[154] By and large, the annual accounting concept is followed quite rigorously and events which change the tax treatment of an item in a subsequent year are reflected in that year rather than through a recomputation of the tax liability for the

148. Sec. 446(b).
149. Secs. 453, 453A, and 453B. Generally, if a taxpayer holds installment debt in excess of USD 5 million, the taxpayer must pay an interest charge on the deferred tax.
150. Sec. 451(b) and (c).
151. Secs. 1272-1275.
152. Treasury Regulations issued under Sections 1272-1275 provide detailed rules for application of the original issue discount provisions.
153. Secs. 467 and 468A. Section 467 also authorizes regulations that would apply original issue discount principles to deferred payments for the performance of services. To date, no such regulations have been proposed.
154. With some exceptions, partnerships, S corporations, and personal service corporations must use the calendar year. Secs. 706(b), 1378, and 441(i).

earlier year. Here too, however, there are exceptions which treat integrated transactions on a unified basis even if they take place over several tax years.[155]

In general, income must be calculated and tax paid in US dollars.[156] This is true for both US taxpayers taxable on their worldwide income and foreign taxpayers taxable on income from US sources. The US rules regarding transactions in foreign currency are discussed in Chapter 13.

2.9 STATUTE OF LIMITATIONS, INFORMATION REPORTING, AND PENALTIES

In general, a three-year statute of limitation applies to tax matters.[157] A special six-year period applies if the taxpayer omits from gross income an amount in excess of 25% of the income shown on the return and the omitted amount is not disclosed in the return.[158] There is no time limit if a return is not filed or if the return is false or fraudulent. The taxpayer likewise has three years from the time the return was filed or two years from the time the tax was paid, whichever is later, to file a claim for refund.[159] Tax deficiencies carry an interest rate geared to the prevailing interest level as do successful refund claims.

The US Federal income and payroll taxes collect over USD 3.5 trillion annually. Administration of these taxes relies substantially on third-party information reporting of taxpayers' wages, investment income, and various categories of business income in addition to taxpayers' filing of tax returns.[160] Information returns are particularly important for administering the US income tax in relation to income from foreign corporations controlled by US persons, foreign corporations carrying on business in the United States, US corporations controlled by foreign persons, and foreign financial assets owned by US individuals.[161] There are a wide variety of civil and criminal penalties for tax underpayments, failure to file information returns, and tax evasion. Due to the low rate of audits of individual income tax returns (less than 1% per year), increased reliance has been placed on civil penalties imposed on taxpayers and tax advisors even though no tax evasion is involved.[162] Additional disclosure requirements have also been imposed in an attempt to curb tax shelters.[163]

To deal specifically with tax evasion by US taxpayers using foreign institutions, Congress adopted the Foreign Account Tax Compliance Act ("FATCA").[164] FATCA in very general terms requires foreign financial institutions (FFIs) to report financial assets held by US taxpayers. To "encourage" compliance by FFIs, FATCA imposes a

155. *See, e.g.*, Sec. 1341.
156. Sec. 6316.
157. Sec. 6501(a).
158. Sec. 6501(e).
159. Sec. 6511(a).
160. Secs. 6041-6060.
161. Secs. 6038-6038D.
162. Secs. 6651-6724.
163. Secs. 6111-6112.
164. Secs. 1471-1474.

30% withholding tax on payments of US source income to noncomplying FFIs or their clients even if such payments would otherwise not be subject to US tax.[165]

165. Section 1473(1) provides an exception from the withholding requirement for income effectively connected with a US trade or business. *See* Chapter 5 for a discussion of income effectively connected with a US trade or business.

CHAPTER 3

Jurisdictional Principles

As noted in Chapter 2, Section 1 of the Internal Revenue Code imposes a tax on the "taxable income" of every individual. Taxable income in turn is derived from the Section 61 definition of gross income, i.e., "all income from whatever source derived." The term "source" embraces within its meaning both the type of income derived and the geographical location to which the income is assigned under the Internal Revenue Code. As a result, in the first instance, the literal scope of the US income tax on *individuals* is to tax all individuals in the world on their worldwide income! However, subsequent provisions make it clear that the assertion of worldwide taxing jurisdiction is only meant to include individuals who are US citizens or residents.[1] For these taxpayers, US taxing jurisdiction is based on their personal relationship or status with respect to the US; the geographical source of their income is irrelevant.

Trusts and estates, whose taxation in very general terms approximates that of individuals, are likewise subject to US worldwide taxing jurisdiction if they are "domestic" entities.[2] A trust is a "domestic" entity if a US court is able to exercise primary supervision over the trust's administration and one or more US persons can control all substantial decisions of the trust.[3] An estate is "domestic" if a balancing of several factors, such as the residence of the decedent, the residences of the estate beneficiaries, and the location of the estate's assets, shows that the trust has sufficient contacts with the US.[4]

Nonresident aliens and foreign trusts and estates are also subject to US tax. For such taxpayers, however, the US tax jurisdiction is based on the geographic source of

1. *See* Chapter 5 section 5.5.2 for a discussion of the rules for determining whether an individual is a US resident.
2. *See* Chapter 2 section 2.4, Chapter 5 section 5.8, and Chapter 8 section 8.3 for the income tax treatment of domestic and foreign trusts.
3. Sec. 7701(a)(30)(E).
4. Rev. Rul. 81-112, 1981-1 C.B. 598 (applying Sec. 7701(a)(30)(D) and (a)(31) by examining several factors to determine whether the estate of a US citizen who had lived overseas for twenty years had sufficient US contacts to be treated as "domestic").

the taxpayer's income. These taxpayers, in general, are only subject to tax on income from sources within the US. Their business income from US sources is taxed in much the same way as that of a US citizen or resident, while their investment income is subject to a special set of tax rules.[5]

A partnership is "domestic" if it is "created or organized in the United States or under the laws of the United States or of any State."[6] Partnerships are treated as flow through entities regardless of whether they are domestic or foreign.[7] As a result, the focus of many US tax rules is not on whether the partnership is domestic or foreign, but rather on the residence of the partners and the source of income allocated to the partners.[8] Individual partners who are US residents will in general be taxable on their share of the partnership's income from all sources, regardless of whether the partnership is domestic or foreign. An individual partner who is not a US resident is generally only taxable on the partnership's income that is sourced in the US regardless of whether the partnership is domestic or foreign.[9]

The assertion of US worldwide tax jurisdiction with respect to corporations is based solely on the place of incorporation. A corporation incorporated under the laws of some other country is treated for US tax purposes as a foreign corporation. Foreign corporations, like nonresident alien individuals, are subject to US tax on income from US sources.[10]

While the US asserts taxing jurisdiction over the foreign income of its citizens and residents, it uses foreign tax credits to alleviate the so-called international double taxation that may arise when another country also seeks to tax a portion of that income. The credit is available to US citizens and residents and domestic corporations who pay taxes on foreign income to other countries.[11] Since 2017, certain US domestic corporations are also permitted in some circumstances to receive tax-free dividends from foreign corporations in which they own at least 10% of the stock if the dividends are attributable to non-US source income.[12]

The US in some instances also looks to the nationality or residence of a foreign corporation's *shareholders* in determining the appropriate pattern of taxation. In the case of a foreign corporation controlled by US shareholders, the normal US jurisdictional rules, which would allow deferral of US tax on the foreign income earned by a foreign corporation until its distribution to its US shareholders, are modified for certain types of undistributed income of the foreign corporation. In such cases, the US

5. *See* Chapter 5 sections 5.5 and 5.8, which discuss US taxation of nonresident individuals and foreign trusts, respectively.
6. Sec. 7701(a)(4).
7. *See* Chapter 5 section 5.7.1.
8. Classification as domestic or foreign partnership, however, can have other effects on the partnership. *See* Chapter 4 section 4.2.1 (discussing special source rules for interest paid by foreign partnerships), Chapter 5 section 5.7 (discussing taxation of foreign partnerships and partners), and Chapter 5 section 5.9 (discussing special disclosure and withholding obligations that might apply to domestic and foreign partnerships).
9. *See* Chapter 5 section 5.7.2.
10. *See* Chapter 5 section 5.6.
11. Foreign tax credits are discussed in Chapters 9 and 10.
12. Sec. 245A. Such dividends are discussed in Chapter 6.

shareholders of the "controlled foreign corporation" are subject to tax on their allocable share of the corporation's income, even though it is not currently distributed to them.[13] The US shareholders are permitted, however, to claim a credit for any foreign income tax paid by the controlled foreign corporation with respect to such undistributed income.[14] Special treatment is also provided for "passive foreign investment companies" (PFICs), by imposing an interest charge on deferred US taxes when a distribution is made (or applying certain elective alternative approaches to achieve rough equivalence to current taxation of a PFIC's earnings).[15]

A number of provisions are intended to protect the assertion of US taxing jurisdiction, such as Section 482 (according the IRS authority to allocate income and deductions among enterprises controlled or owned by the same interests in order clearly to reflect income)[16] and Section 367 (imposing a tax in certain situations where a US person enters into what would otherwise be a tax-free organization, reorganization, or liquidation involving a foreign corporation).[17]

The US has entered into a number of bilateral tax treaties that modify the above general pattern of US income taxation of international transactions.[18]

The foregoing discussion describes in the broadest terms the general pattern of US rules dealing with foreign income and foreign taxpayers. That general description masks technical provisions that are extraordinarily complex in interpretation and operation. To some degree, this complexity is to be expected since international transactions themselves—especially as conducted by multinational corporations—are necessarily complex.

The greatly increased complexity added by legislation in the last few decades has strained the ability of taxpayers to comply with, and tax administrators to enforce, the US rules that apply to international transactions. Yet, this legislation has been in response to strains on the ability of the income tax to cope with the effects of: (i) advances in modern information and communications technology, (ii) advances in transportation and logistics, (iii) globalization of capital, technology and production markets, and (iv) vastly increased sophistication of multinational tax planning, often guided by advisory firms that are either global themselves or networked globally for a project.

In the following chapters, we turn to an analysis of the most important of these provisions and the technical problems that have arisen in implementing them, viewed both from the standpoint of the tax administrator and from the standpoint of taxpayers who must live and operate within those rules.

---

13. *See* Chapter 6. In one sense, the controlled foreign corporation provisions introduce a different test to determine whether a corporation is a "domestic" corporation, i.e., the place of incorporation test gives way to one focusing on the residence or nationality of the shareholders. However, this generalization is not completely accurate, because it is the US shareholder and not the corporate entity that is subject to US tax. Some of the policy considerations behind the controlled foreign corporation provisions are considered in Chapter 6 sections 6.1 and 6.2.
14. *See* Chapter 9 section 9.5.
15. *See* Chapter 8 section 8.2.
16. *See* Chapter 12.
17. *See* Chapter 7.
18. *See* Chapter 14.

The provisions discussed in this volume are those in the US laws as of our writing. We would be remiss, however, to disregard altogether how substantial changes in the business and tax environment have been pushing countries around the globe to consider, separately and together, fundamental changes in international taxing jurisdiction. The United States, while markedly different economically from most countries, is not immune to these pressures on its international tax rules.

The global international tax rules (on which the US rules are based) were formulated in an era when manufacturing was dominant, leading to the sale of tangible goods as the baseline transaction paradigm used in the income tax. Finance was based on separate national currencies, each tethered by a fixed relation to a gold standard. Trade was between national markets, often separated by oceans, and countries were only recently linked by telephone cables. Accordingly, business and trade were overwhelmingly bilateral between countries. The international tax treaty network developed to mitigate double taxation followed that bilateral paradigm. As a result of these and other factors, the predominant form of business organization and geographic distribution of a business's organizational "footprint" was a corporation established in each country in which business was conducted. Under these conditions, the jurisdictional rules set out for US taxation are sensible and reasonably robust to abuse.

The extraordinary rise in fluidity with which international investment and business can be conducted in today's knowledge-based economies has eroded the assumptions and conditions that underlay key rules developed in that early era:

- Residence, of corporations in particular, was stable and linked to a single primary country in the early era. Today, corporate residence is readily changed. Moreover, use of different entity classifications has become an essential tool of sophisticated tax planning.
- The classification and assignment of income and deductions in the early era involved relatively few and straightforward income categories and expense allocations. Income categories were thought to have a reasonable nexus with a geographic source or place where economic activity was conducted. Today, the advent of modern contracting permits categories to be finessed or substituted and assets to be sliced into different ownership elements and tranches of risk. Large portions of business activity are knowledge-based and rely on intangible value for which legal and tax frameworks are inchoate. In the current business environment, it is far more difficult to reliably identify income with a category and a geographic source leaving room for tax planning.[19]
- International business activity and trade were fundamentally bilateral in the early era because of the costs and inefficiencies of communications, transport, and finance. Today, multiple entities and multiple countries are used to house

19. Indeed, there is reason to question whether Schanz-Haig-Simons income can be considered to have a geographic source from an economic perspective. Hugh J. Ault & David F. Bradford, *Taxing International Income: An Analysis of the U.S. System and Its Economic Premises*, in TAXATION IN THE GLOBAL ECONOMY 11, 31-32 (Assaf Razin & Joel Slemrod eds., U. Chi. Press 1990).

> supply chains, group finance hubs, and management service entities.[20] Entities are arranged strategically to earn income so as to minimize global tax bills. Structures using principal and commissionaire arrangements, intellectual property holding companies (including patent boxes), and remote digital platforms are used to shift substantial amounts of income out of countries where there is physical presence or to avoid physical presence altogether.

These changes have served as fodder for the sophisticated taxpayer as well as the tax advisory industry to minimize taxes in source and residence jurisdictions.

The shift to value-added taxes (VAT) from tariffs and sales taxes, which is the most significant global change in taxation over the past fifty years, addressed some of these pressures. The transaction-based, and near universal destination-based, design of the VAT mitigated international pressures as it raised substantial revenue.[21] The VAT, however, imposes a lower burden on capital than on labor, increasing pressure on income and wealth inequality. Moreover, as commonly implemented, the VAT has enforcement challenges and its positive efficiency attributes are undermined when countries fail to implement timely refunds. Importantly for this volume, the United States is unlikely in the short to medium time frame to follow other countries in adopting a Federal VAT or shifting its state tax regimes away from the sales tax.

The 2008 global financial crisis and resulting austerity shone a light on income tax revenue losses due to hidden offshore wealth of high net worth individuals and aggressive base erosion and profit shifting by multinational companies taking advantage of income tax pressure points. This led to political pressures in multiple countries that caused the G20 and OECD to initiate projects to combat tax evasion from offshore accounts (the Global Forum for Transparency and Information Exchange for Tax Purposes) and tax avoidance through income base erosion and profit shifting (BEPS) by multinationals. After agreeing to 15 "action items" to combat BEPS, that project morphed into the Inclusive Framework of over 130 countries. The G20/OECD Inclusive Framework currently has under consideration additional proposals to attack BEPS, referred to as Pillar 2 proposals, and to expand the jurisdiction of countries to tax large multinational companies on remote digital activities that derive material income from a country without a physical presence (i.e., a permanent establishment) in the country, referred to as Pillar 1 proposals.

The additional BEPS Pillar 2 changes under consideration by the G20/OECD are lightly modeled on two US provisions added in 2017, an anti-base erosion minimum tax (discussed in Chapter 5 section 5.10) and the current inclusion of global low-taxed intangible income (GILTI) (discussed in Chapter 6). The Pillar 1 changes under consideration by the G20/OECD are more fundamental and would expand the ability of countries to tax certain remote digital businesses that make sales into a country without a physical presence. Future changes in US jurisdiction to tax remote business activity likely will parallel those gaining consensus among countries in the G20/OECD

20. R. Baldwin, The Great Convergence: Information Technology and the New Globalization, 114-141 (Harv. U. Press 2016).
21. The Modern VAT, 4-13 (eds. Liam Ebrill, Michael Keen, Jean-Paul Bodin, and Victoria Summers, IMF 2001).

Inclusive Framework, albeit the motivation for changes in each country varies in part according to local conditions.

We briefly consider here how the pressure points sought to be addressed in the Pillar 1 and Pillar 2 proposals manifest in the United States and consider why future changes likely will follow in their direction. Broadly, the United States shifted decades ago from being a net capital exporter to being a very large net capital importer. There is a stark disparity, however, between the US net portfolio capital position, which is deeply in deficit, and the US net direct investment position, which continues to be positive, meaning that US foreign direct investment (FDI) outbound stock is larger than the stock of inbound FDI. The inbound FDI is large in absolute terms, however, and the United States is a very substantial market country not just for imports of goods but also for inbound FDI, including from investment hubs. The top fifteen sources of US inbound FDI stock include Ireland, the Netherlands, Switzerland, Bermuda, and Singapore. These same countries, along with Luxembourg, also are the top fifteen fastest growing sources of US inbound FDI flows.[22] Accordingly, US national interest and its business tax base are not fundamentally divergent from that of other developed countries with respect to BEPS issues.

Like other developed countries, the US tax base is exposed to remote economic activity outside the reach of its taxing jurisdiction. At the sub-Federal level, states in the United States have struggled with the issue of remote sellers from other states (and outside the United States) selling goods into a state without being subject to a sales and use tax or an income tax. The US Supreme Court's *Wayfair* overruled a prior decision that had placed constitutional restrictions on a state's ability to tax remote sales into a state.[23] The Court's reasoning should apply equally to protect the ability of the Federal government to expand its tax jurisdiction to remote sellers.

Over time, if the US income tax is to be retained as the primary US tax instrument, changes eventually will be necessary to respond to the pressure points described, including the ability to tax remote sellers, in order to continue to raise revenue at the scale required. While the size of the US domestic market shields the United States from immediate or extreme tax base pressures from BEPS, it is likely that the significant jurisdictional changes sought by countries in the rest of the world will find their way into the US rules. We look forward to reviewing those changes, however, in a future edition of this volume.

22. US International Trade Administration, Select USA Stats for 2019, available at https://www.selectusa.gov/FDI-in-the-US.
23. *South Dakota v. Wayfair*, 138 S. Ct. 2080 (2018) (involving an out-of-state internet seller of home goods).

CHAPTER 4

Source Rules

4.1 GENERAL

The Code in Sections 861-865 and the regulations issued thereunder present detailed rules for determining the source of income for US tax purposes. The exclusive function of these rules is to establish whether income is derived from sources within the United States ("US source income") or from sources without the United States ("foreign source income"). Other sections of the Code dictate the operative results that flow from the source determination.

The most important substantive areas that depend on the source rules are: (1) the tax treatment of nonresident aliens and foreign corporations, which, in general, are taxed only on US source income; and (2) the limitations applicable to the foreign tax credit allowed to a US taxpayer, which are fixed by the amount of the taxpayer's foreign source income, determined under US source rules.[1] In general, the same source rules apply regardless of the taxpayer's status, though in some cases the source of a particular item of income depends on whether a foreign taxpayer or a US taxpayer receives it.

1. Income as defined for tax purposes does not have a clear relationship to a geographic source. *See* Hugh J. Ault & David F. Bradford, *Taxing International Income: An Analysis of the U.S. System and Its Economic Premises*, in TAXATION IN THE GLOBAL ECONOMY 11, 12-16 (Assaf Razin & Joel Slemrod eds., 1990) (observing that the Schanz-Haig-Simons income concept is "not susceptible to characterization as to source at all" but attaches to a taxpayer that consumes and owns assets). The two purposes described for the Code's source rules are principally for allocating primary and residual taxing rights between countries. The Code's source rules are instrumental and may differ according to whether the rule is being employed to determine the right of the US to tax income of a nonresident or to defer to another country's primary right to tax income and allow a foreign tax credit in relation to that income. Contrast, for example, the use of the place of title passage as the source for sales of inventory by a US person (Sec. 865(b)) with the overriding rule that a nonresident's sale of inventory attributable to a US office will be US source irrespective of title passage (Sec. 865(e)(2)).

In addition, the applicability of a number of other Code provisions depends on whether income is determined to be from US or foreign sources.[2]

4.2 APPLICATION OF SOURCE RULES TO SPECIFIC ITEMS OF GROSS INCOME

Sections 861 and 862 set forth rules for determining the source of specified types of gross income.[3] Section 865 has special rules for gross income from the sale of personal property. Section 863 provides source rules for items of income that are not otherwise specified.

2. Source rules play an important role in new tax regimes adopted in the 2017 Tax Act, including GILTI, the exemption for foreign dividends paid to a 10% corporate US shareholder under Section 245A, and FDII. *See* Chapter 6 sections 6.4 and 6.5 and Chapter 11 section 11.2.2.2 for discussions of GILTI, the new dividend exemption, and FDII. The following two paragraphs provide a brief description of GILTI and FDII.

   The new "GILTI" regime, which is discussed in detail in Chapter 6, now allows a portion of the earnings of controlled foreign corporations ("CFCs") to be exempt from US taxation entirely—both as the CFC earns it and, later, when it is distributed to its US corporate shareholders as a dividend. (Individual US shareholders continue to have US tax deferred on this amount as it is earned by the CFC, but it becomes taxable when the CFC distributes it to them.) At the same time, the GILTI regime now taxes US shareholders currently on amounts of income earned by the CFC that exceed the amounts that are tax-free regardless of whether such income is distributed. It reduces the effective US tax on such income, however, from 21% to 10.5% (before taking account of certain deductions and foreign taxes) for US corporate shareholders.

   The new FDII regime, which is discussed in Chapter 11, reduces from 21% to 13.125% the effective US tax on income of a US corporation arising from foreign sales and services according to a formula that seeks to apply the reduced tax rate to the US corporation's foreign income that is attributable to its intangible property. To that end, the formula treats income exceeding 10% of the corporation's domestic tangible assets as though attributable to intangible property. Then, the formula estimates the portion of this income due to intangible property that should be treated as foreign and secure the benefit of lower taxation. This amount is the same portion of total income from intangible property (calculated per the formula) as the corporation's foreign income from sales and services provided to foreign persons for foreign use bears to the corporation's total income. The reduced tax on profits in excess of 10% of domestic tangible assets is intended to encourage US corporations to not transfer intangible property overseas. The incentive is intended instead to encourage US corporations to retain intangible property in the US and license such property overseas.
3. The reader should be aware that a host of difficult definitional problems lurk behind the seemingly straightforward list of income items set forth in sections 4.2.1-4.2.7. For example, the term "interest" includes not only direct interest paid but also imputed interest under Section 483 and original issue discount under Section 1273 (*see* Chapter 2 section 2.8). "Dividend" is a term of art in US tax law, being defined in Section 316 as distributions of the corporation's earnings and profits (*see* Chapter 2 section 2.2.5). Because Treas. Reg. Sec. 1.861-3(a)(1) refers to Section 316, it is possible for some distributions to be treated as dividends for corporate law purposes, but still not constitute "dividends" for source tax rule purposes. Conversely, a distribution which is treated as a dividend under Section 316 (even though in corporate law terms it is not a dividend) is a dividend for source rule purposes. There is also an uncertain and much litigated line in US tax jurisprudence between compensation for personal services and receipts from royalty income or the sale of intangible property. The classification of the receipt under US tax principles will determine which of the source rules described in sections 4.2.3, 4.2.4, or 4.2.6 will be applicable.

4.2.1 Interest

In general, interest received on an obligation issued by a US resident[4] or domestic corporation constitutes US source income.[5] There is, however, an important exception to the general rule that applies to obligations issued before August 10, 2010.[6] If 80% or more of the US obligor's gross income is derived from the active conduct of a foreign trade or business, then the interest on an obligation issued by such obligor before August 10, 2010 is treated as foreign source in its entirety when received by an unrelated party.[7]

Interest received from a foreign branch of a US bank is foreign source income.[8] Interest received from a foreign obligor, in general, is treated as foreign source to the recipient. However, interest received from a US branch of a foreign corporate obligor is treated as US source.[9]

Special rules apply to foreign partnerships. If a foreign partnership, which has a US trade or business, is not predominately engaged in the active conduct of a trade or business outside the US, then all the interest paid by it will be US source to the recipient.[10] In contrast, if the partnership is predominately engaged in the active conduct of a trade or business outside the US, then only the interest paid by the US trade or business of the foreign partnership is treated as US source to the recipient.

For purposes of the foreign tax credit, interest paid by a US-owned foreign corporation to its US shareholders is treated as US source interest income to the

4. IRS Chief Counsel Advice Memorandum 201205007 (Oct. 18, 2011) provided guidance on the source of interest income received from US citizens and resident aliens living outside the United States. It observed that Treas. Reg. Section 1.861-2(a)(1) treats interest paid by a US "resident" as US source income and that Treas. Reg. Section 1.861-2(a)(2)(i) defines a US "resident" to "include ... an individual who at the time of payment of the interest is a *resident* of the United States" (emphasis added). It concluded that the *residence* of a US citizen or lawful permanent resident for purposes of sourcing their interest paid should be determined at the time the interest payment is made by applying the "substantial presence test" found in Treas. Reg. Section 301.7701(b)-1 through (b)-9. *Id.* As discussed in Chapter 5 section 5.5.2.2, the "substantial presence test" determines a taxpayer's residence in part based on the duration of the taxpayer's presence in the country. Thus, a US citizen who is present in a foreign country for a significant period of time would be treated as a resident in that country and interest paid by that person to a foreign lender would not be US source.
5. Sec. 861(a)(1). Interest paid by a US bank to a foreign recipient is US source income but is exempt from US tax. *See* Chapter 5 section 5.5.5.1. *See also* the discussion of the exemption for US source "portfolio" interest income discussed in Chapter 5 section 5.5.5.3.
6. Pub. L. No. 111-226, Sec. 217(d)(2)(A) (2010) (repeal Sec. 861(a)(1)(A) and 861(c)).
7. The determination whether the exception is applicable is made by considering the ratio of active foreign business income to the total income of the US obligor for the three-year period preceding the year in which the interest is paid (the "testing period"). The exception does not apply to interest payable to a related person. Pub. L. No. 111-226, Sec. 217(d)(2)(B) (2010).
8. Sec. 861(a)(1)(A)(i).
9. Section 884(f)(1)(A) treats such interest as "paid by a domestic corporation" thus giving it a US source. Source rules for interest income are thus the same whether a US branch or a US subsidiary of a foreign corporation pays the interest. *See* Chapter 5 section 5.6.6.1 for a discussion of the attribution of interest payments to a US branch.
10. Sec. 861(a)(1)(B).

shareholders to the extent that it is allocated to US source income of the paying corporation.[11]

4.2.2 Dividends

Dividends from US corporations constitute US source income regardless of the income composition of the corporation.[12]

Dividends from foreign corporations generally will be foreign source income. However, dividends paid by a foreign corporation conducting a trade or business in the US constitute US source income if 25% or more of the corporation's gross income from all sources was, for the preceding three years, effectively connected with the conduct of a trade or business in the US. If the 25% limit is exceeded, a portion of the dividend is US source income that is the same as the proportion of the corporation's gross income that is effectively connected with a US trade or business.[13] For foreign tax credit purposes, Section 904(h) treats dividends from a US-owned foreign corporation as US source income to the extent derived from US source income of the paying corporation.

Although the 2017 tax reform did not change the source rules for dividend income, it introduced a 100% "dividends received deduction" ("DRD") for US corporations receiving foreign source dividends from an 10% owned foreign subsidiary.[14] On its own, the new DRD could signal a shift by the US away from worldwide taxation and toward territorial taxation, with potential implications for the significance of source. Two important caveats complicate such a conclusion. First, the US international tax system prior to the 2017 tax reform was neither worldwide nor territorial in its net effects, and in some circumstances, afforded a measure of tax planning for some US taxpayers that was more advantageous than either. Second, the 2017 tax reform not only added this foreign DRD (a shift toward territorial taxation), but it also introduced a new tax (the GILTI tax[15]) for US shareholders on certain low-taxed foreign source income of their foreign subsidiaries (*see* Chapter 6 section 6.4)—which may function as a global minimum tax.

4.2.3 Personal Services Income

In general, US source income includes all income derived from personal services performed in the US, regardless of the residence of the payer, where the contract was

11. Sec. 904(h). This rule prevents the US shareholder from "converting" US source income to foreign source interest income by routing it through a US-owned foreign corporation.
12. Sec. 861(a)(2). Special rules apply to pre-2011 dividends paid to foreign shareholders where the domestic corporation has substantial foreign business income. Post-2010, certain transition rules apply. *See* Chapter 5 section 5.5.5.2.
13. Sec. 861(a)(2)(B). These dividends are not subject to US withholding because the foreign corporation will be subject to the branch profits tax discussed at Chapter 5 section 5.6.5.
14. Sec. 245A. *See* Chapter 6 section 6.5.
15. *See supra* note 2, above, for a brief description of GILTI.

entered into, or where the payment was made.[16] However, compensation derived from services performed within the US will constitute foreign source income if: (1) it is received by a nonresident alien who is temporarily in the US for not more than ninety days in a year, (2) it does not exceed USD 3,000, and (3) the services are performed for a foreign payer not engaged in a trade or business in the US (or for a foreign business operation of a US person).[17]

Compensation for personal services performed outside the US is foreign source income.[18]

4.2.4 Rents and Royalties

All rents and royalties from property, tangible and intangible, located or used in the US are US source income.[19] Included are rents or royalties for the use in the US of intangible assets such as patents, copyrights, and secret processes.[20] Proposed regulations now seek to distinguish software transactions not on the cloud from those that

16. *Dillin v. Commissioner*, 56 T.C. 228, 244 (1971) ("source income is determined by the situs of the services rendered, not by the location of the payor, the residence of the taxpayer, the place of contracting, or the place of payment.").
17. Sec. 861(a)(3). The foreign employer will not be regarded as engaged in a US trade or business by virtue of the activities of the employee that are examined for purposes of applying the source rule. Treas. Reg. Sec. 1.861-4(a)(3). It is important to note that provision of "personal services" is not limited to individuals. A corporation can provide personal services such as advertising services. *See, e.g.*, *Tipton and Kalmbach, Inc. v. U.S.*, 480 F.2d 1118 (10th Cir. 1973) (corporation contracted to provide engineering services was providing personal services).
18. Sec. 862(a)(3). Treas. Reg. Sec. 1.861-4(b)(1) and (2) provide that where services are performed in part within and in part without the US an apportionment of the amount paid between US and foreign sources must be made "on the basis that most correctly reflects the proper source of income under the facts and circumstances of the particular case." Apportionment on a time basis is one, but not the only, acceptable method of apportionment under the Regulation. For examples of application of the allocation rules in personal services situations, *see* Rev. Rul. 87-38, 1987-1 C.B. 176 (compensation paid to nonresident alien hockey player allocated based on time); *Stemkowski v. Commissioner*, 690 F.2d 40 (2d Cir. 1982) (hockey player's income allocated between Canada and the US on the basis of all days of service, including training camp and playoffs). Special rules apply to services rendered in connection with international transportation. *See* Secs. 861(a)(3) (last sentence) and 863(c).
19. Sec. 861(a)(4). In Rev. Rul. 80-362, 1980-2 C.B. 208, the Internal Revenue Service took the position that the royalty source rule applied to source royalty payments in the US where a foreign third party received the payments from a foreign licensee which had in turn relicensed the intangible for use in the United States. In *SDI Netherlands BV v. Commissioner*, 107 TC 161 (1996), the Tax Court rejected the "cascading" royalty approach of Rev. Rul. 80-362 in a somewhat similar factual situation. The interposed foreign company, which received royalties from both US and foreign sources, was not a "conduit" and the court refused to "flow through" the source of the royalties received by the company to the royalties paid in order to make them partially US source.
20. Transfers of rights to intangibles often have elements of license, sale, and personal services intertwined in the same transactions. The exact classification of the amounts received is important since the applicable source rules are different for each category. *See, e.g.*, *Goosen v. Commissioner*, 136 T.C. 547 (2011) (examining whether endorsement fees received by a high-profile professional golfer should be "characterized as solely personal services income, solely royalty income, or part personal services income, part royalty income"); *Garcia v. Commissioner*, 140 T.C. 141 (2013) (concluding that the taxpayer-golf pro's endorsement

involve cloud computing in an effort to continue to reflect changing technology and commercial behavior.[21]

If the transfer of the rights to the intangible is treated as a sale rather than a license for tax purposes, the royalty source rule (and not the sale source rule, *see* section 4.2.6) applies to any payments that are contingent on factors such as use and productivity.[22]

Rents and royalties from property located or used (or for the privilege of using) outside the US are foreign source income.[23]

4.2.5 Gains from Disposition of Real Property

Gains from the disposition of "United States real property interests" constitute US source income. Gains from sales of real estate located outside the US are foreign source income.[24]

4.2.6 Gains from Sale of Personal Property

As a general rule, gain from the sale of personal property is sourced at the residence of the seller.[25] There are, however, a number of exceptions to the general rule.

---

income was to be characterized as 65% royalties and 35% personal services). Similar characterization issues arise concerning the classification of payments received in connection with computer programs. *See infra* note 21.

21. Treas. Reg. Sec. 1.861-18 provides detailed rules and numerous examples to resolve the many classification issues that arise in transactions involving computer programs. For example, suppose that a taxpayer has the copyright on a computer program and grants a right to a foreign customer to make fifty copies of the program for use by its employees at one location (a "site license"). Is the transaction a license, generating foreign source royalty income, or should it be viewed as the equivalent of the sale of fifty disks, which would be treated under the rules on sourcing sales income discussed in section 4.2.6? Example 10 of the Regulation treats a site license as a sale of the copyrighted property and not a license. Proposed regulations would change the location of the sale of the site license from the place where title was transferred to the place where the download/installation on the end user's device occurred. Prop. Treas. Reg. Sec. 1.861-18(f)(2)(ii). Additionally, the proposed regulations would expand the reach of the software regulations to cover digital content. Prop. Treas. Reg. Sec. 1.861-18(a)(3) and -18(h) Ex. 21.

    Proposed regulations issued in August 2019, Prop. Treas. Reg. Sec. 1.861-19, acknowledge that the existing regime for software was not fully suited to cloud computing, and instead offered guidance specific to those transactions. The Preamble to these proposed regulations describes cloud computing as involving "access to property or use of property, instead of the sale, exchange, or license of property, and therefore typically would be classified as either a lease of property or a provision of services." The proposed regulations are formally classification rules, not sourcing rules, and they apply for purpose of key international provisions including Sections 59A, 245A, 250, 267A, 367, 482, and 1059A. In general, Prop. Treas. Reg. Sec. 1.861-19 uses a multifactor test to determine whether income from cloud computing constitutes a lease of property or a provision of services, with the likelihood that services will often be the prevailing classification. Prop. Treas. Reg. Sec. 1.861-19(c) (2019).

22. Sec. 865(d)(1)(B).
23. Sec. 862(a)(4).
24. Secs. 861(a)(5) and 862(a)(5).
25. Sec. 865(a). For purposes of applying this source rule, special provisions determine the residence of an individual that depend in part on the location of his "tax home," a term that is

With respect to inventory (i.e., property held for sale to customers), the rule for sourcing gain depends on the type of inventory. If the taxpayer has purchased inventory to resell (i.e., serves as a "middleman"), then gain generally is sourced at the place where the sale takes place.[26] The regulations provide that the place of sale is generally the country in which the rights, title, and interest of the seller pass. If the seller retains a bare legal title, then the sale occurs where the risk of loss passes. If tax avoidance was the primary purpose for structuring a transaction in a particular manner, the Treasury will look to all the surrounding circumstances to determine where the substance of the sale occurred.[27] However, there remains quite a bit of planning flexibility for taxpayers whose inventory is sourced subject to this "title passage" rule.

Property both produced and subsequently sold either entirely within the US or entirely outside the US similarly is taxed where the sale takes place (which is also where the production has taken place).

The 2017 Tax Act revised the sourcing of produced inventory where production occurs in full or in part in the US and the sale outside, or the reverse. Such income will now in general be sourced under new Section 863(b) "solely on the basis of production activities with respect to the property."[28]

---

used in Section 162(a)(2) and is the subject of frequent dispute between taxpayers and the IRS. Sec. 865(g)(1)(A)(i). A corporation is a resident of the country under the laws of which it is created. Sec. 865(g)(1)(A)(ii).

26. Treas. Reg. Sec. 1.861-7(a). This rule is colloquially known as the "title passage" rule. *See US v. Balanovski*, 236 F.2d 298 (2d Cir. 1956) (embracing the bright line title passage principles); *see also AP Green Export Company v. US*, 284 F.2d 383 (Cl. Ct. 1960) (same).
27. Treas. Reg. Sec. 1.861-7(c). Despite this language in the regulations suggesting potential scrutiny of the context behind title passage cases, courts seem to consistently embrace title passage outcome.
28. Sec. 863(b). Prior to the statutory change in 2017, income from inventory produced within the US and sold outside (or the reverse) was allocated partly to US source and partly to foreign source under Section 863. A taxpayer could elect under Treas. Reg. Sec. 1.863-3(b) between the "50/50" method and the "Independent Factory Price" ("IFP") method to source income from export sales of manufactured goods. Treas. Reg. Sec. 1.863-3(a)(2) and (b). A third method, based on the taxpayer's books and records, was available with the consent of the IRS. Under the 50/50 method, one-half of the taxpayer's gross income was considered attributable to "production activity" and one-half to "sales activity." If all of the production activities were in the US, all of the production income was US source. If there were production activities both within and outside the US, the income was allocated on the basis of the relative tax basis of the production assets. Treas. Reg. Sec. 1.863-3(c)(1)(ii). With respect to the sales activities, the income was allocated according to the title passage rule (section 4.2.6), unless the property was sold for consumption in the US in which case the income will be US source. Treas. Reg. Sec. 1.863-3(c)(2).

    The second pre-2017 Tax Act method for allocating income between production and sales activities—the IFP method—was available for taxpayers with regular sales through independent distributors. The sales price to the independent distributor determined the amount of the income attributable to production activities with the remainder attributed to sales. For example, if a taxpayer produced goods with a cost of goods sold at USD 80 and sold them to an unrelated distributor for USD 100, then the US source production income was USD 20. If the taxpayer also sold the same or similar goods directly for USD 110 to a retail outlet, the US source production was USD 20 and the foreign source sales income was USD 10. Treas. Reg. Sec. 1.863-3(b)(2)(iv) Ex. 1.

    Gain on depreciable property is sourced under the inventory rule except that gain attributable to previously taken depreciation deductions is sourced in the US if the depreciation

In general, other gain attributable to a sale by an office or other fixed place of business established outside of the taxpayer's country of residence has its source where the office is located.[29] A special rule in Section 865(e)(2) governs nonresidents who make a sale of personal property or inventory through their US office or other fixed place of business: income from that sale is sourced in the US. Thus, in the case of a nonresident with foreign manufactured inventory sold through their US office/fixed place of business, the new Section 863(b) source rule (sourcing all income based on where production occurred) will *not* apply. Instead, the special office or fixed place of business rule in Section 865(e)(2) prevails. Treas. Reg. Section 1.865-3(d) provides that the default method for allocating income attributable to the US office/fixed place of business under Section 865(e)(2) is to allocate 50% of such income to the place of production and 50% to the US office/fixed place of business.[30]

Gain on the sale of stock in an affiliated foreign corporation realized by a US resident is sourced outside the US if the foreign corporation derives the bulk of its income in the country in which the sale takes place.[31]

The 2017 Tax Act confirmed that gain or loss incurred by a nonresident or foreign corporation on the sale of its interest in a partnership engaged in US trade or business will be treated as effectively connected—to the extent a sale of the partnership's underlying assets would have been so treated.[32] This legislative change confirmed the IRS' established position which had been undermined by a 2017 Tax Court case.[33]

4.2.7 Insurance Underwriting Income

Income derived from insuring US risks is US source income. All other underwriting income is foreign source income.[34]

4.3 APPLICATION OF SOURCE RULES TO OTHER ITEMS OF INCOME

Section 863(a) gives the fiscal authorities broad power to allocate or apportion between US and foreign sources items of gross income other than those enumerated above.[35]

Where an item of income lacks a clear source rule in the tax law, the IRS and the courts often seek to analogize the payment to one for which there is clearer guidance

---

was taken as a deduction against US source income. Sec. 865(c).

29. Sec. 865(e). In the case of a US resident, the gain must be subject to a foreign tax of at least 10%. In the case of a nonresident with a US office, the gain will not be US source under this rule if the property is sold outside the US and an office of the taxpayer in the foreign country materially participated in the sale. *See* Chapter 5 section 5.3.2.4.
30. Treas. Reg. Sec. 1.865-3(d). The regulations provide that the default rule is to allocate income 50/50 between the place of production and the place of sale, but the seller may elect to use the books and records method.
31. Sec. 865(f).
32. Sec. 864(c)(8).
33. *See Grecian Magnesite Mining, Industries & Shipping Co. v. Commissioner*, 149 T.C. 63 (2017).
34. Sec. 861(a)(7).
35. *See* Rev. Rul. 89-67, 1989-1 C.B. 237, applying this authority to determine the source of a payment made as a scholarship, fellowship, or an award for puzzle solving activities.

on source. For example, in *Bank of America v. United States*, 680 F.2d 142 (Ct. Cl. 1982), the court relied on sourcing by analogy to determine the appropriate source for fees charged by the bank for confirmed letters of credit, banker's acceptances, and negotiations regarding export letters of credit. In particular, the court examined the degree to which each fee was or was not sufficiently comparable to interest and thus should be sourced accordingly.

Guarantee fees also created sourcing challenges until Congress adopted a rule. Such fees can be generated when a parent corporation guarantees a loan for its subsidiary, thereby earning a guarantee fee. Initially, the source of such fees was the subject of some dispute. In *Container Corp. v. Commissioner*, 134 T.C. 122 (2010), the court determined that guarantee fees earned by the Mexican parent of a US subsidiary for guaranteeing the subsidiary's debt were more akin to services income than interest and thus were foreign source. Effectively overriding the result in this case, Congress added Section 861(a)(9) providing that guarantee fees received from a domestic corporation (or a noncorporate resident) will be US source.

Regulations under Section 863(a) have been issued dealing with the source of income from "notional principal contracts" where payments are calculated on a notional principal amount and based on some external index.[36] Such income is generally sourced at the residence of the taxpayer unless the contract is associated with a business abroad.

Taxable scholarships are sourced based on the residence of the payer. (Scholarship payments made for the performance of services are sourced under the service income source rules.) However, a special rule treats as foreign source any payments by a US grantor to a foreign person for activities to be performed outside the US, thus avoiding a potential US tax on much US-based educational support.[37]

Regulations concerning natural resources extracted in the US and sold outside the US give a US source to all of the income. If additional production is performed by the taxpayer outside the US before the sale, the Regulations allocate the income between US and foreign sources based on the fair market value immediately prior to the additional production.[38]

Section 863 also contains rules to allocate income from transportation and communications to sources within and without the US.

36. Treas. Reg. Sec. 1.863-7. These source rules do not apply, however, to notional principal contracts that index dividend payments. Temp. Reg. Sec. 1.863-7T(a)(1). Proposed regulations indicate that such contracts will be sourced in the US if the indexed dividends are from US corporations. Prop. Treas. Reg. Sec. 1.871-15 (2012).
37. Treas. Reg. Sec. 1.863-1(d)(2)(iii).
38. Treas. Reg. Sec. 1.863-1(b).

4.4 ALLOCATION OF DEDUCTIONS TO ARRIVE AT TAXABLE INCOME

4.4.1 Background

The foregoing rules have involved the determination of the source of "gross income." The proper allocation of deductions to arrive at taxable income from a US or foreign source is an independent question. Sections 861(b), 862(b), 863(a), and 863(b) each contain provisions granting broad authority to the Treasury to issue regulations for the allocation of deductions, losses, and expenses between US and foreign sources.

Thus, unlike the statutorily based provisions for determining the source of gross income items, the rules with respect to the allocation of deductions are contained primarily in Treasury Regulations. The length and complexity of the allocation of deduction regulations have grown substantially since the first serious attempt to develop regulations was made in 1977.

The regulations provide general rules applicable to all types of deductible expenditures. In addition, specific rules are detailed for certain types of deductible items, notably interest, research and development costs, and overhead expenses.

4.4.2 General Rules

Under the general rules of the Regulations,[39] deductions must first be allocated to a "class" of gross income to which the deductions "definitely relate." The classes of gross income include the types of income described in section 4.2. In some cases, however, the Regulations group several of those income items into a single class (e.g., gains derived from dealings in property) and also add some additional classes of income. As a basic proposition, deductions are to be allocated to a class of gross income based on the "factual relationship" between the deductions and the class of gross income. It is not necessary that in a given year the taxpayer actually have realized income in the class to which the deductions relate; it is only necessary that the property or activity has generated, or will reasonably be expected to generate, gross income. Thus, for a given year, deductions allocable to a class of income may exceed the income actually realized in that class.[40]

Once deductions have been allocated to the appropriate class of gross income, it may then be necessary to make an apportionment of the deductions within each class of income. When required, such apportionment occurs between the "statutory grouping" of gross income and the "residual grouping" of gross income within each class of income. A statutory grouping is comprised of the gross income from a specific source that must be determined in order to apply other sections of the Code. For example, consider a US corporation that has both US and foreign source income because it is engaged in a business in the US and another country. The class of gross income is

39. Treas. Reg. Sec. 1.861-8.
40. Treas. Reg. Sec. 1.861-8(a)(2), (3); 1.861-8(b); and 1.861-8(d)(1).

income derived from business.[41] If it is necessary to determine the corporation's foreign tax credit limitation under Section 904, the relevant statutory grouping is foreign source income and the residual grouping is US source income. If instead a nonresident taxpayer were conducting business in the US, the statutory grouping would be "effectively connected income" (*see* Chapter 5 section 5.3) and the residual grouping would be all other income. Thus, the items of income assigned to a particular statutory grouping depend upon which operative section of the Code is under consideration.[42]

Apportionment of deductions between a statutory grouping and the residual grouping is required in two situations:

(1) where a class of income to which deductions are allocated is in part in the statutory grouping and in part in the residual grouping; and
(2) where the class of income contains more than one statutory grouping.

If a class of gross income is entirely within one grouping, no apportionment is required.

As in the case of the rules governing the allocation of deductions to particular classes of income, the apportionment of deductions between statutory and residual groupings is to be made on the basis of the "factual relationship" of the deductions and the groupings. Factors are provided that are to be taken into account in effecting an apportionment, such as a comparison of the units sold that are attributable to each grouping, a comparison of the gross sales and receipts attributable to each grouping, or the costs of goods sold attributable to each grouping. Deductions not definitely related to any class of gross income must be apportioned on the basis of gross income in the statutory grouping to total gross income[43] but given the specificity of the apportioning rules, this type of deduction presumably will occur infrequently.

An example will illustrate the operation of the allocation and apportionment rules:

Example

Assume that a foreign taxpayer's sole business is manufacturing trucks abroad and selling the trucks in the US through a US sales branch and in other countries through other foreign branches. The US sales branch constitutes a US trade or business (or, in treaty terminology, a permanent establishment). The foreign taxpayer will be taxed on a net basis on the US source income effectively connected to its US sales business. Thus, the foreign taxpayer must first determine its US source income from the sale of goods into the US. Then the foreign taxpayer must determine what expenses are deductible against its US source income to calculate net income that will be taxed at the applicable rates.

Step 1—determining the US source income of the foreign taxpayer: Post 2017 tax reform, the general source rule for manufactured inventory sources the income exclusively to the location of production (*see* section 4.2.6). Applied here, that

41. Treas. Reg. Sec. 1.861-8(a)(3)(ii).
42. Treas. Reg. Sec. 1.861-8(a)(2), (4). *See* Treas. Reg. Sec. 1.861-8(f) for a partial list of operative sections of the Code.
43. Temp. Treas. Reg. Sec. 1.861-8T(c)(1); Treas. Reg. Sec. 1.861-8(c)(3).

would result in the income being foreign source. However, assuming the taxpayer's US sales branch constitutes an office or other fixed place of business, then the special rule in Section 865(e)(2) applies and supersedes other sourcing rules (*see* section 4.2.6). As discussed in section 4.2.6, Treas. Reg. Section 1.865-3(d) provides that the default method for apportioning income attributable to the US location under Section 865(e)(2) is to apportion 50% of such income to the place of production (the foreign country where the trucks were produced) and 50% to the US office/fixed place of business.[44] The income apportioned to the US sales branch will be considered effectively connected to the foreign manufacturer's US trade or business and taxed on a net basis. So, the next step is to determine what deductions may be taken against this gross income amount.

Step 2—determining the expenses that can be deducted from the US source income of the sales branch: The expense allocation and apportionment rules require that the expenses first be allocated to the class of gross income and then apportioned between the statutory and residual grouping. The class of gross income is income derived from the business of selling trucks and expenses are allocable to that class. Next, apportionment of the expenses between the statutory grouping and residual grouping is required. The statutory grouping is the US source income from the truck business and the residual grouping is the foreign source income. All sales expenses, therefore, would be apportioned between the US source and foreign source income based on their factual relationship to the two groupings. If the taxpayer has any general management expenses, those expenses would similarly be apportioned between the US source and foreign source income based on the factual relationship between such expenses and the groupings.

4.4.3 Special Rules

The foregoing general allocation rules are modified in the case of certain specified types of deductions. The most important of these are the deductions for interest, research and development costs, and stewardship expenses.

4.4.3.1 Interest

4.4.3.1.1 General

Interest expense generally is required to be allocated to all classes of gross income.[45] The provision is based on the theory that money is fungible.[46] In a few narrowly

44. Treas. Reg. Sec. 1.865-3(d). The regulations provide that the default rule is to allocate income 50/50 between the place of production and the place of sale, but the seller may elect to use the books and records method.
45. *See* Temp. Treas. Reg. Sec. 1.861-9T(a). The allocation and apportionment rules which apply to interest (including original issue discount, *see* Chapter 2 section 2.8) also apply to "interest equivalents," defined as any expense or loss which is "substantially incurred in consideration of the time value of money." Temp. Treas. Reg. Sec. 1.861-9T(b)(1)(i). Thus, the implicit interest element in some currency and interest rate swaps is treated as interest expense for purposes of the allocation and apportionment of deduction rules.
46. *See* Temp. Treas. Reg. Sec. 1.861-9T(a): "[I]n general, money is fungible and ... interest expense is attributable to all activities and property regardless of any specific purpose for incurring an obligation on which interest is paid ... . The fungibility approach recognizes that all activities

defined cases, however, the fungibility theory is abandoned and interest expense is allocated to a specific item or class of income.[47] Once interest expense has been allocated to a class of income, it must be apportioned between the statutory grouping and the residual grouping. The apportionment method to be applied is the asset method.[48] Under this method, to determine the amount of interest expense to be apportioned to foreign source income, for example, the taxpayer's total interest expense is multiplied by a fraction, the numerator of which is the tax book value (or "tax basis") of the assets used in producing foreign source income and the denominator of which is the tax book value of the taxpayer's total worldwide assets. The balance of the interest is apportioned to US source income.[49] Until the 2017 Tax Act, US taxpayers had the option of using the FMV method for valuing assets for the interest apportionment.[50] This option was eliminated in 2017.[51]

4.4.3.1.2 Elective Worldwide Allocation

The existing interest expense allocation rules have been criticized because, while they apply on a consolidated group basis domestically, they do not take into account interest

---

and property require funds and that management has a great deal of flexibility as to the source and use of funds. When [money is borrowed for a specific purpose, such] borrowing will generally free other funds for other purposes, and it is reasonable under this approach to attribute part of the cost of borrowing to such other purposes." *Compare* the discussion in Chapter 2 section 2.3.2.5.2.

47. Under Temp. Treas. Reg. Sec. 1.861-10T(b), interest on "nonrecourse" debt, i.e., debt on which the borrower is not personally liable, is generally allocated to the income from the property securing the debt if certain conditions are met. The same approach is taken for interest expense incurred in connection with certain "integrated financial transactions." In such cases, the interest is allocated directly to the corresponding income amount. Thus, if the taxpayer incurs a borrowing to invest in a financial asset, the return on which will be used to amortize the debt, the interest expense will not be required to be apportioned if a number of technical conditions are fulfilled. Treas. Reg. Sec. 1.861-10T(c). In addition, where a US parent corporation borrows money that it "on-lends" to its foreign subsidiary, it may be required to allocate some of the third-party interest expense directly to the foreign source interest income it receives from the subsidiary. These rules, dealing with "excess related group indebtedness," are extremely complex and are intended in very general terms to approximate the results which would have been obtained if the foreign subsidiary had borrowed directly (where all of its interest expense would have been allocated to foreign source income) rather than from the US parent. Treas. Reg. Sec. 1.861-10(e).
48. Sec. 864(e)(2).
49. In addition, Section 864(e)(3) specifically requires that assets generating tax-exempt income are not to be taken into account in making the allocation. Further, in determining the tax basis of stock in a foreign corporation held by a US corporation, the basis must be increased by any undistributed earnings of the foreign corporation accumulated while the taxpayer has held the stock. Also, for an affiliated group of domestic corporations, the members of the group are treated as a single corporation, thus allocating the total interest expense of the group over the group's total assets. This group rule prevents US taxpayers from isolating interest expense in a member of the domestic group that does not have any foreign source income. Treas. Reg. Sec. 1.861-8(d)(2)(C)(1) treats GILTI and FDII income as exempt to the extent of the Section 250 deduction allowed. *See supra* note 2, for a brief description of GILTI and FDII. *See* Chapter 6 section 6.4.3 and Chapter 11 section 11.2.2.2 for detailed discussions of the application of Section 250 to GILTI and FDII income.
50. *See* Temp. Treas. Reg. Sec. 1.861-9(h).
51. Sec. 864(e)(2).

expense incurred by members of the group that are foreign corporations. This "water's edge" approach has the effect in some cases of overstating the amount of interest expense allocated to foreign source income for foreign tax credit purposes since interest expense incurred by foreign subsidiaries is in effect ignored.

In response to this problem, Congress enacted in 2004 a provision that would allow US taxpayers to elect to take foreign interest expense into account in determining foreign source taxable income. Under Section 864(f)(1), interest expense paid to third parties by foreign subsidiaries would reduce the amount of domestically incurred interest expense which the domestic group must allocate to foreign source income for foreign tax credit limitation purposes.[52] Although the provision was supposed to take effect in 2009, its effective date had been repeatedly postponed and the provision was repealed in 2021.[53]

4.4.3.1.3 *Foreign Taxpayers*

In response to the special situation of foreign corporate taxpayers with US branches, particularly banks, Treas. Reg. Section 1.882-5 applies a different set of interest expense allocation rules to such entities. These rules adopt a concept of the fungibility of capital (rather than of money). The taxpayer is required in effect to establish the appropriate amounts of "equity" and "debt" capitalization in the US branch and allocate the interest expense accordingly. In outline, the "debt" capitalization is determined by first valuing the assets of the US branch, using the approach of the branch profits tax discussed in Chapter 5 section 5.6.5. "US-connected liabilities" are then calculated, on an elective basis, either by using the actual worldwide ratio of liabilities to assets of the foreign corporation or a fixed ratio (50% in the case of nonbanks and 95% for banks). The applicable ratio is applied to establish the level of US-connected liabilities. This amount of liability is then compared with the amount of liability actually shown on the US branch's books. If the booked liabilities exceed the US-connected liabilities under the allocation approach, the interest expense generated

52. To *see* how Section 864(f)(1) would have operated, consider a US corporation that has USD 100 of US assets and owns a foreign subsidiary, which itself has USD 100 of foreign operating assets. The US corporation incurs USD 15 of third-party interest expense in the US. The foreign subsidiary has USD 5 of third-party interest expense abroad. Under the "water's edge" approach of current law, USD 7.5 of the interest expense would be allocated to foreign source income (USD 15 of domestically incurred interest expense multiplied by 50%, the ratio of USD 100 foreign assets to USD 200 total assets of the US corporation) and the USD 5 of expense incurred by the foreign subsidiary would be ignored. Under the elective worldwide approach, the allocation would be made on the basis of the total worldwide interest expense and worldwide assets. Thus, the allocation would be USD 20 of worldwide interest multiplied by 50% (the ratio of USD 100 foreign operating assets to 200 worldwide group assets), which would result in USD 10 of interest expense allocated to foreign source income. However, the USD 5 of interest expense incurred abroad in the foreign subsidiary, while not being directly deductible in the US, is in effect "credited" against the US taxpayer's domestic interest expense that must be allocated against foreign source income. Thus, only USD 5 of interest expense (USD 10 of expense determined on the basis of worldwide assets less the USD 5 of interest paid abroad) would be allocated to foreign source income, as contrasted with USD 7.5 under the "water's edge" approach.
53. Sec. 9671, The American Rescue Plan Act of 2021.

on those liabilities is correspondingly reduced, in effect allocating an additional portion of the foreign corporation's equity capital to the US operations. In the converse situation, where US-connected liabilities exceed booked liabilities, the head office is deemed to have partially funded the US office with capital borrowed elsewhere and the interest deduction is increased by attributing additional interest expense to the excess US-connected liabilities. An alternative method of interest calculation takes into account the situation where the US branch (typically a bank) has foreign currency dominated assets.[54] The treaty aspects of the interest expense allocation rules for foreign taxpayers are discussed at Chapter 14 section 14.5.4.

In 1999, the interest allocation and apportionment rules in Treas. Reg. Section 1.882-5 (as in effect during the taxpayer years at issue) were held to violate the US-UK treaty.[55] The Regulation's formulary approach to interest expense allocation was viewed as inconsistent with the obligation under the treaty to determine the foreign taxpayer's US branch income and expenses as if it were a separate entity. Current Treas. Reg. Section 1.882-5(a)(2) permits a nonresident taxpayer to use a different method (i.e., one other than that provided in the regulation) for determining the interest expense attributable to "the business profits of [its] permanent establishment" if "expressly provided by or pursuant to a US income tax treaty or accompanying documents (such as an exchange of notes)."

For individual foreign taxpayers, Temp. Treas. Reg. Section 1.861-9T(d)(2) provides that interest expense will only be deductible if the liability generating the interest expense is shown on the taxpayer's books or is secured by US property. In addition, no deduction is allowed to the extent that liabilities exceed 80% of the value of the US assets, thus in effect requiring a 20% "equity" investment in the US business.

4.4.3.1.4 Anti-abuse

Two changes introduced in the 2017 Tax Act have placed greater limits on taxpayer's ability to currently deduct interest. First, although US tax law has long included a formula-based cap on current year deductions for interest under certain circumstances (*see* Section 163(j) prior to 2018), the 2017 Tax Act significantly revised and restructured this limit on interest deductions in Section 163(j). Under the old formulation, the limits primarily impacted US taxpayers making interest payments for foreign related parties. Under the revised frame, the scope of the limit on interest deductions reaches more broadly. These changes are discussed in Chapter 2 section 2.2.2.5.

Second, the new Base Erosion and Anti-abuse Tax in Section 59A, discussed in Chapter 5 section 5.10, introduces an additional tax for US corporations found to have made excessive deductible payments (including interest) to certain foreign related parties. The tax is effectively structured as a kind of alternative minimum tax collected in addition to all other taxes otherwise due.

54. Treas. Reg. Sec. 1.882-5(e).
55. *Nat'l Westminster Bank, PLC v. United States*, 44 Fed. Cl. 120 (1999). Various issues in the case continued on through litigation, ending in. *Nat'l Westminster Bank, PLC v. United States*, 512 F.3d 1347 (Fed. Cir. 2008). *See* Chapter 14 section 14.5.4.

4.4.3.1.5 Partnerships

Special rules apply to partnerships. The general rule is that a partner's distributive share of the interest expense of a partnership is considered related to all the income-producing activities and assets of that specific partner, including that partner's pro rata share of partnership assets.[56] One exception applies, however, for limited partners and corporate general partners with less than a 10% interest in the partnership and requires that they allocate their share of partnership interest expense to their distributive share of partnership gross income.[57] Another exception applies if the interest expense is generated by nonrecourse debt of the partnership or if the proceeds from the debt that generated the interest expense are used to acquire an interest-paying investment that is coterminous with the interest-paying investment.[58] In that case, the interest expense must be allocated to income generated by the asset purchased with the nonrecourse debt or generated by the interest-paying investment.

4.4.3.2 Research and Experimentation Expenses

Special rules are also provided for the treatment of research and experimentation expenses.[59] The Regulations are based on the premise that research and experimentation "is an inherently speculative activity, that findings may contribute unexpected benefits, and that the gross income derived from successful research and experimentation must bear the cost of unsuccessful research and experimentation."[60] New 2020 regulations for R&E expenses now emphasize that "successful R&E expenditures ultimately result in the creation of intangible property that will be used to generate income."[61] As a result, research and experimentation expenditures are considered under the regulations to be definitely related to "gross intangible income ["GII"] ... reasonably connected to" the relevant the product category. Thus, R&E expenditures are allocable to GII "as a class related to the" product category and apportioned per the regulations.[62] Effectively, the new regulations replace the old approach of generally allocating R&E expenses to all classes of gross income related to the product category, with a new approach that allocates the expenses only to the GII related to the product category. In making this shift, the regulations adopt a fairly expansive definition of GII, but GII does not include "dividends or any amounts included in income under sections 951 [Subpart F and 956 inclusions[63]], 951A [GILTI income[64]], or 1293 [PFIC qualified electing fund inclusions[65]]."[66]

56. Temp. Treas. Reg. Sec. 1.861-9T(e)(1). Partnership interest expense, however, must be allocated to specific assets of the partnership, if the interest is generated by nonrecourse debt or is part of an integrated financial transaction. *Id.*; Temp. Treas. Reg. Sec. 1.861-10T.
57. Temp. Treas. Reg. Sec. 1.861-9T(e)(4).
58. Temp. Treas. Reg. Sec. 1.861-9T(e)(1); 1.861-10T. *See supra* note 47 at section 4.4.3.1.1.
59. The tax law previously referred to such expenses as "R&D" or "research and development" expenses.
60. Treas. Reg. Sec. 1.861-17(b)(1).
61. *Id.*
62. *Id.*
63. *See* Chapter 6 section 6.3.

Product categories are specified and include such classifications as mining, construction services, transportation services, and the like. For manufactured products, the classification is in terms of groups such as engines and turbines, drugs, lighting and wiring. The income that is considered related to a product category includes not only sales income but also royalties and dividends as well in the appropriate circumstances.

Once the allocation of the deduction to classes of income related to product categories has been made, the deduction then may have to be apportioned between the relevant statutory grouping of gross income and the residual grouping of gross income. First, for foreign tax credit purposes, 50% of the R&E expenses "is apportioned exclusively to the residual grouping of US source GII" if researching and experimentation accounting for "at least" 50% of the expenditures occurred in the US. Conversely, if research and experimentation accounting for "more than" 50% of the R&E expenditures occurred outside the US then 50% of such expenses is apportioned to foreign source GII in the product code.[67]

This 50% rule reflects the theoretical view that R&E costs are more likely to be of benefit in the country in which the expenses are incurred. It also responds to the practical consideration that foreign jurisdictions may be reluctant or unwilling to allow a deduction for R&E costs incurred outside the jurisdiction. In these circumstances, a US apportionment to foreign source income would not be matched by a corresponding deduction in the foreign jurisdiction.

After the exclusive geographical allocation is made, the remaining costs are apportioned based on gross receipts from sales of products or services.[68] Thus, for example, if a US taxpayer incurred USD 500 of R&E costs in the US and had total gross receipts of USD 2,000 from sales, leases, or services related to GII within the statutory grouping (with USD 1,600 of the gross receipts from in the US), then USD 250 of the R&E costs would be assigned to US source income under the exclusive apportionment rule and the remaining USD 250 would be assigned USD 50 to foreign income and USD 200 to US income on the basis of gross receipts. In applying the gross receipts formula, appropriate adjustments are made to take into account certain gross receipts generated by controlled subsidiaries expected to benefit from the intangible property generated by taxpayer's R&E.[69]

Final Regulations under Section 250[70] (most specifically the FDII regime introduced by the 2017 Tax Act[71]) continue to allow use of the "exclusive apportionment

64. *See supra* note 2, for a brief description of GILTI and Chapter 6 sections 6.2 and 6.4 for detailed discussions.
65. *See* Chapter 8 section 8.2.
66. Treas. Reg. Sec. 1.861-17(b)(2).
67. Treas. Reg. Sec. 1.861-17(c).
68. Treas. Reg. Sec. 1.861-17(d)(1).
69. Treas. Reg. Sec. 1.861-17(d)(4).
70. Preamble to Treas. Reg. Sec. 1.250, 85 Fed. Preamble to Treas. Reg. Sec. 1.250, 85 Fed. Reg. 4302, 43047 (July 15, 2020). Although Section 250 covers both FDII and GILTI, the exclusive apportionment issue was relevant only for FDII because the 2020 R&E rules explicitly state that since GII does not include GILTI income, no R&E will be apportioned to the foreign source

rule" when apportioning R&E expenses for purposes of Section 250 (this despite a different approach taken in the proposed Section 250 Regulations[72]).

4.4.3.3 *Stewardship and Other Expenses*

The Regulations provide specific rules (although not in the detail employed for interest and research and development deductions) for home office or stewardship costs attributable to dividends received from a foreign corporation,[73] legal and accounting fees and expenses,[74] income taxes,[75] losses on the sale, exchange or other disposition of property,[76] damage awards (along with prejudgment interest and certain settlement payments),[77] and the net operating loss deduction.[78] The introduction in the 2017 Tax Act of the new Section 250 deduction (which pertains to FDII[79]) required guidance on how that deduction would now be allocated and apportioned for purposes of the foreign tax credit.[80]

Section 864(e)(6) requires that expenses incurred by an affiliated group of domestic corporations be allocated on a consolidated basis unless the expenses are directly related to a specific income-producing activity, thus preventing the US

---

income in the GILTI category. Treas. Reg. Sec. 1.861-17(d)(1)(iv). *See* Chapter 6 section 6.4.3 and Chapter 11 section 11.2.2.2 for discussions of the application of Section 250 to GILTI and FDII income.

71. *See supra* note 2 for a brief description of FDII and Chapter 11 section 11.2.2.2 for a detailed discussion.
72. Prop. Treas. Reg. Sec. 1.250(b)-1(d)(2)(i) (2019).
73. Treas. Reg. Sec. 1.861-8(e)(4).
74. Treas. Reg. Sec. 1.861-8(e)(5).
75. Treas. Reg. Sec. 1.861-8(e)(6).
76. Treas. Reg. Section 1.861-8(e)(7) provides that losses on the disposition of a capital asset shall be allocated to "the class of gross income to which the asset ordinarily gives rise." In *Black & Decker Corp. v. Commissioner*, 986 F.2d 60 (4th Cir. 1993), the court applied this Regulation to allocate the loss on the sale by a US corporation of stock of a foreign subsidiary to foreign source income since the class of gross income to which the loss related would have been dividends from the subsidiary stock. Given that such dividends on the subsidiary stock would have been foreign source income, the loss should reduce foreign source income. The court disregarded the fact that no dividends were actually paid on the stock and rejected the taxpayer's argument that the purpose of establishing the subsidiary was not to generate foreign source dividends but to promote the sale of the taxpayer's US-produced products in foreign markets.

    Since gains on the sale of capital assets are typically sourced to the residence of the taxpayer, in situations like *Black & Decker*, there is an asymmetry between the treatment of gains and losses. In Section 865(j)(1), Congress expressly authorized (or more accurately invited) the Treasury to issue regulations dealing with the treatment of losses on sales of personal property. Treas. Reg. Section 1.865-2 provides that loss on the sale of stock will in general be sourced in the same way as gain, that is, to the residence of the taxpayer. To prevent "dividend stripping" of foreign income in the form of a dividend followed by a domestic loss on the sale of the stock, a recapture rule is provided that treats the loss as foreign source to the extent of dividends received within two years before the sale. Treas. Reg. Sec. 1.865-1 provides similar source rules for personal property other than stock but modifications are made to reflect the different nature of the property, e.g., for depreciable machinery and equipment.
77. Treas. Reg. Sec. 1.864-8(e)(5)(ii) and (iii).
78. Treas. Reg. Sec. 1.861-8(e)(8).
79. *See supra* note 2 for a brief description of FDII and Chapter 11 section 11.2.2.2 for a detailed discussion.
80. Treas. Reg. Sec. 1.861-14(e)(4).

taxpayer from isolating expenses in subsidiaries which have no foreign source income.[81]

81. The regulations currently apply Section 846(e)(6) in select areas, which include calculating limits and reductions in the foreign tax credit under Sections 904 and 907. Temp. Treas. Reg. Sec. 1.861-14T(b)(1). The regulations also specify that Section 846(e)(6) does not apply to the computation of subpart F income of controlled foreign corporations and the computation of effectively connected taxable income of foreign corporations. Temp. Treas. Reg. Sec. 1.861-14T(b)(2).

CHAPTER 5

Income Taxation of Nonresident Aliens and Foreign Corporations

5.1 INTRODUCTION

Different tax regimes apply to US source income of a nonresident or foreign corporation depending on whether such income relates to the conduct of a US trade or business. If the US source income is "effectively connected" with a US "trade or business," it is taxed in the same manner as income earned by a US resident and is subject to the rules discussed in Chapter 2 sections 2.2 and 2.3.[1] This means that gross income is reduced by allowable deductions and is then subject to taxation at graduated rates for individuals and at 21% for corporations. In contrast, income not effectively connected with a US trade or business that constitutes "fixed or determinable annual or periodic" (FDAP) income is taxed at a flat rate of 30% on gross income without the benefit of any deductions.[2] (FDAP income generally consists of investment income, such as dividends, interest, rents, and royalties, but does not include capital gains.)[3]

1. Secs. 871(b), 882(a), and 884.
2. Secs. 871(a) and 881.
3. It may be useful to review the statutory landscape of provisions governing the taxation of foreign persons (generally, a nonresident alien individual or a foreign corporation). The taxation of foreign persons is governed by rules in Chapter 1, Subchapter N of the Code. Secs. 861-999. Thus, for a foreign person, gross income is defined in Sections 872 (for a nonresident alien) and 882(a)(1) (for a foreign corporation). These provisions cut back for foreign persons the general Section 61 gross income definition encompassing worldwide income to include only gross income effectively connected with a US business and US source gross income that is not effectively connected. Similarly, Sections 873 and 882(c) limit allowable deductions to those relating to effectively connected income (and, for nonresident individuals, very limited nonbusiness deductions). Otherwise, deductions are not allowed against non-effectively connected US source gross income. In the case of foreign persons, taxes imposed under Section 1 (on individuals) and Section 11 (on corporations) only apply to effectively connected taxable income and are collected based on the filing of a tax return. Secs. 2(d), 11(d), and 6012. *See* section 5.9.1. In this manner, foreign persons only are subject to net basis taxation on income from a US business. Foreign

The amount of a taxpayer's income and related expenses will determine the tax consequences of classifying a taxpayer's US source income as "effectively connected" with a US trade or business or, alternatively, as FDAP income. Taxpayers who have relatively small amounts of US source income or significant expenses may prefer that such income be treated as effectively connected with a US trade or business to take advantage of the graduated tax rates for individuals, the 21% for corporations, and deductibility of expenses. However, the tax rates for some types of FDAP income are often reduced significantly below the statutory 30% rate by treaties (*see* Chapter 14 section 14.6) so it is always necessary to consult the relevant tax treaty.

A number of structural building blocks are involved in determining whether a foreign person's income is effectively connected with a US trade or business. It is necessary to analyze: (1) the nature and source of the taxpayer's income; (2) the taxpayer's activities in the US, i.e., whether it is engaged in a US trade or business; and (3) the relation between its income and its US activities, i.e., whether its income is "effectively connected" with a US trade or business. Source of income and income classification issues were discussed previously in Chapter 4. The following materials first discuss the trade or business concept and the effectively connected concept, and then examine in more detail the pattern of taxation for nonresident aliens, foreign corporations, partnerships, and trusts. In Chapter 14, the impact of tax treaties on the domestic taxing rules will be considered.

5.2 THE "TRADE OR BUSINESS" CONCEPT

5.2.1 Background

A foreign taxpayer that is engaged in a US trade or business has achieved a certain level of economic penetration in the US. It is not merely a passive investor but has become a direct participant in the economic life of the country.

The significance of a US trade or business for the tax treatment of foreign persons has varied over the years. The US tax system has long distinguished between the investment income from US sources of a foreign taxpayer and the business income attributable to the foreign taxpayer's trade or business carried on in the US.[4] The investment income, i.e., the FDAP income, has generally been subject to a flat rate of

---

persons' non-effectively connected US income is taxed on a gross income basis, but only to the extent specified in Sections 871 and 881, which encompass FDAP income. *See* sections 5.5.3 and 5.6.2. Because US source capital gains are not identified in those sections, except for certain intangible gains, or within the case law interpretation of FDAP, a foreign person is not taxed on these capital gains or indeed any other noneffectively connected gross income not specified as FDAP (including foreign source gross income). Since FDAP prescribes the limit of US ability to tax non-effectively connected income, cases have interpreted FDAP income to have a broad scope, though not so broad as to reach capital gain. *See* cases cited at *infra* note 65. Finally, the gross basis tax is collected, at least initially, by requiring the payor of income to withhold the tax under Chapter 3 of the Code. Secs. 1441-1464. *See* section 5.9.2.

4. *See* Stanford G. Ross, *United States Taxation of Aliens and Foreign Corporations: The Foreign Investors Tax Act of 1966 and Related Developments*, 22 TAX L REV. 277, 282 (1967) (flat rate tax on gross FDAP income added in 1936).

tax on gross income, withheld at the source, while the net business income has been taxed at regular individual or corporate rates. However, prior to 1966, if a foreign taxpayer was engaged in a US trade or business the so-called force of attraction principle applied. Under this principle, the US taxed investment income at regular rates, even though it had no connection with the foreign taxpayer's US trade or business. The investment income was "attracted" to the US trade or business and taxed accordingly.

Under current law, only investment income that is effectively connected with the conduct of a trade or business in the US is subjected to the full graduated individual or corporate rates applicable to business income. The mere existence of a US trade or business is not sufficient to subject the investment income to the normal tax rates. Investment income not effectively connected with a US trade or business that is FDAP income in general is taxed at the 30% statutory rate or lower treaty rates. While the existence of a trade or business in the US does not affect the taxation of unrelated investment income, the trade or business concept plays an important role in the US taxation of foreign individuals and corporations. It determines the basic pattern under which the foreign taxpayer's income will be taxed, as discussed more fully in sections 5.5 and 5.6.

5.2.2 The Existence of a Trade or Business

Although the term "trade or business" is employed in several different sections of the Internal Revenue Code, the statute does not contain a general definition of the phrase. Instead, the determination whether an activity constitutes a "trade or business" is largely left to a case-by-case resolution by the fiscal authorities and the courts.[5] In the context of the rules governing foreign individuals and corporations, the fundamental distinction to be drawn is between commercial activity carried on in the US with some regularity versus passive investment.[6] The polar models are a manufacturing plant operated in the US and the simple receipt of dividends paid on stock in a US company. But between these clear extremes, there is an infinite variety of activities which must be placed either in the trade or business or in the investment category.

Section 864(b) currently provides one clear rule for the performance of personal services: "[T]he term 'trade or business within the United States' includes the performance of personal services within the United States at any time within the taxable year, … ." It also provides exceptions from trade or business status in three situations:[7]

5. The Supreme Court has held that the term "trade or business" can have different meanings depending on which Code sections are involved. *Snow v. Commissioner*, 416 US 500 (1974). *See also Commissioner v. Groetzinger*, 480 US 23, 27 n. 8 (1987) ("We caution that in this opinion our interpretation of the phrase 'trade or business' is confined to the specific sections of the Code at issue here. We do not purport to construe the phrase where it appears in other places.").
6. *See, e.g., Continental Trading, Inc. v. Comm.*, 265 F.2d 40 (9th Cir. 1959).
7. Under the statutory language the performance of services in the United States (outside of the limited exceptions) is a hair trigger for having a US trade or business.

(1) The performance of personal services for a nonresident employer is not a US trade or business under the same conditions that determine that compensation for personal services constitutes foreign source income[8] (*see* Chapter 4 section 4.2.3).
(2) Trading in stocks, securities, or commodities through a US broker for the trader's own account or for the account of others, is not a US trade or business if the trader does not maintain a US office or fixed place of business through which the transactions are effected.[9]
(3) Even if the trader maintains a US office or fixed place of business, trading in stocks, securities, or commodities for the foreign investor's *own account*, whether effected in the US directly or through agents is not a US trade or business.[10] This result holds even if the US office is its principal place of business.[11]

Other statutory provisions treat certain activities as a trade or business:

(1) Section 871(c) provides that certain foreign students, teachers, and exchange visitors "shall be treated as" engaged in a trade or business.[12]

8. Sec. 864(b)(1); Treas. Reg. Sec. 1.864-2(b).
9. Sec. 864(b)(2)(A)(i), 864(b)(2)(B)(i), and 864(b)(2)(C); Treas. Reg. Sec. 1.864-2(c)(1) and (d)(1).
10. Sec. 864(b)(2)(A)(ii). The exemption for traders with a US office does not apply to dealers in stock or securities. Sec. 864(b)(2)(B)(ii); Treas. Reg. Sec. 1.864-2(c)(2)(i), (ii), and (d)(2). It is unclear to what extent this exception applies to venture capital investments where the foreign investor (or a partnership in which he is a partner) may be substantially involved in research, management, and other activities in connection with the investment. In *Sun Capital Partners III, LP v. New England Teamsters & Trucking Indus. Pension Fund*, 724 F.3d 129 (1st Cir. 2013), the court held that private equity funds conducted "trades or businesses" within the scope of the Employee Retirement Income Security Act of 1974 (ERISA). As discussed in *supra* note 5, however, the Supreme Court has stated that "trade or business" can have different meanings depending on the statute involved. As a result, the issue for purposes of Section 864(b) remains unresolved.
11. Sec. 864(b)(2)(A)(ii) and 864(b)(2)(C). Prior to the 1997 Act, which adopted Section 864(b)(2)(A)(ii), a foreign corporation that had its principal office in the US was treated as engaged in a US trade or business when trading for its own account. Treas. Reg. Section 1.864-2(c)(2)(iii) provides examples of corporate functions that constitute a "principal office." The quite detailed and formalistic rules in the Regulation established guidelines for a foreign investment company that desired to avoid US trade or business status by locating its principal office outside the US. This guidance led to the creation of the so-called offshore investment funds, through which foreign investors invested in US stocks, bonds, and commodities. If properly structured, profits on sales would be free of US capital gains tax (because, as explained in section 5.3.2, only capital gains effectively connected with the conduct of a US trade or business are subject to US tax). In addition, if the country selected for incorporation had a favorable treaty with the US, the US tax on dividends and interest could be reduced or eliminated. These results made the offshore funds attractive to foreign investors but the benefits could only be realized if certain administrative tasks were performed offshore to avoid the "principal office" limitation. The 1997 Act eliminated this requirement, thus allowing offshore funds to carry on all of their activities in the US that qualify for the exception without being characterized as engaging in a US trade or business.
12. Treas. Reg. Sec. 1.871-9.

(2) Sections 871(d) and 882(d) permit foreign individuals and corporations that own US real estate to elect to treat the income therefrom as trade or business income. The election applies only to real estate investments that, absent the election, would not constitute a trade or business under generally applicable principles.[13]

(3) Section 897(a) provides that gain or loss from the disposition of a "United States real property interest" shall be taxed "as if the taxpayer were engaged in a US trade or business" (*see* section 5.4).

(4) Section 875 provides that a nonresident alien or a foreign corporation that is a partner in a partnership (or the beneficiary of an estate or trust) engaged in a US trade or business is considered also to be engaged in a US trade or business. However, creators of trusts are not considered to be engaged in a US trade or business merely because the trustee is engaged in a US trade or business.[14]

Apart from these specific statutory rules, the determination whether an activity constitutes a trade or business is made on a case-by-case basis, taking into account such factors as the taxpayer's motive (profit versus personal), quantitative aspects (frequency, substantiality, and duration of the activities), and qualitative aspects (business versus investment).[15]

5.2.3 The Location of a Trade or Business in the United States

Since no Code provision offers a comprehensive definition of when a trade or business is located within (or without) the US, the issue is determined on the basis of all relevant facts and circumstances. On the one hand, a foreign producer that ships directly to US

---

13. Treas. Reg. Sec. 1.871-10 details the procedures to be followed in making the election. *See also* Treas. Reg. Sec. 1.882-2(a). No other type of income is granted such an option. Rev. Rul. 74-63, 1974-1 C.B. 374. A similar election is provided in many US income tax treaties. *See* Chapter 14 section 14.7.
14. Treas. Reg. Sec. 1.875-2(b).
15. *See, e.g.*, Rev. Rul. 73-522,1973-2 C.B. 226 (nonresident alien who visited the US once during the year to negotiate leases on real estate he owned was not engaged in trade or business); *Di Portanova v. US*, 690 F.2d 169 (Ct. Cl. 1982) (working interest in minerals did not involve a US trade or business).

    An interesting issue is the extent to which activities undertaken through the Internet will constitute a US trade or business. Traditionally, soliciting US sales without any physical presence in the US does not amount to performance of a trade or business in the US. *Cf. Piedras Negras Broadcasting Co. v. US*, 43 B.T.A. 297, aff'd 127 F. 2d 260 (5th Cir. 1942). But perhaps the concept of physical presence is outdated in light of the technological developments which make it increasingly irrelevant. For some current thinking on the question, *see* OECD/G20 BASE EROSION AND PROFIT SHIFTING (BEPS) PROJECT, TAX CHALLENGES ARISING FROM DIGITALISATION—REPORT ON PILLAR ONE BLUEPRINT (Oct. 14, 2020); US TREAS. DEPT., WHITE PAPER ON TAX POLICY IMPLICATIONS OF GLOBAL ELECTRONIC COMMERCE (November 1996); OECD, ADDRESSING THE TAX CHALLENGES OF THE DIGITAL ECONOMY—ACTION 1: 2015 FINAL REPORT (2015). The same issue arises in connection with permanent establishments in the treaty context and is discussed in Chapter 14 section 14.5.2.

customers does not have a trade or business located in the US.[16] At the other extreme, if a foreign corporation has its principal office in the US and conducts all its activities there, it will obviously have a business situs in the US.[17] But most situations will not be so clear cut and have to be resolved by examining the extent of the corporation's business functions carried on in the US.

The Internal Revenue Code and the Regulations provides a few specific examples. Thus, as noted in section 5.2.2, the performance of personal services in the US constitutes a trade or business located in the US.[18] Also, a foreign investor in the US can be considered to have a trade or business in the US when it is trading for the account of others in stocks or securities through a broker or agent if the investor effects investment transactions through an office or fixed place of business located in the US. In addition, Section 864(c) and the Regulations issued thereunder, which set forth the "effectively connected" definition, contain a number of examples illuminating the business location issue. Those examples are considered in section 5.3.2.[19]

5.2.4 Impact of Treaties on US Trade or Business

The 2016 US Model Treaty provides that the US will only tax a foreign taxpayer's US trade or business income if such income is "attributable to a "permanent establishment" in the US.[20] Many other treaties, such as the OECD Model Treaty, have similar provisions. The "trade or business" concept is somewhat analogous to the "permanent establishment" concept adopted in US tax treaties. Similarly, "effectively connected" corresponds to the notion of income "attributed to" the permanent establishment. *See* Chapter 14 section 14.5.4.

As will be discussed in Chapter 14, the requirement that a permanent establishment exist as a precondition to taxing US trade or business income decreases the likelihood that such income will be subject to tax in the US. While a determination that a foreign individual or corporation maintains a permanent establishment in the US will generally mean that a US trade or business exists, the reverse is not the case. The trade or business concept is broader than the permanent establishment rules and, therefore, a foreign individual or corporation may be engaged in a trade or business in the US, but still be found not to maintain a permanent establishment there.[21]

---

16. *See* Rev. Rul. 73-158, 1973-1 C.B. 337. But if the sales are effected through the foreign corporation's resident US agent, the foreign corporation may have a US-located business. Rev. Rul. 70-424, 1970-2 C.B. 150.
17. For examples, *see* Treas. Reg. Sec. 1.864-3(b).
18. Sec. 864(b).
19. For examples, *see* Treas. Reg. Sec. 1.864-3(b).
20. US Model Income Tax Convention, Art. 7.1 (2016).
21. *See, e.g., de Amodio v. Commissioner*, 299 F.2d 623 (3d Cir. 1962).

5.3 THE "EFFECTIVELY CONNECTED" CONCEPT

5.3.1 General

The third of the critical definitional aspects of the US system for taxation of nonresident aliens and foreign corporations is the "effectively connected" concept. If a nonresident alien or foreign corporation has derived income from US sources (under the rules described in Chapter 4) and if that individual or corporation is engaged in a trade or business in the US (under the rules described in section 5.2), then the actual tax treatment of the income depends on whether the income is effectively connected with the conduct of a trade or business in the US.[22] Section 864(c) and the Regulations issued thereunder prescribe the tests to be utilized in determining whether or not income is effectively connected with a US trade or business.

The "effectively connected" rules involve four categories of US source income: (1) gain or loss from the sale or exchange of capital assets, (2) fixed or determinable annual or periodical gains, profits or income (described in Sections 871(a)(1) and 881(a)(1)), (3) gain or loss from the disposition of US real property interests,[23] and (4) all other income, gain or loss. The US system of imposing tax on such income derived by nonresident aliens and foreign corporations will be discussed in greater detail in sections 5.4 and 5.5. However, it will be useful to summarize the general pattern of taxation (Tables 5.1 and 5.2) at this point to demonstrate the results that flow from a determination that a particular class of US source income either is or is not income effectively connected with a US trade or business.

22. In general, if a nonresident alien or foreign corporation at no time during the taxable year is engaged in a trade or business in the US, no income will be treated as effectively connected income. Sec. 864(c)(1)(B). However, if income that is attributable to the sale or exchange of property or the performance of services is received in a year in which the foreign person is not engaged in a trade or business but would have been treated as effectively connected if it had been received in an earlier year, then the income will remain effectively connected. For example, if the foreign person sells US business assets for deferred payments and receives the payments in a later year after the US business has been terminated, the gain will remain effectively connected. Sec. 864(c)(6). Similarly, if property ceases to be used in a US trade or business and is sold within ten years, the gain on the sale will remain effectively connected. Sec. 864(c)(7). This latter rule is of course extremely difficult to enforce if the property is removed from the United States.
23. Under Section 897(a), gain from disposition of US real property interests is deemed to be effectively connected. *See* section 5.4.

Table 5.1 Nonresident Alien's US Income

	Nonresident Aliens Conducting Trade or Business in US	
Category of Income	*If Income Is Effectively Connected*	*If Income Is Not Effectively Connected*
1. Capital gains other than US real property gains	Net income taxed at US individual income or AMT tax rates	No US tax unless the individual is in the US for 183 days[a]
2. Fixed or determinable income (FDAP)	Net income taxed at US individual income or AMT tax rates	Gross income taxed at flat 30% rate[b]
3. US real property gains	Net income taxed at US individual or AMT tax rates[c]	Treated as effectively connected income
4. Other income	Net income taxed at US individual income or AMT tax rates	Treated as effectively connected income

a. Normally, in these circumstances the individual would be classified as a resident and thus subject to tax on worldwide income. *See* discussion at section 5.5.2. Thus, the rule is only applicable to special categories of aliens such as students and diplomats.
b. Some items of fixed or determinable income are explicitly exempted from tax. *See* section 5.5.5. The 30% rate is often reduced by treaty. *See* Chapter 14 section 14.6.
c. As discussed in section 5.4, real property gains recognized by nonresident aliens are treated as "taxable excess" for purposes of the AMT without the benefit of the AMT exemption that applies to other types of income. *See* Chapter 2 section 2.3.4 for a description of the AMT and taxable excess.

Table 5.2 Foreign Corporation's US Income

	Foreign Corporations Conducting Trade or Business in US	
Category of Income	*If Income Is Effectively Connected*	*If Income Is Not Effectively Connected*
1. Capital gains	Net income taxed at regular corporate rate	No US tax
2. Fixed or determinable income (FDAP)	Net income taxed at regular corporate rates	Gross income taxed at flat 30% rate
3. US real property interest gains	Net income taxed at regular corporate rate	Treated as effectively connected income
4. Other income	Net income taxed at regular corporate rates	Treated as effectively connected income

Thus, in general terms, the effectively connected concept divides US source income between a foreign taxpayer's two pockets. Income that is effectively connected (or is so treated) is placed in the taxpayer's business pocket and taxed at full US rates on a net basis; FDAP income that is not effectively connected is placed in the taxpayer's "investment" pocket and taxed at a flat rate on a gross basis.

5.3.2 Capital Gains and Fixed or Determinable Income

Section 864(c)(2) prescribes two tests for determining whether US source capital gain income and FDAP income are effectively connected with the conduct of a US trade or business. The term "capital gain income" refers to gains (or losses) derived from the sale of exchange of a capital asset.[24] The term "fixed or determinable income" refers in general to interest, dividends, rents, salaries, wages, premiums, annuities, compensations, remunerations, emoluments, and certain other gains.[25]

The tests to be applied to these two categories of income are: (1) the "asset use" test and (2) the "business activities" test.

5.3.2.1 The "Asset Use" Test

The "asset use" test is employed primarily to determine whether US source passive investment income, such as interest, constitutes effectively connected income.[26] An asset will be considered to be used in the conduct of a US trade or business—and the income, gain or loss derived therefrom is effectively connected—if any one of three conditions is satisfied:[27]

(1) The asset is held for the principal purpose of promoting the present conduct of a trade or business in the US.
(2) The asset is acquired and held in the ordinary course of business conducted in the US. Assume for example, the US branch of a foreign taxpayer commonly sold its products by taking notes receivable in payment. Interest income on the notes would constitute effectively connected income.
(3) The asset is otherwise held in a "direct relationship" to the trade or business conducted in the US.[28] The requisite "direct relationship" exists if the asset is presently needed in the business. Thus, in the above example, assume the US branch factory requires a large cash balance to conduct its business. However, the amount required varies through the year as the result of the cyclical

24. The term "capital asset" is defined in Section 1221. *See* Chapter 2 sections 2.2.3 and 2.3.2.2. For materials on the tests employed to determine whether an asset is (or is not) a capital asset, *see* Daniel L. Simmons, Martin J. McMahon, Bradley T. Borden, and Bret Wells, *Federal Income Taxation*, 868-934 (8th ed. Foundation Press 2020).
25. Sections 871(a) and 881(a), discussed in sections 5.5 and 5.6, define "fixed or determinable income." *See also* Treas. Reg. Sec. 1.1441-2(b).
26. Treas. Reg. Sec. 1.864-4(c)(2)(i). The regulations take the position that stock generally cannot meet the asset use test. Stock held by a foreign insurance company in a foreign or domestic corporation, however, can be treated as an asset used in a US trade or business unless the foreign insurance company owns 10% or more of the stock in such foreign or domestic corporation. Treas. Reg. Sec. 1.864-4(c)(2)(iii).
27. Treas. Reg. Sec. 1.864-4(c)(2)(ii).
28. Treas. Reg. Sec. 1.864-4(c)(2)(iv).

> nature of the business. The US branch therefore invests the cash in short-term notes during these periods. Interest earned on the notes will be effectively connected income since the notes are required to meet present business needs. In contrast, if the cash were invested in securities in preparation for a future diversification or expansion by the US branch, its interest income would not be effectively connected since the notes would not be held to meet the present needs of the business.[29]

In addition, the Regulations create a presumption that a "direct relationship" exists if: (1) the asset was acquired from funds generated by the US trade or business; (2) the income from the asset is retained in the business; and (3) personnel in the US who are actively involved in the business exercise significant management and control over the investment of the asset. This presumption is, however, rebuttable by the taxpayer. Therefore, in the foregoing example, even if the investment securities were acquired out of funds generated by the US branch business, interest payments were retained in the business, and the managing officers of the US branch were responsible for supervising the investment, the income from the securities would not be effectively connected because the fact that the securities were acquired to meet future rather than present needs of the business would rebut the presumption of a "direct relationship" created by the Regulations.[30]

5.3.2.2 *The "Business Activities" Test*

The "business activities" test is applied primarily to determine if income derived by dealers in stocks or securities, investment companies, those engaged in the business of licensing patents, and service businesses constitutes effectively connected income.[31] As in the case of the "asset use" test, the objective of the "business activities" test is to determine whether passive income—dividends, rents, royalties, etc.—"arises directly from" the US trade or business. Detailed rules are provided in the Regulations for application of the test to banking, financing, and similar businesses conducted in the US.[32]

5.3.2.3 *Other Income*

Section 864(c)(3) treats US source income other than capital gains and FDAP income as effectively connected income if the taxpayer conducts a trade or business in the US.[33] Such income will therefore be taxed at graduated US rates after appropriate deductions even though it has no actual connection at all with the trade or business actually

29. Treas. Reg. Sec. 1.864-4(c)(2)(v), Exs. (1) and (2).
30. Treas. Reg. Sec. 1.864-4(c)(2)(v), Ex. (2).
31. Treas. Reg. Sec. 1.864-4(c)(3).
32. Treas. Reg. Sec. 1.864-4(c)(5). *See* Rev. Rul. 86-154, 1986-2 C.B. 103 (securities held by branch of foreign bank in the US; various situations distinguished).
33. Sec. 864(c)(3).

conducted in the US. To this extent, after 1966 the "force of attraction" principle still has a limited application.[34] For example, suppose a foreign corporation sells two products to customers that it does not manufacture.[35] It establishes a US branch to sell one of the products in the US. The other product is sold directly to US customers by the corporation's foreign home office, with the foreign home office shipping directly to the US customers and title to the products passing in the US. The sales income of the foreign home office is treated as effectively connected income even though it in fact has no connection with the business actually conducted by the US branch.[36]

5.3.2.4 *Foreign Source Income Effectively Connected with a US Business*

The preceding materials have discussed the rules applied by the US to determine whether its full tax rates should be applied to US source income derived by nonresident aliens or foreign corporations. The detailed nature of those rules is intended to provide guidance and a relatively high degree of certainty so that foreign investors can determine in advance the tax consequences of US investment. In addition, the particularity of the rules is designed to insure that the United States is not utilized as a tax haven.

In furtherance of this latter objective, certain categories of *foreign source* income are treated as effectively connected with the conduct of a US trade or business and hence subject to full US tax rates. In general, foreign source income is not treated as effectively connected income (Section 864(c)(4)(A)). However, Section 864(c)(4)(B) details specific types of income that will be treated as effectively connected with a US trade or business even though the income is determined to arise from a foreign source under the rules discussed in Chapter 4. The types of foreign source income selected for this special treatment include those that are especially susceptible to manipulation by taxpayers to obtain tax advantages. In the absence of Section 864(c)(4)(B), transactions might be arranged so that the income was treated as from a foreign source under the source rules, even though the transaction in fact had substantial economic ties to the US. For example, suppose that a branch of a foreign taxpayer arranges to sell inventory with title passing outside the US to a customer that will use the inventory in

34. This remaining application is colloquially referred to as the "residual force of attraction" rule.
35. Such items are not capital assets since they would be characterized as inventory (Section 1221(3)), and, therefore gain from their sale is not capital gain.
36. Treas. Reg. Sec. 1.864-4(b). *See* Treas. Reg. Sec. 1.864-4(b) Example (3) (Foreign corporation's US source income from sales of wine to US customers without involvement of its US trade or business selling electronic equipment is effectively connected income). As discussed in section 5.2.2, above, an alien individual or foreign corporation who is a partner in a US partnership that is engaged in a US trade or business is also considered to be engaged in a US trade or business. Under Treas. Reg. Section 1.875-1, a nonresident partner is subject to full US income tax on any effectively connected income if the partnership "at any time during the taxable year" was engaged in a US trade or business. As a result, a nonresident alien or foreign corporation that becomes a limited partner on the last day of a taxable year could subject previously earned "other income" to full US tax since such income is treated as effectively connected income if the taxpayer is engaged in a US trade or business. *See Vitale v. Commissioner*, 72 TC 386 (1979), for an application of this result under pre-1966 law to a nonresident alien.

the US. Section 864(c)(4)(B) will treat income from the sale of such inventory as effectively connected to a US trade or business.

Foreign source income will be treated as effectively connected with a US trade or business if it is "attributable" to an "office or other fixed place of business" in the US. Both of the quoted terms are defined in the statute (Section 864(c)(5)) and given detailed content by the regulations.

The foreign source income that can be treated as effectively connected income if the above conditions are satisfied includes: (1) rents or royalties and gain or loss from intangible property which is located or used outside the US if derived from the active conduct of a trade or business in the US,[37] (2) dividends or interest and gain or loss from stocks or securities which are derived in the conduct of a US trade or business either by banks or other financial institutions or by a corporation whose principal business is trading in stocks or securities for its own account,[38] (3) the sale of personal property outside the US that the purchaser will use in the US,[39] and (4) the economic equivalent of income in either of the first two categories.[40] Thus, for example, if the US branch of a foreign bank makes a loan to a Mexican borrower, the interest income may be taxed under Section 864(c)(4) if the statutory tests are met despite the fact that the interest income technically has a foreign source.

Treating such income as effectively connected with a US trade or business can be seen as a modification of the otherwise applicable source rules discussed in Chapter 4. Put another way, the types of income covered by Section 864(c)(4)(B) have such a relationship to the US that they should be treated as US source income and taxed accordingly. However, instead of formally changing the source rules in these situations, Section 864(c)(4)(B) applies the effectively connected concept to what is still technically foreign source income. This choice of technique has some important implications. For example, in some of its income tax treaties, the US has obligated itself to tax only US source income of foreign taxpayers. In such cases, the treaty provisions can prevent the application of the effectively connected concept to what is still technically foreign source income.

Section 865(e)(2) does change the source rules for income from the sale of personal property (including inventory) attributable to a foreign taxpayer's US office. In general, such income is treated as having a US source even though the sale occurs outside the US if the sale is arranged through the US office. The income is treated as effectively connected US source income (regardless of where the title to the property passes) and is subject to tax under Section 882 (or Section 871(b) if a nonresident individual). One effect of this rule is to allow the US to tax such income in certain

37. Sec. 864(c)(4)(B)(i).
38. Sec. 864(c)(4)(B)(ii).The regulations exempt income derived from incidental investment activity—portfolio investments—and specifically state that a holding company is not a corporation whose principal business is trading in stocks or securities. Treas. Reg. Sec. 1.864-5(b)(2). In addition, income described in categories (1) and (2) in the text does not constitute effectively connected income if the recipient owns more than 50% of all the voting stock of the corporate payor or if the income constitutes subpart F income. Treas. Reg. Sec. 1.864-5(d).
39. Sec. 864(c)(4)(B)(iii).
40. Sec. 864(c)(4) (flush language).

circumstances under tax treaties that restrict the US taxing right to US source income.[41] However, if a foreign office of the taxpayer participates materially in the sale and the property is sold for use outside the US, the income will have a foreign source and will not be subject to US tax.[42]

5.4 GAINS FROM THE DISPOSITION OF REAL PROPERTY INTERESTS

Prior to 1980, properly advised foreign investors in US real estate could generally dispose of the property free of any US tax on the capital gain. A variety of techniques were used to achieve this result. These tax plans generally took advantage of the fact that, under normally applicable US tax rules, the US imposed no tax on capital gains, including gains from the disposition of real estate, unless the taxpayer was engaged in a US trade or business or, in the case of individuals, was present in the US for 183 days during the taxable year. The rapid increase in the level of foreign investment in US real estate and agricultural operations which took place in the late 1970s led to closer scrutiny of these transactions by the US Government. Part of the response to the situation was the enactment of the Foreign Investment in Real Property Tax Act ("FIRPTA") of 1980.

Under Section 897, gain or loss realized by a nonresident alien individual or foreign corporation from the "disposition" of a "United States real property interest" is taxed as if the foreign investor were engaged in a US trade or business and as if the gain or loss were effectively connected to that trade or business.[43] Such gain realized by a nonresident alien individual is treated for AMT purposes as "taxable excess"[44] subject to the AMT without the benefit of the exemption amount (Chapter 2 section 2.3.4) that applies to other types of AMT income.[45] For foreign corporations, the regular corporate rate generally will be applicable.

A "United States real property interest" may be either: (1) a direct interest in real property located in the US, or (2) an interest (other than solely as a creditor) in a domestic "United States real property holding corporation" (USRPHC). An USRPHC is a corporation in which the fair market value of US real property interests owned by the corporation equals or exceeds 50% of the sum of the fair market value of the

41. It also affects the foreign tax credit allowed to foreign persons. Sec. 906 (Chapter 9 section 9.4.4).
42. Sec. 865(e)(2)(B). Section 865(e)(2), which was enacted after Section 864(c)(4), diminishes the role of Section 864(c)(4)(B)(iii), which also addresses the sale of inventory outside the US. Section 864(c)(4)(B)(iii) continues to apply, however, to sales of inventory by individuals who are "US residents" for purposes of Section 865 (Chapter 4 section 4.2.6, note 25) because they have a principal place of business in the US but are nonresidents under Section 7701(b) (section 5.5.2).
43. Sec. 897(a)(1).
44. *See* Chapter 2 section 2.3.4 for a discussion of "taxable excess."
45. Sec. 897(a)(2). This will generally not create an adverse tax effect if the gain is long-term capital gain since the AMT rates for long-term capital gains are equal to the preferential rates for long term capital gains under the regular income tax. Sec. 55(b)(3). However, there will be an adverse tax effect if the gain from the US real property interest is ordinary income or short-term capital gain and the taxpayer is in an income tax bracket below 26%. In that situation, the AMT rates of 26% or 28% imposed on the gain will be higher than rates that would have otherwise applied. Sec. 872(a)(2).

corporation's US real property interests plus its foreign real property interests plus all other assets used in its trade or business.[46] If, under the foregoing test, a corporation was a domestic USRPHC at any time during the five years preceding the disposition of the taxpayer's shares in the USRPHC, the gain (or loss) recognized by the foreign taxpayer is subject to tax under Section 897.[47] Special rules apply to investment in US real estate through a real estate investment trust (REIT).[48]

Thus, where a foreign investor owns US real estate directly or through a US corporation that is an USRPHC, gain on a sale or exchange of either the property or the stock will be fully subject to US tax. Moreover, the techniques discussed in Chapter 2 sections 2.2.3 and 2.2.5 for exchanging property on a tax-free basis generally are not available unless the property received in the exchange is such that the gain on its sale would be subject to US tax. The Act gave the Treasury broad authority to issue regulations which determine the extent to which the various nonrecognition provisions discussed in Chapter 2 will or will not apply to exchanges of US real estate interests or stock in a domestic USRPHC.[49]

Different rules apply where the US real property interest is owned by a foreign corporation. The gain on disposition of stock in a foreign corporation which owns a US real property interest is not subject to tax under Section 897.[50] Instead, tax is deferred until the corporation itself disposes of the interest whether by sale or exchange, dividend distribution, or distribution pursuant to a redemption or liquidation.[51] The tax is then imposed on the corporation.[52] The gain subject to tax is the difference between

46. Sec. 897(c). Special "look-through" rules are applied so that a corporation is treated as owning its pro rata share of the relevant assets of corporations controlled (50%) by it. Attribution rules are applied to determine whether the requisite 50% control exists.
47. The disposition of the stock in a domestic USRPHC is not taxable, however, if within the five-year period: (i) the corporation disposed of all of its US real property in taxable transactions prior to the disposition of the stock, and (ii) the corporation was not a RIC or a REIT. Sec. 897(c)(1)(B).

    There is also an exception if the stock of the USRPHC is publicly traded and the selling shareholder owns 5% or less of the stock. Sec. 897(c)(3).
48. *See* Chapter 2 section 2.7.2. Dividend distributions by a REIT attributable to real estate operating income are taxed as normal dividends; dividends attributable to gains on the disposition of US real property interests by the REIT retain that character in the hands of foreign investors but are not taxed as effectively connected income if: (1) the distribution is received with respect to a class of stock that is publicly traded on a US securities market and (2) the foreign investor does not own more than 5% of the class of stock. Sec. 897(h)(1). REIT shares are treated as US real property interests unless 50% or more in value of the stock of the REIT is held directly or indirectly by US persons. Sec. 897(h)(2) and (h)(4)(B). Similar pass-through rules apply to real estate investments by a RIC (Chapter 2 section 2.7.1).
49. Sec. 897(e); Temp. Treas. Reg. Sec. 1.897-6T.
50. Stock in a foreign corporation, however, is treated as a US real property interest for purposes of testing the USRPHC status of a US corporation if such corporation owns directly or indirectly US real property interests whose fair market value equals or exceeds 50% of the sum of: (i) the fair market value of such corporation's US real property interests, (ii) its foreign real property interests, and (iii) all other assets used in its trade or business. Sec. 897(c)(4)(A).
51. The foreign corporation may avoid gain recognition under Section 897 upon the distribution of a US real property interest if the distributee takes the same basis as the foreign corporation, the distributee would be subject to US taxation if he were to immediately dispose of the property interest and certain reporting requirements are satisfied. Sec. 897(d)(2); Temp. Reg. Sec. 1.897-5T(c)(2).
52. Sec. 897(d)(1).

the fair market value of the interest at the time of distribution and its adjusted basis. Neither statutory tax-free exchanges nor the use of tax treaty elections, discussed above, can be used to avoid US tax on the disposition of US real property interests by a foreign corporation.

The FIRPTA provisions are reinforced by withholding requirements, as discussed at section 5.9.2.2. Treaty implications of the legislation are considered in Chapter 14.

5.5 TAXATION OF NONRESIDENT ALIENS

5.5.1 General

The general pattern of taxation discussed in sections 5.2, 5.3, and 5.4 applies to *nonresident* aliens. *Resident* aliens are taxed on their worldwide income in the same manner as US citizens (*see* Chapter 2). Thus an individual's status as resident or nonresident is a crucial element in establishing the appropriate taxing regime. The following material deals with the determination of resident or nonresident status and then examines in more detail the rules for the taxation of nonresident aliens. The special rules that may apply when a long-term permanent resident abandons her residence are considered in section 5.5.7.

5.5.2 Determination of Status as Resident or Nonresident

Section 7701(b) has detailed rules to determine the resident or nonresident status of aliens.[53] In general, an alien will be treated as a US resident if she meets any of the following three tests:

(1) the permanent residence test;
(2) the substantial presence test;
(3) the first year election.

In all other circumstances, she will be treated as a nonresident.

---

53. Prior to the enactment of Section 7701(b) in 1984, an alien's status as resident or nonresident was a factual question involving her intention with respect to the length and nature of the stay in the US. An intention to remain for an indefinite period was sufficient to establish residence while an intention to leave the US after a relatively short period established nonresidence. The question of residence was frequently litigated and the courts considered a variety of factors in determining the alien's intention. The following are some representative cases: *Siddiqi v. Commissioner*, 70 TC 553 (1978) (resident alien status where taxpayer entered the United States for an expected stay of 4-5 years to study architecture; compensation earned from temporary employment taxable at full US tax rates); *Jellinek v. Commissioner*, 36 TC 826 (1961) (nonresident alien status despite filing a declaration of intention to become a US citizen where the taxpayer returned to the foreign country within a short period of time because of lack of US employment opportunities); *Park v. Commissioner*, 79 TC 252 (1982) (taxpayer resident where he had substantial business and social connections to US despite fact that visa limited stay).

5.5.2.1 The Permanent Residence Test

If an alien has the status of having been lawfully accorded the privilege of residing in the US under US immigration laws,[54] she is treated as a resident alien until such status has been revoked or otherwise terminated. Resident treatment under this test does not require that the alien actually be present in the US at any time during the year in question. The taxpayer's status as a "resident" under this rule continues unless the immigration status is "rescinded or administratively or judicially determined to have been abandoned."[55]

5.5.2.2 The Substantial Presence Test

Even if an alien does not have permanent resident status, she will be treated as a resident for tax purposes for the current year if:

(1) such individual was present in the US on at least thirty-one days during the calendar year; and
(2) the sum of the number of days on which the individual was present in the US during the current year, plus one third of the number of days the individual was present in the US the prior year, plus one sixth of the number of days the individual was present in the US two years ago equals or exceeds 183 days.[56]

Even if the alien individual meets this total days present calculation, she can avoid resident status if she: (1) is present in the US present fewer than 183 days in the current year, (2) can establish that she has her "tax home" (generally her principal place of business) in a foreign country, and (3) has a closer connection to that country than to the US.[57] Thus, the substantial presence test depends significantly on what counts as a day present in the US. As an initial matter an alien is treated as "present" in the US for any day such individual is physically present at any time during the day.[58] However, a number of statutory exemptions are available that allow an individual to

54. In general, this means that an alien holds a valid "green card" entitling her to unrestricted permanent residence in the United States. Sec. 7701(b)(6); Treas. Reg. Sec. 301.7701(b)-1(b)(1).
55. Treas. Reg. Sec. 301.7701(b)-1(b)(1). Thus, an alien who continues to hold a green card after leaving the United States and moving to a foreign country will still be treated as a US resident until steps are taken to formally abandon her US resident status. *See* Treas. Reg. Sec. 301.7701(b)-1(b)(3) for the steps necessary to obtain a formal determination of abandonment of resident status.
56. Sec. 7701(b)(3)(A).
57. Sec. 7701(b)(3)(B). *See* Treas. Reg. Sec. 301.7701(b)-2 for the factors to be considered in establishing the "closer connection." To take advantage of the "closer connection" exception, the taxpayer must file a statement with the IRS detailing the basis for the claim. Absent a properly filed statement, the exception is generally not available. Treas. Reg. Sec. 301.7701(b)-8.
    Thus, for example, if an alien was present in the US for 66 days in 2019, 33 days in 2020 and more than 161 days in 2021, she would be resident in the US for 2021 unless she could meet the "closer connection/tax home" test. Under the substantial presence test, an alien can spend up to 121 days each year in the US without being considered a resident.
58. Sec. 7701(b)(7)(A).

not count certain days that the individual was in fact in the US. For example, any days present in the US when the taxpayer qualified as an "exempt individual" do not count towards the substantial presence test.[59] Exempt individuals are, generally speaking, teachers, students and trainees, and foreign government officials.[60] Additionally, if an individual is in transit between two points outside the US, and is physically present in the US fewer than twenty-four hours, then the individual is not treated "present" in the US on any day during that transit period.[61] Special rules govern the first and last year of residency and allow an individual to be treated as a resident for part of the year and a nonresident for the remainder of the year. Specifically, residence begins at the time the alien is first present in the US and continues for the remaining portion of that calendar year. Residence ends on the day that the alien leaves the US if the alien at that time has a closer connection to a foreign country than to the US and is not a resident at any time during the next calendar year.[62]

5.5.2.3 The First Year Election

An alien individual who satisfies neither the permanent residence test (the "green card" test) nor the substantial presence test in a given year may nonetheless be able to elect resident status for that year under certain circumstances. Why might an individual *want* resident status for tax purposes? Depending on the type of income being earned by the taxpayer (and whether the taxpayer is earning income outside the US), it may be more advantageous to be taxed as a resident on taxable income (income reduced by certain deductions) with graduated tax rates, than to be taxed as a nonresident on certain types of gross income at a flat rate without the benefit of deductions (*see* sections 5.5.3 and 5.5.4).

To make this first year election, the taxpayer: (1) must not be a resident under the other two tests this year, (2) must not have been a resident the year before, (3) must meet the substantial presence test *next* year, (4) must have been present in the US for at least thirty-one consecutive days in the year of the election, and (5) must be present in the US for 75% of the period beginning with the first day of the thirty-one day consecutive period and ending with the last day of the election year.[63] The election, which is made on the individual's tax return, cannot be made until the individual has satisfied the substantial presence test in the following year.[64]

59. Sec. 7701(b)(3)(D)(i) and 7701(b)(5).
60. Sec. 7701(b)(5).
61. Sec. 7701(b)(7)(C). Treas. Reg. Section 301.7701(b)-3 sets forth detailed rules for determining days of physical presence. There are also exceptions for situations where the taxpayer is prevented from leaving due to a medical condition that arose while the individual was in the US. Sec. 7701(b)(3)(D)(ii).
62. Sec. 7701(b)(2)(A), (B), and (C).
63. Sec. 7701(b)(4)(A).
64. Sec. 7701(b)(4)(E).

5.5.3 Income Taxed at 30% Rate

If a nonresident alien individual is not engaged in a US trade or business, a flat rate of 30% is imposed on five categories of income from US sources:

(1) Fixed or determinable annual or periodic income (generally passive investment income such as dividends, interest, and royalties from patents and copyrights).[65]
(2) Original issue discount on certain debt obligations.[66]
(3) The excess of capital gains over capital losses if the taxpayer has been present in the US for 183 days or more during the taxable year.[67] If this rule does not apply, a nonresident alien's capital gains are not subject to the 30% tax.[68]
(4) Gains from the sale or exchange of intangibles such as patents and copyrights to the extent that the gains are contingent on the productivity, use or disposition of the property sold.[69]
(5) 85% of Social Security benefits.[70]

The 30% rate is applied to income of the type discussed above even when the nonresident alien is engaged in a US trade or business, as long as the income is not "effectively connected" under the tests outlined in section 5.3.[71]

65. The items of income are specified in Section 871(a)(1)(A). *See also* Treas. Reg. Sec. 1.871-7(b). The phrase "fixed or determinable annual or period income" has been given a very wide interpretation. *See, e.g., Commissioner v. Wodehouse,* 337 US 369 (1949) (lump sum payment for literary rights). For a history of the provision, *see Barba v. US,* 2 Cl. Ct. 674 (1983). Section 1441 requires that US payers of fixed or determinable income that is not effectively connected income withhold US tax on that income at a rate of 30%. *See* section 5.9.2.1.

    With respect to transactions involving patents, know-how, and other intangibles, royalties paid under a license agreement are subject to the 30% withholding tax. In addition, if the transfer of the intangible is formally structured as a sale rather than a license, but payments are contingent on the productivity or use of the intangible, the transaction is treated as a license and the payments are subject to withholding as royalties. *See* Sec. 871(a)(1)(D).
66. *See* Chapter 2 section 2.8. Under Section 1273, original issue discount is deemed to accrue currently during the period that an original issue discount obligation is outstanding. Such accrued discount income is taxed to nonresidents at the time any payments (whether principal or interest) are made on the obligation. In addition, any accrued but untaxed discount income is taxed when the obligation is sold. Sec. 871(a)(1)(C). No tax is imposed on original issue discount obligations which have a term of 183 days or less. Sec. 871(g)(1)(B)(i).
67. Sec. 871(a)(2). This section has limited application in light of the present statutory definition of resident. *See* section 5.5.2. In normal circumstances, an alien who was present in the US for 183 days or more would be treated as a resident and subject to tax at normal rates on his worldwide income and Section 871(a)(2) would have no application. The provision could apply, for example, to students and foreign government officials who are exempted from the residence definition but who meet the Section 871(a)(2) test.
68. Treas. Reg. Sec. 1.1441-2(b)(2). As a result, such gains will, in general, escape US taxation unless effectively connected with a US trade or business or treated as such, *see* sections 5.3.2, 5.4, and 5.5.3.
69. Sec. 871(a)(1)(D).
70. Sec. 871(a)(3).
71. Treas. Reg. Sec. 1.871-8(b)(1).

Where the income is subject to the 30% rate, the tax is imposed on gross income.[72] Thus, no deductions are allowed even though attributable to the income subject to tax.[73] In the case of capital gains, the tax is imposed on the gain reduced by losses.

5.5.4 Income Taxed at Full US Progressive Tax Rates

All income of a nonresident alien that is (or is treated as) effectively connected with the conduct of a US trade or business is subject to the progressive US tax rates normally applicable to residents.[74] As in the case of US individuals, the rates are applied to taxable income (rather than to gross income as in the case of items described in section 5.5.3). Thus, gross income (as defined in Section 872) is reduced by the deductions that are "connected with income" which itself is "effectively connected" income (as specified in Section 873).[75] In addition, Section 873 allows gross income to be reduced by one personal exemption, the deduction for charitable contributions, and personal casualty losses even though these items are not so "connected."[76] Finally, various credits against tax are allowed.[77]

5.5.5 Exempt Income

Section 871 exempts from tax some categories of US source income received by nonresident aliens that otherwise would be within the scope of the gross basis tax.

72. Secs. 871(a)(1) and 881.
73. A nonresident alien who is a bona fide resident of Puerto Rico and in certain other circumstances may by filing a return claim the benefit of deductions for casualty losses for property located in the United States and charitable contributions, and, when available (after 2025), personal exemptions, even when not attributable to income effectively connected to a US trade or business. Secs. 873(b) and 874(a). These are rare cases.
74. Gains, realized by the individual, from the disposition of US real property interests are deemed to be effectively connected income. Sec. 897(a)(2). *See* section 5.4.
75. The rules for allocating and apportioning deductions are those set forth in Treas. Reg. Sec. 1.861-8 and following and 1.863-1 through 5, discussed in Chapter 4 section 4.4. No deduction is allowed for an expenditure that is allocable to an item exempt from tax. *See* Treas. Reg. Sec. 1.873-1(a)(1) and (5). Section 874 requires a nonresident alien to file a return in order to obtain the benefit of the deductions allowed by Section 873. *Brittingham v. Commissioner*, 66 TC 373 (1976), held that even though some return is filed, no deductions are allowed if it is not a "true and accurate" return. *See also Espinosa v. Commissioner*, 107 TC 146 (1996) (no deductions where timely return not filed; no waiver for "good cause" allowed).
76. A nonresident alien is not given the benefit of the standard deduction amount discussed in Chapter 2 section 2.3.2.6 because personal deductions are generally not allowed to such taxpayers. Sec. 63(c)(6)(B).

    In addition, if the nonresident is married, the preferential married person's rate schedule is not available. If a nonresident is married to a US citizen or resident, however, Section 6013(g) and (h) permit the spouses to elect to treat the nonresident spouse as a US resident and file a joint return. They are required to include their worldwide income but are then entitled to claim personal exemptions for themselves and qualified dependents, the standard deduction amount, tax credits, the married persons rate schedule, etc., just as in a joint return filed by married US citizens or residents.
77. Treas. Reg. Sec. 1.871-8(d). *See* Chapter 2 section 2.3.3.

5.5.5.1 Bank Deposits

Interest on bank deposits with US banks paid to nonresident aliens is exempt from tax if such interest is not effectively connected with the alien's US trade or business. Prior to 1986, the exemption was effected by treating such interest as foreign source income; the 1986 Act modified the source rules to treat such interest as US source income and made the exemption from tax explicit (Section 871(i)(2)(A)).

5.5.5.2 Dividends from Foreign Business Income

Prior to January 1, 2011, a "look-through" rule applied to dividends paid by a US corporation with significant foreign income. The pre-2011 version of Section 871(i)(2)(B) provided that if a domestic corporation derived 80% or more of its income from an active foreign business in the three-year testing period preceding the year in which it paid a dividend, the portion of the dividend deemed to be paid out of its foreign business income was not subject to tax under Section 871(a). Thus, for example, if a domestic corporation had 90% of its income in the testing period from an active foreign business and paid a dividend to a nonresident alien shareholder, only 10% of the dividend would be subject to tax under Section 871.[78]

This "look-though" rule was generally repealed for taxable years starting in 2011, but certain corporations to which the old rule applied remain covered by the prior rules.[79]

5.5.5.3 Portfolio Interest

Section 871(h) exempts from tax under Section 871(a) US source "portfolio interest" received by a nonresident alien. The interest qualifies as portfolio interest if the obligations are issued in registered form and if the US borrower paying the interest receives a statement from the beneficial owner of the interest that the recipient is not a US person.[80] The interest, however, cannot be received from a corporation or partnership in which the recipient has a 10% or greater interest, thus targeting the exemption at interest on a portfolio-type investment.[81]

The enactment of the exemption for portfolio interest by the US was an important initial step in the "race to the bottom" with respect to source taxation of interest income

78. *See* the pre-2011 version of Sec. 871(i).
79. Sec. 871(l). To retain coverage under the prior rules, the corporation must have satisfied the old rule for its 2010 taxable year, must not have added a substantial line of business since Aug. 10, 2010 and must show to the satisfaction of the IRS that at least 80% of its gross income from all sources is active foreign business income.
80. Sec. 871(h)(2); Treas. Reg. Sec. 1.871-14. The requirements for determining whether a debt obligation is in registered form are discussed in Notice 2012-20, 2012-1 C.B. 574 (2012).
81. Sec. 871(h)(3). When indebtedness is held by a partnership, regulations apply the 10% ownership test at the partner level. Treas. Reg. Sec. 1.871-14(g)(3). It may be questioned whether debt held by a partnership that also owns a controlling interest in the issuer should give rise to portfolio interest treatment to any of its partners.

generally. The race at least has been limited, however, by the repeal of the portfolio interest exemption for bearer bonds as part of an effort to eliminate tax evasion through cross-border arrangements. Interest paid on bearer bonds issued after March 18, 2012 is no longer treated as exempt portfolio interest.[82]

The portfolio interest exemption also does not apply to bank loans made in the ordinary course of business out of deference to concerns regarding competition with banks operating directly in the United States. In addition, the definition of portfolio interest does not include "contingent" interest where the interest is determined by reference to income, cash flow, sales, etc., of the debtor or a related person[83]

5.5.5.4 Capital Gains

Capital gains are not fixed or determinable income. As a result, capital gains of a nonresident who does not meet the 183-day presence test of Section 871(a)(2) and that are not connected with a US trade or business are generally not taxable.[84]

5.5.6 Treaties

Treaty provisions agreed to by the US and another country may modify the rules described above (*see* Chapter 14).

5.5.7 Taxation of Nonresident Aliens Who Are Former US Citizens or Legal Permanent Residents

Prior to June 17, 2008, US citizens and residents who expatriated (and satisfied certain conditions) continued to be taxed for ten years at normal rates on all US source income. The scope of US source income for these purposes was broadened substantially. The general purpose of the expatriation regime was to ensure that residents who held appreciated property did not seek to exit the US tax system just before selling the property (and thereby avoid US tax on income that effectively had been earned while the taxpayer was a US resident but had not been taxed due to the US' realization based tax system). In 2008, Congress largely supplanted Section 877 and adopted a "mark-to-market" regime to address the consequences of expatriation.[85] Section 877A treats certain US citizens and long-term US resident aliens who expatriate as having sold all their property for fair market value on the day before the date of expatriation. All gain

82. P.L. 111-147, Sec. 502(b)(1) and (f) (2010).
83. Sec. 871(h)(4)(A).
84. The capital gain distributions of a mutual fund (regulated investment company) are also exempt from tax. Rev. Rul. 69-244, 1969-2 C.B. 215. However, gains from the sale of certain intangible properties, such as patents, trade secrets, and copyrights, are subject to a 30% tax if the gains are contingent on the productivity of the intangibles. Secs. 871(a)(1)(D) and 881(a)(4). *See* sections 5.5.3 and 5.6.2. In effect, such gains are treated as though they represent license payments.
85. Section 877 was not repealed because it continues to apply in narrow situations. *See, e.g.*, section 5.5.7.2.

from the deemed sale is taken into account in the taxable year of the deemed sale "notwithstanding any other provision" of the Code.[86] Taxpayers are permitted to use losses from the deemed sale to the extent otherwise permitted in the Code to offset gains (Section 877A(a)(2)(B)).[87] The first USD 600,000 of net gain, adjusted annually for inflation after 2008, is not taxed.[88]

5.5.7.1 *Covered Expatriates: Former US Citizens*

The mark-to-market scheme of Section 877A applies to "covered expatriates," which includes a US citizen who has relinquished US citizenship and has certain levels of income or wealth. A former US citizen is a "covered expatriate" if: (1) his or her average tax liability for the five preceding years exceeds USD 124,000 (adjusted for inflation, USD 171,000 in 2020), (2) his or her net worth exceeds USD 2 million, or (3) the individual fails to certify that he or she has complied with all US income tax obligations for the preceding five years.[89]

5.5.7.2 *Covered Expatriates: Former US Residents*

Under Section 877A(g), "long term" permanent resident aliens who cease to be lawful permanent residents (*see* section 5.5.2.1) are treated in general in the same way as expatriating citizens. An alien is a "long term" permanent resident if she had this status for eight of the fifteen years prior to abandonment of residence status.[90] Similar rules apply if the alien remains a permanent resident (i.e., keeps her green card) but moves to a country which has a tax treaty which would prevent the US from asserting personal tax jurisdiction under the treaty[91] (*see* Chapter 14 section 14.4).

A separate rule applies under Section 7701(b)(10) to any resident alien (whether or not a lawful permanent resident) who, having been a resident for at least three years, abandons his residence and reestablishes residence within three years. In that situation, Section 877 applies to subject the taxpayer to tax on all US source income during the interim years.

5.5.7.3 *Deferral of Payment*

Section 877A(b) provides that a covered expatriate may make an irrevocable election to defer the payment of tax on gain arising from the deemed sale until his death or such

86. Sec. 877A(a)(2)(A). Special rules apply to defer taxation of certain deferred compensation items, tax-deferred accounts and interests in certain complex trusts. Sec. 877A(c).
87. Section 877A(a)(2)(B) also eliminates restrictions on deducting losses from wash sales for purposes of determining the expatriate's gains.
88. Sec. 877A(a)(3). The inflation adjusted amount in 2021 is USD 744,000.
89. Sec. 877A(g)(1)(A) and 877(a)(2). Limited exceptions are provided for persons with dual citizenship and certain minors. Sec. 877A(g)(1)(B).
90. Sec. 877A(g)(1), (2), and (5); Sec. 877(e)(2).
91. Sec. 7701(b)(6).

time that he actually transfers the property. Interest is imposed on the amount of tax deferred. The deferral election is made on an asset-by-asset basis. To make the election, the covered expatriate must provide adequate security and irrevocably waive any right under any US treaty that would preclude assessment or collection of any tax imposed by Section 877A. If the IRS subsequently determines that the security provided for the deferred tax no longer qualifies as adequate security, the deferred tax and interest will become due immediately, unless the covered expatriate corrects such failure within thirty days.[92]

5.6 TAXATION OF FOREIGN CORPORATIONS

5.6.1 General

The US method of taxation of foreign corporations follows in most respects the rules applicable to nonresident alien individuals. Thus, in general, US source investment income is taxed at a flat 30% rate if it is not effectively connected with the conduct of a US trade or business or at the normal corporate rate of 21% if it is effectively connected. The classification rules discussed at Chapter 2 section 2.1.2 determine whether a foreign organization will be subject to tax as a corporation.

5.6.2 Income of Foreign Corporations Taxed at 30% Rate

If a foreign corporation is not engaged in a US trade or business during the taxable year, a tax of 30% is imposed on its gross income from US sources that consists of: (1) fixed or determinable annual or periodic income; (2) original issue discount; and (3) gains from the sale or exchange of intangibles such as patents and copyrights to the extent that the gains are contingent on the productivity, use or disposition of the property sold.[93]

Even though a corporation is engaged in a US trade or business, income of the type described in the preceding paragraph is taxed at the 30% rate if it is not effectively connected with the conduct of the US trade or business.

5.6.3 Income of Foreign Corporations Taxed at Normal Corporation Tax Rates

The taxable income of a foreign corporation that is (or is treated as)[94] effectively connected with the conduct of a US trade or business is taxed at the normal US

92. Notice 2009-85, 2009-2 C.B. 598, provides additional detail about the application of Section 877A, including the election to defer payment of tax.
93. Sec. 881(a)(4). The definition of fixed or determinable annual or periodic income in Section 881(a) follows that in Section 871(a) discussed in section 5.5.3.
94. Gains from the disposition of US real property interests by a foreign corporation are treated as effectively connected with the conduct of a US trade or business. The term "disposition" includes dividend distributions and distributions pursuant to a redemption or liquidation. *See*

corporate rates. In determining taxable income, the starting point is gross income which is effectively connected with the US trade or business. Deductions are allowable to the extent that they are "connected with income" that is itself effectively connected income.[95] A charitable contribution deduction is allowed whether or not it is so connected.[96] In addition, credits against tax are allowed.

5.6.4 Exempt Income

Interest on bank deposits, portfolio interest, dividends from US corporations from foreign business income, and capital gains are exempt from tax if not effectively connected with a US trade or business (*see* section 5.5.5).

5.6.5 Branch Profits Tax

5.6.5.1 Background

Prior to 1986, dividends paid by a foreign corporation conducting a trade or business in the US constituted US source income if 50% or more of the corporation's gross income for the preceding three years was effectively connected with the US trade or business.[97] The amount of the US source dividend depended on the ratio of the effectively connected income to the total amount of income in the testing period. As US source income, the dividend was subject to tax in the hands of a nonresident alien or foreign corporate shareholder and the foreign distributing corporation was required to withhold US tax at the 30% rate on the distribution. This so-called second level dividend tax was difficult to administer since it required calculation of the corporation's worldwide income and imposed a withholding liability on a foreign corporation making a distribution to foreign shareholders. In addition, through proper planning, liability for the tax could be avoided by keeping the foreign corporation's income below the 50% threshold. The 1986 Act substantially eliminated the second level dividend tax and replaced it with the branch profits tax of Section 884, leaving the second-level dividend tax applicable only in very limited situations. The 2004 Act completely repealed the second level dividend tax.

5.6.5.2 Structure of the Branch Profits Tax

Section 884 imposes a 30% tax on a foreign corporation's "dividend equivalent amount" which is defined as the foreign corporation's effectively connected earnings

also section 5.3.2.4, which describes situations in which foreign source income can be treated as effectively connected with a US trade or business.

95. Sec. 882(c)(1).
96. *Id.*
97. Sec. 861(a)(2)(B) (former version).

and profits.[98] This tax is in addition to the regular corporate income tax but, since the tax is based on earnings and profits, the corporate income tax is in effect deductible from the branch profits tax base. Thus, if a foreign corporation has USD 100 of effectively connected earnings before corporate tax, it would pay USD 21 of regular corporate tax and then USD 23.7 of branch profits tax ((100-21) X 0.30) for a total tax burden of USD 44.70 (USD 21 regular corporate tax plus USD 23.70 branch profits tax). Dividend distributions by the foreign corporation, even if constituting US source income under Section 861(a)(2), are correspondingly not subject to tax when paid to its foreign shareholders.

The branch profits tax can be deferred and, in certain circumstances, avoided altogether if the earnings potentially subject to tax are reinvested in the US business. Technically, under Section 884(b)(1) the amount of effectively connected earnings is reduced by the increase in "US net equity" for the year. US net equity is essentially the net investment in the assets used in the US trade or business.[99] Thus, in the example above, if the foreign corporation had USD 500 of net US assets at the beginning of the year and USD 579 at the end of the year, no branch profits tax would be due. The USD 79 of net earnings are deemed to have been reinvested in the US business.[100] If, however, the branch profits tax for a prior year has been avoided through reinvestment and in the current year there is a reduction in US net equity, then the amount of the reduction is included in the branch profits tax base for the current year. Thus, to continue the above example, if in the following year the foreign corporation had an additional USD 79 of earnings after regular corporate tax and US net equity at the end of the year of USD 500, both the USD 79 of current earnings and the USD 79 of previous earnings on which tax had been deferred would be subject to the branch profits tax in that year.

If the foreign corporation completely terminates its US trade or business, the resulting decrease in US net equity will not trigger an imposition of the branch profits tax on any earnings which had previously escaped the tax through reinvestment.[101]

98. As discussed at Chapter 2 section 2.2.5, earnings and profits is a technical US tax concept that is similar to but not identical with book income less income taxes paid. The notion that a branch can have its own earnings and profits apart from those of the corporation as a whole was unknown in US tax law until introduction of the branch profits tax. For aspects of the determination of the dividend equivalent amount, *see* Treas. Reg. Sec. 1.884-1(b). A foreign corporation's gain on the sale of stock in a USRPHC is excluded from effectively connected earnings and profits for purposes of the branch profits tax. Sec. 884(d)(2)(C).

99. The calculation is made in terms of tax basis and not fair market value. Sec. 884(c)(2). *See* Treas. Reg. Sec. 1.884-1(c).

100. The calculation of US net equity is not based on a tracing of the earnings but on the total change in the overall US investment. Thus, if the foreign corporation in fact remitted the USD 79 of earnings to the home office but later in the same year transferred an additional USD 79 of funds to the branch for investment in the business, no branch profits tax would be due. Earnings are in effect "stacked" first against any increase in US net investment regardless of the actual source of the funds used for the investment. *See* Treas. Reg. Sec. 1.884-1-(b)(2).

If a foreign corporation is a partner in a partnership that has effectively connected earnings and profits, its share of those earnings is subject to the branch profits tax. Treas. Reg. Sec. 1.884-0(a).

101. Temp Treas. Reg. Sec. 1.884-2T. The theory behind this approach is that if the investment had been made through a US corporation that had reinvested its earnings and then subsequently

5.6.5.3 *Treaty Aspects*

In general, the branch profits tax is not imposed where its application would conflict with a US treaty obligation (Section 884(e)). This is the case where a treaty contains a nondiscrimination clause that prohibits "less favorable" treatment for the permanent establishment of a treaty country taxpayer when compared with a similarly situated US person. If the branch profits tax applied to the permanent establishment, the foreign taxpayer would be subject to both the regular corporate tax and the branch profits tax while a similarly situated US corporation would only pay the regular corporate tax.[102] Thus in these circumstances the branch profits tax is not imposed. However, the treaty limitation only prevents the imposition of the tax if the foreign corporation is a "qualified resident" of the treaty country, i.e., the corporation is not being used by residents of third countries for "treaty shopping."[103] Other aspects of the "treaty shopping" problem and the branch profits tax are discussed at Chapter 14 section 14.4.

---

liquidated, no dividend withholding tax would have been imposed on the liquidating distribution since the liquidating distribution is treated as capital gain. Since the branch profits tax is a replacement for the shareholder level withholding tax, parallel treatment requires that the tax not be imposed when the foreign corporation's US branch operations are in effect "liquidated" through a termination of the US business. The branch can also be "liquidated" by transferring its assets to a US subsidiary corporation in a tax-free transaction. In the latter case, the accumulated earnings on which branch profits tax has not been paid carryover to the transferee corporation, thus supporting future dividend payments. *See* Temp. Treas. Reg. Sec. 1.884-2T(d). Rules are provided, similar to a corporate liquidation-reincorporation situation, to restrict complete termination treatment where assets of a terminated branch are used within three years in a US trade or business. Temp. Treas. Reg. Sec. 1.884-2T(a)(2)(i)(B).

102. It could be argued that since the branch profits tax is really a surrogate for the second level shareholder tax, the foreign corporation is in no different position than a US corporation with foreign shareholders where the corporate level tax applies to the corporate level profits and the withholding tax to corporate distributions. However, the Internal Revenue Service took the position that imposition of the branch profits tax, which technically falls on the foreign corporation and not the shareholders, does in fact constitute impermissible discrimination. Treas. Reg. Section 1.884-1(g)(3) gives a list of those treaties that prevent the imposition of the branch profits tax. If the treaty permits the imposition of the branch profits tax but stipulates certain conditions for its imposition, the tax will only be applied if the conditions are met. In addition, if the treaty provides for a reduced rate of tax for dividends paid by US subsidiaries to foreign corporate parents, that rate rather than the 30% rate will be used for the branch profits tax. Sec. 884(e)(3)(A); Treas. Reg. Sec. 1.884-1(g)(4).

103. Under the statute, a foreign corporation is a "qualified resident" and thus is potentially entitled to treaty protection if more than 50% of its stock is owned by treaty country residents (or US persons) and less than 50% of its income is used to meet liabilities to third-country residents. Sec. 884(e)(4) and Treas. Reg. Sec. 1.884-5. Foreign corporations whose stock (or whose parent's stock) is publicly traded on an established securities market in the treaty country are automatically treated as qualified residents. Corporations that cannot meet these "safe haven" tests can still be treated as qualified residents if they are engaged in an active business in the treaty country and in the US. Treas. Reg. Sec. 1.884-5(e). If a taxpayer satisfies the limitation on benefits article of a treaty adopted after the enactment of the statutory rule and otherwise qualifies for the benefits of the treaty, the later treaty will take precedence over the statutory qualified resident rule. Treas. Reg. Sec. 1.884-1(g)(1)(ii).

5.6.6 Branch Interest Tax

5.6.6.1 General

In addition to the second level dividend tax described at section 5.6.5, prior to 1986 the US also imposed a second level tax on interest paid to foreign recipients by a foreign corporation with substantial amounts of US effectively connected income.[104] The 1986 Act eliminated the second level interest tax and replaced it with the branch interest tax of Section 884(f).[105] Under Section 884(f)(1)(A) interest that is "paid by" a US branch is treated as if it were paid by a domestic corporation. That is, it will be deemed to be US source interest income under Section 861(a)(1) and subject to tax under Sections 871(a) and 881(a) when received by foreign persons (unless some exception, for example, the exemption for portfolio interest applies). The statute does not indicate how to determine when interest is "paid by" the branch but extensive regulations have been issued that deal with the question. In general, interest will be "paid by" the branch if it arises in connection with a liability that is identified in the foreign corporation's books and financial statements as a liability of the US business or is secured by US assets.[106]

Section 884(f)(1)(B) provides a special rule where the amount of the interest "paid by" the branch under Section 884(f)(1)(A) is less than the amount of the interest expense deduction allocated to the branch under Treas. Reg. Section 1.882-5 (*see* Chapter 4 section 4.4.3.1). In this situation, the foreign corporation must pay tax on the difference between the "paid" interest and the "allocated" interest as if the difference were paid to it by a US subsidiary. That is, the difference is treated as interest from US sources, subject to tax as non-effectively connected US source interest income which the foreign corporation is deemed to have received, and that does not qualify for the portfolio interest exemption. The basic idea behind this special provision is that the US should be able to claim taxing jurisdiction over the amount of interest that is being deducted from the effectively connected corporate tax base. If the foreign corporation had invested in the United States through a US corporation, any interest paid by the US corporation would have been deductible from the corporate tax base but would have been subject to tax in the hands of the related party recipient. Section 884(f)(1)(B) reaches a similar result by treating the foreign corporation as the deemed recipient of the "excess" allocated interest that has been deducted in determining the amount of the effectively connected branch income.

For example, suppose that a US branch books and pays interest expense of USD 100 to a foreign lender. The USD 100 of interest would be treated as US source interest income and would be taxable to the foreign lender under either Section 871 or 881 (assuming no exceptions were applicable). The US branch would be required to

104. Sec. 861(a)(1)(C) (former version). This section made the interest US source and hence subject to tax under Sections 871 and 881. It was repealed by the 1986 Act.
105. Technically the section refers to interest paid by a "US trade or business" of a foreign corporation rather than by a "branch" but the tax is usually referred to as the branch interest tax.
106. Treas. Reg. Sec. 1.884-4(b)(1).

withhold tax at the 30% rate under Section 1441. Suppose, in addition, that the amount of interest expense allocated to the branch under Treas. Reg. Section 1.882-5 (Chapter 4 section 4.4.3.1) in calculating its effectively connected income is USD 150. The USD 50 of "excess" interest is deemed to have been received by the foreign corporation as non-effectively connected US source interest income and is taxable at the 30% rate under Section 881(a). Thus, all interest expense that was deducted for purposes of determining the effectively connected income of the branch would have been subject to tax as US source interest income.[107]

5.6.6.2 *Treaty Aspects*

Section 884(f)(3) deals with the treaty aspects of the branch interest tax and provides rules similar to those applicable to the branch profits tax. If a foreign corporation with a branch in the US is a "qualified resident" of a treaty country that has a treaty provision prohibiting the US from imposing tax or reducing the rate of tax on interest paid by a treaty country corporation, then either no tax or the reduced rate of tax will be imposed under Section 884(f)(1)(A). If the foreign corporation is not a qualified resident of the treaty partner but pays interest to a foreign person who is entitled to treaty benefits, the recipient of the interest will be taxed in accordance with the terms of the treaty between the US and the recipient's country (assuming in turn that the recipient is a qualified resident of that country).[108]

5.6.7 Penalty Taxes Applicable to Foreign Corporations and Domestic Corporations with Foreign Shareholders

5.6.7.1 *Accumulated Earnings Tax*

5.6.7.1.1 Foreign Corporations with US Income

As discussed at Chapter 2 section 2.2.6.1, Section 531 imposes a penalty tax on corporations which accumulate income to avoid the shareholder level tax. While the accumulated earnings tax does not apply to foreign corporations owned by foreign shareholders, it does apply to foreign corporations that have at least one US shareholder and US source income.[109]

107. For a case illustrating the operation of the branch interest tax, *see Taiyo Hawaii Company v. Commissioner*, 108 TC 590 (1997).
108. Sec. 884(f)(3)(B).
109. Treas. Reg. Sec. 1.532-1(c). Although Treas. Reg. Section 1.532-1(c) refers only to US source income, it is possible that the accumulated earnings tax also applies to effectively connected income that is not US source income.

5.6.7.1.2 Foreign Shareholders in Domestic Corporations

In general, dividends paid by a US corporation to a foreign shareholder would be subject to US tax in the shareholders' hands and thus the domestic corporation could in principle be subject to the accumulated earnings tax if it did not make distributions. However, the fact that the shareholder level dividend tax in many cases would be at a reduced treaty rate would be relevant in determining if the retention of earnings was to avoid the shareholder level tax.

5.6.7.2 Personal Holding Company Tax

Foreign corporations are not subject to the personal holding company provisions discussed at Chapter 2 section 2.2.6.2.[110] However, the provisions do apply to US corporations with foreign shareholders regardless of the level of foreign ownership or the source of the US corporation's income.

5.6.8 Comparison of Branch and Subsidiary Operations

As the preceding material has indicated, there are a number of differences between the taxation of foreign investment in the US through a branch of a foreign corporation and investment carried out through a US subsidiary. As regards the underlying corporate tax, business income is taxed at the same rates but the computation of the tax base differs. For a foreign branch, the source rules of Sections 861-865 determine the amount of gross income and the allocable share of deductions is established by Treas. Reg. Sections 1.861-8 and 1.882-5. For a US subsidiary, the tax base is generally its worldwide income.[111] Its share of income and deductions from dealings with related parties is determined on a direct basis under the arm's length principles of Section 482 (discussed in Chapter 12).

A second "level" of tax is collected from the business income of the branch through the imposition of the branch profits tax. That tax is payable currently to the extent that the US profits are not reinvested in the US business. The second level of tax on a US subsidiary's income is only collected when the US corporation actually distributes the income to the foreign shareholder. Thus the payment of the tax may be deferred, though excessive accumulations of income may run afoul of the accumulated earnings tax.

Historically, the bulk of foreign investment in the US has been through US subsidiaries. Branch operations have been mainly limited to foreign banks and other financial institutions that must operate in that form for regulatory reasons. Real estate investment in branch form has also been common. The extensive use of US subsidiaries has resulted in part for commercial reasons and in part because of the uncertainties

110. Sec. 542(c)(5).
111. As discussed in Chapter 6 section 6.5.1, however, some US corporations are allowed a 100% DRD for the foreign source portion of a dividend from foreign corporations in which they own at least 10% of the stock. Sec. 245A.

surrounding branch income determination. Generalizations about the appropriate investment structure, however, are difficult to make. For example, treaty benefits discussed in Chapter 14 may alter the domestic rules in favor of one form of investment over the other. For individual or closely held private investment, estate tax considerations must also be taken into account (*see* Chapter 15). And naturally the tax regime in the investor's own country and its interaction with the US system must also enter into the analysis. The basic point is that the failure to coordinate more closely branch and subsidiary taxation makes the overall taxing pattern transactionally elective.

5.7 TAXATION OF FOREIGN PARTNERSHIPS AND FOREIGN PARTNERS

5.7.1 Foreign Partnerships

Since the US does not treat a partnership as a separate taxable entity (*see* Chapter 2 section 2.5), the partnership, whether foreign or domestic, simply serves to pass through partnership income and loss to the partners. In determining whether this pass-through pattern of taxation applies to a foreign legal organization, the entity classification rules discussed at Chapter 2 section 2.1.2 are applicable. Thus under the elective "check-the-box" rules, a foreign entity that is treated as a partnership under foreign law may be a corporation for US purposes. While such "hybrid" treatment has always been possible in principle, the ease of creating such entities under the "check-the-box" approach have made such structures much more common and raise both planning opportunities and traps for the unwary. The appropriate treatment of such "hybrid" entities involves a number of complex issues (*see* Chapter 14 section 14.4.1.2.).

5.7.2 Foreign Partners in a US or Foreign Partnership

The taxation of a foreign partner on the income of a US or foreign partnership depends on the nature of that income. Under the conduit principle of partnership taxation, the partnership income retains its character in the hands of the individual partner. Thus, for example, if the partnership has income that is effectively connected with its US trade or business, the foreign partner is taxable on his share of such income under the rules described in sections 5.3-5.6. The partnership's US trade or business is attributed to the foreign partner.[112] Gain or loss of a foreign person from the disposition of a directly or indirectly held partnership interest generally is treated as effectively connected with a US trade or business to the extent of the partner's share of gain that would have been effectively connected had the partnership sold its assets.[113]

---

112. Sec. 875(1).
113. Sec. 864(c)(8). This provision was adopted in the 2017 Tax Act to override the result in the Tax Court decision in *Grecian Magnesite Mining Co. v. Commissioner*, 149 T.C. No. 3 (2017), *aff'd*, 926 F.3d 819 (D.C. Cir., 2019), which concluded that the gain was non-effectively connected gain from the sale of a capital asset. The Tax Court rejected the position in Rev. Rul. 91-32,

If the partnership has US source non-effectively connected FDAP income, a foreign partner will be taxed on its distributive share of the income on a gross income basis under Section 871 or 881. If the partnership has income which, if received by the foreign partner directly would not be subject to tax, for example, non-effectively connected income from foreign sources, the foreign partner is not subject to tax on her share of such income. The foreign partner is taxed at the time the income is received or accrued by the partnership, depending on the partnership's method of accounting (*see* Chapter 2 section 2.5).

5.8 TAXATION OF FOREIGN TRUSTS AND FOREIGN BENEFICIARIES

5.8.1 Foreign Trusts

5.8.1.1 Classification Issues

A trust or other similar arrangement created under foreign law may be classified as a trust for US tax purposes under the Regulations discussed at Chapter 2 section 2.1.2.[114] If the purpose of the arrangement is to protect or conserve property for the beneficiaries, it will be treated as an "ordinary" trust and taxed according to US trust taxation principles. However, if the purpose of the arrangement is to associate to carry on a business and divide the profits, it will not be treated as a trust for tax purposes despite the fact that it is legally organized in trust form.[115]

Assuming that the arrangement is classified as a trust, Section 7701(a)(30) and (31) provide rules for determining its status as "domestic" or "foreign."[116] A trust will be domestic if: (a) a court in the US is able to exercise primary supervision over the administration of the trust, and (b) US fiduciaries have authority to control all "substantial decisions" concerning the trust. All other trusts are treated as foreign. For example, consider a trust formed under US law that is subject to the supervision of a US court and has two trustees, one foreign person and one US person. That trust will be

1991-1 C.B. 107, that gain or loss recognized by a foreign person upon its disposition of a partnership interest generally constitutes effectively connected income or loss to the extent of the foreign person's distributive share of unrealized gain or loss of the partnership attributable to effectively connected property of the partnership. The Government only appealed the Tax Court decision with respect to its alternative argument that the gain was attributable to Grecian's US office. In a highly textual exegesis, the D.C. Circuit looked to whether the sale of the interest itself, as opposed to the activity increasing the value of the interest, was attributable to the US office, and siding with the Tax Court, concluded the US office was not a material factor in the realization of the gain.

114. As in the cases of foreign corporations, however, its treatment under foreign law is not determinative of the US tax classification.
115. Treas. Reg. Sec. 301.7701-4. Businesses operating in the legal form of trust are generally taxed as corporations (*see* e.g., *Hynes v. Commissioner, 74* TC 1266 (1980)), though classification as a partnership is also possible. There is very little authority on the classification of foreign legal entities organized in civil law jurisdictions which do not have the common law trust as an indigenous legal institution.
116. Prior to the changes in Section 7701(a)(30), cases and rulings looked at a number of factors including place of activity, residence of trustees, place of administration, and the like to determine the status of a trust.

treated as a foreign trust if, as is usually the case, the trust instrument provides that decisions are to be made by a majority of the trustees, since the single US trustee lacks the requisite control.[117]

5.8.1.2 *Taxation of Foreign Trusts*

As discussed at Chapter 2 section 2.4, simple trusts are in general treated as modified conduits. This result is accomplished by including amounts received by the trust in trust income initially but then giving the trust a deduction for the income which is distributed in the same year to beneficiaries.[118] The trust beneficiary includes the currently distributed amount in income and such current income retains the same character that it had in the hands of the trust.[119] If a domestic trust accumulates its income (a so-called complex trust)[120], the income is taxable to the trust in the year received. When the trust distributes the accumulated income in a subsequent year, it is not permitted to claim a deduction and the beneficiary is not taxed on the distribution.[121] In general, if a trust has current income, it is treated as distributing such current income before distributing any accumulated income.[122]

In the case of a foreign trust, US source income and income effectively connected with a US trade or business is initially taxed to the trust.[123] As is the case with US trusts, however, the foreign trust deducts that income if it distributes it to the US beneficiary in the current year.[124] The US beneficiary includes *all* the income currently distributed to her or him, not just the amount of US source or effectively connected income, since US residents are taxable on all their income.[125] If the foreign trust accumulates income and then distributes it in a later year to a US beneficiary, the income is taxed to the trust when received and then taxed again to the beneficiary when distributed in a later year with a credit for the trust level taxes.[126] All the accumulated income that is later distributed to the beneficiary is treated as ordinary—accumulated capital gains of the trusts do not retain their character in the hands of the US beneficiary.[127] In order to discourage the accumulation of income by the trust, an interest charge is also added to

117. *See* Treas. Reg. Sec. 301.7701-7(d)(1)(v) Example 1.
118. Sec. 661(a).
119. Sec. 662(a) and (b).
120. *See* Chapter 2 section 2.4.
121. Sec. 641(a).
122. This is accomplished through the mechanism of "distributable net income." Secs. 643(a), 661(a), and 662(a).
123. Sec. 641(b).
124. Sec. 661(a).
125. This is accomplished through a modification to the distributable net income ("DNI") rules under Section 643(a)(6) for foreign trusts, so that all income collected from any source by the trust, including foreign source income, will be included in the trust's DNI. Section 662(a) in turn requires the US taxpayer to include the distribution in income to the extent is consists of DNI.
126. Sec. 667(d)(1)(A).
127. *Compare* Sec. 667(e), which retains the character of trust income that is distributed to foreign beneficiaries. *See* section 5.7.2.

the tax payable by the distributee for the period the trust had accumulated such income.[128]

The treatment of foreign trusts with US grantors and US beneficiaries is discussed at Chapter 8 section 8.3.

5.8.2 Taxation of Foreign Beneficiaries

Income which is distributed currently by a trust (whether foreign or domestic) is treated in the hands of the foreign beneficiary as having the same character as it had in the hands of the trust.[129] Thus the taxation of the beneficiary depends on whether the income was foreign source investment income, US source effectively connected income, etc. If the income is accumulated by a foreign trust initially and then distributed to foreign beneficiaries, it retains its tax character when ultimately received by the beneficiary; any taxes paid by the trust are included in the beneficiaries' income and in effect credited against their final tax liability.[130] However, if the tax paid at the trust level exceeds the tax due at the beneficiary level, no refund is available to the beneficiary.[131]

5.8.3 Foreign Grantor Trusts

As discussed at Chapter 2 section 2.4, normally if the grantor of a trust retains certain control over or rights to the trust property, he will remain taxable on the trust income. This principle, when applied to nonresident grantors, led to significant tax avoidance possibilities through which a nonresident could establish a grantor trust with US beneficiaries (often with property "given" to the grantor by the beneficiaries) and the trust could then make distributions to the beneficiaries that would not be subject to US

128. Sec. 668(a). *See* Michael A. Heimos, PORTFOLIO 854-4TH T.M., US TAXATION OF FOREIGN ESTATES, TRUSTS AND BENEFICIARIES Sec. V. E. (2020), for a detailed description of how the interest charge is calculated. In addition to the interest charge, a "throwback rule" causes the tax payable by the distributee in effect to be determined at the recipient's highest marginal tax rate for the year in which the income was earned by the trust. Sec. 667.

129. Sec. 662(a), (b), and Sec. 667(e). *See* Rev. Rul. 81-244, 1981-2 C.B. 151 (interest income on US bank deposit received by trust and distributed to nonresident beneficiary kept that character in the beneficiary's hands); *Martin-Montis Trust v. Commissioner*, 75 TC 381 (1980) (same). Where the income is investment income that is normally taxed on a gross basis to the foreign recipient, there is a question as to whether the amount includible when received as a trust distribution is reduced by the expenses incurred at the trust level. One case has allowed such treatment (under a prior version of the statute), but the result seems inconsistent with the general principles of pass-through taxation. *See Wittschen v. Commissioner*, 5 TC 10 (1945).

130. Sec. 667(d) and (e).

131. Sec. 666(e). This rule makes the timing of distributions important. For example, if a US trust with foreign source income distributes the income currently to its foreign beneficiary, there will be no tax at the trust level (because of the distribution deduction) and no tax at the beneficiary level (because the income is foreign source). However, if the income is accumulated and later distributed, it will be taxed to the US trust. Neither the trust nor the beneficiary can obtain a refund for the trust level tax when the income is distributed. The same principles apply to accumulated capital gains. *See, e.g., Maximov v. United States*, 373 US 49 (1963).

tax.[132] The grantor theoretically would be subject to US tax on the trust income but could control the trust investment policy to avoid that tax. Often foreign tax would be avoided as well if the foreign jurisdiction treated the trust as a separate taxable entity. To counter such arrangements, Section 672(f) in general eliminates from grantor trust classification any trust (foreign or domestic) if the trust's income is not taken currently into account by a US person.[133] Thus, a trust established by a nonresident that would not qualify as a grantor trust because of Section 672(f) will be subject to the normal pattern of taxation, including the special rules applicable to foreign trusts with US beneficiaries discussed at section 5.8.1.

5.9 PROCEDURAL ASPECTS

5.9.1 Return and Disclosure Requirements

Every nonresident alien or foreign corporation that is engaged in a US trade or business must file a US tax return.[134] This return must be filed even though the taxpayer has no taxable income in its US trade or business. A US return must also be filed if the foreign taxpayer's US tax liability has not been completely covered by withholding at source. The filing of a return is a prerequisite for the allowance of any deductions otherwise available under the Code and, in addition, there are penalties for failure to file.[135] The return is generally due on or before the fifteenth day of the sixth month following the close of the taxable year (June 15 for calendar year taxpayers). Special rules apply for employment income. In some cases estimated tax payments may be required.

There are a number of provisions requiring disclosure of information to various governmental agencies by foreign persons doing business in the US. Section 6038A requires information concerning transactions between a US corporation in which at least 25% of the stock is owned by a foreign person and any "related parties."[136] The section is intended to help in policing intercompany pricing practices between related

---

132. *See* Rev. Rul. 69-70, 1969-1 C.B. 182 (income of foreign grantor trust set up by a nonresident alien was taxable to the grantor and not to the trust or the US resident beneficiary). For special rules treating foreign trusts set up by US persons as grantor trusts, *see* Chapter 8 section 8.3.2.
133. The special rules disqualifying the trust as a grantor trust do not apply if the trust would otherwise have qualified as a grantor trust because of the grantor's unrestricted power to revoke the trust or if the income of the trust can only be distributed to the grantor during his lifetime. Sec. 672(f)(2). Other aspects of the grantor trust rules as they apply to foreign grantors are described in Treas. Reg. Sec. 1.672(f)-1(a).
134. Treas. Reg. Sec. 1.6012-1(b) and 2(g).
135. Secs. 874(a), 882(c)(2), 6651, and 6652. Treas. Reg. Secs. 1.874-1(b)(2) and 1.882-4(a)(3)(ii) waive the filing deadline if the non-filer acted in good faith.
136. The detailed requirements of Section 6038A are set out in Treas. Reg. Section 1.6038A-1. A foreign corporation that has at least 25% of its stock owned by one foreign person is required to furnish to the Service the information described in Section 6038A(b). This information includes: (1) the name of each person that is a "related party" and that has had any transaction with the reporting corporation, (2) the nature of the relationship with that party, and (3) the nature of "any transactions" between the two corporations. Many foreign-owned multinational groups with US operations have complained about the burdensome nature of the reporting requirements, especially in the light of the substantial penalties for noncompliance. *See* Treas. Reg. Sec. 1.6038A-4(a)(3).

parties under Section 482 (*see* Chapter 12 section 12.3). In addition, Sections 6038A and 6038C also require foreign corporations conducting business in the US to provide information that will enable the IRS to determine application of the Base Erosion Anti-Abuse Tax ("BEAT") under Section 59A, which is discussed in section 5.10.[137]

Another provision, Section 6039C, authorizes the Treasury Department to issue regulations requiring the disclosure of ownership by foreign persons of US real property interests but no regulations have as yet been issued. Instead, withholding requirements, discussed below in section 5.9.2.2, are imposed by Section 1445 and the Regulations issued thereunder on persons purchasing real property interests from foreign taxpayers.[138] In addition, other nontax provisions also involve disclosure obligations. For example, the Agricultural Foreign Investment Disclosure Act of 1978 (7 USC Sections 3501-3508) deals with foreign investment in agricultural land, the International Investment Survey Act of 1976 (22 USC Sections 3101-3108) imposes reporting requirements for foreign investors in US businesses, and the US Foreign Account Tax Compliance Act[139] requires certain foreign financial institutions, including foreign banks and foreign investment funds, to disclose information regarding accounts and investments held or owned by US citizens and residents.

5.9.2 Withholding at Source

5.9.2.1 Fixed or Determinable Income

Sections 1441 and 1442 impose a 30% withholding tax on income such as interest, dividends, and other fixed or determinable annual or periodical income paid to a nonresident alien, foreign corporation, foreign partnership, or foreign fiduciary from US sources.[140] In the normal situation, this withholding at source fully satisfies the nonresident taxpayer's US tax liability and no tax return need be filed.

No withholding is required for income that is effectively connected with a US trade or business.[141] This rule mirrors the fact that effectively connected income is not subject to the 30% tax, but is taxed at normal individual or corporate rates. Wages received by a nonresident alien employee for services performed in the US are subject

137. Sec. 6038A(b)(2); Treas. Reg. Sec. 1.6038A-2.
138. Sec. 1445(a); Treas. Reg. Sec. 1.1445-1.
139. Pub. L. No. 111-147, 124 Stat. 71 (2010).
140. Treas. Reg. Sec. 1.1441-5 provides circumstances in which the payer to a foreign partnership, trust, or estate will be excused from withholding. In general, the payer will not be required to withhold if the foreign partnership, trust, or estate has entered into a withholding agreement with the Internal Revenue Service. Treas. Reg. Sec. 1.1441-5 also provides circumstances in which a payer may treat a payment to a foreign partnership, trust, or estate as a payment to the beneficial owners. Amounts paid to domestic partnerships with foreign partners are not subject to withholding by the payer but the partnership is required to withhold on the foreign partner's distributive share of the US source income (whether or not actually distributed). Treas. Reg. Sec. 1.1441-5(b). Similarly, withholding is required on US source income of foreign beneficiaries of a foreign or domestic trust. *Id.*
141. Sec. 1441(c)(1). Withholding by a domestic partnership is required under Section 1446 on its effectively connected income that is allocable to a foreign partner. *See* section 5.9.2.3.

to the usual wage withholding tax imposed on US citizens and residents rather than the 30% rate.[142]

To be subject to withholding under Section 1441, amounts paid must be from sources within the US and thus no withholding is required on non-US source income, for example, wages paid by a foreign employer to a nonresident alien employee who is only temporarily present in the US and meets the tests of Section 861(a)(3) (*see* Chapter 4 section 4.2.3). However, if the income is from US sources, withholding is required even if the foreign employer is not otherwise engaged in a US trade or business.[143]

The 30% withholding rate is often reduced or eliminated in US tax treaties (*see* Chapter 14 section 6).

In general, for any exemption from or reduction in withholding tax to apply, various certifications of the recipient's qualification for the reduction or exemption must be supplied to the US withholding agent. Regulations, which were adopted in 1997 and apply to payments made after 2000, extend this rule to dividends.[144] Thus, the old rule, that had allowed the US withholding agent to rely on the address of the payee of dividends to establish whether withholding is required, no longer applies.[145]

Withholding is not required for payments to "qualified intermediaries," generally foreign financial institutions that have entered into agreements with the Internal Revenue Service.[146] The qualified intermediary agreements set forth the information that the intermediary is required to obtain from the foreign taxpayers and the circumstances in which it is required to disclose such information to the Internal Revenue Service.[147]

5.9.2.2 Disposition of US Real Property Interests

Section 1445 sets forth detailed rules for withholding on the disposition of US real property interests. In general, the transferee of the real property interest is required to withhold 10% of the *amount realized* by the foreign transferor on the disposition of the property. Withholding can be avoided if the transferee receives from the transferor an affidavit that the transferor is not a foreign person or, in the case of the transfer of shares of stock of a domestic corporation, an affidavit from the corporation that it is not a US real property holding corporation.[148] No withholding is required if the stock of a US real property holding corporation is regularly traded on an established securities market. Since the amount required to be withheld is based on the gross amount of the

142. Treas. Reg. Sec. 1.1441-4(b)(1).
143. Sec. 1441(a).
144. *See* Treas. Reg. Sec. 1.1441-1(b).
145. *See* Treas. Reg. Sec. 1.1441-1(b)(1).
146. Treas. Reg. Sec. 1.1441-1(b)(1).
147. Treas. Reg. Sec. 1441-1(e)(5)(iii). In certain cases, a qualified intermediary may elect to take on withholding responsibility directly.
148. Withholding is required if the transferee has actual knowledge that the affidavit is false. Sec. 1445(b)(7). In addition, if any agent of the transferor or transferee has knowledge that the affidavit is false, the agent is required to notify the transferee. If the notification is not furnished, the agent is required to withhold and is liable to the extent of its compensation received in connection with the transaction. Sec. 1445(d).

sales proceeds, it may exceed the tax liability on the foreign transferor's taxable gain. Section 1445(c) provides a mechanism by which the amount to be withheld can be reduced by obtaining an advance determination from the Internal Revenue Service of the maximum amount of the foreign transferor's tax liability. Section 1445(e) provides special rules dealing with withholding on distributions of US real property interests by domestic corporations, partnerships or trusts.[149]

5.9.2.3 *Withholding on Foreign Partners*

Section 1446 requires a partnership (domestic or foreign) to withhold tax at the highest marginal individual or corporate rate on a foreign partner's allocable share of the partnership's effectively connected income regardless of whether such income is distributed. The withheld tax is credited against the partner's US tax liability on the effectively connected income. As discussed previously, the 2017 Tax Act treats a foreign partner's gain on the sale of a partnership interest as effectively connected income to the extent attributable to gain on assets used in a US business (section 5.7.2). The same Act imposes an obligation on purchasers of such interests to withhold 10% of the amount realized on the disposition.[150] In addition, withholding is required by domestic partnerships on a foreign partner's share of non-effectively connected US source fixed or determinable annual or periodic income whether or not the income is distributed.[151]

5.10 BASE EROSION ANTI-ABUSE TAX ("BEAT")

Congress adopted an additional tool, the Base Erosion Anti-Abuse Tax ("BEAT") to prevent corporations (other than mutual funds, REITs and S corporations) conducting business in the US from shifting income outside the US by making deductible payments to foreign related persons.

In general, the BEAT applies to corporations (other than mutual funds, REITs and S corporations) that have gross receipts of at least USD 500 million[152] and that make payments having the potential to erode the US tax base. The BEAT targets payments to related foreign parties that are deductible in calculating the payer's US tax liability and that are not subject to the 30% withholding tax discussed in section 5.6.2.[153] The BEAT

149. Procedures to be followed under Section 1445 are set forth in Treas. Reg. Section 1.1445-5.
150. Sec. 1446(f).
151. Treas. Reg. Sec. 1441-5(b)(2).
152. Sec. 59A(e). The USD 500 million threshold is determined by using only income effectively connected with a US trade or business if the taxpayer is not a US entity. Sec. 59A(e)(2).
153. Sec. 59A(c)(2)(B). For this purpose, deductible payments do not include payments properly included in the taxpayer's costs of goods sold. Sec. 59A(c)(2)(A)(iv); *see also* Tax Cuts and Jobs Act, Conf. Comm., 653 (115th Cong. 1st Sess. Dec. 18, 2017) (stating "base erosion payments do not include payments for cost of goods sold (which is not a deduction but rather a reduction to income).").

is triggered if such payments exceed a threshold amount that is equal to 3% of the taxpayer's total allowable deductions plus certain base erosion tax benefits.[154]

The BEAT in effect is a minimum tax that adds the deductible payments not subject to withholding back to the taxpayer's taxable income. If the BEAT exceeds the taxpayer's regular US income tax, then the taxpayer is required to pay its regular income tax plus the amount by which the BEAT exceeds its regular tax liability. The BEAT rate is 10% from 2019 to 2025, and thereafter is 12.5%.[155]

For example, consider a US corporation that has USD 500 million of gross income and pays deductible royalties to a foreign affiliate of USD 400 million. This deductible payment, which is not subject to withholding, constitutes 100% of the deducible payments and, therefore, exceeds the 3% threshold amount. The corporation's regular tax liability is USD 21 million (21% of USD 100 million), but the BEAT is USD 50 million (10% of USD 500 million). As a result, the corporation would pay USD 50 million to the United States (the regular tax of USD 21 million plus the USD 29 million amount by which the BEAT exceeds the regular tax liability).

5.11 FOREIGN ACCOUNT TAX COMPLIANCE ACT ("FATCA")

In 2010, Congress passed FATCA, which is aimed at reducing tax evasion by US taxpayers holding funds in foreign accounts.[156] FATCA provides for taxation of US source payments to "foreign financial institutions" ("FFIs"), collected by withholding, if US persons are beneficial owners of foreign financial accounts unless the FFI satisfies requirements to disclose the accounts and identity of their owners to the IRS or under certain intergovernmental agreements to their country of residence for potential exchange with the IRS.[157] If an FFI fails to satisfy FATCA's reporting requirements, then the FFI is subject to having a 30% tax deducted and withheld from withholdable payments to the FFI (including gross proceeds from the sale of securities).[158] The tax is an incentive to disclose and was not intended to be collected if there is compliance through reporting of US persons' ownership of accounts.[159]

154. Sec. 59A(c)(4). The base erosion tax benefits added to the numerator are those for certain reinsurance payments to related persons and payments to affiliates in an expatriated entity affiliated group that reduce gross receipts.
155. Sec. 59A(b)(1) and (2).
156. Secs. 1471-1474.
157. A FFI includes any foreign entity that accepts deposits in the ordinary course of a banking or similar business, holds financial assets for the account of others as a substantial portion of its business, or is engaged (or holding itself out as being engaged) primarily in the business of investing, reinvesting, or trading in securities, partnership interests, commodities, or any interest in those. Sec. 1471(d)(5).
158. Sec. 1471(a).
159. Although the tax on income of the FFI (as opposed to its customers) is subject to relief by treaty, relief only can be claimed by refund and no interest will be paid on the overpayment. Sec. 1474(b)(2). These rules were intended to avoid overriding treaties. Much of the tax on withholdable payments relates to income of FFI customers who would have to separately claim treaty relief. Any refund of tax on the FFI's income would take a long time and the withholding of tax would impinge on the FFI's liquidity. For these reasons, the treaty relief feature is largely unused.

Although FATCA was controversial when adopted, and remains controversial as a consequence of its burdens on US citizens living abroad, other countries have adopted analogous rules under a common reporting standard regime. A major complaint of other countries regarding FATCA is that the United States has not possessed (and has not been able to exchange under IGAs) certain information it demands from FFIs including beneficial ownership of certain entities. This may change in the future as the US implements new beneficial owner disclosure rules regarding interest holders of LLCs, as well as corporations and other similar entities, enacted as part of the Corporate Transparency Act in 2021.

CHAPTER 6

Treatment of Foreign Business Operations and Investments by US Persons

6.1 INTRODUCTION

The materials in this chapter deal with special rules that apply to foreign business operations by US persons.

Prior to the 2017 Tax Act, the US employed a global tax system that taxed US residents and corporations on all their income regardless of where such income was earned. In contrast, most other countries employ an exemption system that does not tax the profits earned by its resident corporations in foreign countries. Exemption tax systems are sometimes also called territorial tax systems.

Although the US employed a global tax system, the income of a foreign corporation controlled by US shareholders prior to the 2017 Tax Act was in general not included in the shareholder's income until distributed to them, either in the form of a dividend or as a liquidation distribution. As a result, many controlled foreign corporations ("CFCs") deferred distributing profits to their US shareholders if the profits could be reinvested in countries with low tax rates. An important exception to the general rule that profits were not taxed until distributed was subpart F.[1]

The subpart F provisions, which are still in effect after the 2017 Tax Act, attempt to curb the use by US shareholders of CFCs that act as a "base" for accumulating income in low-tax countries from passive investments and from transactions with related parties. (Income from the related party transactions and passive investments is called subpart F income.[2]) The subpart F provisions seek to discourage this by requiring the CFC's US shareholders to recognize the CFC's subpart F income on their

1. The subpart F provisions are in Sections 951-965.
2. *See* Sec. 952(a), which defines subpart F income.

US tax returns each year regardless of whether the CFC actually distributes that income.[3]

Subpart F has a specific definition for the type of CFCs to which it applies. It defines a "controlled foreign corporation" that is subject to its rules as a foreign corporation in which "US shareholders" own more than 50% of the voting power or value of the CFC's stock.[4] A "US shareholder" is in turn defined as a US person that owns at least 10% of the voting power or value of the CFC's stock.[5]

Until the 2017 Tax Act, the subpart F rules, which will be discussed in detail in section 6.3, were the primary provisions that taxed US shareholders immediately on the income of their CFCs. As a result, the opportunity to defer US taxation of non-subpart F income often encouraged CFCs in low-tax jurisdictions to accumulate such income indefinitely rather than have it subjected to a US tax when distributed to US shareholders.

The 2017 Tax Act not only retained subpart F but also adopted a hybrid system, called "GILTI,"[6] which taxes a portion of the non-subpart F income of US CFCs before such income is actually distributed to US shareholders.[7] In effect, GILTI, which is discussed in detail in section 6.4, divides the non-subpart F income of CFCs into two portions. The first portion is the CFC's income that is equal to 10% or less of its tangible assets. That portion is not taxed in the US as earned by the CFC and is exempt from taxation when distributed to the CFC's US corporate shareholders.[8] (Distributions to shareholders, who are *individuals*, however, are not exempt from taxation.)

GILTI treats differently the second portion of the CFC's non-subpart F income, which is the amount of the CFC's income in excess of 10% of its tangible assets. GILTI taxes corporate and individual US shareholders annually on their share of that second portion regardless of whether such income is distributed to them.[9] A reduced tax rate applies, however, to corporate shareholders.[10] In effect, GILTI eliminates deferral of US taxation on that second portion of the CFC's non-subpart F income, i.e., the portion that exceeds 10% of its tangible assets.

Why is this hybrid tax regime called GILTI, which is the acronym for Global Intangible Low-Taxed Income? The GILTI tax regime in effect is assuming that income in excess of 10% of a CFC's tangible assets must be attributable to the CFC's *intangible assets*. In other words, the income in excess of 10% is literally *the* GILTI, the global intangible low-taxed income. Since intangible assets can easily be located anywhere, Congress determined that subsidizing the income generated by such assets in low-tax countries would encourage locating such assets there even though such location might

3. Sec. 951(a). The US shareholders who recognize subpart F income do not recognize any further income when such income is actually distributed to them. Sec. 959(a).
4. Sec. 957(a).
5. Sec. 957(c).
6. The acronym, GILTI, stands for Global Intangible Low-Taxed Income.
7. Sec. 951A(a).
8. *See* Secs. 951A(b), (c), and 245A.
9. Sec. 951A(a). Since the shareholders have already been taxed on the GILTI, they are not taxed when it is ultimately distributed. Sec. 959(a).
10. Sec. 250(a).

not be required for nontax competitive reasons.[11] As a result, the GILTI is taxed, although at a favorable rate for corporate US shareholders.

As a result of the 2017 Tax Act, the US system has three approaches to taxing the income of US-owned foreign corporations: (1) Subpart F taxes certain US shareholders annually on the subpart F income of US CFCs regardless of whether such income is distributed to them. (2) The foreign source income of CFCs that is not subpart F income and does not exceed 10% of the subsidiary's tangible assets escapes US taxation entirely when earned by the foreign corporation and subsequently distributed to its corporate US shareholders. (3) The amount of the CFC's income that exceeds a 10% return on its assets (the GILTI) is taxed annually to US shareholders regardless of whether it is distributed.

6.2 REASONS FOR THE PARTIAL SHIFT FROM DEFERRAL TO CURRENT TAXATION AND DIVIDEND EXEMPTION

As discussed above, prior to the adoption of subpart F in 1962, the US did not tax a shareholder on most foreign earnings of a foreign corporation until distributed as a dividend.[12] By 1962, when US tax rates were high and the US was a net exporter of capital following the Second World War, US multinationals engaging in international business activities were using a variety of "base company" planning techniques to avoid US taxes on their foreign income. The subpart F rules were introduced in 1962 to restrict this planning and resulting revenue loss to the United States, as well as to countries on the other side of the base company planning. By 2017, however, global trade and economic activity and global business practices had changed dramatically from the early 1960s. Attitudes in the US toward international tax rules also had shifted significantly toward more laissez-faire tax treatment for US multinationals.

As discussed in section 6.1, above, this change in attitude resulted in the current complex system that simultaneously exempts some of a foreign subsidiary's earnings while at the same time expanding current taxation of earnings in excess of a 10% return on tangible assets, the GILTI. To appreciate the forces that shaped this approach, a brief introduction to the foreign tax credit, capital export neutrality, and capital import neutrality is required.

As will be discussed in detail in Chapter 9, the foreign tax credit is the mechanism adopted by the US to apply properly its tax rules when US citizens or corporations derive income from other countries. A foreign tax credit allows a taxpayer who pays an income tax to a foreign country to reduce her US tax liability by the amount of tax paid to the foreign country. For example, consider a US taxpayer subject to a 37% income tax who earns USD 100 in a foreign country that taxes such income at 20%. The US

11. *See* HR Rep. No. 409, 115th Cong., 1st Sess. 388-389 (2017).
12. A limited exception applied in the form of foreign personal holding company rules adopted in 1937 to frustrate the use of a foreign corporation by wealthy individuals as a foreign incorporated pocketbook. Secs. 551-558, repealed by the American Jobs Creation Act, Pub. L. 108-357, Sec. 413(a)(1) (2004) (hereinafter the "2004 Act"). The personal holding company rules continue to apply in respect of domestic income. Secs. 541-547.

taxpayer will be allowed a USD 20 tax credit for the foreign tax she paid to reduce her US tax liability on that 100 of income to 17 (USD 37 tentative tax minus USD 20 credit).[13]

One basic purpose of the foreign tax credit is to achieve tax neutrality in deciding whether to invest in the US or abroad. Such neutrality is called "capital export neutrality." The basic idea of capital export neutrality is that a US business should have identical aggregate tax liabilities regardless of whether income is earned in the US or abroad.

Consider, for example, a US corporation that wishes to expand into a new line of operations. It might accomplish this expansion in three different ways: (1) through a branch or division in the US, (2) through a wholly owned US subsidiary that will operate in the US, or (3) through a foreign branch that will operate in a foreign country. The US tax system is neutral among these three choices. A single US tax will be imposed on the profits of the operation if conducted through a US division or subsidiary in the US[14], and an identical aggregate tax consisting of the US tax and foreign tax will be imposed on the profits of the foreign branch.

To illustrate that the tax aggregate tax liability is identical in all three scenarios, assume that the new business line earns USD 100, that the US corporation is subject to a 21% US tax on its income, and that income earned in the foreign country will be subject to a 20% foreign income tax. The USD 100 income earned by the US branch in the US or the US subsidiary in the US will incur a USD 21 single tax liability.[15] The income earned by the foreign branch in the foreign country will be subject to a foreign tax of USD 20 and US tax of USD 1 (the USD 21 tentative tax reduced by the USD 20 foreign tax credit), resulting in an aggregate tax of USD 21. In all three cases, the aggregate tax liability paid is the same, USD 21. Capital export neutrality is achieved because the tax impact of investing in the US or the foreign country is the same. The US corporation's decision to invest at home or abroad can be based on economic considerations, not tax considerations.

If, instead of the three above scenarios, the US corporation considers using a foreign subsidiary for its expansion, the situation changes markedly. Prior to the 2017 Tax Act, the US tax on the foreign subsidiary's non-subpart F earnings in general was imposed only when the earnings were distributed to the subsidiary's US shareholder.[16]

---

13. As discussed in Chapter 10, a limitation on the foreign tax credit prevents a taxpayer from claiming a credit that is greater than the US tax that would be owed on the foreign income. For example, if the foreign country taxed the USD 100 of income at a 40% rate, the taxpayer subject to a 37% US tax would be limited to claiming a USD 37 credit against her US tax liability. The difference of USD 3 in some cases can be used against US tax on other foreign income. If not so used, the "excess credit" in some cases can carryover to other years.
14. While a US subsidiary is a juridical entity separate from its US parent, only one level of tax will apply to its earnings because the distribution of those earnings will not be taxable to the US parent either because of the 100% DRD (*see* Chapter 2 section 2.2.2.2) or because the US parent elected to file a consolidated return (*see* Chapter 2 section 2.2.5).
15. As discussed in *supra* note 14, only one level of tax will apply to the US subsidiary's earnings.
16. An exception, discussed in section 6.2.2, applied to Passive Foreign Investment Companies (PFICs) for US shareholders not taxed under subpart F. The 1997 Act excluded a CFC's 10% US shareholders from the reach of the PFIC rules. Pub. L. 105-34, 111 Stat. 788 §1121.

Once distributed and included in income, the "deemed paid" (or "indirect"[17]) foreign tax credit provisions, discussed in Chapter 9 section 9.5, allowed the US corporate shareholder to claim a credit for the foreign taxes paid by the foreign subsidiary with respect to the distributed income. Even with the benefit of the indirect tax credit, however, the corporate US shareholder could increase its after-tax return by causing the subsidiary to accumulate and reinvest its income in the foreign country if the foreign tax rate was lower than the US rate. In that situation, capital export neutrality would not be achieved because tax considerations favored expanding the US corporation's operation through a foreign subsidiary operating in a low-tax jurisdiction.

Why allow deferral if it violates capital export neutrality? One potential answer is that it helps achieve "capital import neutrality." Capital import neutrality seeks to have US businesses operating in a foreign country bear the same aggregate tax burden as the local businesses. To achieve full capital import neutrality no US tax should be paid on a foreign subsidiary's foreign earnings. The US system of imposing a US tax, but delaying it until the US parent received the earnings, could be viewed as a subsidy by the US Government to achieve partial capital import neutrality.

The rules in subpart F that eliminate deferral in certain situations help limit the subsidy for capital import neutrality to activities for which competitive neutrality is likely to outweigh tax avoidance factors. That is, the income is attributable to the subsidiary's conduct of an active trade or business in the foreign country in which it resides. In these situations, the subsidy helps the subsidiary compete with local companies operating in the same country. Contrast that situation with one in which a subsidiary incorporated in country A is buying from a related party located in country B and selling that item in country C. The business operation in country A does not need to be protected if it can be located anywhere. Thus, the income earned by the subsidiary in country A is treated as subpart F income and is immediately taxable to the subsidiary's US shareholder.[18]

While the subpart F rules helped define the limits of the deferral subsidy, over time, the focus of the rules on whether a CFC was engaged in actual business operations in its place of incorporation proved ineffective. Transfer pricing strategies and, later, the ease of manipulating entity classification and reliance on entities that might be disregarded for US tax purposes, reduced the effectiveness of the subpart F rules. Even as the restrictions of subpart F eroded over the years through self-help and legislative and regulatory relaxations, US multinationals argued that deferral was not sufficient because they would have to pay a US tax when the foreign subsidiary distributed its earnings to the US parent. They asserted a competitive need to not just

17. This is called an "indirect credit" because the corporate US shareholder did not itself pay the foreign tax upon which the credit is based. Rather, the credit is calculated based on the foreign tax paid by the CFC on the income that it then distributed to the corporate US shareholder.

18. As discussed in section 6.3.4.1, such income would be a type of subpart F income called foreign base company sales income. Sec. 954(d). Note that where the CFC is merely buying from one related party and then selling to another party, it is acting as a conduit and may be used to shift income to a low-tax jurisdiction. Thus, completely apart from broader considerations of limiting the subsidy for capital import neutrality to legitimate business operations, the subpart F provisions also support US transfer pricing rules designed to restrict transactions that artificially shift profits outside the US.

defer US taxes, but to exempt altogether earnings on their foreign operations in order to compete effectively.[19] The elimination of US taxes would fully achieve capital import neutrality because only then would the tax burden for the US-owned subsidiaries be identical to their competitors in the foreign country.

Following the adoption of the subpart F rules in 1962, many tax analysts in the US favored the total repeal of tax deferral on income realized by CFCs on the grounds that the subsidy implicit on the remaining deferral was unnecessary and should be repealed. The multinational business community, on the other hand, supported academic work and pushed proposals that were resolutely in the opposite direction to move the United States to a territorial or dividend exemption system. The debate about the importance of achieving capital import neutrality remained unresolved.[20]

Unfortunately, the current hybrid approach adopted in the 2017 Tax Act has not resolved the issue. In the 2017 Tax Act, Congress did not select between current taxation, deferral, or exemption. Rather, it chose all three.[21] This choice has not achieved capital export or import neutrality, but has achieved significant complexity.

6.2.1 Brief Overview of How GILTI Applies to Controlled Foreign Corporations

The complexity of GILTI requires a brief overview before delving into the details. To begin to understand the GILTI regime, it is necessary to distinguish between the treatment of corporate US shareholders and individual US shareholders.

19. While in recent years other industrial countries also adopted controlled foreign company rules similar to subpart F to protect their own tax bases, especially given the proliferation of low-tax countries and arrangements enabling income shifting, developments in European Court of Justice case law under EU treaties limited their scope to cases of clear tax avoidance. *Cadbury Schweppes and Cadbury Schweppes Overseas* (Case C-196/04 Sept. 12, 2006) ("Articles 43 EC and 48 EC must be interpreted as precluding the inclusion in the tax base of a resident company established in a Member State of profits made by a CFC in another Member State, where those profits are subject in that State to a lower level of taxation than that applicable in the first State, unless such inclusion relates only to wholly artificial arrangements intended to escape the national tax normally payable.").
20. In December 2000, the US Treasury Department released a study on subpart F, "The Deferral of Income Earned Through US Controlled Foreign Corporations." In summary, the Study concluded that capital export neutrality was the preferable policy whether viewed from a global or national welfare perspective; the subpart F regime was still required to protect important US tax policy objectives; and there was no convincing evidence that the regime adversely affected the competitiveness of US multinationals. The Study considered, but did not recommend, alternatives to subpart F ranging from total repeal of deferral to eliminating application of subpart F to sales and services transactions between related foreign corporations. The National Foreign Trade Council published in 2001 a two volume study urging a shift to exemption. National Foreign Trade Council, *International Tax Policy for the 21st Century* (December 2001). In 2006 the American Bar Association Tax Section Task Force on International Tax Reform published a report recommending expansion and strengthening of subpart F and other changes that would increase taxation of foreign business income. ABA Tax Sec. Task Force on Intl Tax Reform, *Report of the Task Force on International Tax Reform*, 59 Tax Lawyer 649 (2006).
21. *See generally* Michael J. Graetz, *Foreword - The 2017 Tax Cuts: How Polarized Politics Produced Precarious Policy*, 128 YALE L.J. F. 315, 328 (2018) ("Faced with the choice between these two very different regimes for taxing the foreign income of the U.S. multinationals [current taxation or exemption], Congress chose both.").

The non-subpart F earnings of a CFC that do not exceed a 10% return on the CFC's tangible assets are not taxable to the CFC's corporate US shareholders as earned. The CFC's non-subpart F earnings in excess of the 10% return (i.e., the GILTI) are immediately taxable to the corporate US shareholder. A corporate US shareholder is allowed, however, a 50% deduction with respect to that amount.[22] As a result, the effective tax rate applied to the GILTI is 10.5% (50% of the 21% US corporate tax rate). In addition, a corporate shareholder is able to claim a foreign tax credit (an "indirect" credit[23]) for the foreign income taxes paid by the CFC on the portion of the CFC's income that the subpart F or GILTI rules requires the corporate shareholder to recognize.[24] Any distribution of the subpart F income or GILTI to the corporate US shareholder is not taxable under Section 959 since it has already been taxed. Also, distributions of the non-subpart F income that also is not GILTI (i.e., the income that is less than a 10% return on the CFC's tangible assets) are not taxable to corporate US shareholders if the requirements of Section 245A are met.

Thus, for a corporate US shareholder of a CFC, the CFC's earnings can be thought of as falling into three buckets: (1) subpart F income taxed at 21% before an indirect credit for foreign income tax, (2) GILTI taxed at 10.5% before an indirect credit for foreign income tax, and (3) a 10% return on tangible investment not taxed as earned and not taxed when distributed due to a 100% Section 245A dividends received deduction ("DRD").

An individual US shareholder, like a corporate US shareholder, is not taxed on non-subpart F earnings of a CFC that do not exceed a 10% return on the CFC's tangible assets. Similarly, individual US shareholders are taxed currently on subpart F income and the GILTI, but, unlike a corporation, both categories of income are taxed at full marginal rates. Moreover, unlike the case with corporate shareholders, there is no indirect credit for any foreign income tax paid by the CFC on such income. The subsequent distribution of subpart F income or the GILTI to an individual US shareholder is not taxable under Section 959 since the shareholder has already included it in income.[25] Finally, unlike corporate US shareholders, the CFC's income that was not immediately taxable to the shareholder as subpart F income or GILTI is taxable at full rate when distributed to the individual shareholder unless the dividend is a "qualified dividend" eligible for a lower rate.[26]

Thus, for a noncorporate US shareholder of a CFC, the CFC's earnings can again be thought of as falling into three buckets: (1) subpart F income taxed to the noncorporate US shareholder at full marginal rates as earned by the CFC, (2) GILTI

22. Sec. 951A(a) and (b); Sec. 250(a).
23. As discussed in *supra* note 17, above, this is called an "indirect credit" because the corporate US shareholder did not itself pay the foreign tax upon which the credit is based. Rather, the credit is calculated based on the foreign tax paid by the CFC on the income that GILTI required the corporate US shareholder to recognize.
24. Sec. 960. The indirect credit for the taxes paid by the CFC on its GILTI are limited to 80% of the CFC's GILTI. Sec. 960(d). *See* Chapter 10 section 10.2.1.
25. Moreover, the individual US shareholder is permitted to claim a credit for any foreign withholding taxes that apply to the actual distribution of the CFC's income. Secs. 901(b)(1) and 960(b).
26. Qualified dividends are discussed in Chapter 2 section 2.3.2.2.

taxed at full marginal rates to the noncorporate US shareholder as earned by the CFC, and (3) a 10% return on tangible investment not taxed as earned but taxed at full rates when distributed to the noncorporate US shareholder (unless eligible for the lower rate applicable to "qualified dividends"[27]).

Table 6.1 summarizes these rules.

Table 6.1 Summary of Tax Treatment of Subpart F Income and GILTI for Corporate and Noncorporate US Shareholders of CFCs

	Non-GILTI and Non-subpart F Income	*GILTI (Income Greater than 10% of Tangible Assets)*	*Subpart F Income*	*Indirect Tax Credit for GILTI and Subpart F Income*	*Non-GILTI and Non-subpart F Distributions*
Corporate US Shareholders	Not taxed as earned by CFC	Taxed at 10.5% rate as earned by CFC	Taxed at 21% rate as earned by CFC	Yes[a]	Not Taxed
Noncorporate US Shareholders	Not taxed as earned by CFC	Taxed at ordinary rates as earned by CFC	Taxed at ordinary tax rates as earned by CFC	No	Taxed at ordinary rates unless "qualified dividend"[b]

a. The corporate US shareholders indirect credit for the taxes paid by the CFC with respect to the GILTI is limited to 80% of the CFC's GILTI. Section 960(d). *See* Chapter 10 section 10.2.1.
b. Qualified dividends are discussed in Chapter 2 section 2.3.2.2.

An "in between" case of current taxation and deferral applies to an individual US shareholder who makes an election under Section 962 relating to subpart F income and GILTI in a particular year. In such a case, the subpart F and GILTI inclusions are taxed currently under the rules and at the rates that would apply to domestic corporations. The Section 962 election allows the individual US shareholder's notional corporation to claim the indirect credit[28] with respect to the subpart F and GILTI inclusion and the 50% deduction for the GILTI inclusion.[29] The resulting amount determines the tax the US shareholder has to pay in the current year. When such inclusions are actually distributed, the individual US shareholder recognizes income to the extent the distribution exceeds any tax the individual paid on inclusion of the subpart F income and GILTI.[30] The effect of the Section 962 election then is to mimic what would happen if the individual US shareholder had held the CFC stock through a domestic corporation.[31]

27. *Id.*
28. The electing shareholders indirect credit for the taxes paid by the CFC with respect to the GILTI is limited to 80% of the CFC's GILTI. Sec. 960(d). *See* Chapter 10 section 10.2.1.
29. Sec. 962(a); Treas. Reg. Sec. 1.962-1(b)(1)(i).
30. Sec. 962(d).
31. An unresolved issue is whether under Section 962 an actual dividend to the individual US shareholder from the CFC could qualify for the reduced capital gain tax rate if the CFC were a qualified foreign corporation (*see* Chapter 2 section 2.3.2.2) where a subpart F inclusion does not

6.2.2 Non-controlled Foreign Corporations

If a foreign corporation is not a CFC, foreign corporate earnings are currently taxed to a US person only if the foreign corporation is a passive foreign investment company (PFIC) as discussed in Chapter 8. Otherwise, a US person's share of the foreign corporation's earnings are deferred from US tax until distributed. The subsequent distribution of the foreign source portion of the untaxed earnings generally is exempt to a corporate US shareholder who owns at least 10% (by vote or value) of the foreign corporation.[32] In contrast, the earnings are subject to full US taxation when distributed to a less than 10% corporate shareholder and to individuals.[33]

6.2.3 Summary

The picture that results is one of inordinate complexity that arises from a reform implemented almost exclusively through addition of new provisions with minimal adaptation of existing rules. There was no effort at fundamental reform based on clearly articulated policy objectives. This was in significant part because the 2017 Tax Act was the fruit of a legislative process conducted largely without hearings (or meaningful Treasury Department input) by a single party controlling all three branches of government almost entirely within the fourth quarter of 2017 to provide a noteworthy legislative achievement in advance of an election year for Congress. Revenue considerations mandated by the budget reconciliation process used to avoid the need for votes from the other party caused numerous arbitrary design decisions whose principal policy justification was to curb the aggregate revenue loss from the legislation to the required budgetary limit of USD 1.5 trillion over ten years.

While this may explain the complexity of the rules, it does not assist in their understanding. To increase understanding of the rules, sections 6.3, 6.4, and 6.5 will further discuss subpart F, GILTI, and the dividend exemption, respectively. Chapters 9 and 10 will explore the foreign tax credit and its limitations in greater detail.

6.3 BUSINESS OPERATIONS THROUGH FOREIGN CORPORATIONS CONTROLLED BY US PERSONS: SUBPART F

6.3.1 The Structure of Subpart F

Section 951(a) requires a "US shareholder" to include in income each year its pro rata share of the CFC's subpart F income. As discussed in more detail in section 6.3.2, a "US

qualify. *See Rodriguez v. Commissioner*, 722 F.3d 306 (5th Cir. 2013) (subpart F inclusion from a qualifying foreign corporation is not a dividend qualifying for capital gain rate treatment); *Smith v. Commissioner*, 151 T.C. 41 (2018) (denying capital gain rate to actual dividend from Hong Kong CFC to individual US shareholder by reason of Section 962 election where CFC is not a qualified foreign corporation).

32. Secs. 245A and 951(b). The exemption is not allowed for distributions on shares held for 365 days or less or dividends for which a deduction is allowed to the distributing foreign corporation.
33. Such shareholders are allowed to claim a credit for foreign taxes withheld on the distributions. Sec. 901(a).

shareholder," in general, is a US person that owns 10% or more of the "total combined voting power" of all classes of voting stock or 10% or more of the total value of shares of all classes of stock of a CFC.[34]

Section 957(a) defines a CFC to which the subpart F rules apply as a foreign corporation in which more than 50% of either the total combined voting power of all classes of voting stock or the total value of all stock is owned by "US shareholders" on any day during the taxable year of the CFC.[35] Note that the 50% control test is determined by only counting US shareholders who own 10% or more of the vote or value of the CFC.

Subpart F taxes the CFC's US shareholder on the subpart F income earned during the year by the CFC.[36] When such income is subsequently distributed as a dividend, no further tax is imposed.[37] An indirect foreign tax credit is granted to a corporate US shareholder for the foreign income taxes paid by the CFC with respect to the distributed subpart F income (and the US shareholder includes the amount of the deemed foreign tax credit in income as well).[38] In order to avoid a second tax if the shares are disposed of, the basis of the US shareholder's stock in the CFC is increased by the amount of subpart F income and is decreased by subsequent distributions of such income.[39] Within this deceptively simple statutory framework lie a host of definitions, exceptions, limitations, and qualifications.

6.3.2 Tax Treatment of US Shareholders

A "US shareholder" is any US person (citizen, resident, partnership, corporation, estate, or trust)[40] who owns directly or is treated as owning ("constructive ownership") at least 10% of either the total combined voting power[41] of all classes of stock entitled to vote in a CFC or the total value of the CFC.[42] The US shareholder is taxed on its pro rata share[43] of the CFC's undistributed subpart F income.[44]

Constructive ownership of the stock of a CFC can result if a US person is a stockholder, partner, or beneficiary of a corporation, partnership, trust, or estate that owns stock in a CFC.[45] In general, constructive ownership of CFC stock is determined

34. Sec. 951(b).
35. Sec. 957(a).
36. Sec. 951(a).
37. Sec. 959(a).
38. Secs. 960(a) and 78.
39. Sec. 961(a) and 961(b).
40. Secs. 951(b), 957(c), and 7701(a)(30). Section 957(c) modifies the definition in the case of corporations organized in US possessions.
41. As to what constitutes "voting power," *see* Treas. Reg. Sec. 1.951-1(g)(2).
42. Sec. 951(b). In the 2017 Tax Act, the 10% ownership test was modified by the addition of an alternative value component.
43. Sec. 951(a)(2). For the definition of pro rata shares, *see* Treas. Reg. Sec. 1.951-1(e).
44. The constitutionality of Section 951 was upheld in *Garlock, Inc. v. Commissioner*, 489 F.2d 197 (2d Cir. 1973) (unconstitutionality argument "borders on the frivolous in the light of this court's decision in *Eder v. Commissioner*, 138 F.2d 27, 28 (1943)"); *Estate of Whitlock. Commissioner*, 494 F.2d 1297 (10th Cir. 1974); *Dougherty v. Commissioner*, 60 TC 917 (1973).
45. Sec. 958.

by applying the attribution rules of Section 318, although some modifications are made.[46] While the attribution rules may push a US person above the 10% stock ownership level, it is only taxed on its pro rata share of subpart F income based on the stock it owns directly (or indirectly through a foreign entity).[47]

6.3.3 Definition of a CFC

A CFC is a foreign corporation in which more than 50% of either the total combined voting power of all classes of stock entitled to vote or of the total value of all stock[48] is owned by "US shareholders," i.e., US persons owning directly or by attribution 10% of the vote or value of the CFC's stock.[49] Thus, CFC status may be avoided if eleven unrelated US shareholders own ratably 100% of the voting stock and value of a foreign corporation or if one or more US shareholders own exactly 50% of the voting stock and 50% of the total value of all stock of a foreign corporation, the balance being owned by foreign shareholders. A foreign corporation is a CFC if the more-than-50% test is met on any one day during the taxable year.

46. Sec. 958(b); Treas. Reg. Sec. 1.958-2. In general, under Section 318, a person is considered to be the owner of stock owned by close relatives (spouse, children, etc.), by his 50% controlled corporation, or by a partnership or trust of which he is a partner or beneficiary. For purposes of subpart F, the percentage of stock ownership deemed to be controlling is reduced from 50% to 10%. In a significant change, the 2017 Tax Act repealed the rule in former Section 958(b)(4) that restricted attribution from a non-US person to a US person. This has expanded the circumstances in which a foreign corporation with foreign shareholders will be a CFC. Pub. L. 115–97, title I, §§ 14213(a), Dec. 22, 2017, 131 Stat. 2217.
47. Sec. 958(a).
48. Prior to 1986, only the voting stock requirement was employed to determine whether the 50% test was satisfied. This test led to some controversy where the *value* of the stock held appeared to be more than 50% although actual stock ownership was 50% or less. *See, e.g.*, Rev. Rul. 70-426, 1970-2 C.B. 157; *Garlock, Inc. v. Commissioner, supra* note 44; *Estate of Weiskopf v. Commissioner*, 64 TC 78 (1975); *Koehring Co. v. United States*, 583 F.2d 313 (7th Cir. 1978) (holding that more than 50% test was met although nominal stock ownership by US persons was 50% or less). *But compare CCA, Inc. v. Commissioner*, 64 TC 137 (1975) (holding the control test not satisfied where the US shareholders owned exactly 50% of the stock and the foreign shareholders possessed real powers). The addition of the "value" test in 1986 resolved the legal issue, though factual disputes over the correct value remain.
49. Secs. 951(b) and 957(a). The 50% figure is reduced to 25% in the case of certain insurance subsidiaries. Sec. 957(b). The IRS will examine the substance of the corporation's voting arrangements to determine whether US shareholders hold more than 50% of the combined voting power of all classes entitled to vote. In *Framatome Connectors U.S.A., Inc. v. Commissioner*, 118 T.C. 32 (2002), *aff'd in unpublished opinion*, 108 Fed. App. 683 (2d Cir. 2004), the court held that a US corporation owning 50% of a Japanese corporation's shares could not rely on substance over form to claim it held more than 50% of the combined voting power of a Japanese corporation under a control premium theory. The court alternatively rejected the claim where there were two 25% Japanese shareholders and the corporation's articles required that 80% of the voting shares approve most corporate actions.

6.3.4 Income Taxable to US Shareholders

A US shareholder of a CFC must include in income two principal types of income:[50]

(1) its pro rata share of the CFC's subpart F income; and
(2) the amount determined with respect to the shareholder under Section 956, i.e., the earnings invested by the CFC in US property for the year.

6.3.4.1 Subpart F Income

The first major category of income currently taxable to a US shareholder, and the most important, is the US shareholder's pro rata share of the CFC's "subpart F income."[51] Subpart F income, as defined in Section 952,[52] consists of two principal categories of income:

(1) insurance income;[53] and
(2) foreign base company income.[54]

(*See also* section 6.3.7, for additional special categories of subpart F income.) Even if income is within one of the two categories, it does not constitute subpart F income if it is effectively connected with the conduct of a US trade or business of the CFC (unless such income is exempt from tax by treaty or is taxed at a reduced rate by treaty).[55]

---

50. Sec. 951(a)(1). As discussed in section 6.3.4.2, corporate US shareholders have effectively been exempted from application of the investment of earnings in US property rules for post-2017 Tax Act years.
51. A CFC's subpart F income includes its share of income from a partnership to the extent such income would have been subpart F income if received directly by the CFC. Treas. Reg. Sec. 1.952-1(g).
52. A CFC's subpart F income cannot exceed its current earnings and profits as defined in Section 964(a). Sec. 952(c)(1)(A). Deficits in earnings and profits from prior years generally cannot be used to reduce the current year's earnings and profits unless the deficits arose in the same activity. If the limitation of Section 952(c)(1)(A) applies in one year and there is an excess of earnings and profits over subpart F income in a later year, that excess is recharacterized as subpart F income in the later year. Sec. 952(c)(2).

    Generally, a CFC's earnings and profits are computed in the same manner as those of a US corporation. See Treas. Reg. Sec. 1.964-1. Subpart F income does not include earnings and profits that are attributable to foreign income that is blocked from repatriation by, for example, currency regulations of the foreign country. Treas. Reg. Sec. 1.964-2. In general, US tax rules apply to determine the gross income and taxable income of a CFC. Treas. Reg. Sec. 1.952-2. Foreign currency fluctuations can affect the amount of a corporation's earnings and profits for subpart F purposes, see Chapter 13 section 13.2 and Treas. Reg. Sec. 1.964-1(a)(2) and (3).
53. Sec. 952(a)(1). This category of subpart F income is defined in detail in Section 953; it is not discussed further in this book.
54. Sec. 952(a)(2).
55. Sec. 952(b).

Subpart F income that is distributed to the US shareholders is in general not treated as a dividend.[56] The distribution, however, is classified as "previously taxed earnings and profits" and excluded from gross income under Section 959.[57]

The term "foreign base company income" (FBCI) is defined in great detail in Section 954 and the Regulations.[58] The basic arrangement addressed by these rules is one in which a US parent creates a foreign subsidiary in a country that imposes tax at a relatively low rate. The parent sells products to the subsidiary (the foreign base company) which then makes the sale to the ultimate customer. The various "sale" prices can be manipulated so that most of the profit winds up in the subsidiary in the low-tax country, thus avoiding both US and foreign tax. The same kind of arrangement can be structured involving the provision of services for a related party. The FBCI rules focus on sales or services provided outside the country of incorporation of the CFC since it is in those cases that the CFC is being used as a "base" company. Another situation at which the FBCI rules are aimed is the use of a foreign corporation to accumulate passive investment income. FBCI includes four categories of income:[59]

(1) *Foreign personal holding company income (FPHCI).* This income consists of: (i) dividends, interest, rents and royalties;[60] (ii) net gains from the sale or

56. Sec. 959(d); Treas. Reg. Sec. 1.959-4; Prop. Treas. Reg. Sec. 1.959-4.
57. Treas. Reg. Sec. 1.959-2(a); Prop. Treas. Reg. Sec. 1.959-2(a). Keeping track of "previously taxed earnings and profits" (PTEP) is complex. In Notice 2019-1, the IRS announced that taxpayers need to maintain 16 different accounts to calculate PTEP. Notice 2019-1, 2019-2 IRB 275 (2018).
58. Treas. Reg. Sec. 1.954-1.
59. Previously, subpart F income also included foreign base company shipping income, which was eliminated from the base company income definition in the 2004 Act, and foreign base company oil related income, which was repealed in the 2017 Tax Act.
60. Treas. Reg. Sec. 1.954-2(a)(1). There are a number of exceptions and special rules involving FPHCI. In 1997 Congress adopted a "temporary" exception to FPHCI for income derived from conducting an active banking or insurance business in the country in which the CFC was incorporated. Sec. 954(h) and (i). The "temporary" exception was expanded in the 2004 Act to include situations where the CFC itself is not actively engaged in the financing business but the activities are performed on its behalf by related parties. The "temporary" exception was finally made permanent in 2015. Protecting Americans from Tax Hikes Act of 2015, P. L. 114–113, div. Q, title I, § 128(b) (Dec. 18, 2015).

    Another special rule involves gain on the sale of a partnership interest. Such gain is normally FPHCI but is excluded from the definition if the CFC is a 25% or greater partner in the partnership. In that case, the character of the gain is determined by "looking through" to the underlying assets held by the partnership. Sec. 954(c)(4).

    In addition, generally excluded from FPHCI are dividends, interest, rents, and royalties received by a CFC from related persons organized and operating a trade or business in the CFC's country of incorporation. (However, if an interest, rent, or royalty payment decreased the payer's own subpart F income, the exclusion is not applicable.) Sec. 954(c)(3)(A) and (B); Treas. Reg. Sec. 1.954-2(b). In another exception, rents and royalties received from unrelated persons are excluded if derived in the active conduct of the CFC's trade or business. Sec. 954(c)(2)(A); Treas. Reg. Sec. 1.954-2(c) and (d).

    Section 954(d)(3) defines the term "related person" for these purposes generally in terms of more than 50% voting power or value. Section 954(d)(3) includes within the scope of related persons partnerships that control foreign corporations and partnerships controlled by foreign corporations.

exchange of property which gives rise to the income described in (i)[61] or which does not give rise to any income;[62] (iii) gains from certain commodities transactions;[63] (iv) gains from certain foreign currency transactions;[64] and (v) income which is the equivalent of interest (e.g., loan commitment fees).[65]

(2) *Foreign base company sales income,* which consists of income from property purchased from or sold to a related person if the property is manufactured outside *and* sold for use outside the CFC's country of incorporation.[66]

---

61. Section 954(c)(1)(B)(i) excludes gain that is attributable to property that gives rise to banking or insurance income excluded from FPHCI. Sec. 954(c)(1)(B)(i), 954(h), and 954(i).
62. Gains from sales of property in this category that constitute inventory in the hands of the taxpayer or which are realized by a dealer in such property are not included since they are derived from non-passive business activity. Sec. 954(c)(1)(B)(iii) (last sentence).
63. Sec. 954(c)(1)(C). Prior to the 2004 Act, gains on commodities transactions constituted FPHCI unless the CFC was an active producer or handler of commodities. The 2004 Act expanded the scope of the exception to include hedging transactions as well as gains on commodities used in the normal course of the taxpayer's business, even if the CFC is not a producer or handler.
64. Sec. 954(c)(1)(D); Treas. Reg. Sec. 1.954-2(g). The foreign currency gains that give rise to subpart F income are the excess of gains over losses from "section 988 transactions." Section 988 transactions are described in Chapter 13 section 13.3.1.
65. Sec. 954(c)(1)(E); Treas. Reg. Sec. 1.954-2(h).
66. Sec. 954(d)(1). If the CFC purchases property from a related party but sufficiently transforms the property to constitute "manufacturing" by it, then the sale of that property does not result in foreign base company sales income. Treas. Reg. Sec. 1.954-3(a)(4). It is relatively easy for high technology companies to satisfy this rule by locating operations in low-tax countries.

    In some instances, a branch of the CFC may be treated as if it were a subsidiary, and hence a related person, so that the subpart F rules apply to sales transactions where the CFC is treated as making sales on behalf of a related party, its branch (normally such transactions are ignored for US tax purposes). Section 954(d)(2) states that if a branch "has substantially the same effect as if such branch ... were a wholly owned subsidiary..., [then] the income attributable to carrying on ... [the branch's] activities ... shall constitute foreign base company sales income of the controlled foreign corporation." See Treas. Reg. Sec. 1.954-3(b). In Whirlpool Financial Corp. v. Commissioner, 154 T.C. No. 9 (May 2, 2020), the Tax Court determined that a Luxembourg CFC with a Mexican manufacturing branch had foreign base company sales income arising from the Luxembourg CFC's sale of goods manufactured by its Mexican branch. The Tax Court reasoned that the establishment of the Mexican branch had substantially the "same effect" as "a wholly owned subsidiary" within the meaning of Section 954(d)(2). This "same effect" arose because the Luxembourg CFC would not be taxable on income earned by the Mexican branch since Luxembourg had a territorial tax system and had agreed that the Luxembourg CFC would not be taxable on gain arising from the sale of goods manufactured by the Mexican branch. The Tax Court thought that Luxembourg's agreement to not tax such gain was the same as treating the Mexican branch as "a wholly owned subsidiary" because foreign subsidiaries are separate taxable entities. The Tax Court stated:

    > Where a CFC was chartered in a country that employed a territorial tax system, the CFC's conduct of business through a branch outside of the CFC's home country and earning only income sourced there could have 'substantially the same effect' as if that income were earned by a subsidiary under U.S. tax rules. That is because... the income [of a subsidiary] typically would not be currently taxable to its ultimate owner (viz., the branch's home office or the subsidiary's parent). As the Senate Finance Committee explained, the branch rule was intended to capture sales income where 'the combined effect of the tax treatment accorded the branch, by the [CFC's] country of incorporation * * * and the country of operation of the branch, is to treat the branch substantially the same as if it were a subsidiary corporation organized in the country in which it carries on its trade or business.
    >
    > S. Rept. No. 87-1881, supra at 84, 1962-3 C.B. at 790.

(3) *Foreign base company services income*, which is income derived from performing services outside the CFC's country of incorporation for or on behalf of a related person.[67]
(4) *Personal services contract income*, which is income of so-called rent-a-star companies earned when the CFC makes available the services of its 25% or greater shareholder and the person paying for the services has the right to designate such stockholder to perform the services or such stockholder actually performs the services or is required to perform the services.[68]

In each category of income, the amount of FBCI is reduced by the deductions properly allocable thereto.[69]

The statute provides certain exceptions for income that otherwise would constitute FBCI:

(1) If the gross FBCI of a CFC for the taxable year is less than the lesser of 5% of its total gross income or USD 1 million, then the CFC shall be considered to have no FBCI. Conversely, if the gross FBCI for the taxable year exceeds 70% of the CFC's gross income, then all of its gross income less allocable deductions is considered FBCI.[70]
(2) FBCI does not include any item of income if the taxpayer (generally the US parent) can establish that the income was subject to an *effective* tax rate in a foreign country that was greater than 90% of the maximum *marginal* US corporate tax rate and the taxpayer elects the exclusion (the "high-tax election").[71] The high-tax election has been extended by regulation to income that otherwise would be tested income to determine GILTI. Under conformity rules, an election would apply to both categories of income.[72] Income that is subject to the high-tax election and excluded from FBCI also is excluded from GILTI and as a result is eligible for the Section 245A foreign DRD when the earnings are distributed to a corporate US shareholder.

67. Sec. 954(e); Treas. Reg. Sec. 1.954-4. The regulations consider a sale of services with "substantial assistance" of a related party to be services performed for or on behalf of a related party. This rule has been substantially cut back in Notice 2013-7, 2007-5 IRB 410 to permit greater use of services from related persons.
68. Sec. 954(c)(1)(H). This category of FBCI was added in 2004 in connection with the repeal of the foreign personal holding company rules. *See supra* note 12 in section 6.2.
69. Sec. 954(b)(5). The rules for allocating deductions are described Chapter 4 section 4.4.
70. Sec. 954(b)(3) and (4).
71. Sec. 954(b)(4). The provision applies only at the taxpayer's election. Treas. Reg. Sec. 1.954-1(d)(1)(i). The purpose of the provision is to exclude from subpart F treatment situations where income may have been routed through a related corporation but only a limited US tax advantage is gained thereby. Taxes paid to a foreign country are, of course, determined by its tax rules, but income is determined under US tax rules. The comparison of a foreign effective tax rate to the US marginal rate has obvious conceptual difficulties and, among other things, can have the effect of denying the benefit of the exclusion where a foreign country provides significant subsidies through its tax system rather than directly.
72. Treas. Reg. Sec. 1.951A-2(c)(7); Treas. Reg. Sec. 1.951A-2(c)(1)(iii), cross-referencing Treas. Reg. Sec. 1.954-1(d)(1) and (6).

6.3.4.2 *Earnings Invested in US Property*

The second major category of CFC's income that Section 951(a)(1) subjects to current taxation to the US shareholders is the amount determined under Section 956, which, in general, refers to the earnings and profits of the CFC invested in US assets.[73] The effect of Sections 951(a)(1) and 956 is to treat certain investments of a CFC's earnings in US assets as resulting in income to the CFC's US shareholders. Even if a CFC had no "subpart F income," it often would like to make its income available to shareholders without the shareholders incurring a tax in order to perpetuate deferral of US tax. Various strategies exist that the CFC might employ to have its shareholders enjoy the benefits of its income without incurring a tax. For example, the CFC could loan its earnings to a US shareholder. Without Sections 951(a) and 956 there would be no US tax, but the US shareholder would have the use of the funds in just the manner that would have been produced had a dividend in fact been paid.

Sections 951(a) and 956 have lost some of their "bite" after the 2017 Tax Act. Corporate US shareholders are now able to receive income distributions tax-free due to the Section 245A DRD. Individual US shareholders, in contrast, are still taxed on income distributions of non-GILTI and non-subpart F income, and, therefore, still prefer deferral of US tax on earnings not taxed under Subpart F and GILTI. As a result, Sections 951(a) and 956 in effect police the boundary of the deferral advantage for individual US shareholders.

Unlike other types of subpart F income subject to Section 951(a), Section 956 does not refer directly to an amount that would have been included as a dividend, but rather identifies a tentative amount to include in the income of the US shareholder that is the lesser of:

(1) the excess of:
  (a) the shareholder's pro rata share of the average amount of US property held by the CFC (determined quarterly by reference to the property's tax basis), over;
  (b) the shareholder's pro rata share of earnings and profits of the CFC which have previously been taxed under Sections 951 and 956;

  or

(2) the US shareholder's pro rata share of the "applicable earnings" of the CFC, i.e., the sum of its current and accumulated earnings and profits, reduced by any distribution made during the year and by any earnings and profits previously taxed under Sections 951, 956, or 965.[74]

In more straightforward language, the total earnings and profits of the CFC are reduced by amounts previously taxed under Sections 951, 956, and 965. Then, if there

73. Sec. 951(a)(1)(B).
74. Sec. 956(a) and (b).

has been any additional investment in US property, any remaining earnings and profits are deemed to have been used to make the investments.[75]

US "property" is defined to include, among other items, the following:

(1) tangible personal property located in the US (excluding certain oil and gas drilling rigs, certain transportation property, and property intended for export from the US);[76]
(2) stock of a related US corporation (i.e., the corporation invested in is itself a shareholder of the CFC or US shareholders of the CFC own 25% or more of the voting stock of the corporation in which the investment is made);[77]
(3) obligations of a US person (excluding debt of an unrelated corporation as determined in (2), money, bank deposits, obligations of the US Government, and some obligations arising in the ordinary course of trade or business);[78] and
(4) the right to use in the US patents, copyrights, secret processes, etc. acquired or developed by the CFC for use in the US.[79]

If the US shareholder is a corporation, the amount otherwise determined under Section 956 for the taxable year of the CFC is reduced to the extent that the US shareholder would be allowed a deduction under Section 245A if the US shareholder had received a distribution from the CFC equal to the tentative Section 956 amount.[80] The result, as mentioned above, is that corporate US shareholders have effectively been exempted from these rules addressing investment of earnings in US property for years after the 2017 Tax Act.

75. Former Section 956A previously required current inclusion in a US shareholder's income of earnings and profits invested in "excess passive assets," whether those assets were US or foreign property. The provision was repealed in 1996, primarily because of its excessive complexity but also because a number of multinationals were approaching the 50% passive asset limitation and made its repeal a political priority.
76. Sec. 956(c)(1)(A), (c)(2)(B), (D), and (G).
77. Sec. 956(c)(1)(B) and (b)(2)(F). Investment in the stock of "unrelated" US corporations is thus excepted from the rule. However, by virtue of the attribution rules, stock owned by the CFC is attributed to the US shareholder. As a result, any 25% investment by the CFC is automatically covered by Section 956.
78. Sec. 956(c)(1)(C), (c)(3)(A) and (C), (c)(3). *See Sherwood Properties, Inc. v. Commissioner*, 89 TC 651 (1987) (advance by CFC to related party not in ordinary course of the CFC's business). Indirect transactions are also covered by Section 956. *See* Rev. Rul. 90-112, 1990-2 C.B. 186 (US property owned by either a domestic or foreign partnership in which the CFC is a partner constitutes US property of the CFC for purposes of Section 956); Treas. Reg. Sec. 1.956-1(e)(2) (pledges and guarantees by a CFC are treated as an investment in the obligation that is guaranteed); and Sec. 956(c)(3). The 2004 Act expanded the exclusions from the definition of US property by exempting securities held by a dealer for sale to customers and obligations issued by a US person that is not a domestic corporation. Sec. 956(c)(2)(K). At the same time, the Act narrowed the scope of the exclusion for "deposits" by narrowing the definition of "banking business." Sec. 956(c)(2)(A).
79. Sec. 956(c)(1)(D).
80. Treas. Reg. Sec. 1.956-1(a)(2).

6.3.5 Foreign Tax Credit

Section 960 provides an indirect foreign tax credit for income taxed to a US shareholder under the subpart F rules. These rules are described in Chapter 9 section 9.5. Individual US shareholders can obtain the benefits of the Section 960 credit by electing to be taxed at corporation rates on their income taxable under subpart F.[81]

6.3.6 Distributions and Adjustments to Basis

Generally, Section 961(a) increases a US shareholder's basis in CFC stock by the amount of income included under Section 951 (as if the dividend had been paid and then recontributed to the CFC). Section 959 reduces such basis by amounts actually distributed that constitute previously taxed earnings (basis having previously been increased at the time the tax was imposed). Those distributions are correspondingly tax-free.[82]

If the amount of previously taxed earnings received in a year exceeds basis, the excess is taxed as a capital gain.[83]

6.3.7 Denial of Deferral Benefits for Boycott Income and Foreign Bribes and to Achieve Other US Foreign Policy Objectives

There are three additional categories of subpart F income that are based on policy issues quite different from those discussed in section 6.3.4, above.

Section 952(a)(3) treats CFC earnings and profits attributable to participation in or cooperation with an international boycott as subpart F income that are currently taxable to the CFC's US shareholder.

Section 952(a)(4) includes in a CFC's subpart F income an amount equal to the sum of illegal bribes, kickbacks, and other payments (as defined in Section 162(c)) that are paid by or on behalf of a foreign corporation directly or indirectly to any official, employee, or agent of a foreign government. In addition, in computing the earnings and profits of a CFC, no deduction is allowed for such payments. Note that the amount of income that is taxable to the US shareholder under Section 952(a)(4) is not the income produced as a result of the bribe, but the amount of the bribe itself.

Under Section 952(a)(5), a CFC's subpart F income includes income derived from any foreign country during any period in which Section 901(j)[84] is applicable. For example, income from a foreign country that the Secretary of State has designated as a country that supports terrorism constitutes subpart F income under this provision.

81. Sec. 962. Subsequent distributions of the income, however, are taxable to the extent the distribution exceeds the amount of tax paid by the individual on the subpart F income.
82. Secs. 961(a), (b)(1), and 959(a).
83. Sec. 961(b)(2).
84. *See* Chapter 10 section 10.5 note 41.

6.3.8 Disposition of Stock in a Controlled Foreign Corporation: Section 1248

6.3.8.1 Background

Under Section 1248, enacted in 1962 in connection with subpart F, a US shareholder's gain on the disposition of stock in a CFC[85] that otherwise would be treated as capital gain must be reported as dividend income to the extent of the shareholder's share of the foreign corporation's earnings and profits accumulated after 1962. At the time of the enactment of Section 1248, corporate and individual capital gains were subject to a preferential tax rate, while dividends were taxed at higher rates as ordinary income. Section 1248 reflected the policy judgment that it was inappropriate for the US shareholder to receive the benefit of both deferral of US tax on the earnings of a CFC (to the extent permitted by subpart F) and also receive preferential capital gain treatment on the disposition of the foreign corporate stock.

The provision has lost much of its original purpose because corporate capital gains are now taxed as ordinary income. Moreover, dividends paid to individual stockholders by foreign corporations are generally taxed at the same preferential rates as capital gains if the foreign corporation's stock is traded on a US stock exchange or the corporation is covered by a treaty that requires adequate exchanges of information.[86] In addition, corporate shareholders holding 10% or more of the stock in a CFC would often prefer that Section 1248 apply because Section 1248 recharacterizes the gain from the disposition of CFC stock as a dividend, which in general will not be taxable under Section 245A.[87] The result is that Section 1248 generally preserves the relatively neutral treatment of preferential capital gains and dividends for individuals and favorable treatment of foreign dividends for corporations.

6.3.8.2 Scope of Coverage

Section 1248 applies to any sale or taxable exchange by a US person of stock in a CFC and to any corporate distribution to such person for which capital gain treatment is provided.[88] The foreign corporation must be a CFC as defined in the subpart F

85. Section 1248 can also be relevant in situations involving the acquisition of a US corporation with foreign subsidiaries where the transaction is treated as a deemed sale by the US corporation of its assets (i.e., its stock in the foreign subsidiaries). *See* Treas. Reg. Sec. 1.338-4(h)(3).
86. Sec. 1(h)(11)(c). The favorable 20% tax rate does not apply to dividends paid by a foreign corporation that is a passive foreign investment company under Section 1297 (section 8.2). Notice 2011-64, 2011-2 C.B. 231, lists treaties that Treasury deems to have satisfactory information exchange requirements.
87. Sec. 1248(j). Treas. Reg. Section 1.245A-5(e) reduces the Section 245A dividend deduction by the amount of subpart F income or GILTI income that will escape US taxation as a result of the transaction. In addition, the Section 245A dividend deduction is decreased by earnings and profits generated by transactions between related parties to take advantage of gaps in the effective dates of various provisions in the 2017 Act. Treas. Reg. Sec. 1.245A-5(b) and (c).
88. That is, liquidations covered by Section 331 and redemption distributions which are given capital gain treatment under Section 302. As stated in Chapter 2 section 2.2.5, redemption of

provisions and the US person selling or exchanging the stock must own at least a 10% interest in the voting stock of the corporation. For Section 1248 to apply, the corporation need not be a CFC at the time of the sale or other disposition, however, as long as it was a CFC at any time during the five-year period preceding the sale.

6.3.8.3 *Calculation of Tax*

Under Section 1248, the gain recognized on the sale or exchange of stock in the CFC is included "as a dividend" in the income of the selling US shareholder to the extent of the shareholder's share of the earnings and profits of the foreign corporation accumulated after December 31, 1962 during the period that the stock sold was held by the selling shareholder.[89] A US corporate shareholder that satisfies the one-year holding period requirement may claim a 100% DRD on the earnings includible under Section 1248 but the foreign taxes associated with the earnings may not be claimed as credits.[90] In calculating the earnings and profits of the foreign corporation, there are some special rules applicable only to Section 1248.[91] Section 1248 is coordinated with the subpart F and GILTI rules by excluding from the earnings and profits subject to Section 1248 any earnings and profits previously included in the US taxpayer's income under subpart F or GILTI.[92] Amounts included under Section 1248 are treated as previously taxed income under Section 959(e) and thus are not taxable again when actually distributed to a purchasing US shareholder.

6.3.9 Deemed Repatriation Tax on Deferred Earnings

The deferral of US tax on CFC earnings prior to the 2017 Tax Act triggered an accumulation of trillions of dollars of untaxed earnings, notwithstanding the opportunity under a 2004 repatriation holiday for a CFC to distribute untaxed earnings at low effective rates of US tax.[93] Instead of an elective repatriation, the 2017 Tax Act sought

---

stock involving related persons can give rise to dividend treatment under Section 304. In the controlled foreign corporation context, this treatment can be beneficial in generating exempt foreign dividends to the US parent of CFCs. Section 304(b)(5) imposes limitations on the ability to achieve dividend treatment from transactions in which foreign corporations are involved.

89. Section 964(e) likewise includes as a dividend any gain realized by a CFC on the sale of stock in another foreign corporation to the same extent the gain would have been treated as a dividend to a US shareholder under Section 1248 if the CFC were a US person.
90. Secs. 1248(j) and 245A(d).

    Section 1248(b) contains a limitation on the tax imposed on individuals who dispose of stock in a controlled foreign corporation in a transaction subject to Section 1248. Very generally, the US individual shareholder's tax liability is limited to the liability she would have incurred if: (1) the foreign corporation had been taxed as a domestic corporation with an allowance for the foreign tax credit for foreign corporate taxes paid and (2) the shareholder was taxed at capital gains rates on the liquidation of the corporation.
91. *See* Sec. 1248(d).
92. Secs. 1248(d)(1), 951(a), and 951A(f)(1).
93. The 2004 tax holiday permitted earnings inclusion to be reduced by an 85% deduction at a time when the statutory corporate tax rate was 35%. It is believed that over USD 300 billion was repatriated as a result of the tax holiday. There was controversy over the extent to which the

through a mandatory deemed repatriation to tax the deferred earnings to pull revenue into the ten-year budget period and pay (from a budgetary perspective) for the loss of revenue expected from a lower corporate tax rate. An administratively favorable feature of the one-time inclusion was to clean out old earnings and profits. This permitted implementation of a new regime that taxed most CFC earnings currently and reduced the need to track historic earnings and associated tax attributes, other than previously taxed earnings. The tracking of the different categories of previously taxed earnings, however, has become very complex.

Section 965 increases the subpart F income of a "deferred foreign income corporation" in the last taxable year starting before 2018.[94] The increase is the greater of the CFC's "accumulated post-1986 deferred foreign income" as of (i) November 2, 2017 or (ii) December 31, 2017. A deferred foreign income corporation (DFIC) is any foreign corporation with a 10% corporate US shareholder,[95] which aligns with the scope of the new Section 245A dividend exemption rule discussed in section 6.4. The increase in subpart F income is taxed to US shareholders of the DFIC for the year in which the DFIC year ends.

Section 965 taxes the accumulated income of the DFICs at reduced rates by permitting the corporate shareholder to deduct a portion of the inclusion. This deduction results in an effective tax rate of 15.5% applied to the portion of the inclusion that is equal to the US shareholders' share of the DFIC's aggregate foreign cash and cash equivalents. An effective rate of 8% applies to remaining portion of the inclusion.[96] The higher tax rate applied to the portion of the Section 965 inclusion equal to the DFIC's cash assets reflects a view that the investment of deferred earnings in cash assets was less desirable and more suggestive of avoidance of US tax than investment in business assets. A proportionately reduced deemed paid foreign tax credit is allowed against the inclusion.[97] To further ameliorate the tax law change, taxpayers are allowed to elect to defer the time for paying the resulting US tax over eight years without interest. In addition, the schedule of required tax payments is back loaded to increase the value of the deferral.[98]

---

repatriations led to the increased domestic investment, employment or research and development by firms anticipated by supporters of the holiday. Dhammika Dharmapala, Fritz Foley, and Kristin Forbes, *Watch What I Do, Not What I Say: The Unintended Consequences of the Homeland Investment Act*, 66 J. of Finance 753, 756 (2011) (finding that USD 0.60-0.92 per repatriated dollar was spent in shareholder payouts in 2005 and subsequently, which was not one of the investments permitted to qualify for the reduced holiday effective rate). This finding has been contested. Thomas J. Brennan, *Where the Money Really Went: A New Understanding of the AJCA Tax Holiday*, 38-40 Nw. Law & Econ Research Paper No. 13-35 (2014) (extending the analysis to non-top-20 firms, firms spent USD 0.59 per repatriated dollar on uses permissible under the AJCA).

94. Sec. 965(a).
95. Sec. 965(d) and (e).
96. Sec. 965(c).
97. Sec. 965(g).
98. Sec. 965(h). The deferral of tax payments would be ended and the payments accelerated if payment is untimely or the taxpayer liquidates, sells substantially all of its assets or ceases business.

The statute authorizes and regulations have adopted anti-avoidance rules designed to prevent avoidance planning into the lower tax rates.[99] The earnings included are treated as previously taxed earnings and the basis of the DFIC shares is increased under the usual subpart F rules, but there is no requirement that these earnings be distributed. The very large amounts of previously taxed earnings and ongoing installment payments are an important legacy of the deemed repatriation tax.

6.4 GLOBAL INTANGIBLE LOW-TAXED INCOME (GILTI)

6.4.1 Background

As briefly discussed earlier, the 2017 Tax Act added a 100% dividends-received by a corporate US shareholder in Section 245A. At the same time, the Act also required income inclusions under subpart F and GILTI because of concerns about income shifting. The GILTI provisions were added to require inclusions from a CFC of non-subpart F foreign income exceeding a 10% return on tangible assets of the CFC and of income excluded from subpart F by reason of the high-tax election.[100] The GILTI provisions allow a US corporate shareholder to claim a 50% deduction against this income inclusion, so that the effective US tax rate before credits is 10.5%.[101] Corporate US shareholders are also allowed to claim an indirect foreign tax credit for the income taxes that the CFC paid on the corporate US shareholder's income inclusion.[102] The combined effect of all this is to create a form of minimum tax on foreign income.

The 2017 Tax Act's international provisions were not as solicitous toward individual US shareholders as they were toward corporate US shareholders. An individual US shareholder of a CFC must include GILTI in income but is *not* allowed the 50% deduction and may *not* claim indirect foreign tax credits (for taxes paid by the CFC) against the inclusion. In addition, an individual US shareholder is not allowed a 100% dividend-received deduction under Section 245A. As partial relief, an individual US shareholder may make a Section 962 election to tax the GILTI and subpart F inclusions at corporate rates.[103] Such an election permits the electing individual US shareholder to claim the 50% deduction against GILTI and the deemed paid foreign tax credits against the GILTI and subpart F income.[104] If an individual US shareholder makes the Section 962 election, however, she must recognize income when such GILTI

99. Sec. 965(o)(2); Treas. Reg. Sec. 1.965-4(b)(1), (f).
100. Sec. 951A. The high-tax election, which is discussed is 6.3.4.1, allows a CFC to elect not to have its income treated as FBCI and GILTI if it can establish that the income was subject to an *effective* tax rate in a foreign country that was greater than 90% of the maximum *marginal* US corporate tax rate and the taxpayer elects the exclusion (the "high-tax election").
101. Sec. 250(a). This effective rate also disregards allocable expenses of the shareholder, which do not reduce the Section 250(a) deduction but are allocable to determine the foreign tax credit limitation discussed in Chapter 10.
102. Sec. 960. *See* section 6.2.1, which briefly discusses the indirect credit, and Chapter 9 section 9.5.1, which discusses the indirect credit in detail.
103. Sec. 962. *See* section 6.2.1.
104. Secs. 962(a); Treas. Reg. Sec. 1.962-1(b)(1)(i).

and subpart F income is distributed to her to the extent the distribution exceeds any tax she paid upon inclusion of the subpart F income and GILTI.[105]

6.4.2 Shareholder Level Determination of GILTI

Although GILTI is an inclusion from a CFC, the GILTI amount is determined at the shareholder level in a complex set of calculations.

The starting point is to determine the net income, called "tested income," and the net loss, called "tested loss," for each of the US shareholder's CFCs.[106] Each CFC's gross income (with certain exclusions listed in Section 951A(c)(2))[107] is reduced by allocable deductions to determine the CFC's "tested income" or "tested loss."[108] The determination of a CFC's tested income and loss can be summarized as follows:

All of a CFC's gross income
<u>Less: Section 951A(c)(2) exclusions</u>
All of a CFC's gross income after exclusions
<u>Less: CFC's deductions allocable to this gross income</u>
CFC's tested income or tested loss

Each US shareholder then aggregates its pro rata share of the tested income and loss from its CFCs.[109] The statute refers to any resulting net income as "net CFC tested income."[110] This approach allows losses from a CFC with "tested losses" to offset what would be an inclusion from a profitable CFC with "tested income," without having the complexities of a consolidating the results of CFCs or a CFC group relief regime.[111]

---

105. Sec. 962(d).
106. Section 951A(c)(2) defines "tested income" and "tested loss."
107. The items of gross income excluded from the calculation of tested income under Section 951A(c)(2) include:
    - US source income effectively connected with a US trade or business unless the income is exempt by treaty;
    - gross income used to compute subpart F income;
    - income excluded from subpart F under the high-tax election and under regulations the GILTI high-tax election;
    - a dividend from a related person; and
    - foreign oil and gas extraction income.
108. Sec. 951A(c)(2).
109. A US shareholder's pro rata share of tested income is in general the amount it would have received had the CFC distributed such income to its shareholders. Treas. Reg. Sec. 1.951A-1(d)(1); Sec. 951(a)(2). To determine a US shareholder's share of tested loss, the tested loss is treated in general as though it were income and distributed to the shareholders. A US shareholder's share of the tested loss is in general equal to the amount it would have received in the distribution of the income into which the loss has hypothetically been converted. Treas. Reg. Sec. 1.951A-1(d)(4); Sec. 951(a)(2); Treas. Reg. Sec. 1.951-1(b)(1) and (e)(1).
110. Sec. 951A(c).
111. A CFC's tested loss does not reduce a CFC's earnings and profits for purposes of the earnings limitation on subpart F income in Section 952(c). Sec. 951A(c)(2)(B)(II).

Recall that only income in excess of 10% of its tangible business assets is the GILTI that is taxed. As a result, the "net CFC tested income" calculated above must be adjusted downward to account for this 10% return and to calculate the GILTI. This is accomplished by calculating the "net deemed tangible investment return" ("NDTIR") for each US shareholder. In general, the NDTIR is 10% of the US shareholders share of the "qualified business asset investment" ("QBAI") of those CFCs that had tested income.[112] The QBAI of each CFC is the CFC's average adjusted basis at the end of each quarter in depreciable property used in a trade or business.[113] These calculations can be summarized as follows:

Net CFC Tested Income
Less: Net Deemed Tangible Investment Return (NDTIR), i.e. 10% of QBAI
GILTI

A corporate, but not an individual, US shareholder is then allowed a deduction equal to 50% of the GILTI inclusion in order to calculate its tax liability for the GILTI.[114]

The GILTI taxed to the US shareholders is added to their bases in their CFCs that had tested income. The allocation to each CFC with tested income is in proportion to the ratio of the shareholder's share of tested income from such CFC to the aggregate of all the shareholder's tested income from all its CFCs with tested income.[115] It is also necessary to keep track of other tax items for the CFCs that are affected by GILTI, such as the indirect foreign tax credits allowed in respect of the GILTI inclusion and earnings not taxed by reason of the net deemed tangible investment return reduction. The IRS has asked for help in trying to determine ways to keep the accounting as simple as possible.[116]

6.4.3 Shareholder Level Taxation of GILTI

6.4.3.1 Corporate US Shareholder

A corporate US shareholder is allowed a 50% Section 250 deduction against the GILTI inclusion.[117] The Section 250 GILTI deduction is reduced if the combined Section 250

112. Sec. 951A(b). CFCs that have tested loss are not counted in determining QBAI. In calculating the NDTIR for each CFC with net CFC tested income, a reduction is required for interest expense that did not give rise to income taken into account in determining the shareholder's net tested income. Sec. 951A(b)(2). A US shareholders share of a CFC's QBAI is in general calculated in the same way as its share of tested income is determined, which is discussed in the text accompanying *supra* notes 108-110. Treas. Reg. Sec. 1.951A-1(d)(3)(i).
113. Sec. 951A(d)(1): Treas. Reg. Sec. 1.951A-3(b).
114. Sec. 250.
115. Sec. 951A(f)(2); Treas. Reg. Sec. 1.951A-5(b)(2)(i). Proposed regulations had also required US shareholders to reduce their bases in CFCs that had tested losses. The theory was that allowing tested losses to offset tested income would create a double benefit unless the US shareholder's bases in the tested loss CFCs were reduced. The final regulations did not contain this rule, although the IRS has said that it continues to study the issue. TD 9866, 2019-29 IRB 261, 294.
116. Notice 2019-1, 2019-2 IRB 275 (2018).
117. Sec. 250(a)(1)(B). The Section 250 deduction is 50% for taxable years that begin before Jan. 1, 2026, and then declines to 37.5%.

deductions for GILTI and foreign-derived intangible income (FDII), discussed in Chapter 11, exceed the US shareholder's taxable income.[118]

As discussed in Chapter 9 section 9.5.1, a corporate US shareholder is allowed an indirect credit under Section 960 for 80% of the foreign income taxes paid by the CFC attributed to the GILTI inclusion.[119]

When the GILTI is eventually distributed to a corporate US shareholder it is not subject to a second tax. As is the case with subpart F income, a distribution from these earnings is classified as "previously taxed earnings and profits" and excluded from gross income under Section 959.[120]

6.4.3.2 *Individual US Shareholder*

An individual US shareholder must include GILTI in income in the same manner as a corporation, except that an individual is not allowed a 50% deduction under Section 250. In addition, an individual is not eligible for a deemed paid credit for foreign income taxes paid by the CFC in light of the objective of that provision to mitigate two levels of corporate tax.[121] As is the case with corporate US shareholders (*see* section 6.4.3.1), distributions of the GILTI are classified as "previously taxed earnings and profits" and excluded from gross income under Section 959.[122]

If all or a part of the GILTI inclusion is subject to an effective rate of foreign tax allowing it to be eligible for the GILTI high-tax election and the taxpayer chooses that option, the earnings would not be taxed by the United States until distributed. In such case, the dividend would be taxed at the individual's marginal tax rate, unless the foreign corporation is eligible for the benefits of a US income tax treaty and other conditions for qualified dividend income are satisfied. In that case, the dividend would be eligible for a preferential capital gain tax rate.[123]

6.5 FOREIGN DIVIDEND EXEMPTION

6.5.1 Corporate US Shareholder's Section 245A DRD

Section 245A, added in the 2017 Tax Act, permits corporate US shareholders to claim a 100% DRD for the foreign source portion of a dividend from a "specified 10-percent

118. Sec. 250(a)(2)(A).
119. Sec. 960(d).
120. Treas. Reg. Sec. 1.959-2(a); Prop. Treas. Reg. Sec. 1.959-2(a).
121. An individual would be eligible to claim a credit under Section 901 for foreign withholding tax imposed on the distribution of those earnings when subsequently distributed. Secs. 901 and 903. As discussed in section 6.2.1, if the individual made a Section 960 election in the year of the GILTI inclusion, or paid no foreign taxes in that year, and made the election in the year of the distribution, Section 960(c) provides that the Section 904 limitation is increased by the amount of and in the category of the tax. The tax generally would be in the same foreign tax credit limitation category as the income. Treas. Reg. Sec. 1.904-6(b).
122. Treas. Reg. Sec. 1.959-2(a); Prop. Treas. Reg. Sec. 1.959-2(a).
123. Sec. 1(h)(11). If the dividend is eligible for the preferential capital gain rate, the special foreign tax credit limitation provisions of Section 904(b)(2) would apply.

owned foreign corporation."[124] Dividends to which the provision applies include Section 1248 gain (section 6.3.8) and a dividend paid to a partnership in which a corporate US shareholder of the foreign corporation is a partner.

The corporate US shareholder must have a 365-day holding period for the stock (including the ex-dividend date) in order to qualify for the deduction.[125] In addition, the dividend cannot be a "hybrid dividend" from a controlled foreign corporation for which the foreign corporation receives a deduction or other foreign tax benefit in calculating its foreign tax.[126]

The foreign source portion of a dividend is determined by the ratio of undistributed foreign earnings to total undistributed earnings based on the earnings and profits at the end of the year without taking account of distributions during the year.[127] No foreign tax credit is allowed for foreign taxes actually or constructively paid with respect to the portion of a dividend for which a Section 245A deduction is allowed and the foreign tax may not be deducted for US tax purposes.[128]

6.5.2 Dividends from Controlled Foreign Corporations

As discussed in section 6.2, a large portion of the earnings of a CFC will be taxed currently under subpart F and GILTI. The subsequent distribution of those earnings to corporate or individual US shareholders is not taxable under Section 959.[129]

The remaining CFC earnings will be the earnings equal to a 10% return on tangible investment, those subject to the high-tax election and earnings not taxed under GILTI because of losses of other CFCs. The distribution of those remaining CFC's earnings to a corporate (but not an individual) US shareholder will be eligible for the 100% DRD under Section 245A, assuming that its conditions are satisfied.

6.5.3 Effective Date and Extraordinary Transactions

The effective date for Section 245A is for dividends received from foreign corporations after December 31, 2017. The GILTI rules first became effective for taxable years of CFCs beginning after December 31, 2017 (and years of US shareholders in which or with which the CFC year end falls). This left a "window" (also known as the "doughnut hole") for fiscal year taxpayers to plan certain extraordinary transactions between

124. A "specified 10-percent owned foreign corporation" is a foreign corporation that is not a PFIC that has a corporate US shareholder. Sec. 245A(b). A US shareholder is a US person who owns, directly, indirectly or constructively, 10% or more of the total combined voting power of all classes of voting stock of the foreign corporation, or 10% or more of the total value of shares of all classes of the foreign corporation's stock. Sec. 951(b).
125. Sec. 246(c).
126. Sec. 245A(e). Section 245A(e) defines a "hybrid dividend" as a dividend that would otherwise qualify for a deduction under Section 245A and "for which the controlled foreign corporation received a deduction (or other tax benefit) with respect to any income ... taxes imposed by any foreign country or possession of the United States."
127. Sec. 245A(c)(1).
128. Sec. 245A(d).
129. *See* sections 6.3.4.1 and 6.3.4.2.

January 1, 2018 and the start of a CFC's fiscal year that could create favorable tax attributes while triggering earnings that would be exempt. The IRS has promulgated regulations under GILTI and Section 245A that deny benefits to these attributes.[130] These adjustments to tax attributes will have ongoing effects for many years for affected companies.

130. Treas. Reg. Secs. 1.951A-3(h)(2) and 1.245A-5(c).

CHAPTER 7

Formation, Reorganization, and Liquidation of Foreign Corporations: Section 367

7.1 BACKGROUND

As discussed briefly in Chapter 2 section 2.2.5, the US does not tax shareholders and their corporations in a number of transactions involving corporate formations and reorganizations. In qualifying transactions, a shareholder's recognition of gain or loss on stock received from a corporation in the transaction is deferred until a sale or exchange at some subsequent date.[1] Similarly, a corporation's recognition of gain (or possibly loss[2]) on assets transferred to it in the transaction is deferred until the assets are disposed of in a taxable transaction by the acquiring corporation.

If it were possible to utilize one of these tax-free techniques to transfer appreciated property beyond the US taxing jurisdiction to a foreign corporation, US taxpayers could easily avoid paying US tax on the appreciation. Taxpayers could recognize losses, however, by disposing of the depreciated assets in a taxable transaction. To address this problem, Section 367(a) provides that transfers to foreign corporations will not qualify for tax-free treatment or will be tax-free only if certain conditions are met. Technically, Section 367(a) achieves this result by providing that unless various statutory requirements are met, a foreign corporation "shall not be considered to be a

1. *See* Sec. 351, which applies to corporate formations, and Sec. 354(a)(1), which applies to corporate reorganizations. Securities may also be received tax-free in corporate reorganizations so long as the principal amount of the securities received does not exceed the principal amount of the securities transferred. Sec. 354(a)(2).
2. As discussed in note 68 in Chapter 2 section 2.2.5, Section 362(e) generally restricts the ability of a corporation to deduct losses on property that was transferred to it in a tax-free transaction where the transferred property had a fair market value below its tax basis at the time of the transfer.

corporation" for purposes of the various sections providing for nonrecognition of gain in transactions involving corporations.

Section 367(b) applies to reorganizations and liquidations of foreign corporations where earnings and profits of the foreign corporation might directly or indirectly be repatriated without the imposition of a US tax.[3] Prior to the 2017 Tax Act, distributions of earnings and profits from a foreign corporation to US shareholders were generally taxed as dividends. Regulations issued under Section 367(b) prevented the use of various corporate nonrecognition provisions to avoid the tax on such dividends. After the 2017 Tax Act, however, dividends from foreign corporations to corporate US shareholders are generally not taxable, either because they have already been taxed to such shareholders as subpart F income and GILTI[4] or because they qualify for the 100% dividends received deduction ("DRD") under Section 245A.[5] As a result, the potential for abuse addressed by Section 367(b) has diminished significantly. Presumably, Treasury will amend regulations issued under Section 367(b) to reflect this.

Section 367 also provides special rules for the transfer of intangibles to foreign corporations in Section 367(d).

7.1.1 Section 351: Formation of Corporation and Transfers of Stock to Controlling Stockholders in Exchange for Property

To understand Section 367, it is helpful to review the rules that govern tax-free corporate transactions in situations where Section 367 does not apply. This section 7.1.1 and sections 7.1.2 and 7.1.3, below, briefly review such transactions.[6]

Under Section 351, no gain or loss is recognized in a transaction in which property is transferred to a corporation in exchange for stock of the corporation if, after the transfer, the transferor owns at least 80% of the voting stock and all other classes of stock of the corporation.[7] As a result, without Section 367, it would be relatively easy to transfer appreciated property to a foreign corporation in a tax-free transaction.

7.1.2 Reorganizations

In general, the Internal Revenue Code permits certain corporate reorganizations to proceed on a tax- free basis both to the shareholders and the corporation involved.[8] In addition, corporate tax "attributes" such as earnings and profits and net operating

3. Section 367(b), like Section 367(a), accomplishes this by authorizing the Treasury to issue regulations treating a foreign corporation as though it were not a corporation for purposes of the various sections allowing nonrecognition in corporate liquidations and reorganizations.
4. Sec. 959(a). *See* Chapter 6 sections 6.3.1 and 6.4.3.1, which discuss the treatment of distributions of amounts previously taxed as subpart F income or GILTI.
5. Chapter 6 section 6.5.1.
6. These transactions are also discussed in Chapter 2 section 2.2.5.
7. Chapter 2 section 2.2.5.
8. Secs. 354, 361, and 368.

losses generally carryover in the reorganization transaction.[9] Under the basic statutory patterns, six general types of tax-free reorganizations are permitted. They are:

(1) *Type A:* A merger or consolidation in compliance with US federal or state law or the law of foreign country, as where Corporation X is merged into Corporation Y or Corporations X and Y consolidate into Corporation Z.
(2) *Type B:* The acquisition by one corporation of an 80% interest in the voting stock of another corporation solely in exchange for the voting stock of the acquiring corporation. The shareholders of the acquired corporation thus become shareholders of the acquiring corporation.
(3) *Type C:* The acquisition by one corporation of substantially all of the assets of another corporation in exchange for the voting stock of the acquiring corporation. The acquired corporation which receives the stock must distribute the stock to its shareholders in liquidation and they then become shareholders of the acquiring corporation.
(4) *Type D:* The creation of a new corporation to which are transferred some or all of the parent's assets with the shares of the new corporation distributed to the parent's shareholders.
(5) *Type E:* A change in the capital structure of an existing corporation, for example, the exchange of common stock for a new class of stock.
(6) *Type F:* A mere change in the identity, form, or place of organization of the corporation.

In all of these transactions, Section 361 provides that the corporation transferring its assets or shares does not recognize gain or loss and Section 354 provides similar nonrecognition treatment for shareholders exchanging their shares in connection with the reorganization transaction. The type A, B, and C reorganizations thus provide a variety of techniques for undertaking corporate acquisitions of appreciated property on a tax-free basis.[10] The provisions and their judicial interpretations are quite complex,

9. Sec. 381. The carryover of built-in losses is restricted, however, by Section 362(e). *See supra* note 2.
10. There are also provisions that permit tax-free acquisitions in situations where the acquiring corporation may want to use its subsidiary to acquire the target. In a "forward triangular merger," the acquiring company will form a subsidiary and the target company will be merged into the subsidiary with the target's stockholders receiving stock from the parent acquiring company. To be tax-free, this transaction must satisfy the requirements for an A reorganization. Sec. 368(a)(2)(D). In a "reverse triangular reorganization," the acquiring company will form a subsidiary that is then merged into the target company with the result that the target survives as a subsidiary of the acquiring company. The former stockholders of the target receive stock in the acquiring company. To be tax-free, the former stockholders of the target must have transferred at least 80% of their voting stock and each class of nonvoting stock for voting stock of the acquiring company and the requirements for an A reorganization must also be satisfied. Sec. 368(a)(2)(E). Acquisitions are often structured as reverse triangular reorganizations because the target company survives as a subsidiary of the acquiring company. In contrast, in a forward triangular merger, the target company is merged into the subsidiary of the acquiring company and the subsidiary is the surviving company.

    Two other types of triangular reorganizations may also be used. In a triangular C reorganization, the acquiring company will form a subsidiary that will acquire all the assets of

but the basic principle behind the sections is that if the shareholders of the acquired corporation continue their investment in the form of stock in the acquiring corporation, the transaction should not be subject to current taxation.

7.1.3 Liquidations

Under Sections 332 and 337, the liquidation of a subsidiary by a corporate parent owning at least 80% of the voting stock of the subsidiary (and 80% of the stock value) is tax-free to the subsidiary and the parent corporation.

7.2 APPLICATION OF SECTION 367(A)

7.2.1 General

In the context of the above transactions, Section 367 distinguishes between two types of transfers involving foreign corporations. First, Section 367(a) generally requires recognition of any built-in gain (but not losses) on transfers involving property moving from the US transferor to a foreign corporation (so-called outbound transfers). It also specifies certain transfers which can be made on a tax-free basis. Second, Section 367(b) grants broad regulatory authority to the IRS to promulgate regulations setting forth the principles under which non-outbound transactions involving foreign corporations will qualify for tax-free treatment. The law in this area is governed almost exclusively by extensive and complex regulations issued under both Section 367(a) and (b).

7.2.2 "Outbound" Transfers

Section 367(a)(1) states as a general rule that *all* transfers by US persons of appreciated property to a foreign corporation will result in recognition of gain except to the extent that regulations provide otherwise.[11] Thus, the normally tax-free transactions described in section 7.1 become taxable on any gain realized on the transfer of property

the target company in exchange for voting stock of the acquiring company's parent company that the target company then distributes to its stockholders in complete liquidation. Sec. 368(a)(1)(C) and 368(b). In a triangular B reorganization, stock of the target company is acquired in exchange for voting stock of the acquiring company's parent company. Sec. 368(a)(1)(B) and 368(b).

11. The character and source of the gain are determined as if the US transferor had sold the property to the foreign transferee. Treas. Reg. Sec. 1.367(a)-1(b)(4)(A).

    It is possible for Section 367(a) to apply to a transaction that appears to involve only US corporations. Consider a forward triangular merger in which US Corp. A merges into US Corp B, a subsidiary of Foreign Corp. F, and the shareholder of US Corp. A receives the stock of Foreign Corp. F. This transaction is treated as an "indirect stock transfer" subject to Section 367(a). It is characterized as though the shareholder of US Corp. A transferred its stock for stock in US Corp F. *See* Treas. Reg. Sec. 1.367(a)-3(d)(1)(i) and 1.367(a)-3(d)(3) Ex. 1. Similar "indirect stock transfers" for other types of reorganizations are also described in Treas. Reg. Section 1.367(a)-3(d).

to a foreign corporation, unless an exception is applicable.[12] Although Section 367(a)(1) eliminates nonrecognition of gain, it does not change the nonrecognition rules for losses. While Section 367(a) will require gains to be recognized on assets that have a fair market value greater than their tax basis, the nonrecognition rules described in section 7.1 will continue to prevent the recognition of losses on the transfer of assets with a diminished fair market value.

7.2.3 Transfers of Assets Other than Intangibles or Stock and the Branch Loss Recapture Rule

Prior to the 2017 Tax Act, a transfer of assets to a foreign corporation to be used in the active conduct of a foreign trade or business qualified for an exception that permitted nonrecognition treatment.[13] The 2017 Tax Act repealed this once very important exception. As a result, unless some other exception applies, the transfer of appreciated assets will now trigger gain recognition regardless of whether the assets are part of a trade or business. It is important to note that Treasury has not yet amended the regulations that implemented the prior exception for trade or business assets. Consequently, advisors consulting the regulations for post-2017 transactions should confirm whether the regulation has been revised to reflect current law.

The transfer of assets comprising a trade or business to a foreign corporation may also trigger the recognition of additional income that is "recapturing" previously deducted losses. The concern that motivated these additional income "recapture" provisions is that the transferred trade or business assets might have generated losses prior to the transfer that reduced the transferor's US tax liability. The transfer of such assets to a foreign corporation will often mean that any subsequent income those assets generate will be subject to no or reduced amounts of US taxation.[14]

Two potentially overlapping "recapture" provisions might apply: Sections 904(f)(3) and 91. Section 904(f)(3) requires a taxpayer who transfers assets that are used in its foreign business to a US or foreign buyer to recognize income in certain circumstances if the taxpayer has "overall foreign losses." A taxpayer's "overall foreign losses" are, in general, the amount by which the taxpayer's foreign source deductions have exceeded the taxpayer's foreign source gross income for the current year and prior years (Section 904(f)(1)). In other words, overall foreign losses represent, in general, losses that offset the taxpayer's *US source income*. If a taxpayer transfers assets used in a trade or business predominantly outside the US, the taxpayer is required to recognize as US source income an amount equal to any built-in gain in any of the transferred

12. Some exceptions to the general gain recognition rule are discussed in sections 7.2.5, 7.2.6, and 7.2.7.
13. Prior version of Sec. 367(a)(3). Thus, for example, the transfer by a parent corporation of machinery and equipment to a foreign subsidiary to be used in manufacturing could be done on a tax-free basis prior to 2018. However, the active trade or business exception did not apply to transfers of inventory, foreign currency, installment obligations, or property leased to third persons. Prior version of Sec. 367(a)(3)(B).
14. *See* Chapter 6 section 6.2.1 discussing the tax treatment of non-subpart f income of CFCs.

foreign assets or the taxpayer's overall foreign losses, whichever is lesser (Section 904(f)(3)).

The other recapture provision, Section 91, in general, requires a US corporation to include in income some of the losses incurred after December 31, 2017 that it deducted for US tax purposes.[15] Section 91 applies when a US corporation transfers substantially all the assets of a foreign branch[16] to a "specified 10-percent owned foreign corporation" if such US corporation is a "US shareholder" after the transfer. A "US shareholder" is defined the same as in subpart F (*see* Chapter 6 section 6.3.2).[17] It is a shareholder that owns stock comprising at least 10% of the corporation's total combined vote or 10% of the total value of all stock of the corporation after the transfer.[18] A "specified 10-percent foreign corporation" is a foreign corporation in which a US corporation is a US shareholder.[19]

Section 91 "recaptures" as US source income[20] losses previously deducted by the branch that Section 91 classifies as a "transferred loss amount."[21] In general, a "transferred loss amount" equals the extent to which the post-2017 branch losses exceed any taxable income recognized by the branch in a taxable year after it incurred the loss, any gain recognized on transfer of the branch assets to the specified 10-percent foreign corporation,[22] and any amount recognized under Section 904(f)(3) in the transfer.[23] Note that since the "transferred loss amount" of Section 91 is reduced by income triggered by Section 904(f)(3), Section 91 is only recapturing the losses not covered by Section 904(f)(3), i.e., losses that offset *foreign source income*.[24]

---

15. Sec. 91. An earlier version of Section 367(a)(3) had similar rules that applied to losses incurred prior Jan. 1, 2018.
16. Section 91(a) refers to the pre-2017 Tax Act version of Section 367(a)(3)(C) for the definition of "foreign branch." Regulations issued under old Section 367(a)(3)(C) define foreign branch:

    > For purposes of this section, the term "foreign branch" means an integral business operation carried on by a US person outside the United States. Whether the activities of a US person outside the United States constitute a foreign branch operation must be determined under all the facts and circumstances. Evidence of the existence of a foreign branch includes, but is not limited to, the existence of a separate set of books and records, and the existence of an office or other fixed place of business used by employees or officers of the U.S. person in carrying out business activities outside the United States. Treas. Reg. Sec. 1.367(a)-6T(g)(1).

17. Sec. 951(b).
18. Secs. 91(a), (b)(1), and 951(b).
19. Secs. 91(a) and 245A(b). Passive foreign investment companies (Chapter 8 section 8.2) that are not controlled foreign corporations are excluded from "specified 10-percent foreign corporations."
20. Sec. 91(a) and (d).
21. Sec. 91(b).
22. Sec. 91(c). This amount of gain is reduced, however, to the extent that gain would have been recognized under Sec. 367(a)(3)(C) for losses incurred prior to Jan. 1, 2018, had that provision not been repealed. P.L. 115-97, 131 Stat. 2054, 2194 (2017). This has the effect of increasing the amount of gain recognized under Section 91 and, in effect, recapturing those earlier losses.
23. Sec. 91(b) and (c).
24. *See* Jeff Maydew and Julia Skubis Weber, *Foreign Branch Incorporations After the TCJA*, 160 TAX NOTES 1871, 1876 (Sept. 24, 2018).

Consider a very simple example to illustrate the interaction of Sections 367(a), 904(f)(3), and 91.[25] Suppose US Parent, a US corporation, has a foreign branch that conducts a trade or business in country X. The foreign branch had USD 150 of losses in 2020 for which US Parent claimed a deduction against other foreign source income on its US return in 2020. (Note that since the USD 150 loss offset foreign source income and not US source income, it is not an overall foreign loss governed by Section 904(f)(3).) On January 1, 2021, US Parent transferred all the tangible assets of the foreign branch to a newly formed foreign subsidiary. The assets had a built-in gain of USD 100.

Section 367(a)(1) requires US Parent to recognize the USD 100 of built-in gain on the transfer since Section 367(a)(1) negates the nonrecognition rule in Section 351. The source of this gain will be determined under Sections 862 and 865.[26] In addition, Section 91 requires US Parent to recognize USD 50, which represents the difference between the USD 150 branch loss and the USD 100 gain recognized under Section 367(a). Section 91(d) treats this USD 50 of gain as US source gain. There are no "overall foreign losses" and, therefore, Section 904(f)(3) does not apply, since the losses did not offset US source income.

In the foregoing example, if the USD 150 branch loss had offset US source income, it would have been characterized as an "overall foreign loss," which is recaptured under Section 904(f)(3), not Section 91. US Parent would still recognize USD 100 of gain under Section 367(a)(1). It would also recognize USD 50 of income under Section 904(f)(3), which is treated as US source (Section 904(f)(3)(A)(i) and 904(f)(1)). Although Section 91 technically also applies, Section 91 would not recapture the overall foreign losses because the amount of income triggered by Section 91 is reduced by the income that was recognized under Section 904(f)(3) (Section 91(b)(2)(B)).

7.2.4 Transfers of Intangibles

Section 367(d) provides a special rule for intangible property. It taxes gain on transfers of intangible property that would otherwise not be taxable under the provisions discussed in section 7.1.[27] The gain is calculated as though the transferor had sold the intangible property for royalty payments for the asset's useful life that are contingent

25. This example is based on an example in JT. COMM. ON TAXATION, GENERAL EXPLANATION OF PUBLIC LAW 114-97 354 (December 2018).
26. Treas. Reg. Section 1.367(a)-1(b)(4)(i) sources gain under Section 367 by characterizing the exchange as though it occurred between the transferor and the foreign corporation. Chapter 4 discusses the source rules that apply to various types of property. Gain from the sale of real estate located outside the US is foreign source. Sec. 862(a)(5). Gain from depreciable personal property will in general be US source to the extent of depreciation recapture. Sec. 865(c). And gain in excess of depreciation recapture will be sourced where title passes. Sec. 865(c)(2).
27. "Intangible" property is defined in Section 367(d)(4) and includes patents, know-how, copyrights, licenses, contracts, goodwill, going concern value, work force in place and "any other item the value of which is not attributable to tangible property or the services of any individual." The quoted language was added in the 2017 Tax Act to the definition of intangible to address concerns that certain decisions in transfer pricing cases did not take account of the full range of intangible value transferred under cost sharing arrangements. *See* Chapter 12, section 12.4.2.

on property's productivity, use, or disposition. The deemed royalty payments must commensurate with the income attributable to the transferred property[28] and are taxed as ordinary income.[29] Such income is treated as foreign source income to the same extent that an actual royalty payment for the transferred intangible would be considered foreign source income.[30]

7.2.5 Transfers of Stock

Special rules also apply to the transfer of stock to a foreign corporation. The regulations generally provide that a transfer of stock to a foreign corporation pursuant to Section 351 (section 7.1.1) or in a tax-free reorganization (section 7.1.2) will be taxable, but then provide several exceptions in situations where the US will be able to tax the deferred gain in the future. To understand the rules, it is necessary to distinguish between two types of transfers of stock that may occur in a tax-free reorganization. The first type of transfer is one described in Section 354 in which the *stockholders* in one company in a tax-free reorganization exchange their stock for stock of another company that is also a party to the tax-free reorganization. For example, if the requirements for a B reorganization are satisfied, Section 354 permits the stockholders of the acquired company to exchange tax-free their stock for stock of the acquiring company. The other type of transfer of stock that may occur in a tax-free reorganization is described in Section 361 and involves a *corporation* that is a party to the reorganization transferring its assets, including stock that it may hold in another company, to the acquiring company in exchange for the acquiring company's stock.[31] For example, if the requirements for a tax-free C reorganization are satisfied, Section 361 allows the acquired company to transfer tax-free its assets, including any stock that it may hold in another company, to the acquiring company in exchange for stock of the acquiring company.

The Section 367(a) Regulations distinguish between transfers of stock to a foreign corporation under Section 351 or 354, on the one hand, and under Section 361, on the other hand. If a US person transfers stock in a foreign corporation under Section 351 or under Section 354 in a tax-free reorganization to a foreign corporation, the transfer will not be taxable in situations where the transferor either: (1) owns less than 5% of the transferee foreign corporation after the transaction, or (2) agrees with the IRS to pay a

28. Sec. 367(d)(2).
29. Sec. 367(d)(2)(C).
30. *See* H.R. Rep. No. 105-148 pp. 537-8 (1997); S. Rep. No. 105-33 pp. 208-9; H.R. Rep. No. 105-220 p. 628 (1997). The income can also qualify for look-through treatment under Section 904(d)(3)(C) for purposes of determining the appropriate foreign tax credit basket. Sec. 367(d)(2)(C). *See* Chapter 10 section 10.2. In addition, the deemed royalty may qualify for the lower (13.125%) tax rate for foreign-derived intangible income ("FDII") if the other FDII requirements are satisfied. Treas. Reg. Sec. 1.250(b)-3(b)(16) and 1.250(b)-4(d)(2)(iv)(B)(Ex. 8). *See* Chapter 11 for a discussion of FDII.
31. Since Section 361 applies to the transfer of assets held by a corporation that is a party to a reorganization, it applies only to those reorganizations in which the acquired company is transferring assets. These reorganizations are A, C, D and F reorganizations described in section 7.1.2 and the related triangular reorganizations described in *supra* note 10.

tax on the unrecognized gain in the event the transferee disposes of the stock within five years (a so-called gain recognition agreement).[32] If stock in a US corporation is transferred to a foreign corporation pursuant to Section 351 or Section 354, the transfer may be tax-free if several conditions are satisfied.[33] First, all US transferors must have received no more than 50% of the transferee foreign corporation in the transaction. Second, persons who are directors, officers, or own at least 5% of stock in the US corporation cannot own more than 50% of the transferee foreign corporation. Third, either the US transferor must own no more than 5% of the transferee foreign corporation or, if it owns more, must enter into a gain recognition agreement. Fourth, the transferee foreign corporation must have engaged in an active trade or business outside the US for thirty-six months prior to the transfer. Lastly, the value of the transferee corporation must at least equal the fair market value of the US corporation.[34]

Stricter rules apply when a US corporation transfers stock to a foreign corporation in the context of Section 361 because the transferor corporation often disappears in the types of reorganizations to which Section 361 applies.[35] Thus, when a domestic corporation transfers stock of a US or a foreign corporation to a foreign corporation in a Section 361 transfer, the exchange will be taxable unless conditions exist that will enable the IRS to collect in the future any gain on the transferred stock. The regulations require that five or fewer US corporations own at least 80% of the transferor corporation and that the US shareholders who own 5% or more of the stock of the foreign transferee corporation agree to recognize gain when the foreign corporation disposes of the transferred stock.[36] To the extent that stock in the foreign transferee is not owned by US stockholders owning 5% or more of the foreign transferee, the US transferor must recognize gain immediately on the transfer of the stock.

7.2.6 Spin-Offs

Outbound transfers of stock of a subsidiary corporation pursuant to a "spin off" transaction under Section 355 (a Type D reorganization described in section 7.1.2) are

32. Treas. Reg. Sec. 1.367(a)-3(b). It is important to note, however, that successfully running the gauntlet of Section 367(a) Regulations will not assure tax-free treatment. It is also necessary to satisfy Section 367(b), which may require that Section 1248 income (Chapter 6 section 6.3.8), with respect to the transferred stock be recognized in two situations. In very general terms, one situation arises when the transferred stock was subject to Section 1248, but the stock received is not, and the other situation arises when the transferee receives nonparticipating preferred stock in the exchange, in effect bailing out the earnings of the transferred stock. *See* Treas. Reg. Sec. 1.367(a)-3(b)(2) and 1.367(b)-4(b)(1) and (2). As will be discussed in section 7.3, an important purpose of Section 367(b) prior to the 2017 Tax Act was to ensure that US persons owning stock in a foreign corporation could not permanently avoid including in income the foreign corporation's earnings and profits. However, the adoption of Section 245A has significantly reduced the impact of Section 1248 for corporate US shareholders since Section 245A allows such shareholders to receive dividend income tax-free.
33. Treas. Reg. Sec. 1.367(a)-3(c).
34. This requirement is referred to as the "substantiality" test in the regulations. Treas. Reg. Sec. 1.367(a)-3(c)(3)(iii).
35. For example, in an A reorganization, the acquired company is merged into the acquiring company and, in a C reorganization, the target company transfers its assets to the acquiring company in exchange for stock and then liquidates.
36. Treas. Reg. Sec. 1.367(a)-3(e)(3)(i) and (iii).

taxable if the subsidiary is a foreign corporation, except to the extent the distributing corporation can prove that the distributees are US citizens, residents, or corporations.[37] If the subsidiary is a US corporation, the distribution is not taxable.[38]

7.2.7 Liquidations

Outbound transfers of property to a foreign parent corporation on the liquidation of an 80% controlled US subsidiary corporation result in gain recognition unless the foreign parent continues to use the distributed property in a US trade or business and waives any benefits that might otherwise be available under a tax treaty with respect to the taxation of income and gain from such property.[39]

7.3 SECTION 367(B) AND THE REPATRIATION OF EARNINGS AND PROFITS

An important theme that ran through the US tax rules governing cross-border transactions prior to the 2017 Tax Act was the expectation that income earned by the foreign subsidiary of a US corporation would at some point be taxed by the US at ordinary rates. A key provision in achieving this goal was Section 367(b), which reverses the approach of Section 367(a). Section 367(b) provides that corporate formation, reorganization, and liquidation transactions not involving an outbound transfer of property are eligible for nonrecognition under the general rules except as provided in regulations issued under Section 367(b).[40] An important purpose of Section 367(b) was to ensure that US persons owning stock in a foreign corporation could not permanently avoid including in income the corporation's earnings and profits when the foreign corporation's earnings were repatriated through transactions that might otherwise be tax-free or when the stock was sold.

After adoption of the 2017 Tax Act, the future role of Section 367(b) is unclear and, as of this writing, regulations have not been revised. Earnings distributed by a controlled foreign corporation to its 10% US shareholders that have already been taxed to those shareholders under GILTI, subpart F, or a deemed repatriation are not taxable again when distributed (*see* Chapter 6 section 6.2).[41] Moreover, after adoption of the 2017 Tax Act, foreign source earnings that were not taxed to the shareholder under subpart F or GILTI are also generally tax-free under Section 245A when distributed to

---

37. Sec. 367(e)(1); Treas. Reg. Sec. 1.367(e)-1(b)(1) and 1.367(e)-1(d).
38. Sec. 367(e)(2); Treas. Reg. Sec. 1.367(e)-1(c).
39. Treas. Reg. Sec. 1.367(e)-2(b)(2)(i). Another exception allows a liquidating US subsidiary to distribute real estate located in the US tax-free on the theory that the ultimate disposition of that property will be taxable under Section 897 (*see* Chapter 5 section 5.4). Treas. Reg. Sec. 1.367(e)-2(b)(2)(ii). A third exception permits a liquidating US subsidiary to distribute the stock of a US subsidiary where it owns 80% of that subsidiary and certain other requirements are satisfied. Treas. Reg. Sec. 1.367(e)-2(b)(2)(iii).
40. Treas. Reg. Sec. 1.367(b)-1 to 1.367(b)-13.
41. Secs. 959(a), 951A(f)(1), and 965.

10% US shareholders that are corporations.[42] The result is that the primary abuse targeted by Section 367(b) has been substantially reduced, since most distributions of earnings to 10% corporate US shareholders are no longer taxable. It remains to be seen whether the rules under Section 367(b) applicable to reorganizations and liquidations of foreign corporations will be changed to reflect this.

In this section, we describe application of the Section 367(b) Regulations that may require a US person holding stock in a foreign corporation to recognize income upon the repatriation of foreign earnings and profits of a foreign corporation. In section 7.4, we will describe the manner in which the Section 367(b) Regulations act as a backstop to Section 1248, which requires US shareholders in a CFC to recognize as dividend income the portion of their gain attributable to their share of the foreign corporation's earnings and profits when they sell their stock.

In general, the Section 367(b) Regulations allow transactions to proceed on a tax-free basis as long as it is possible to ensure that the foreign earnings will ultimately be taxable to US persons holding stock in the foreign corporation. In some cases, this result is achieved by attributing the tax characteristics of the corporation whose stock is exchanged to the stock received on the exchange. Where such attribution is not possible, the exchanging shareholder may have to recognize income to the extent of its share of the earnings as the price for having the rest of the transaction treated as tax-free.[43] To assure compliance, US taxpayers are required to submit notice of the transaction and specified information to the IRS.[44]

The repatriation of the foreign earnings of a foreign corporation might occur as the result of an inbound liquidation or reorganization. Suppose, for example, that US Corp owns all the stock of F Corp, a foreign corporation, and decides to liquidate F Corp. Normally, the transaction would be tax-free under Section 332. At the time of liquidation, F Corp has USD 100 of earnings and profits that have not been subject to US tax.[45] F Corp also has other appreciated assets that, when distributed to US Corp, would cause US Corp to realize USD 200 of gain on a disposition. The Section 367(b) Regulations state that US Corp must recognize the USD 100 of F Corp's earnings and profits as dividend income, but the balance of the transaction (the USD 200 of gain) is tax-free.[46] Note, however, that Section 245A should generally result in the amount treated by the regulations as a taxable dividend as being nontaxable.[47] As a result, the entire transaction is likely tax-free.

42. As discussed in Chapter 6 section 6.5, Section 245A allows a deduction for dividends of foreign source income from a "specified 10-percent owned foreign corporation" to 10% US shareholders. *See infra* note 47, for a discussion of some of the situations in which the DRD may be reduced.
43. *See, e.g.*, Treas. Reg. Sec. 1.367(b)-3(b)(3) and 1.367(b)-4(b).
44. Treas. Reg. Sec. 1.367(b)-1(c).
45. The regulations refer to earnings and profits that have not yet been subject to US tax as the "all earnings and profits amount." Treas. Reg. Sec. 1.367(b)-2(d)(1) and (2).
46. Treas. Reg. Sec. 1.367(b)-3(b)(3)(i) and -3(b)(3)(ii) Ex. 1. The USD 200 gain inherent in F Corp's assets is preserved by carrying over the basis of F Corp's assets to US Corp. Sec. 334(b)(1).
47. Regulations adopted on Aug. 20, 2020, reduce the DRD for distributions received from a CFC where the dividend recipient reduced its ownership interest in the CFC (so-called extraordinary reductions). Treas. Reg. Sec. 1.245A-5(a), (b), and (e). The concern is that Section 951(a) only requires US shareholders to include subpart F income and the GILTI on the last day of the year.

A similar result occurs in a reorganization. For example, suppose that US Corp has two subsidiaries, US Sub and Foreign Sub. US Corp has unrealized gain of USD 80 in its stock in Foreign Sub and Foreign Sub had USD 20 of earnings and profits. US Sub acquires all the assets of Foreign Sub in a D reorganization, issuing shares in US Sub to Foreign Sub, which then liquidates and distributes the additional shares of US Sub to US Corp. The Section 367(b) Regulations require US Corp to include the USD 20 of repatriated foreign earnings and profits in income as a dividend.[48] Note, however, that Section 245A should again result in the amount treated by the regulations as a taxable dividend as being nontaxable.[49] The remainder of the transaction is also tax-free. Foreign Sub recognizes no gain on the exchange of its assets for US Sub stock and no gain on the distribution of US Sub stock to US Corp under Section 361. Similarly, US Corp recognizes no gain under Section 354 on the receipt of the additional shares in US Sub in exchange for its shares in Foreign Sub.[50]

7.3.1 Outbound Transfers to Other Entities

Other provisions also prevent US persons from shifting gains in appreciated property by transferring such property outside the US. Section 684 requires that a US person always recognize gain on the transfer of appreciated property to a foreign trust[51] or

---

Consequently, a US shareholder transferring its stock could avoid its share of such income with respect to the transferred stock so long as the transfer does not close the corporation's taxable year. At the same time, the transferring stockholder could claim a full dividends received deduction for a dividend distribution received with respect to the transfer. To prevent this, the regulations reduce the amount of the DRD by the amount of subpart F income and GILTI that the transferor avoided. The regulations do not reduce the dividends receive deduction, however, if the transfer occurred in a liquidation. Treas. Reg. Sec. 1.245A-5(e)(2)(i)(C). The reason is that in a liquidation, the transferring US shareholder has to include its full share of subpart F income and the GILTI because the liquidating corporation's taxable year closes on that date. *See* Treas. Reg. Sec. 1.245A-5(e)(2)(i)(C). Thus, in the text's example, F Corp should be able to claim the DRD for the entire USD 100 dividend.

The same recently adopted regulations also reduce the Section 245A dividend by the amount of earnings and profits generated by sales of a CFC's property to related parties during a time that there was a gap in the effective dates of various provisions in the 2017 Tax Act. Treas. Reg. Sec. 1.245A-5(b) and (c).

48. Treas. Reg. Sec. 1.367(b)-3(b)(3)(i) and (b)(3)(ii) Ex. 2.
49. We believe that Treas. Reg. Sec. 1.245A-5(a), (b), and (e) should not result in a decrease of the DRD in this transaction since the liquidation closes Foreign Sub's taxable year and, as a result, US Corp would recognize any subpart F income or GILTI realized during the taxable year. *See supra* note 47.
50. Treas. Reg. Sec. 1.367(b)-3(b)(3)(ii) Ex. 2. If US Corp owned less than 10% of the stock of Foreign Sub (with the result that it is not a US shareholder), a different tax result would occur. US Corp would have to recognize all USD 80 of the gain it realized in the reorganization unless it elects to recognize its share of Foreign Sub's earnings and profits as dividend income. Treas. Reg. Sec. 1.367(b)-3(c). Note that in this situation US Corp could not use Section 245A to avoid recognizing the dividend income since it would not be a 10% US shareholder.
51. The term "foreign trust" is discussed in Chapter 5 section 5.8.1.1. A trust is classified as a "foreign trust" if: (a) a court in the US cannot exercise primary supervision over the administration of the trust, or (b) US fiduciaries lack authority to control all "substantial decisions" concerning the trust. *See* Sec. 7701(a)(30).

foreign estate[52]. In addition, new regulations, in general, require a US person transferring appreciated property to a partnership (foreign or domestic) to recognize gain if one or more foreign persons related to the transferor are partners, and they and the transferring partner own at least an 80% interest in partnership.[53] A de minimis rule allows the transferring partner to avoid gain recognition if all property transferred to the partnership during the taxable year has built-in gain of less than USD 1 million.[54] Moreover, the transferor may avoid gain recognition if the partnership agrees to make certain allocations of income that will minimize the possibility that US tax will be avoided on the built-in gain and agrees to undertake certain notice requirements.[55] Reporting requirements similar to that imposed on US shareholders of CFCs are imposed on US partners in foreign partnerships.[56]

7.4 SECTION 1248 AND SECTION 367(B)

As discussed in Chapter 6 section 6.3.8, Section 1248, which was adopted at the same time as subpart F, reflected the policy judgment that it was inappropriate for the US shareholder to receive the benefit of both deferral of US tax on the earnings of a controlled foreign corporation (to the extent permitted by subpart F) and also receive preferential capital gain treatment on the disposition of the foreign corporate stock. As we noted earlier, the provision has lost much of its original purpose. Dividends paid to individual stockholders by foreign corporations are generally taxed at the same preferential rates as capital gains if the foreign corporation's stock is traded on a US stock exchange or the corporation is covered by a treaty that requires adequate exchanges of information.[57] In addition, corporate shareholders holding 10% or more of the stock in a CFC would often prefer that Section 1248 apply because the gain from the disposition of CFC stock that Section 1248 recharacterized as a dividend in general will not be taxable under Section 245A.[58] In contrast, gain that is not recharacterized as

52. Section 7701(a)(31)(A) defines a "foreign estate" as an estate that is taxed only on its income effectively connected with a US trade or business and not its other income. The determination whether an estate will be taxed on its income other than effectively connected income and, thereby, treated as a "domestic" estate, is a multifactor test discussed in Chapter 3.
53. Treas. Reg. Sec. 1.721(c)-2(b). The regulations exclude cash equivalents and securities from this gain recognition rule. *See* Treas. Reg. Sec. 1.721(c)-1(b)(6), which defines "excluded property" to include cash equivalents and securities.
54. Treas. Reg. Sec. 1.721(c)-2(c).
55. Treas. Reg. Sec. 1.721(c)-2, -3, and -6.
56. Sec. 6038B; Treas. Reg. Sec. 1.6038B-2.
57. Sec. 1(h)(11)(c).The favorable 20% tax rate does not apply to dividends paid by a foreign corporation that is a passive foreign investment company under Section 1297 (Chapter 8 section 8.2) or by a corporation that is a "surrogate foreign corporation" as defined in Section 7874(a)(2)(B). (*See* section 7.5, for a discussion of "surrogate foreign corporations.") Notice 2011-64, 2011-2 CB 231, lists treaties that Treasury deems to have satisfactory information exchange requirements.
58. Sec. 1248(j). Treas. Reg. Section 1.245A-5(e) reduces the Section 245A dividend deduction by the amount of subpart F income or GILTI income that will escape US taxation as a result of the transaction. In addition, the Section 245A dividend deduction is decreased by earnings and profits generated by transactions between related parties to take advantage of gaps in the effective dates of various provisions in the 2017 Tax Act. Treas. Reg. Sec. 1.245A-5(b) and (c).

a dividend will usually be taxable to the corporate shareholder as capital gain at a rate of 21% since there is no preferential rate for corporate capital gains.

As mentioned in section 7.3, one of the objectives of the regulations under Section 367(b) is to ensure that US persons owning stock in a foreign corporation could not permanently avoid paying US tax on the corporation's earnings and profits when the foreign corporation's earnings were repatriated through transactions that might otherwise be tax-free. In section 7.3, we discussed application of Section 367(b) where the earnings and profits and other assets of a foreign corporation were distributed to shareholders.

The Section 367(b) Regulations also apply to transactions in which a US shareholder exchanges stock in a CFC for stock in a foreign corporation that will not qualify as a CFC. Under the regulations, if a Section 351 transaction or tax-free reorganization results in a US shareholder exchanging stock that would be taxable under Section 1248 for stock that will not be subject to Section 1248, the transaction will be taxable as a dividend to the extent of the US shareholder's share of foreign earnings and profits.[59] As is the case discussed above in section 7.3, however, such a dividend to a corporate US shareholder will often not be taxable under Section 245A.

For example, consider a situation where US Corp wholly owns Foreign Sub, which has earnings and profits of USD 20. US Corp has no current subpart F or GILTI income. Since US Corp wholly owns Foreign Sub, Foreign Sub is a CFC, and the stock US Corp owns in Foreign Sub is subject to Section 1248. In a tax-free C reorganization, Foreign Acquirer transfers some of its voting stock to Foreign Sub in exchange for all of Foreign Sub's assets. Foreign Sub then liquidates and distributes the stock in Foreign Acquirer to US Corp. The Foreign Acquirer voting stock received by US Corp does not represent more than 50% of the voting power or value of Foreign Acquirer stock. As a result, Foreign Acquirer is not a CFC and Section 1248 does not apply to US Corp's stock in Foreign Acquirer. To prevent US Corp from never having to recognize Foreign Sub's USD 20 of earnings and profits, the Section 367(b) Regulations require that US Corp recognize as dividend income the USD 20 of Foreign Sub's earnings and profits.[60] But note that US Corp would likely avoid taxation of that income by virtue of Section 245A.[61]

Guidance from the IRS about the continued role of Section 367(b) in policing Section 1248 would be helpful.

7.5 INVERSIONS

In a corporate inversion, a US corporation will seek to change its residency to avoid US tax. There are many ways to accomplish this. For example, as the first step in a plan to

59. Treas. Reg. Sec. 1.367(b)-4(b)(1)(i).
60. Treas. Reg. Sec. 1.367(b)-4(b)(1)(i) and 1.367(b)-4(b)(1)(iii) Ex. 1. Another set of rules applies to tax-free spin-off transactions that might otherwise be used to avoid Section 1248. *See* Treas. Reg. Sec. 1.367(b)-5.
61. *See supra* note 47, for a discussion of situations in which the Section 245A deduction may be reduced.

invert, stockholders in a US corporation might transfer their stock to a foreign corporation in exchange for the foreign corporation's stock.[62] The stockholder's exchange of stock in the US corporation for the foreign corporation would be taxable under Section 367(a) unless the requirements discussed in section 7.2.5 are satisfied. In addition, if the US corporation were subsequently liquidated into the acquiring foreign corporation, such liquidation would be taxable unless the exception for nonrecognition described in section 7.2.7 applies.

Another way to accomplish the inversion would be for the US corporation to merge into the foreign corporation or transfer all its assets to the foreign corporation with the stockholders of the US corporation receiving stock in the foreign corporation. In that situation, the US corporation would, in general, be taxed on any gain realized in the transfer of its assets.[63] In addition, the stockholders of the US corporation would be taxed on any gain realized in their exchange of stock in the US corporation for the foreign corporation unless the requirements for nonrecognition discussed in section 7.2.5 are satisfied.

The potential for gain recognition described above may not be a deterrent to implement an inversion, if the stock price in the US corporation is depressed and the US corporation has losses that could offset any gains recognized in the transaction. Section 7874, which was adopted in 2004, creates additional tax "costs" to discourage inversions.[64]

Section 7874 applies to "expatriated entities." An "expatriated entity" is, in general terms, a US corporation or partnership that transferred its assets to a foreign corporation that qualifies as a "surrogate foreign corporation."[65] Section 7874(a)(2)(B) defines a "surrogate foreign corporation" as a foreign corporation that:

(1) acquired substantially all the assets held by a US corporation or substantially all the properties constituting a trade or business of a US partnership;
(2) has at least 60% of its ownership interests held by former owners of the expatriated entity;[66] and

62. *See* Bruce N. Davis, 919-3RD TAX MANAGEMENT PORTFOLIO, *U.S.-to-Foreign Transfers Under Section 367(a)*, Sec. IV.C.3 for a discussion of the various ways in which an inversion might be implemented.
63. Treas. Reg. Sec. 1.367(a)-1(b)(1). *See* section 7.2.5 for a possible exception to gain recognition on the transfer of stock to a foreign corporation.
64. In a wave of inversions by publicly traded US corporations preceding the 2016 adoption of debt-equity regulations, which stopped further inversions, the most common transactional approach involved a transfer of stock in the US corporation in exchange for stock a foreign parent corporation. Corporate managements recommending these transactions accepted shareholder level gain taxation on the basis that many shareholders were tax-exempt in the US or were foreign shareholders not taxed on the gains. *See* Leonard E. Burman, Kimberly A. Clausing and Lydia Austin, *Is U.S. Corporate Income Double Taxed?* 70 NAT. TAX J. 675 (2017); Steven M. Rosenthal and Lydia S. Austin, *The Dwindling Taxable Share of U.S. Corporate Stock*, 151 TAX NOTES 923 (2016).
65. Sec. 7874(a)(2)(A).
66. The determination of the percentage of equity in the foreign surrogate corporation that carries over from the expatriated entity can become quite complex because stock owned by affiliates of the surrogate foreign corporation is in general disregarded. *See* Treas. Reg. Sec. 1.7874-1 for

(3) does not directly, or indirectly through its affiliates, have substantial business activities in the foreign country in which it is created or organized.

If, after the inversion, the former owners of the expatriated entity own at least 60%, but less than 80%, of the surrogate foreign corporation, then any income recognized by the expatriated entity in the inversion cannot be offset by its net operating losses or credits (other than foreign tax credits) for a ten-year period beginning at the time of the inversion.[67] This, in effect, postpones the ability of the expatriated entity to avoid recognizing any gains realized in the inversion by applying, for example, its net operating loss carryovers.

If the former owners of the expatriated entity own 80% or more of the surrogate foreign corporation, Section 7874(b) treats that foreign corporation as a US corporation for all US income tax purposes. This effectively eliminates any tax advantage that might have been obtained by the inversion.

There are additional tax disincentives for inversions. A director, officer, or 10% shareholder of an expatriated entity is liable for a 20% excise tax on the value of stock-based compensation held when the entity expatriated if any stockholders in the expatriated entity recognized gain in the inversion.[68] In addition, dividends paid by the surrogate foreign corporation are not eligible for classification as qualified dividends that are taxed at the preferential capital gains rate[69] unless the surrogate foreign corporation is treated as a US corporation under Section 7874(b).[70]

The 2017 Tax Act added two additional disincentives to inversions. If a surrogate foreign corporation engages in an inversion within ten years after the effective date of the 2017 Tax Act, and is not classified as a domestic corporation, any reduced effective rate of repatriation tax (discussed in Chapter 6 section 6.3.9) will be recaptured at a full 35% rate.[71] Finally, payments for costs of goods sold to a related surrogate foreign corporation (that is not classified as a domestic corporation) by a taxpayer subject to the BEAT (discussed at Chapter 5 section 5.10) will be classified as a base erosion payment if the inversion is after November 17, 2017.[72]

circumstances in which stock ownership by affiliates is included in the denominator, but not the numerator, of the fraction used to calculate the percentage ownership.

67. Sec. 7874(a)(1), (d)(1), and (e)(1).
68. Sec. 4985. More than one inverting US corporation "grossed-up" affected managers for this additional tax cost on their compensation. David I. Walker, *Another (Critical) Look at the Inversion Excise Tax*, 151 TAX NOTES 947 (2016).
69. *See* Chapter 2 section 2.3.2.2 for a discussion of qualified dividends.
70. Sec. 1(h)(11)(C)(iii).
71. Sec. 965(l).
72. Sec. 59A(d)(4).

CHAPTER 8

Foreign Investment Activities by US Persons Utilizing Foreign Corporations

8.1 BACKGROUND

The subpart F rules, although primarily focused on corporate investment in foreign business activities, also apply to investment income realized by foreign corporations controlled by 10% or more US shareholders, i.e., CFCs.[1] GILTI includes all other income of a CFC except for a 10% return on QBAI and except for high-taxed income. However, these provisions do not apply where the US shareholder's interest in the foreign company realizing passive income is less than 10%. In addition, the CFC rules generally do not reach foreign investment by US taxpayers where US control of the investment does not exist.

As a result, subpart F and GILTI do not limit the deferral of US investor-level tax available through investment in widely held foreign investment companies, for example, foreign mutual funds. Absent any special rules, the US investor's earnings could accumulate abroad free from US tax until distributed or realized indirectly through sale of the shares. Congress responded to this situation in 1986 by enacting the passive foreign investment company (PFIC) rules, which deal more directly with this

1. Treas. Reg. Sec. 1.954-2(a)(1); Chapter 6 section 6.3.4.1. This type of income was also covered by the foreign personal holding company provisions (former Sections 551-558) which were repealed in 2004 in order to simplify the regime dealing with closely held foreign investment companies. Those provisions, a predecessor of the subpart F regime, taxed the passive income of closely held foreign corporations with concentrated US individual ownership. They overlapped substantially with the subsequently enacted subpart F rules, though the shareholding and income requirements were somewhat different. As part of the repeal, one important category of income, personal services income from contracts involving the services of a principal shareholder, is now covered by the definition of foreign personal holding company income and taxed under subpart F. *See* Chapter 6 section 6.3.4.1.

problem.[2] While the rules are primarily directed at US investment in foreign mutual funds, their scope is much broader and they are potentially applicable to a wide range of situations.

PFIC status is sometimes an unintentional status that could be (or should be) avoided. Where it is not possible to avoid PFIC status because of the business model for the investment, e.g., an investment in a foreign mutual fund, it is important that US investors are aware of the PFIC status so as to take advantage of alternative tax regimes available to the US investor.

8.2 PASSIVE FOREIGN INVESTMENT COMPANIES

8.2.1 Definition of Passive Foreign Investment Company (PFIC)

Under Section 1297(a), a foreign corporation is a PFIC if: (1) 75% or more of its gross income is "passive"[3], *or* (2) 50% or more of the value of its assets (measured either in terms of fair market value or adjusted basis)[4] generate passive income. Unlike the subpart F rules, there are no minimum shareholder ownership requirements and no *de minimis* rules.[5] In applying the income and assets tests, there is a "look through" to the income and assets of any foreign corporation in which the potential PFIC owns 25% or more of the stock.[6] If the combined income and assets (disregarding the 25% stock interest as an asset and any dividends paid on the stock as income) do not meet the threshold tests, then the corporation will not be classified as a PFIC. The look-through rule protects most holding companies with operating subsidiaries from being classified as a PFIC.[7] Special rules provide an exception from PFIC status if the foreign corporation meets the tests only temporarily, as in a start-up or change of business situation where the concentration of passive income or assets is atypical.[8]

2. Former Section 1246, which had taxed gain on the sale of a foreign investment company's stock as ordinary income to the extent of the shareholder's share of accumulated earnings and profits, was essentially supplanted by the PFIC rules and was formally repealed in 2004.
3. Section 1297(b) defines "passive" by reference to the types of income classified as foreign personal holding company income in Section 954(c) (*see* Chapter 6 section 6.3.4.1) with certain modifications.
4. The determination of the 50% amount is based on the fair market value of the corporation's assets if the corporation is publicly traded. If the corporation is a controlled foreign corporation that is not publicly traded, the determination is based on the adjusted basis of the assets. For all other corporations, fair market value is used unless the corporation elects to use the adjusted basis of its assets. Sec. 1297(a)(2) and (e).
5. Section 1298(a) has a set of attribution rules that attribute PFIC stock to US shareholders through intervening entities.
6. Sec. 1297(c).
7. For an application of the look-through rule, *see* Rev. Rul. 87-90, 1987-1 C.B. 216. The look-through rule only affects the status of the top tier foreign holding company. If the subsidiary corporation, tested solely on the basis of its own income and assets, meets the PFIC tests it will be classified as a PFIC with the result that, under the attribution rules of Section 1297, the US shareholder will be treated as a shareholder in a PFIC. This is true even if the holding company is not itself a PFIC, e.g., because a sufficient amount of income and assets of other subsidiaries is not passive.
8. Sec. 1298(b)(2) and (3). These exceptions are narrow and of limited practical utility.

Once a corporation is classified as a PFIC while a US person is a shareholder in the corporation, it remains a PFIC for later years as to that shareholder, even if it does not meet the definitional tests in those years.[9] The US shareholder can purge stock of its PFIC "taint" by electing to realize gain on the PFIC shares as if they had been disposed of on the last day of the last year in which the corporation qualified as a PFIC, thus avoiding PFIC status for future years.[10] This "once a PFIC, always a PFIC" rule does not apply in the case of a qualified electing fund, discussed at section 8.2.3, if the US shareholder did not hold shares when the foreign corporation was a PFIC or made a purging election immediately before it became a qualified electing fund in the hands of the shareholder.

8.2.2 Imposition of an "Interest Charge" on US Shareholders

Unlike subpart F, the PFIC provisions do not tax the US persons holding stock in a PFIC currently on their share of PFIC income.[11] Rather, recognizing that the deferral of US tax on the PFIC income is in effect a loan from the US government to the shareholder in the amount of the deferred tax liability, the PFIC rules impose an interest charge on the deferred taxes.[12]

More technically, Section 1291 provides for the computation of a "deferred tax amount" when a PFIC makes an "excess distribution."[13] An "excess distribution" is the amount of any current distribution that exceeds the "normal" level of the PFIC's distributions.[14] This amount is treated as having been received *ratably* over the period that the US shareholder has held the stock and is taxed at the highest marginal rates applicable for those years. An interest charge (based on the interest rate applicable to income tax deficiencies) is then imposed on the amount of tax attributable to each year, with the amount of interest a function of the number of years between the year to which the distribution is allocated and the year of actual distribution.[15]

For example, assume that a PFIC earns a total of USD 500 over a five-year period during which it makes no dividend distributions. At the end of year five, the entire USD 500 is distributed. Since the corporation has made no distributions in the past, the entire USD 500 is an excess distribution. A ratable amount (USD 100) of the distribution is allocated to each of the five years involved (regardless of the years in which the income was actually earned). For the income allocated to year five, no special rules

9. Sec. 1298(b)(1).
10. *Id.*
11. Because the PFIC rules apply regardless of the level of US ownership, it was thought unfair to tax the US shareholders in the PFIC directly when they might have only a minority interest which could not influence distribution policy.
12. This interest charge technique is also used in connection with accumulation distributions from foreign trusts. *See* section 8.3.3.
13. Sec. 1291(a)(1), (b), and (c).
14. "Excess distribution" is defined in Section 1291(b)(1) and (2) as a distribution in excess of 125% of the corporation's average distributions for the past three years. Excess distributions from past years are not included in the 125% base.
15. Sec. 1291(c). The interest is measured from the due date of the tax return for the year to which the income is allocated to the due date for the year of actual distribution.

apply since that income is being taxed currently. However, for the USD 100 allocated to each of the preceding four years, a tentative tax is calculated based on the highest marginal rate of tax applicable to the taxpayer in each of those years. This tax for each year is then increased by an interest charge based on the length of time that the tax has been deferred. Thus, for the amount allocated to year one, the tax would be increased by four years of compound interest. The sum of the deferred taxes plus interest for each of the prior four years is added to the tax liability determined for the income allocated to year five.[16]

The same interest charge principles apply under Section 1291 to gain on the sale of stock in a PFIC.[17] Thus, if in the above example, the corporation had made no distributions and the taxpayer sold the PFIC stock in year five for USD 750 gain (the additional USD 250 of gain being attributable to unrealized appreciation in the PFIC assets), USD 150 (USD 750 divided by 5) would be allocated to year 5. The other USD 600 of the gain (that portion not allocated to year five) would be "thrown back" ratably to prior years and subject to tax at prior years' rates together with the interest charge.[18]

The IRS issued proposed regulations almost thirty years ago that address the sale of PFIC stock held by an intervening entity and attributed to a US person under the PFIC attribution rules. The proposed regulations would treat the sale by the entity of the PFIC stock as a sale by the US person.[19] This means, for example, if the regulations ever become final, then the sale by a foreign holding company of the stock of a subsidiary that qualified as a PFIC would be directly taxable to the US person holding stock in the holding company and would be subject to the interest charge.[20]

8.2.3 Qualified Electing Funds

The US person owning stock in the PFIC can elect to have the PFIC treated as a "qualified electing fund" ("QEF").[21] The QEF election can be made on a shareholder-by-shareholder basis, and the election by one US person holding stock does not affect any other shareholder.[22] For the election to be effective, the PFIC must agree to provide to electing shareholders the records necessary for the shareholders to establish their share of the PFIC's income, including its ordinary income and net capital gain for the year computed under US tax principles.[23] The effect of the election is that the electing

16. Sec. 1291(a)(1)(C).
17. Sec. 1291(a)(2).
18. As the example indicates, the interest charge can apply to gain attributable to unrealized appreciation in the PFIC assets and thus goes beyond simply imposing a deferral charge on realized but undistributed earnings.
19. Prop. Treas. Reg. 1.1291-3.
20. *Id.* Prop. Treas. Reg. Sec. 1.1291-2 would also treat distributions to the intervening entity as distributions made to the US person. For a critique of the proposed regulations, *see* KIMBERLY BLANCHARD, 6300 T.M. PFICS, para. V.B.4 (2020).
21. Sec. 1295(a).
22. Sec. 1295(a) and (b). The procedures for making the election are set forth in Treas. Reg. Sec. 1.1295-1.
23. Treas. Reg. Sec. 1.1295-1(g). The PFIC must provide an annual certification statement with this and other information and permission to inspect the PFIC's books. A foreign corporation may

shareholders must include in income currently their share of the PFIC's ordinary income and capital gain.[24] Because the current inclusion eliminates the deferral advantage, later distributions by the QEF are not subject to the interest charge rules of Section 1291.[25] In addition, gain on the disposition the PFIC stock is exempted from Section 1291 if the PFIC has been a QEF at all times the electing shareholder held stock in the QEF.[26] The gain is simply taxed at the shareholder's current rates and no interest charge is imposed. The shareholder in a qualified electing fund can elect to defer tax liability on undistributed PFIC income (with interest) until a distribution is actually made and he has cash to pay the tax.[27]

8.2.4 Mark-to-Market Election

As mentioned in section 8.2.3, in order for a shareholder to make a valid QEF election, the PFIC must agree to provide information to the electing shareholders about their share of PFIC income. Because it might be difficult for a shareholder to persuade a PFIC to agree to provide such information,[28] Congress adopted an alternative to the QEF election. Under Section 1296, a US person holding stock in a PFIC may avoid the rules of Section 1291 by making an election to mark her PFIC stock to market at the close of each taxable year. The election is available only with respect to stock that is "marketable," generally stock that is regularly traded on a national securities exchange or stock of a mutual fund that is always redeemable at its net asset value. An electing shareholder recognizes gain or loss equal to the differences between her adjusted basis in the PFIC stock at the beginning of the taxable year and its fair market value at the end of the taxable year. The deductibility of a mark-to-market loss in a stock is limited to any mark-to-market gains realized by the shareholder in prior years with respect to the same stock.[29] The shareholder's adjusted basis in the PFIC stock is adjusted upward or downward to reflect included gain or deducted losses resulting from the election.[30]

---

decline to provide this information if it does not seek US investors, in which case the QEF election is unavailable to the taxpayer.

24. Sec. 1293(a).
25. Section 1293(d) allows the shareholder to increase her basis in the PFIC shares by the amount of the inclusion and, under Section 1293(c), distributions of previously taxed income are tax-free (with a corresponding reduction in basis).
26. Sec. 1291(d)(1). The requirement that the PFIC have been a QEF at all times the shareholder held stock in the PFIC often prompts taxpayers to make a "protective" QEF election at the time they become a shareholder in the entity even though they are uncertain about whether the entity is, or will become, a PFIC. The procedure for such a protective election is in Treas. Reg. Sec. 1.1295-3.
27. Secs. 1294(a), (g), and 6601. Unlike taxation under Section 1291, the qualified electing fund inclusion is taxed at the actual rates applicable to the taxpayer instead of the highest marginal rate.
28. Staff of Joint Comm. on Taxation, 105th Cong., 1st Sess., GENERAL EXPLANATION OF TAX LEGISLATION in 1997, p. 309 (1997).
29. Sec. 1296(a)(2) and 1296(d).
30. Sec. 1296(b). PFIC stock acquired from a decedent who made the Section 1296 election is not eligible for the step-up in basis under Section 1014. Sec. 1296(i).

Gains or losses realized pursuant to the election are ordinary rather than capital and are sourced in the same manner as if the PFIC stock had been sold.[31]

8.2.5 Relation Between PFIC and Subpart F

A "US shareholder" with stock in a CFC that is also a PFIC is taxed only under subpart F.[32] However, a US person holding less than 10% (by vote or value) in the same corporation remains subject to the PFIC regime.[33] Proposed regulations exempt from the interest charge regime of the PFIC rules distributions of income previously taxed under subpart F or the qualified electing fund rules.[34]

8.3 INVESTMENT THROUGH FOREIGN TRUSTS

8.3.1 Background

In most respects, the basic rules governing taxation of US trusts apply to foreign trusts.[35] Special rules apply, however, to prevent avoidance or deferral of US tax through the use of foreign trusts where US persons are involved.

8.3.2 Foreign Grantor Trusts

Section 679 subjects to the grantor trust rules a US grantor who transfers property to a foreign trust that has a US beneficiary. As a result, the US grantor will be taxed currently on all income earned by the trust, whether distributed or accumulated, that is attributable to the property that the grantor transferred to the trust.

Section 679 applies to all grantors who are US "persons," thus including individuals, corporations, partnerships, trusts, and estates. The section does not apply to: (1) testamentary transfers or (2) property transferred to the trust in a sale or exchange where the transferor receives full fair market value consideration for the property transferred.[36]

A special rule provides that if a nonresident alien transfers property to a foreign trust and, within five years thereafter, becomes a US resident, the individual is treated as having created a grantor trust on the residency starting date and therefore is subject to the rules of Section 679.[37] Conversely, if a US individual creates a US trust which

31. Sec. 1296(c).
32. Secs. 951(c) and 1297(d).
33. Section 951(b) was amended in the 2017 Tax Act to expand the US shareholder definition to include a value text. Prior to the amendment, the definition was based only on voting power.
34. *See* Prop. Treas. Reg. Sec. 1.1291-2(b)(2) (1992).
35. *See* Chapter 2 section 2.4 and Chapter 5 section 5.8.
36. Sec. 679(a)(2)(B). Section 679(a)(3) provides that any note issued for the property by the trust, the grantor, a beneficiary, or any person related to the grantor or beneficiary is disregarded in determining the amount of consideration paid for the transferred property.
37. Sec. 679(a)(4).

then becomes a foreign trust, the individual is treated as having created a foreign grantor trust on the date the trust became a foreign trust.[38]

Section 679 covers indirect as well as direct transfers by US persons. Thus, if a US individual transfers property to a foreign entity which in turn transfers property to a trust with a US beneficiary, the US individual will generally be treated as the grantor of the trust under Section 679.[39]

A foreign trust is treated as having a US beneficiary unless: (1) under the terms of the trust no part of the trust income can be paid to or accumulated for the benefit of a US person,[40] and (2) if the trust were to terminate during the taxable year, no part of the income or corpus of the trust could be paid to or for the benefit of a US person.[41] Attribution rules are applied so that a US beneficiary is present if amounts are paid to or accumulated for the benefit of a controlled foreign corporation, a foreign partnership with a US partner, or another foreign trust with a US beneficiary.[42]

At the time a US person transfers property to a foreign trust it may have no US beneficiary. However, if a US person subsequently becomes a beneficiary of the trust, Section 679 is triggered. In such a case, the US grantor is then treated as the owner of a trust and is taxable on the income attributable to the property originally transferred. Moreover, the trust may have accumulated income which would be taxable to the new US beneficiary if distributed. The grantor must include this accumulated income (attributable to the property he transferred) in her own income in the taxable year a US person becomes a beneficiary, unless the trust distributed all accumulated income before the end of the prior taxable year.[43]

8.3.3 Transfers to and Distributions from Non-grantor Trusts

Section 684 requires that a US person transferring appreciated assets to a foreign trust, which is not a grantor trust, recognize taxable gain. Similarly, gain must be recognized when a US trust converts to a foreign trust.[44] In addition, Section 668 imposes an interest charge on the tax deferral attributable to a foreign trust's accumulation of income. When a foreign trust that is not subject to the grantor trust rules distributes its accumulated income to a US person, interest is added to the tax payable by the distributee for the period the trust had accumulated such income. The total amount due cannot exceed the amount actually distributed by the trust to the beneficiary.[45]

38. Sec. 679(a)(5).
39. Sec. 679(a)(1).
40. Sec. 679(c)(1)(A). Loans of cash or marketable securities to US persons for which a market rate of interest is not charged are treated as payments or accumulations for the benefit of US persons. Sec. 679(c)(6).
41. Sec. 679(c)(1)(B).
42. Sec. 679(c)(2). A beneficiary who became a US person more than five years after the initial transfer in trust is not a US beneficiary. Sec. 679(c)(3).
43. Sec. 679(b).
44. Sec. 684(c).
45. Sec. 668(b).

8.3.4 Procedural Aspects

Compliance with US rules regarding investment and doing business through foreign entities is generally enforced through the filing of information returns. Thus, any US person who controls (50%) a foreign corporation or a foreign partnership must file an annual return which includes information concerning the income and ownership composition of the foreign business entity.[46] Notices and returns must also be filed by any US person who transfers property to a foreign partnership or to a foreign corporation in a transaction discussed in Chapter 7 section 7.1 (such as a corporate reorganization) and by any US person who is an officer, director, or 10% shareholder of a foreign corporation or is a partner in a foreign partnership involved in such transactions.[47] US persons must also report their transfers to foreign trusts[48] and are also required to disclose their interests in all foreign assets (including foreign trusts) if the taxpayer has interests in such assets that in the aggregate exceed USD 50,000.[49] Penalties are imposed for failure to file the various information returns at the time and in the manner prescribed.[50] The US Foreign Account Tax Compliance Act ("FATCA") also requires certain foreign financial institutions, including foreign banks and foreign investment funds, to disclose information regarding accounts and investments held or owned by US citizens and residents.[51]

46. Sec. 6038.
47. Secs. 6038B, 6046, and 6046A.
48. Sec. 6048.
49. Sec. 6038D(a).
50. Secs. 6652, 6677, and 6679.
51. Pub. L. No. 111-147, 124 Stat. 71 (2010). *See* Chapter 5 section 5.11 for a discussion of FATCA.

CHAPTER 9

Taxation of Foreign Source Income of US Persons: The Foreign Tax Credit

9.1 GENERAL

Despite the increasing number of provisions in the US tax law that exempt some of the foreign income of US taxpayers,[1] two fundamental sets of rules are needed to govern taxation of US taxpayers on foreign taxable income from investing or doing business abroad. The first is the foreign tax credit mechanism, discussed in this and the next chapter, which allows US taxpayers a credit against their US income tax liability for foreign income taxes paid on income from foreign sources. The second set is the transfer pricing provisions, which are intended to allocate properly income and deductions between related parties. These rules are discussed in Chapter 12. In addition, there are a number of special provisions that are applicable to the foreign income or foreign activities of US taxpayers, including the limited exemption of dividends paid to 10% domestic corporate shareholders, GILTI and export income for corporate US shareholders and the limited exemption of foreign earned income of US individuals living abroad. These special rules are discussed in Chapters 7 and 11.

9.2 TREATMENT OF FOREIGN TAXES IN GENERAL

US citizens, resident aliens, and domestic corporations who pay income taxes to foreign countries may elect annually either:

1. The new 100% dividends received deduction for foreign dividends in the hands of a 10% domestic corporate shareholder (Chapter 6 section 6.5) and the partial deductions against foreign global intangible low-taxed income (so-called GILTI) (Chapter 6 section 6.4) and foreign-derived intangible income (FDII) (Chapter 11 section 11.2.2) passed in the 2017 Tax Act, as well as the longstanding foreign earned income exclusion (Chapter 11 section 11.2.3.1), represent exceptions (in increasing number) to taxing worldwide income in full.

(1) to deduct those taxes from income as prescribed by Section 164(a);[2] or
(2) to claim foreign income taxes paid or accrued as a credit against US income taxes[3] as allowed under Sections 901-909 and 960.

If the taxpayer elects to utilize the foreign tax credit as to *any* foreign income tax, no foreign *income* tax may be deducted under Section 164. However, the deductibility of all other types of taxes described therein is not affected by the election. Generally speaking, it is to the taxpayer's advantage to elect the foreign tax credit rather than the deduction. The credit produces a dollar-for-dollar offset against US tax liability; the benefit of a deduction is limited to the amount of the foreign income taxes multiplied by the taxpayer's marginal US tax on the income (i.e., generally a maximum reduction for a corporation of 21 cents in US tax for each dollar of foreign tax paid).

9.3 OBJECTIVES OF THE FOREIGN TAX CREDIT

Detailed rules are provided in the Code and Regulations to implement the foreign tax credit mechanism.[4] In considering those rules, it is important to keep in mind the functions that the foreign tax credit plays in the US international tax system.

Given the fact that the US taxes most foreign source income of its tax residents, some recognition must be given to the existence of foreign taxes that are also imposed on that income by foreign countries. Otherwise two interrelated results will follow: (1) a US taxpayer with foreign source income will bear a total tax burden greater than that of a taxpayer with the same income from the US, and (2), foreign investment will be less attractive for a US taxpayer than domestic investment because of the excess burden. The first point is essentially a question of neutral treatment of US taxpayers regardless of the source of their income. It starts from the premise that foreign taxes are the equivalent of US taxes for comparison purposes. The second is a question of the attitude to be adopted regarding the impact that the tax system should have on investment location decisions.

As to the first point, the historic US view has been that neutrality is achieved among US taxpayers if the foreign taxes they pay on foreign source taxable income are treated as equivalent to US taxes they pay on a similar amount of US source taxable

2. Sec. 164(a). US citizens and resident aliens may only deduct foreign taxes incurred in a trade or business. They cannot deduct foreign taxes incurred in a profit-seeking activity that does not rise to the level of a trade or business. Secs. 164(a) and 67(g). (*See* Chapter 2 section 2.3.2.4.) In addition to foreign income taxes, Section 164 also allows deductions for foreign real property taxes and any other foreign taxes incurred. But, again, such expenses must be incurred by individuals in a trade or business. *Id.*
3. Section 901 (by cross-reference to Section 26(b)) precludes utilization of the foreign tax credit to offset certain special US penalty taxes such as, for example, the accumulated earnings tax and the personal holding company tax. The alternative minimum tax is included in the Section 26(b) list of taxes for which the Section 901 credit cannot provide offset. But a separate, modified foreign tax credit applies in calculating the alternative minimum tax. Secs. 55(b)(1)(A) and 59(a).
4. The discussion of the foreign tax credit is necessarily brief and is intended to provide a general outline of the structure and operation of the credit.

income.[5] The foreign tax liability replaces all or a portion of the US tax liability on the foreign source taxable income (i.e., the US tax bill is credited with the amount of foreign income tax paid). Payment of tax directly to the US on that foreign source income is required only to the extent that the US tax due on the foreign source taxable income exceeds the income tax paid to the foreign jurisdiction on the foreign source income. Thus, rough equality of treatment is assured.

Suppose, however, that the foreign taxes exceed the US taxes that would be applicable on the same amount of income. Here, the taxpayer with income from abroad bears a higher tax burden than a US taxpayer with the same amount of income from US sources. Why? Because US tax law limits the credit to the amount of US tax liability on the foreign source taxable income. The additional foreign income tax paid is not allowed to offset US source taxable income (if it were, it would be offsetting US tax due on other income—either US or foreign source—which itself bore no, or little, foreign income tax). This result simply reflects the fact that the foreign effective tax rate is higher than that selected by the US for the taxation of the income (whether domestic or foreign), earned by its tax residents. In such a case, the US is treating its taxpayers equally when viewed from the perspective of the general level of US taxation. Put another way, there is no *international* double taxation as long as the US recognizes the foreign tax liability up to the level of US taxation of the foreign income.

However, when considered from the perspective of the second point, the impact of total tax burden on foreign investment decisions, failure to credit (or refund) foreign taxes when they exceed the level of US taxation (or as a result of a "haircut" on foreign income taxes allowed to be credited) results in an additional tax burden on foreign investment by a US taxpayer when compared with purely domestic investment. A policy of tax neutrality (specifically capital export neutrality[6]) with respect to investment decisions would require a full crediting of foreign taxes without regard to their level in comparison with US domestic taxation. As will be seen, this result is not achieved by the US foreign tax credit mechanism.

The foreign tax credit method of dealing with the existence of a foreign tax liability can of course be contrasted with the exemption system used by many European countries.[7] Under the exemption system, exempting the foreign source income from domestic taxation recognizes the possibility of a foreign tax liability. As a result, international double taxation is by definition avoided, but at the price of losing: (1) equality of treatment of domestic taxpayers regardless of the source of their income when viewed from the perspective of the domestic system, and (2) tax neutrality with respect to foreign versus domestic investment decisions by domestic investors (up to

5. This neutrality view has suffered erosion as evidenced by the provisions described in *supra* note 1, and the 20% "haircut" for the foreign tax credit applied to foreign taxes attributable to GILTI, which is discussed in section 9.5.1, below.
6. Capital export neutrality is discussed in Chapter 6 section 6.2.
7. Similar principles apply in the US with respect to dividends from US-owned foreign corporations eligible for the foreign dividends received deduction in Section 245A.

the limitation on credits for foreign income taxes).[8] Countries that have utilized the exemption method have insured that the foreign operations of their domestic taxpayers will not bear any other tax burden than that imposed by the country of foreign operation. Exemption system countries see this benefit (capital import neutrality) as outweighing the equity of taxing all income the same regardless of source and capital export neutrality factors. The distinction between the two systems can be overstated, however. If a US taxpayer is denied some foreign tax credits because the foreign taxes paid exceed the US limitation, then as to foreign taxes paid in excess of the limit, the US taxpayer is in the same economic position as if the US were an exemption country. For example, if a US taxpayer pays USD 1,000 of foreign tax on USD 4,000 of foreign income and the US tax on that income is USD 800, the extra USD 200 of tax paid to the foreign country is the same amount that would be incurred by the taxpayer if the US were an exemption country. The taxpayer is paying no US tax on the income and bears the higher foreign rate.

The post-TCJA hybrid system of partial exemption and partial current taxation (at lower effective US rate) with a foreign tax credit is unlikely to end ongoing discussion regarding the appropriate treatment of foreign source income earned by resident taxpayers, particularly multinational corporations. Some will continue to advocate for a stronger move in the direction of territoriality and an exemption system—based on the view that this is the direction pursued by most countries and will be necessary to make US businesses competitive and to make the US an attractive jurisdiction for headquarters. A contrary view questions what is meant by "competitiveness" for US-based multinationals, and questions whether a stronger exemption approach would be best for the country overall. Instead, a tighter regime of worldwide taxation with appropriate foreign tax credits, likely will be urged as a more sensible approach in the face of continued tax planning and lower income taxes paid by many multinationals.[9]

The above discussion illustrates that no mechanism has been developed to deal with the problem of overlapping tax jurisdiction that accommodates all of the policy considerations discussed (including equity across different kinds of domestic taxpayers, neutrality regarding the decision between foreign and domestic investment, sacrifice of tax revenue beyond that necessary to prevent double taxation). Therefore, many countries including the US provide other mechanisms (either directly or through the tax system) to achieve the objectives that cannot be realized through their basic structural mechanism for dealing with the problem of multiple jurisdictions taxing the same income.[10]

---

8. In addition, if a foreign exemption system does not disallow expenses incurred to earn the exempt foreign income, the effective foreign rate of tax is reduced. The value of the deduction in the residence country in effect subsidizes the foreign investment.
9. For discussion of these issues, *see* CONGRESSIONAL BUDGET OFFICE, TAXING U.S. MULTINATIONAL CORPORATIONS (January 2013); Edward Kleinbard, *Stateless Income*, 11 FL. TAX REV. 699 (2011).
10. For discussions of the issues, *see* AMERICAN LAW INSTITUTE, INTERNATIONAL ASPECTS OF UNITED STATES INCOME TAXATION (1987). *See also* Jane Gravelle, Congressional Research Service Report R40623, "Tax Havens: International Tax Avoidance" (Jan. 23, 2013) and Jane Gravelle, Congressional Research Service Report RL34115, "Reform of U.S. International Taxation: Alternatives" (Dec. 17, 2010); OECD, TAX CHALLENGES ARISING FROM DIGITALIZATION—REPORT ON PILLAR TWO BLUEPRINT (2020).

9.4 THE DIRECT FOREIGN TAX CREDIT

9.4.1 Eligibility for Tax Credit

9.4.1.1 Persons Eligible

Section 901(b) describes the categories of taxpayers eligible for the credit. US citizens and domestic corporations generally may credit income taxes paid to any foreign country. Alien residents are also entitled to the credit for taxes paid to any foreign country.[11] As discussed in more detail in section 9.4.4, Section 906 allows a credit to nonresident alien individuals and foreign corporations for taxes paid to any foreign country or US possession with respect to income that is effectively connected with a US trade or business (*see* Chapter 5 sections 5.2 and 5.3). Any of the above categories of eligible taxpayers that are members of a partnership, beneficiaries of a trust, or shareholders of an S corporation may also claim as a credit their proportionate share of the qualifying foreign taxes paid by the partnership, trust, or corporation.[12]

9.4.1.2 Taxes Eligible

The credit for foreign taxes is limited to *income* taxes.[13] In general, the character of the foreign tax is determined by its similarity to the US income tax. After years of debate and controversy, detailed regulations were issued in 1983 that deal with the question of when a foreign tax qualifies as an income tax.[14] The determination whether a foreign tax qualifies as an income tax is a crucial part of the foreign tax credit mechanism. In general, Treas. Reg. Section 1.901-2 provides that a foreign levy is an income tax only if: (1) the levy is a "tax," and (2) the "predominant character" of the tax is that of an

11. Section 901(c) authorizes the President by Presidential proclamation to disallow the foreign tax credit to resident aliens who are citizens of a foreign country that does not allow US citizens resident therein a similar credit for taxes paid to the US or other countries. Before the President can take such an action, he must make findings that: (1) the foreign country involved does not allow US citizens a credit similar to the US foreign tax credit, (2) the US has made a request to the foreign country to provide a tax credit to US citizens who are residing in it, and (3) it is in the public interest of the US to allow a foreign tax credit to citizens of the foreign country who are US residents only if the foreign country grants a similar credit to US citizens who are residents of the foreign country.
12. No foreign tax credit is allowed to individual investors in a US entity that is taxed as a C corporation under US rules (*see* Chapter 2 section 2.2 for a description of the US corporate income tax). Treas. Reg. Sec. 1.901-2(f)(1); *see also* Rev Rul. 72-197, 1972-1 C.B. 215 (same result even though the entity may be a valid partnership or trust under foreign law).
13. Technically the credit extends to war profits and excess profit taxes as well but in practice it is the income tax aspect of the credit that is important. The theoretical justification for limiting the credit to income taxes is that such taxes in general are not economically passed on by the US taxpayer in the form of higher prices and thus, with respect to those taxes, true economic double taxation has occurred. Rather than examining each situation to determine if in fact the tax has been passed on, the statute assumes that all (and only) income taxes are borne by the US taxpayer and are thus eligible for the credit. For a discussion of these issues, *see* AMERICAN LAW INSTITUTE, AMERICAN LAW INSTITUTE, INTERNATIONAL ASPECTS OF UNITED STATES INCOME TAXATION 308 (1987).
14. *See* T.D. 7918, 48 Fed. Reg. 46295, Oct. 12, 1983.

income tax in the US sense of the term.[15] A levy is not a tax if the person paying it receives a specific economic benefit from the foreign country as a result of paying the levy.[16]

Moreover, a payment is not a "tax" if that payment is "voluntary." To avoid classification as a voluntary (and thus nontax) payment, taxpayers must exhaust their plausible means to reduce the tax due.[17] In *Procter & Gamble Co. v. U.S.*, 2010 WL 2925099 (SD Ohio 2010), the taxpayer did not pursue whether Japan would in fact reduce the taxes that it had levied on income that Korea had taxed as Korean source. As a result, the court denied the foreign tax credit on the grounds that it was not a tax.[18] In determining which steps to take (and not take) to reduce a foreign levy, a taxpayer may generally rely on advice obtained in good faith from competent foreign tax advisors with full possession of the relevant facts.[19] Final regulations issued in 2011 as part of an effort to combat abusive foreign tax credit transactions provide that taxes paid in the context of a "structured passive investment" are deemed "noncompulsory" payments and thus fail the definition of a creditable tax under Treas. Reg. Section 1.901-2(e)(5)(iv). Determined under a six factor test, "structured passive investment arrangements" are those that enable both the US party and the foreign counterparty to claim a tax benefit (a credit claimed by the US party and a credit, deduction, loss, exemption or other benefit claim by the counterparty).

15. In *PPL Corp. v. Commissioner*, 569 U.S. 329 (2013), the US Supreme Court unanimously concluded that a "U.K. windfall tax" (imposed on previously privatized utility enterprises) was a creditable foreign tax under Section 901. The decision sought to apply the "predominant character test" by employing "a commonsense approach that considers the substantive effect of the tax" on most persons subject to the tax. The UK's characterization was not dispositive. Rather, the decision focused on whether the tax would be an income, war profits or excess profits tax under US tax principles.
16. *See, e.g., Phillips Petroleum Co. v. Commissioner*, 104 TC 256 (1995) (Norwegian tax imposed only on oil producers not for a specific economic benefit). A taxpayer who is subject to a levy which is in part a tax and who also receives a specific economic benefit for part of the levy is a "dual capacity taxpayer." The amount of the creditable portion of the levy for such taxpayer is determined by rules set forth in Treas. Reg. Sec. 1.901-2A. *See Exxon Corp. v. C.I.R.* 113 T.C. 338 (1999), acq. 2001-31 IRB 90 (2001) (treating U.K. North Sea oil taxes as wholly creditable under "facts and circumstances" exception to dual capacity taxpayer rule). In addition, Treas. Reg. Sec. 1.901-2(a)(3) provides that a foreign tax is not creditable if liability for the tax is related to the availability of a credit for the tax against the income tax liability of another country. This provision is aimed at so-called soak up taxes that are imposed by some countries when payments are made to nonresidents operating from a foreign tax credit system country but not when made to other nonresidents. *See, e.g.*, Rev. Rul. 2003-8, 2003-1 C.B. 290 (Costa Rica).
17. Treas. Reg. Sec. 1.901-2(e)(5)(i).
18. Specifically, the District Court concluded that "P & G may not claim a U.S. foreign tax credit for both the Japanese and Korean payments of the same withholding tax on the same royalty income, at least to the extent that those taxes overlap. Given that the Yulchon law firm confirmed the legality of the Korean claims, these claims may be deemed compulsory payments under 26 C.F.R. § 1.901-2. However, the Japanese tax payments cannot be so deemed because P & G did not exhaust all practical and effective avenues of appeal in Japan after Korea lay claim to the same source of income." *Procter & Gamble Co. v. U.S.*, 2010 WL 2925099 (SD Ohio 2010).
19. *See Coca-Cola Company & Subsidiaries v. Commissioner* 149 T.C. 446 (2017) (taxpayer relied on counsel advice in determining whether to change royalty methodology).

A tax satisfies the "predominant character" test if it is likely to reach "net gain."[20] The regulations in turn provide that the net gain requirement is satisfied if the tax is imposed: (1) only on realized gains (although in some situations, such as taxation of imputed rent from home ownership,[21] the requirement is satisfied even though there has not been a realization of gain in the US sense of the term); (2) on no more than gross receipts (i.e., an artificial posted price will not satisfy this element of the test); and (3) on net income (by allowing appropriate recovery of significant costs and expenses incurred to produce the gross receipts).[22]

Under Section 901(i), a levy is not creditable if it is used to provide a subsidy to the taxpayer, a related person, or any party to the actual or a related transaction, if the subsidy is determined by reference either to the amount of the tax or the tax base.[23]

The results reached in the regulations may be changed by tax treaty.[24]

---

20. *See Texasgulf, Inc. v. Commissioner,* 172 F.3d 209 (2d Cir. 1999) (discussion of "net gain" requirement in holding Ontario Mining Tax to be a creditable tax).
21. Rev. Rul. 2002-16, 2002-1 C.B. 740, held that the Netherlands individual income tax was creditable under the US-Netherlands treaty, even though taxable income from savings and investments was determined by an imputed 4% rate of return.
22. The Tax Court has examined empirical data to determine whether amounts approximating significant expenses are recovered for most persons subject to a tax even if an important expense such as interest is not allowed. *Exxon Corp. v. C.I.R.* 113 T.C. 338 (1999), acq. 2001-31 IRB 90 (2001) *Texasgulf, Inc. v. Commissioner,* 172 F.3d 209 (2d Cir. 1999). The IRS has issued proposed regulations that would modify the 1983 regulations rules for determining when a foreign levy is an income tax by adding a "jurisdictional nexus requirement." Notice of Proposed Rulemaking, Guidance Related to the Foreign Tax Credit; Clarification of Foreign-Derived Intangible Income, 85 Fed. Reg. 72078, 72088 (Nov. 12, 2020). The jurisdictional nexus requirement would require a foreign tax to conform to established international norms, including reliance on the arm's length principle and basing taxing rights on the source of income or situs of property, as reflected in the Code and related guidance. Prop. Treas. Reg. Sec. 1.901-2(c). The intent of these rules is to restrict creditability for taxes that overreach jurisdictional boundaries as determined by US principles. The proposed rules also would conform the rules for credibility of foreign income tax conform more closely to the contours of the US income tax in a number of respects. Prop. Treas. Reg. Sec. 1.901-2(b). The proposal acknowledges that the proposed rules may be changed if the United States agrees to changes in jurisdictional taxing norms as part of the G20/OECD Inclusive Framework project on addressing tax challenges from digitalization.
23. There have been a number of cases involving subsidies granted by the Brazilian Government with respect to borrowings by Brazilians from foreign lenders. These cases provide further explication of the subsidy rule. *See, e.g., Nissho Iwai American Corp. v. Commissioner,* 89 TC 765 (1987) (Brazilian subsidy to borrower based on amount of withholding tax imposed on lender reduced taxes paid for foreign tax credit purposes); *Norwest Corporation v. Commissioner,* 69 F.3d 1404 (8th Cir. 1995) (US lender received interest from Brazilian borrowers which, in turn, received subsidies with respect to that interest; US lender entitled to foreign tax credit for withholding tax on the interest less the amount of the subsidy, the court rejecting the IRS view that none of the tax was creditable because of the subsidy); *PNC Fin. Servs. Group v. Commissioner,* 503 F.3d 119 (D.C. Court of Appeals 2007) (although the taxpayer US bank was entitled (as determined in prior litigation) to a foreign tax credit in a net loan transaction to the Brazilian Central Bank which paid withholding tax on bank's behalf, that credit should be reduced by the indirect subsidy). *Compare Foley v. Commissioner,* 87 TC 605 (1986) (direct incentive payments received under Berlin Promotion Law did not reduce taxes paid for foreign tax credit purposes); Rev. Rul. 86-134, 1986-2 C.B. 104 (the Netherlands investment incentives did not reduce taxes paid for foreign tax credit purposes when provided as direct grants but did reduce taxes paid when converted to an identical tax credit provision).
24. For example, the Technical Explanation to the US-Canadian Treaty states that the paragraph 1 of Article XXIV of the Convention "provides a credit for these specified taxes whether or not they

A "foreign country" includes any political subdivision thereof that levies and collects an income tax.[25]

9.4.2 In Lieu of Taxes

Section 903 also permits certain foreign taxes paid in lieu of an income tax to qualify for the credit under Section 901. A tax will be considered as imposed "in lieu of" an income tax if it is in substitution for, and not in addition to, an income tax otherwise generally imposed.[26] The provision's primary impact is to permit withholding taxes imposed by a foreign country on payments of dividends, interest, etc. to US recipients to be creditable against US tax.[27]

9.4.3 Time and Manner of Claiming Credit

Generally, the year in which a taxpayer is entitled to claim the credit is determined by its method of accounting, i.e., cash or accrual. Section 905(a), however, permits a taxpayer to claim the credit in the year the foreign taxes accrued regardless of the method of accounting employed. But, if the foreign tax ultimately determined differs from that claimed as a credit, appropriate adjustments must be made and, if the tax is accrued more than two years from the close of the taxable year to which it related, it only may be claimed as a credit when paid.[28]

---

qualify as creditable under Code section 901 or 903." *Treasury Department Technical Explanation of the Convention Between the United States of America and Canada With Respect to Taxes on Income and on Capital*, effective Jan. 1, 1985 (1980).

25. *See* Treas. Reg. Sec. 1.901-2(g)(2). A possession of the United States is a foreign country for this purpose.
26. Treas. Reg. Sec. 1.903-1 in effect exempts gross withholding taxes on interest, dividends, royalties, etc. from the requirement that the tax be imposed on net income. The Regulations give a number of examples of taxes meeting the "in lieu of" requirement.
27. The absence of standards has permitted the Section 903 credit to be manipulated to allow a foreign tax credit in questionable circumstances to extend economic relief to Puerto Rico. *See* Notice 2011-29, 2011-2 C.B. 663 (declining to contest creditability of Puerto Rico's excise tax under Section 903 pending further study); *see also* Martin A. Sullivan, *Economic Analysis: The Treasury Bailout of Puerto Rico*, TAX NOTES TODAY (Jan. 27, 2014) (describing back door bailout for Puerto Rico). Proposed regulations would modify regulations for determining when a foreign levy is in lieu of an income tax. The proposed regulations would tighten the requirement that the tax be in substitution for a generally applicable income tax and add a jurisdictional nexus requirement that corresponds to the proposed requirement for general income tax credibility described in *supra* note 22.
28. Section 905(c) requires adjustments if foreign taxes accrued in dollars are different in amount when paid (including in dollars if a de minimis threshold is exceeded). If accrued amounts are not paid on or before the date twenty-four months after the close of the taxable year to which such taxes relate they are treated as refunded on that date. If a foreign tax is accrued after that date, the tax only will be allowed as a credit when paid. Treas. Reg. Sec. 1.905-3(a). Treas. Reg. Section 1.905-3T(d)(2) and 4T, which preceded the 2017 Tax Act, provided procedures to be followed in situations in which adjustments are required to be made. Although these temporary regulations expired in 2010, the regulations have been reissued as proposed regulations. These proposed regulations clarify that required adjustments to foreign taxes of a controlled foreign

To be entitled to the foreign tax credit, the taxpayer must submit proof of: (1) the amount of its total foreign source income, (2) the amount of its income from each country and the taxes paid or accrued thereto for which a credit is being taken, and (3) any other information necessary to enable the Internal Revenue Service to verify and compute the credit.[29]

9.4.4 Nonresident Aliens and Foreign Corporations

The US subjects certain foreign source income to US tax (*see* Chapter 5 section 5.3.2.4 above). As noted earlier, one purpose of this provision is to prevent the US from becoming a tax haven as the result of the relaxation of its tax jurisdiction. However, the country of source and/or the country of domicile may also tax the foreign source income that is taxed by the US under its effectively connected concept. Consistent with the purpose of the foreign tax credit, therefore, Section 906 grants a foreign tax credit under Section 901 to nonresident aliens and foreign corporations for taxes paid or accrued to a foreign country or US possession with respect to that income. The limitations applicable to Section 901 likewise apply to the credit allowable under Section 906.

9.5 THE INDIRECT FOREIGN TAX CREDIT

9.5.1 Corporate US Shareholders

The discussion in section 9.4 concerned taxes paid directly by a US (or other qualifying) taxpayer to a foreign country. Section 960 treats foreign income taxes paid by a CFC as deemed paid by a corporate US shareholder of the CFC. As a result, the US corporation becomes entitled to a credit under Section 901 for the CFC's taxes thus deemed paid by it. This credit is commonly referred to as the "indirect" or "'deemed paid' credit" and the creditable foreign taxes as "deemed paid" taxes.[30]

The indirect credit addresses double taxation of a corporate US shareholder on subpart F income and GILTI inclusions from a CFC (*see* Chapter 6), except that only 80% of foreign taxes on GILTI are allowed as an indirect tax credit.[31] The US

corporation also require adjustments to its income and earnings and profits and inclusions under Sections 951 and 951A as well as to Section 78 dividends (discussed at section 9.5.1). Prop. Treas. Reg. 1.905-3(b)(2).

29. Treas. Reg. Sec. 1.905-2 and Rev. Rul. 67-308, 1967-2 C.B. 254 provide guidelines on the kind of evidence that a taxpayer should submit to substantiate a claimed foreign tax credit. Treas. Reg. Sec. 1.905-2(a)(2) and (b)(3) relax some aspects of the substantiation requirements. For a case in which the taxpayer failed to meet the substantiation requirements with respect to foreign withholding taxes, *see Norwest Corporation v. Commissioner,* TC Memo 1995-453.
30. As in the case of the direct credit, the discussion provides an outline of the structure and operation of the indirect foreign tax credit. The amount of the credit is subject to the foreign tax credit limitation described in Chapter 10.
31. Sec. 960(d)(1). The effect of the 20% haircut on GILTI deemed paid foreign tax credits is to require an effective foreign tax rate of at least 125% of the effective US rate on GILTI after the Section 250 deduction before the US tax is eliminated by the deemed paid tax on GILTI

shareholder must include the amount of the deemed paid foreign taxes in its income (the gross-up requirement of Section 78), including in the case of GILTI the 20% share of foreign taxes deemed paid but not allowed as a deemed paid credit.[32] Foreign taxes on residual earnings of a CFC eligible for the Section 245A DRD (after taking account of earnings taxed under subpart F and GILTI) are not allowed as a foreign tax credit.[33]

The Section 960 indirect credit in effect treats the corporate US shareholder as if the CFC had distributed earnings that included the tax due to the foreign country and the US parent had then paid the tax to the foreign country. In concept, CFC income currently included in the corporate US shareholder's income thus is treated comparably for foreign tax credit purposes as profits from direct foreign branch operations.

For example, assume US Corporation X owns all the stock of CFC Y and that CFC Y earns USD 100 of income, half of which is subpart F base company services income (*see* Chapter 6 section 6.3.4).[34] CFC Y pays foreign income taxes of USD 30 on the USD 100 of income, resulting in USD 70 of earnings and profits.[35] Since half of this USD 70 is subpart F income, US Corporation X includes USD 35 (1/2 of USD 70) in income.[36] In addition, Section 78 requires US Corporation X to include USD 15, which is the tax associated with that subpart F income (1/2 of USD 30) and for which an indirect credit will be allowed. In other words, as described above, US Corporation X is treated as though, CFC had distributed USD 50 of the subpart F earnings that included the foreign tax due on such earnings and then paid the foreign tax. US Corporation X is entitled to a foreign tax credit of 15 with respect to the subpart F inclusion.[37] At the end of the year, CFC Y assigns USD 35 representing its subpart F income to the relevant 2020 Previously Taxed Earnings and Profits ("PTEP") account.[38] Assignment to the PTEP

(assuming no foreign withholding tax and no US expenses allocated to GILTI). At the tax rates in effect following the passage of the TCJA, this hurdle rate was 13.125% (10.5% * 125% = 13.125%).

32. Sec. 78. Note that the portion of the Section 78 dividend relating to a GILTI inclusion is offset by a 50% Section 250 deduction.
33. Sec. 245A(d)(1). The prior law concerning the indirect foreign tax credit regime for relieving double taxation with respect to dividends from a foreign corporation (that were not from earnings effectively connected with a US trade or business) became unnecessary with the adoption of the Section 245A dividends received deduction. For tax years beginning before 2018, now repealed Section 902 provided that if a US corporation owned 10% or more of the voting stock of a foreign corporation from which it received a dividend, the US corporation was deemed to have paid the foreign income taxes paid by the subsidiary attributable to that dividend.
34. For simplicity, we will assume that all of the income earned by CFC Y is in the same limitation category or "basket."
35. In calculating the current earnings and profits of a CFC, the CFC's income is reduced by taxes associated with such income. BORIS BITTKER AND JAMES EUSTICE, FEDERAL INCOME TAXATION OF CORPORATIONS & SHAREHOLDERS, Par. 8.04 note 78 (Thompson Reuters 2020).
36. CFC Y's subpart F income is USD 35 (1/2 of 70) and not USD 50 (1/2 of 100), because subpart F income cannot exceed a CFC's "current earnings and profits" (*see* Chapter 6 section 6.3.4.1 note 52), as defined in Section 964(a). Sec. 952(c)(1)(A). CFC Y's current earnings and profits are the USD 100 or income less USD 30 of tax. As discussed in *supra* note 35, a corporation's income is reduced by tax liability associated with such income in calculating the corporation's earnings and profits.
37. Treas. Reg. Sec. 1.960-2(b).
38. Treas. Reg. Sec. 1.960-3(c) and (d). *See* Chapter 6 section 6.3.4.1.

account assures that the USD 35 of subpart F income will not be taxable to US Corporation X when actually distributed.[39]

As illustrated in the previous example, the amount of the indirect credit allowable to a corporate US shareholder is the portion of the CFC's current year foreign income taxes allocable to the subpart F inclusion or GILTI inclusion from the CFC.[40] The earnings attributable to current income inclusions that give rise to the indirect credit may be subject to additional foreign tax in a later year, including when these previously taxed earnings are actually distributed up a chain of CFCs. Section 960(b) provides an indirect credit to a US shareholder for its share of these additional foreign taxes.[41] In order to associate these foreign taxes with the appropriate categories of income, the regulations create an annual PTEP account by taxable year of a CFC and by foreign tax credit limitation category, each further subdivided into PTEP tax groups to track the myriad of circumstances in which the foreign tax may affect distinctly the US shareholder's tax liability.[42] At the US shareholder level, Section 960(c) increases the applicable foreign tax credit limitation in the year an excluded distribution of PTEP is received to the extent the US shareholder had excess limitation with respect to the original inclusion.[43]

The operation of the indirect credit where lower tier subsidiaries are involved is illustrated by the following example: Assume US Corporation A owns all the stock of Foreign Corporation B, which in turn owns all the stock of Foreign Corporation C. Corporation B is a holding company whose only asset is stock in Corporation C. Corporation C has net deemed tangible investment return of USD 50. In 2020, Corporation C had before tax earnings of USD 300 and paid foreign tax of USD 45 leaving earnings and profits of USD 255. Corporation A included in 2020 income a subpart F inclusion of USD 85, which represented USD 100 of Corporation C's pretax earnings less USD 15 of foreign tax, and a GILTI inclusion of USD 127.50 with respect to Corporation C.[44] Corporation C's foreign income tax is apportioned USD 15 to the subpart F Income group (100/300 * 45 = 15), USD 22.5 to the GILTI tested income group (150/300 * 45 = 22.5) and USD 7.5 to the residual income group (50/300 * 45 = 7.5).[45]

Corporation A has a Section 960 credit against US tax of USD 15 in respect of the subpart F inclusion from Corporation C, and of USD 18 in respect of the GILTI inclusion from Corporation C (determined by multiplying the USD 22.5 of GILTI taxes by 80% to reflect the 20% reduction in creditable GILTI taxes).[46] Correspondingly, Corporation A

39. Sec. 959(a).
40. Sec. 960(a); Treas. Reg. Sec. 1.960-2(b) and (c). Income of a CFC is grouped according to the relevant foreign tax credit limitation category, and the CFC's foreign taxes are associated with the relevant category. Treas. Reg. Secs. 1.960-1(d) and 1.904-6.
41. Sec. 960(b).
42. *See* Treas. Reg. Sec. 1.960-3(c).
43. Sec. 960(c).
44. For simplicity, it is assumed that all of Corporation C's income is in the same foreign tax credit limitation category and the foreign income tax base is the same as the US Federal income tax base. *See* Treas. Reg. Secs. 1.904-6 and 1.861-20.
45. Treas. Reg. Sec. 1.960-1(d)(3)(ii) and 1.960-2(b)(2).
46. Sec. 960(d)(1).

must include the deemed paid taxes of USD 37.5 (15 + 22.5 = 37.5) in income under Section 78.[47]

In 2021 Corporation C establishes an annual 2020 PTEP account and establishes a separate PTEP group for the USD 85 subpart F earnings and for the GILTI inclusion of USD 127.5.[48] In 2021 Corporation C paid a dividend of USD 100 to Corporation B which was subject to a withholding tax of USD 10. Corporation C's dividend to Corporation B is not taxed by Corporation B's country of residence and the dividend is excluded from Corporation B's gross income for US tax purposes because it is attributable to previously taxed earnings.[49] The dividend income is added to Corporation B's 2020 PTEP account corresponding to the PTEP account groups from which it derives and the USD 10 of withholding tax paid by Corporation B in 2021 is added to PTEP group taxes with respect to Corporation B's 2020 PTEP account groups.[50] Corporation C's 2020 annual PTEP account groups are correspondingly reduced by the dividend amount. When Corporation B pays a dividend, Corporation A will be deemed to pay its share of the Corporation B PTEP account group tax with respect to the PTEP account from which the dividend arises.[51]

The foreign taxes deemed paid under Section 960 are treated under Section 901 in the same manner as foreign taxes paid directly and are subject to the same limitations.

9.5.2 Individual US Shareholders

Individual US shareholders can obtain the benefits of the Section 960 credit by electing to be taxed at corporation rates on their income taxable under subpart F and GILTI.[52] The shareholder level tax on these amounts is deferred until subsequent distribution of the income, which is then taxable to the extent the distribution exceeds the amount of US tax paid by the individual on the subpart F income.[53] The Section 962 election generally was not useful under pre-TCJA corporate and individual tax rates. The allowance by regulation of the Section 250 deduction against GILTI for purposes of Section 962,[54] however, materially reduces the effective corporate tax rate with respect

47. Sec. 78. Note that 50% of the Section 78 dividend will be offset by a Section 250(a)(1)(B) deduction. The Corporation C foreign income tax attributable to the residual income group will not be allowed as a credit when the earnings are distributed. Sec. 245A(d); Treas. Reg. Sec. 1.960-1(e).
48. Treas. Reg. Sec. 1.960-3(c).
49. Sec. 959(b).
50. *See* Treas. Reg. Sec. 1.960-1(d)(3)(ii).
51. Sec. 960(b)(2).
52. Sec. 962.
53. Sec. 962(d). The Tax Court has rejected a claim that the subsequent distribution should be deemed from a domestic corporation and therefore eligible for treatment as qualified dividend income eligible for the lower tax rate on capital gain. *Smith v. Commissioner of Internal Revenue*, 151 T.C. No. 5 (2018). The *Smith* case did not involve a foreign corporation that would be a qualified foreign corporation whose dividends would be eligible for QDI classification under Section 1(h)(11)(B)(i)(II), though its analysis of the statute suggests that QDI might be available in such a case.
54. Treas. Reg. Sec. 1.962-1(b)(1)(i)(B)(3).

to a Section 962 election and, combined with the availability of the Section 960 indirect credit, means that a Section 962 election will be beneficial in a broader range of cases.

9.6 RESPONSES TO FOREIGN TAX CREDIT ABUSE

9.6.1 Dividend Sale Transactions

Prior to the 1997 Act, taxpayers engaged in a variety of transactions designed to transfer the benefit of the tax credit for foreign withholding taxes from a taxpayer that could not use the credit to one that could. A tax-exempt pension fund, for example, in effect could sell the credit to a taxable entity that was in an excess limit position and thus could benefit from the credit. In simplified form, just before the dividend record date of the stock in a non-US corporation, a US tax-exempt entity would sell its stock in the company to a US bank for an amount that reflected the expected dividend. The bank would receive the dividend and the tax credit for withholding foreign taxes imposed on the dividend by the foreign corporation's government. The tax-exempt organization would receive enough to compensate itself for losing the dividend and would repurchase the stock immediately after the dividend record date for the value of the foreign corporation's stock now reduced because of the declared dividend. The bank would then take a loss on the sale back to the tax-exempt entity. The combination of the loss plus the foreign tax credit insured a profit for the bank in a transaction for which there was no economic purpose other than being compensated for foreign tax credits on dividends that would not have carried a tax credit to the tax-exempt organization.

Congress responded to this obvious tax avoidance transaction (and others similarly designed) by enacting Section 901(k). Under that provision, a US taxpayer cannot claim a foreign tax credit for dividend withholding taxes unless it has held the stock for more than fifteen days during a thirty-one-day period that begins fifteen days before the dividend record date of the stock. (The holding periods are extended for preferred stock to more than forty-five days during a period of ninety-one days beginning forty-five days before the ex-dividend date.)[55] Similar rules apply to withholding taxes imposed on gains and non-dividend income (such as interest, rents, and royalties).[56] An exception for both sets of holding period rules applies to securities dealers who are actively engaged in trade or business in the foreign country if certain qualifying conditions are met.[57] Foreign taxes disallowed as a credit by Section 901(k) may be claimed as a deduction.

55. Sec. 901(k)(3). *See also* Notice 2004-19, 2004-1 C.B. 606, in which strategies to be employed by the Internal Revenue Service in combating abuse of the foreign tax credit rules are set forth; and Notice 2004-20, 2004-1 C.B. 608, describing a particular foreign tax credit transaction identified as abusive by the Internal Revenue Service.
56. Sec. 901(l), introduced in 2004.
57. Sec. 901(k)(4) and (l)(2).

Because the parties to transactions such as that described above typically were unwilling to take a real economic risk of loss, the holding period requirement appears to have been effective with respect to such transactions.[58]

9.6.2 Foreign Tax Credit Generator Transactions

Perhaps the most significant foreign tax credit reforms in recent years have attacked foreign tax credit "generator" transactions. Broadly described, such transactions are structured to manufacture foreign tax credits, but not the corresponding income, to the US taxpayer seeking to claim a foreign tax credit. Although the Service had been challenging a variety of these foreign tax credit transactions (including challenging them on the grounds that they lacked economic substance),[59] Congress stepped in with legislative reforms in 2010. These reforms include codifying the economic substance doctrine and adding provisions to the Code targeting transactions designed to split foreign tax credits from income subject to the foreign tax and to "hype" or increase the foreign tax imposed in relation to the relevant US tax base.[60]

9.6.3 Additional Anti-abuse Provisions

9.6.3.1 The Problem

Although abusive foreign tax credit transactions can be structured in a variety of ways, a common feature has been the use of a hybrid entity that is treated as a pass-through by the US and as a corporation by a foreign jurisdiction. The basic transaction at issue in the *Guardian Industries* case can serve as a useful example of the problem.

In *Guardian Industries Corp. & Subs. v. U.S.*,[61] a US corporation (part of a consolidated group) was the sole shareholder in a Luxembourg company, Guardian Industries Europe ("GIE"). The US shareholder treated GIE for tax purposes (pursuant

58. In a case involving a tax year prior to the enactment of Section 901(k), the court upheld a transaction similar to that described in the text (the entire transaction was completed in five days). *Compaq Computer Corp. v. Commissioner*, 277 F.3d 778 (5th Cir. 2002). The IRS asserted that the transaction had no business purpose other than obtaining tax benefits. *See also IES Indus., Inc. v. United States*, 253 F.3d 350, 356 (8th Cir. 2001).
59. The Service asserted the economic substance doctrine (as well as other judicial doctrines) successfully in a series of cases to challenge the availability of a foreign tax credit where the taxpayer has otherwise met the formal requirements of the statute and regulations. *See, e.g.*, *Wells Fargo & Co. v. United States*, 957 F.3d 840 (8th Cir. 2020) (denying refund for foreign tax credits in STARS transaction and upholding negligence penalty); *Santander Holdings USA, Inc. v. United States*, 844 F.3d 15, 26 (1st Cir. 2016), *cert. denied*, 137 S. Ct. 2295 (2017) (finding STARS transaction lacked substance and remanding); *Bank of N.Y. Mellon Corp.*, 801 F.3d 104 (2d Cir. 2015) *cert. denied*, 136 S. Ct. 1377 (2016) (upholding denial of tax credits and allowing deduction for interest paid); *Salem Fin., Inc. v. United States*, 786 F.3d 932, 951 (Fed. Cir. 2015), *cert. denied*, 136 S. Ct. 1366 (2016) (upholding denial of tax credits and accuracy penalty, allowing deduction for interest paid).
60. Secs. 7701(o), 909, and 901(m).
61. 477 F.3d 1368 (Fed. Cir. 2007).

to the check-the-box regulations[62]) as a disregarded entity.[63] However, GIE remained classified as a separate corporation for Luxembourg tax purposes. GIE served as the Luxembourg parent for several subsidiaries and in 2001 GIE paid Luxembourg income tax on behalf of itself and its subsidiaries. On an amended US tax return, the US shareholder claimed a Section 901 credit for the entire Luxembourg tax paid by GIE (i.e., by virtue of the hybrid status of the entity, which from a US tax perspective was the same entity as the US shareholder). The claimed credit included both the portion attributable to GIE's income and the portions attributable to the income of GIE's subsidiaries. The Service challenged the availability of a Section 901 credit on the grounds that GIE's subsidiaries were legally liable for their own share of income taxes (even though the taxes had been paid by GIE) and thus GIE was not the taxpayer, and not entitled to the credit. Relying on expert testimony regarding the operation of Luxembourg law, the court concluded that GIE and its subsidiaries were not jointly and severally liable for the taxes paid by GIE. Rather, under Luxembourg law, GIE was the taxpayer liable for the tax and thus, constituted the taxpayer entitled to the credit under Treas. Reg. Section 1.901-2(f)(1). This application of what is colloquially referred to as the "technical taxpayer rule," allowed the taxpayers to use the hybrid entity structure combined with Luxembourg law on consolidated groups, to keep the underlying income at the Luxembourg subsidiary level but have the credit available at the GIE level. Thus, the taxpayer achieved separation of the credit and the income—allowing the foreign tax credit to be brought onto the 2001 US return without the corresponding income.

9.6.3.2 Section 909 Foreign Tax Credit Splitter Rules and Technical Taxpayer Regulations

In 2006 Treasury and the Service issued proposed regulations under Section 901 to limit foreign credit planning based on hybrid entities and the technical taxpayer rule.[64] In 2010, Congress enacted Section 909, which tackled some of the same problems underlying 2006 proposed Section 901 Regulations, in part in response to the enactment of Section 909, and in part in response to comments received on the proposed regulations, Treasury and the Service finalized portions of the Treas. Reg. Section 1.901-2 technical taxpayer rules in 2012. In particular, the rules governing consolidated foreign groups (such as the *Guardian Industries* scenario) and similar regimes were

62. *See* Chapter 2 section 2.2.1 for a discussion of the check-the-box regulations.
63. The "check-the-box" regulations, Treas. Reg. Section 301.7701-2(a), permit a wholly owned foreign subsidiary to elect to be treated as a "disregarded" entity. If such an election is made, the US parent and the foreign subsidiary are treated as a single company for US tax purposes.
64. Prop. Treas. Reg. Sec. 1.901-2(f) and (h). The proposed regulations accepted the baseline principle that the taxpayer entitled to the credit is the one upon whom foreign law imposes legal liability. However, the proposed regulations further stated that foreign law is not considered to impose that legal liability unless the person is required to take the corresponding income into account under foreign law. Specific provisions addressed issues of joint and several liability, consolidated groups, hybrid entities, disregarded entities, and reverse hybrid entities.

among the portions finalized.[65] The main effect of these rules is to require that if the foreign tax is imposed on the combined income of two persons (e.g., a corporation and its subsidiaries), then "foreign law is considered to impose legal liability on each such person for the amount of the tax that is attributable to such person's portion of the base of the tax. Therefore, if foreign tax is imposed on the combined income of two or more persons, such tax is allocated among, and considered paid by, such persons on a pro rata basis in proportion to each person's portion of the combined income ... ."

Section 909 basically provides that if there is a "foreign tax credit splitting event" the foreign tax credit "shall not be taken into account ... before the taxable year in which the related income is taken into account" for US tax purposes by the taxpayer. Similar rules govern the availability of the foreign tax credit under Section 960 with respect to an indirect credit.[66]

What is a splitter event? Section 909(d)(1) provides a preliminary definition: "There is a foreign tax credit splitting event ... if the related income is (or will be) taken into account under this chapter by a covered person." Who is a covered person? A covered person, with respect to a person who pays or accrues the foreign tax, includes: (1) an entity in which the payer holds directly or indirectly 10% (vote or value), (2) any person which holds directly or indirectly, at least 10% (vote or value) in the payer, (3) certain other related parties or those specified by the Secretary of Treasury (Section 909(d)), and (4) thus, the key feature of a splitter is having the foreign tax paid or accrued by one person, and the income taken into account by certain kinds of related persons. Importantly, this definition of a splitter event does *not* apply to the case of a timing difference between US and foreign law (Section 909(d)(1)).

The temporary Section 909 Regulations specifically exclude "covered asset acquisitions" (which are discussed in section 9.6.4, below) from the list of foreign tax credit splitter arrangements.[67] "Covered asset acquisitions" are the subject of their own statutory rule also enacted in 2010 in Section 901(m) and therefore are not addressed within Section 909.[68]

9.6.4 Covered Asset Acquisition

The other important foreign tax credit legislation enacted in 2010 was the introduction of the covered asset acquisition rules in Section 901(m). This provision targets cases in which a transaction or election ("covered asset acquisitions") can generate additional basis for US tax purposes, but not create any corresponding increase in the basis of the

65. Treas. Reg. Sec. 1.901-2(f)(3)(i), (ii), and (iii). These rules are generally effective for tax years beginning after Feb. 14, 2012. Treas. Reg. Sec. 1.901-2(f)(3)(i). Some portions of the proposed regulations were not finalized. Specifically, the determination of the person who paid a foreign income tax with respect to the income of a reverse hybrid was covered by Section 909.
66. Sec. 909(b)(1).
67. Temporary Regulations issued in 2012 offer guidance on splitter events for the taxable years after 2010, including an exclusive list of splitter arrangements governed by the Regulations for pre-2011 tax years and post-2011 tax years. T.D. 9577, 77 Fed. Reg. 8127, 8131 (Jan. 14, 2012).
68. *See* T.D. 9577, 77 Fed. Reg. 8127, 8131 (Jan. 14, 2012) (preamble to the Section 909 regulations discussing the treatment of covered asset acquisitions).

asset under foreign tax law. In such cases, there could be foreign tax credits associated with foreign income that would itself not be subject to US tax because of the effect of increased US tax basis in the covered asset acquisition. For example, if a US taxpayer makes a Section 338 election (with a step-up in basis for US tax purposes) in connection with the purchase of stock of a foreign corporation, such a discrepancy in basis can be created.[69] Once the discrepancy is created, the foreign target will have higher income for foreign tax purposes in subsequent years than the US would acknowledge because the foreign target will have smaller depreciation deductions (again, assuming the underlying target assets are appreciated).

In this case, Section 901(m) disallows the "disqualified portion" of the foreign income tax paid or accrued with respect to this basis differential generated in a covered asset acquisition (such as a Section 338(g) election). Thus, to the extent the foreign income tax is higher due the difference in US basis and foreign basis, then that portion of the foreign tax is not permitted a credit under Section 901 or 960.[70]

---

69. The election under Section 338(g) treats the target corporation as if it sold and then repurchased its assets. The "repurchase" at fair market value gives the target an opportunity to increase the basis of all of its appreciated assets. The "price" for this basis increase is that fact that Section 338(g) elections require the target to report not just the "repurchase" but also the deemed sale. To the extent there are appreciated assets the target will have gain to report currently. Although the election has limited use in a domestic context, in the foreign context there are typically no consequences to reporting the "sale" by a target owned by a foreign seller. The foreign jurisdiction does not acknowledge the election and deemed sale, and the US generally has no jurisdiction to impose tax on the foreign target. (Where the target is a CFC and a seller is a US shareholder, the deemed sale gain can be subpart F income or GILTI.) Yet, the basis of assets inside the foreign target would be fair market value (i.e., in the "appreciated" scenario, stepped up) for all relevant US tax purposes.
70. Consider the example from STAFF OF THE JOINT COMM. ON TAX'N, 111 CONG., 2D SESS., TECHNICAL EXPLANATION OF THE REVENUE PROVISIONS OF HR 5982, "THE SMALL BUSINESS TAX RELIEF ACT OF 2010," 16 (JCX-43-10; July 30, 2010). The example:

> To illustrate, assume USP, a domestic corporation, acquires 100 percent of the stock of FT, a foreign target organized in Country F with a "u" functional currency, in a qualified stock purchase for which a section 338(g) election is made. The tax rate in Country F is 25 percent. Assume further that the aggregate basis difference in connection with the qualified stock purchase is 200u, including: (1) 150u that is attributable to Asset A, with a 15-year recovery period for U.S. tax purposes (10u of annual amortization); and (2) 50u that is attributable to Asset B, with a 5-year recovery period (10u of annual depreciation). In each of years 1 and 2, FT's taxable income is 100u for local tax purposes and FT pays foreign income tax of 25u (equal to $25 when translated at the average exchange rate for the year). As a result, the disqualified portion of foreign income tax in each of years 1 and 2 is $5 ((10u + 10u of allocable basis difference / 100u of foreign taxable income) x $25 foreign tax paid). In year 3, FT's taxable income is 140u, 40u of which is attributable to gain on the sale of Asset B. FT's Country F tax is 35u (equal to $35 translated at the average exchange rate for the year). Accordingly, the disqualified portion of its foreign income taxes paid is $10 ((40u (including 10u of annual amortization on Asset A and 30u attributable to disposition of Asset B) of allocable basis difference / 140u of foreign taxable income) x $35 foreign tax paid).

CHAPTER 10

Limitations on the Foreign Tax Credit

10.1 HISTORICAL BACKGROUND

10.1.1 Limitations on the Foreign Tax Credit: Introduction of Baskets

The foreign tax credit almost from its inception has been subject to a limitation on the amount of the credit available to offset US taxes. While the forms of the limitation have varied, the basic purpose of the limitation has always been to prevent the crediting of foreign taxes against the US tax on income from US sources.[1] As a result, foreign source income in a limitation category will be subject to the higher of the effective US or foreign tax rates. Prior to the Tax Reform Act of 1986, the foreign tax credit limitations did not attempt to allocate the actual foreign taxes paid to specific items or classes ("baskets") of income, and then limit the credit to the amount of the US tax on that

1. To appreciate the problem, consider a simple example. Assume the US corporate tax rate is 21% and the foreign corporate tax rate is 30%. If a US corporation earns USD 100 in the US and USD 100 in the foreign jurisdiction, the preliminary US tax due is USD 42 (USD 21 on the USD 100 of US income and USD 21 on the USD 100 of foreign source income). If the US corporation seeks a credit in the US against the foreign tax of USD 30 paid abroad, what would be the effect of granting that foreign tax credit without limitation? The first USD 21 of the USD 30 of foreign tax credit effectively would offset the US tax imposed on the USD 100 of foreign source income. However, the remaining USD 9 of credit would then be reducing the US tax of USD 21 on the USD 100 of *US source income*. This result is considered inappropriate because there is no reason for the US to give up any taxing jurisdiction on US source income. The only obligation as a residence country is to prevent double taxation on foreign source income.

   A related problem occurs when the US corporation earns USD 100 in foreign country Y with a tax rate of 50% and earns USD 100 in foreign country Z with a tax rate of 0%. Fully allowing the foreign tax credits against the US tax imposed on the US corporation's worldwide income of USD 200 would have the effect of allowing the County Y tax to reduce the US tax "imposed" on the Country Z income. Again, there is no reason in that scenario for the US to yield tax jurisdiction. There is no double taxation on the Country Z income so the full US tax should be imposed without reduction. The foreign tax credit limitation (as designed and implemented in various ways over the years) is an effort to prevent the US from surrendering taxing jurisdiction in cases in which elimination of double taxation is not a concern.

income. Rather, the US adopted an approach which in general limited the credit for foreign taxes paid to a portion of the total US tax liability determined by the relation between foreign source income (either on a global basis or an individual country basis) and total income. That system was significantly changed by the 1986 Act. It is helpful to review briefly changes in the US foreign tax credit system over time to understand the reasons behind different limitation regimes and their evolution through the 2017 Tax Act.

Prior to the Tax Reform Act of 1976, a taxpayer could elect to compute the limitation on its foreign tax credit either on a country-by-country basis (the per-country limitation) or by aggregating all taxes paid to all foreign countries (the overall limitation). Generally, taxpayers with losses in some countries and profits in others chose the per-country method because the losses did not prevent the crediting of taxes paid in the profit countries (under the law at the time). However, the overall method was preferable for taxpayers operating at a profit in different countries, some with rates of tax higher than the US and some with rates lower. The overall method allowed the taxpayer to average the high- and low-rate countries and thus utilize currently the excess credits from the higher rate countries.

To illustrate the advantage of averaging high- and low-rate countries, assume that US Corp was subject to a US tax of 40% on its global income and had USD 1 million of income in Country A and USD 1 million in Country B. Also, assume that Country A applied a 50% corporate income tax and Country B a 30% corporate income tax. Consider first what happened under the per-country limitation where each country was treated as a separate basket for calculating the limitation. Although US Corp paid USD 500,000 tax (50% of USD 1 million) to Country A, the per-country method would limit US Corp to a USD 400,000 foreign tax credit (40% of USD 1 million). This would occur because the per-country limitation only permitted a credit up to the amount of US tax attributable to the Country A income. (US Corp is said to be "excess credit" in Country A, since it paid USD 500,000 in taxes to Country A but could only claim a US tax credit of USD 400,000.) US Corp would also claim a credit of USD 300,000 (30% of USD 1 million) for the USD 300,000 income tax it paid to Country B, since the taxes paid to Country B are less than the US tax of USD 400,000 on that income. (US Corp is said to be "excess limitation" in Country B because it only paid USD 300,000 tax in Country B on income that is subject to a USD 400,000 US tax.) In total, US Corp X would have claimed a total of USD 700,000 of credits (USD 400,000 credit for the tax paid to Country A plus USD 300,000 credit for the tax paid to Country B).

Now consider what happened if the overall method were used such that the income from Country A and Country B was combined into a single basket to calculate the tax credit limitation. The combined USD 2 million of income resulted in a limitation of USD 800,000 (40% of USD 2 million). US Corp would be able to claim a full USD 500,000 credit for the tax it paid to Country A and a USD 300,000 credit for the tax paid to Country B. US Corp clearly improved its tax position since in the aggregate it had increased the credit it could claim from USD 700,000 to USD 800,000.

In general, as illustrated above, US taxpayers in the position of being excess credit in some countries and excess limitation in other countries increased the credits they could claim when they averaged the high and low-rate countries by combining the income from such countries in a single basket.

If a US taxpayer incurred some losses, however, it would in general have preferred that the loss country be in a separate basket so that it did not reduce the credit for the countries with income. For example, suppose US Corp has USD 1 million income in Country A, and USD 1 million loss in Country B. Suppose also that the USD million income in Country A was taxed at 40% by Country A and was subject to a 40% US tax. If Country A and Country B were in separate imitation baskets, US Corp could claim the full tax credit of USD 400,000 for the tax paid in Country A. If, however, the income from Country A and B were placed into the same basket, US Corp would not be able to claim any credit since the income in that basket that was subject to US taxation would be zero (the USD million income from Country A reduced by the USD million loss in Country B). (As we will see in section 10.4.1, Section 904(f)(5) now requires that losses from one basket offset income in another for purposes of calculating the limitations with the result that a taxpayer cannot isolate losses in a basket.)

The Tax Reform Act of 1976 eliminated the per-country method and required all taxpayers to use the overall method.[2] This action reflected a congressional view that the combination of deductible losses from some countries and allowable foreign tax credits from others was creating an excessive tax benefit. Apparently, the averaging of rates achieved under the overall method was not seen as creating a similar problem. Requiring all taxpayers to use the overall method insured that foreign losses from a country first reduced other foreign source income before the tax credit mechanism came into play. Even under the 1976 Act approach, however, certain types of income were removed from the overall credit computation, and separate overall credit limit computations were required with respect to these categories or "baskets" of income. Interest income was a notable example of the separate treatment because of the ease with which its source could be manipulated to be foreign source and thereby increase the limitation.

Many expected the 1986 Act's reduction in the top US corporate income tax rate from 46% to 34% (later increased to 35%) to intensify the pressure on the foreign tax credit limitation. This rate reduction, it was assumed, would place many US corporations in a situation where their foreign taxes paid would exceed the US tax on the foreign income, with the result that they would be in an excess foreign tax credit position. Congress feared that this situation in turn would create too great an incentive for US corporations to manipulate receipts and deductions among various categories and sources of income in order to maximize foreign tax credit utilization. To prevent this response (but without going back to the per-country limitation as recommended by

2. The per-country limitation preceding the 1976 act had a significant loophole in that it did not look through dividends received by the US taxpayer to determine the original source of the income. Without a look-through regime, it was possible to use a top-tier foreign holding company as a mixer company and effectively achieve a result comparable to a general limitation. The look-through rules for the foreign tax credit limitation were first adopted on a limited basis in the 1984 Act and then materially expanded in the 1986 Act. Whichever limitation approach is adopted, it is necessary to be able to trace the limitation category through tiers of companies or anti-blending objectives can be easily defeated with use of tiered entities in planning.

the President's reform proposals), the 1986 Act significantly expanded the baskets of income for which separate foreign tax credit limitations must be computed.

In total, following the 1986 Act there were nine baskets including the general limitation basket of income.[3] The traditional overall limitation (now the general limitation basket) was for income derived from manufacturing, production, sales, and services carried out or performed directly by a US corporation or its foreign subsidiaries. The other major baskets included: (1) passive income basket, (2) high withholding tax interest basket,[4] (3) financial services income basket,[5] (4) shipping income basket,[6] (5) basket for dividends from a Domestic International Sales Corporation (DISC),[7] and (6) basket for dividends from a Foreign Sales Corporations (a now-defunct category of foreign subsidiary).

---

3. The justifications for the nine-basket system, which applied until 2007, could be grouped in the following broad categories:

    (1) Types of income that can be easily manipulated by taxpayers from country to country, with a resulting increase in the allowable foreign tax credit at little or no extra tax cost. The special baskets for passive income and for financial services income respond to this problem and in effect deny the use of the basic averaging mechanism to such income.
    (2) Types of income with respect to which the US has granted preferential tax treatment. The basket governing the special limitations with respect to natural resources income responds to this problem. The rules prevent the preferential tax treatment of such income by the US from being used to increase the available foreign tax credit through the impact of the preferences on the limitation mechanism.
    (3) Types of income that are not subjected to the same tax rules abroad as are applied by the US. Failure to take these differences into account again can increase the allowable foreign tax credit at no increased US tax cost or exempt the foreign source income from tax altogether. The rule requiring recapture of overall foreign losses and the high withholding tax and shipping income baskets respond to this problem.
    (4) Income earned in activities that run counter to foreign policy objectives of the US. The rule denying the foreign tax credit for boycott related income responds to this problem by imposing a tax penalty on such income.

    Thus, the various special limitations respond to what have been perceived as defects in the operation of the credit when applied to the particular classes of income involved. The use of the basket approach in turn responds to the averaging effect created by any overall limitation.
4. Interest income (other than export financing interest) that was subject to a withholding tax that was 5% or greater and was imposed on a gross basis was placed in a separate basket. Sec. 904(d)(2)(B) as in effect prior to 2007.
5. Income (other than passive income, export financing interest, or high withholding tax interest) which was derived from the active conduct of a banking, financing, or similar business or from ordinary investment activity by an insurance company was placed in a separate basket. Because of the difficulty of distinguishing passive from active income for financial institutions, the financial services income basket included both types of income if the institution was "predominantly engaged" in the active conduct of a banking, insurance, financing, or similar business. Treas. Reg. Section 1.904-4(e) adopted a very broad definition of qualifying income for financial institutions and provided that the "predominantly engaged" test was met if 80% of an institution's gross income was qualifying income. If a financial entity did not satisfy the "predominantly engaged" test, its passive income remained in the passive income basket.
6. The income in this basket (which included income from aircraft and shipping operations) was that described in Sections 904(d)(2)(D) and 954(f).
7. Subsidiaries of US companies engaged in foreign trade activities through a Domestic International Sales Corporation (DISC) received special treatment that exempted or deferred recognition of some of their income. The US had thought it inappropriate to allow a credit for foreign taxes imposed on income that is in whole or in part excluded from or subject to deferred tax in the US.

After the 1986 Act, most industrialized countries reduced corporate tax rates over time so that by 2004 they largely were lower than the (pre-2018) US rate of 35%. This decreased or eliminated the concerns of pressure on the foreign tax limitation expressed in 1986. As a result, in 2004 Congress reduced the number of limitation categories from nine to two (effective starting in 2007): a passive category income basket and a general category income basket.[8]

10.1.2 The Passive Category Income and General Category Income Baskets

Since 1986, the foreign tax credit limitation in Section 904 has always included both a passive income basket and a general income basket.[9] (As will be discussed in the next section, the 2017 Tax Act added two additional baskets, with the result that there are currently four limitation baskets.) The passive basket holds the items of income that are most easily shifted between US and foreign source as well as between foreign countries.

The formula to calculate the limitation for each basket may be expressed as follows:

Limitation on Credit for Income in a Basket = (US Income Tax on Worldwide Taxable Income) X (Foreign Source Income in the Basket/Worldwide Taxable Income)

For example, suppose that US Corp, subject to a 21% US corporate tax, earns 100 in the US and 100 in Country X, which applies a 25% tax to such income. All the income in Country X is in the general income basket. The US income tax on all US Corp's worldwide income is 42 (21% of USD 200). US Corp's foreign source income in the general income basket is 100 and its worldwide income is 200. Applying the above formula, US Corp's foreign tax credit will be limited to:

(42) X (100/200) = 21

The result is that US Corp has an excess tax credit of USD 4 (the foreign tax of USD 25 minus the limitation of USD 21). An excess foreign tax credit in one basket of income cannot spill over and offset US tax on income in another basket (in US tax jargon, no

---

Accordingly, a separate basket was provided and a separate Section 904(d) limitation computation was required for dividends from a DISC paid from income treated as foreign source. The special treatment for DISCs was replaced with the Foreign Sales Corporations provisions, which have also been repealed.

8. After 2006, income that previously would have been placed in one of the baskets eliminated for 2007 (i.e., a basket other than the passive basket or the general income basket) was assigned to one of the two baskets. Beginning in 2007, dividends from a DISC and were placed in the passive category income basket. Sec. 904(d)(2)(B)(v). Financial services income was placed in the general category income basket. Sec. 904(d)(2)(C). Shipping income generally moved to the general category income basket. High withholding tax interest generally went to the passive category income basket and high-taxed passive income was in the general basket. Sec. 904(d)(2)(B)(iii)(II). Thus, post 2007 the general limitation basket and the passive basket included the categories of income that previously had been assigned to the eliminated baskets.
9. The methodology for allocating a taxpayer's foreign taxes among its baskets of income is spelled out in Treas. Reg. Section 1.904-6.

"cross-crediting" is allowed).[10] Thus, to continue the above example, if US Corp also had income in the passive income basket, it could not use the excess credit from its general income basket to offset the US tax owed on the passive income.

Why retain a separate basket for passive income? We have seen that the US foreign tax credit mechanism contemplates that, if foreign countries impose tax on a US corporation's business income higher than the US effective rate, an excess foreign tax credit will be created. If a taxpayer could allocate additional foreign source income that is taxed at a low rate or not taxed at all to the basket, the averaging effect of the overall limitation fraction would permit the current crediting of the excess foreign taxes paid on the business income. Passive investment income, which is often subject to little or no foreign tax and whose source is readily manipulable, could be used to achieve this result absent some limitation.

For example, assume foreign Country X imposes a tax of 30% on USD 1 million of taxable business income of US Corp. US Corp also has USD 1 million of US source income. All USD 2 million of US Corp's income is taxed by the US at 21%. In the absence of anything else, Section 904(a) would limit the allowable foreign tax credit to USD 210,000, calculated as follows:

(USD 420,000 US Income Tax on Worldwide Taxable Income) × (USD 1,000,000 foreign source income in basket/USD 2,000,000 worldwide income) = USD 210,000 foreign tax credit limitation

Total taxes of USD 510,000 would be paid (USD 300,000 to Country X and USD 210,000 to the US). US Corp would also have a USD 90,000 excess credit.

In an attempt to use the excess credit, suppose US Corp transfers assets generating USD 428,671 in passive income from the US to a branch in foreign Country Y where the tax on the passive income is 0%. US source income is reduced to USD 571,429, and the total foreign source income is increased to USD 1,428,571. The total US tax paid is USD 420,000 (21% times USD 2 million), and the total foreign taxes paid are USD 300,000 (USD 300,000 paid to Country X plus USD 0 to Country Y). If the passive income is placed in the general income basket, the foreign tax credit limitation would then be:

(USD 420,000 US Income Tax) × (USD 1,428,571 foreign source income in basket/USD worldwide 2,000,000) = USD 300,000

The result is that US Corp would fully use the USD 300,000 foreign tax credit. Consequently, it would only pay USD 120,000 to the US (USD 420,000 tentative tax less USD 300,000 foreign tax credit), resulting in a total tax liability of USD 420,000 (USD 120,000 paid to the US and USD 300,000 paid to Country X). Compare this with the USD 510,000 total tax liability it would have incurred before shifting income to Country Y.

10. The excess credit may be carried back and carried forward to be utilized in years when additional foreign source income taxed at less than the US effective rate is realized in the same basket, except there is no carryover in the GILTI basket (*see* section 10.2.3).

US tax law, however, currently prevents Corp X from achieving this tax reduction. Section 904(d)(1)(A) requires that the overall limitation for foreign taxes on passive income be computed separately. Thus, in the above example, the passive income would be placed in the passive income basket, with the result that the US would impose a tax of USD 90,021 (21% of USD 428,671) on the passive income against which a zero credit would be allowed. The US tax on that passive income is not reduced by the excess credit generated on the business income.

The passive income basket, in general, currently includes dividends, interest, annuities, certain rents, and royalties, and net gains from sales or exchanges of property that generated passive income. Technically, "passive income" is defined by reference to the definition of "foreign personal holding company income," discussed at Chapter 6 section 6.3.4.1.[11] The term includes income taxed under the passive foreign investment company rules, discussed at Chapter 8, section 8.2.[12] Additionally, income equivalent to interest, such as loan commitment fees, is also included in the passive income basket. Net gains from commodity transactions are included in the passive basket unless realized by taxpayers actively and regularly engaged in such transactions. The passive basket includes net gains from foreign currency transactions,[13] unless the transactions are directly related to the business needs of the entity.

An important exception to classification as passive income excludes rents and royalties derived from unrelated parties in the active conduct of a trade or business from the definition of foreign personal holding company income.[14] As a result, these items fall into the general limitation income basket. The statute also specifically excludes from passive income basket:[15]

(1) any export financing interest;[16] and
(2) any high-taxed income.[17]

The "high-taxed income" exception is designed to limit use of the passive basket for internal cross-crediting. Contrary to the general assumption underlying the passive income category, i.e., that passive income is subject to low foreign taxes, some passive income is subject to quite high foreign tax, for example, withholding taxes on portfolio dividends. As a result, Congress felt it was not adequate merely to differentiate passive

11. Sec. 904(d)(2)(B).
12. Sec. 1297(b)(1).
13. *See* Chapter 13 section 13.3.
14. For rules regarding related parties and whether rents and royalties were derived from the active conduct of a trade or business, *see* Treas. Reg. Section 1.954-1(e) and 2(d), 1.904-4(b)(2). Under a relaxed rule applicable for foreign tax credit limitation categorization purposes, activity of a member of the same affiliated group (using an 80% affiliation test) is taken into account in determining whether a rent or royalty is active. Treas. Reg. Sec. 1.904-4(b)(2)(iii)(B).
15. Sec. 904(d)(2)(B)(iii).
16. In general, this category included interest derived from financing the sale for use or consumption outside the US of property manufactured or produced within the US so long as no more than 50% of the fair market value of the property is attributable to products imported into the US. Sec. 904(d)(2)(G). Interest that qualified for the exception fell into the general limitation income basket. The purpose of this exception was to avoid adversely affecting the level of US exports.
17. Sec. 904(d)(2)(F).

from other types of income but also passive income subject to low foreign effective tax rates from passive income subject to high foreign effective tax rates.[18] This so-called high-tax kick-out, when it is operative, shifts income that otherwise would have fallen in the passive income basket to the general limitation income basket.

The high-tax kick-out rule operates mechanically and automatically if its conditions are satisfied. Under the rule, the foreign tax paid on the *net* passive income (gross income minus allocable deductions, both as determined under US rules) is compared to US tax on that income.[19] If the foreign tax exceeds the US tax, the passive income is "kicked-out" of the passive basket into the general limitation income basket. For example, assume that a US corporation receives USD 100 in passive income from a foreign corporation that is subject to a 30% withholding tax. Under the US allocation of deduction rules (*see* Chapter 4 section 4.4), assume that USD 50 of the US recipient's expenses is allocated to the USD 100 payment. The USD 50 of net passive income is subject to the high-tax kick-out because the USD 30 of foreign tax on the USD 50 of net income exceeds the US tax of USD 10.5 on that income (21% × USD 50). The high-tax kick-out thus operates when the effective foreign tax rate on passive income (determined under US rules) exceeds the US effective rate on that income, even though the nominal foreign rate is lower than the US rate.

10.2 THE TWO NEW POST-2017 LIMITATION CATEGORIES

The 2017 Tax Act added two new foreign tax credit limitation categories to Section 904(d): a category for amounts includible in income as GILTI (described in Chapter 6 section 6.2.) and a category for foreign branch income.[20] As a result, there are now four baskets: (1) GILTI (discussed below), (2) foreign branch income (discussed below) (3) passive category income (discussed in 10.1.2), and (4) general category income (discussed in 10.1.2).

Importantly, there is no separate category for dividends of a specified 10% owned foreign corporation that in the hands of a corporate US shareholder qualifies for a 100% dividends received deduction ("DRD") under Section 245A. For purposes of the Section 904 limitation, these dividends are treated as exempt income, though at the level of the CFC the current year earnings must be accounted for in determining the foreign source taxable income. The treatment of these earnings for purposes of the foreign tax credit limitation is discussed at section 10.3.1. The dividends from a CFC to a US shareholder who is not eligible for the Section 245A deduction are assigned to a limitation category under the look-through rules discussed at section 10.3.2.

18. This differentiation insures that the US tax on low-taxed passive income will not be absorbed by the foreign tax on high-taxed passive income.
19. Treas. Reg. Section 1.904-4(c)(2) provides rules for the grouping of certain types of income for purposes of the high-tax kick-out rule. These regulations sought to ease the formidable task of applying the rule to each item of passive income.
20. Sec. 904(d)(1)(A) and (B).

10.2.1 The GILTI Category

As discussed in Chapter 9 section 9.5.1, Section 960 allows a corporate US shareholder to claim an indirect credit for 80% of the foreign income taxes paid by the US shareholders corporation attributable to the GILTI inclusion. The GILTI category basket consists of income included, directly or indirectly through a pass-through entity, in the gross income of a US person under Section 951A (discussed at Chapter 6, sections 6.2.1 and 6.4.2) that is not allocated to passive category income under the look-through rules described in section 10.3.[21] The Section 78 dividend amount associated with foreign taxes assigned to the GILTI category also is included in the GILTI category.[22]

Because the amount of a GILTI inclusion is determined at the shareholder level in relation to the US shareholder's net CFC tested income from CFCs with positive tested income (Chapter 6 section 6.4.2), the inclusion must be allocated to the CFCs from which it derives in order to determine what portion of the inclusion, if any, is allocable to the passive category under the look-though rules.[23] The allocation of the GILTI inclusion amount to a CFC is based on the ratio of the US shareholder's pro rata share of the CFC's tested income to the shareholder's total share of tested income of each CFC for the shareholder's year.[24]

By regulation, a taxpayer may elect to exclude from GILTI tentative gross tested income subject to an effective rate of foreign tax that is greater than 90% of the maximum rate of tax specified in Section 11.[25] Where this exclusion applies, the income is neither subpart F income nor gross tested income. These "residual" earnings of the CFC, which also include earnings excluded from GILTI attributable to the US shareholder's net deemed tangible income return and a CFC's tested income offset by tested losses, will be eligible for the foreign DRD when the earnings are distributed as a dividend to a US shareholder. The taxes attributable to these earnings are not allowable as a foreign tax credit.[26]

Another alternative available to an individual is to make an election under Section 962, discussed in section 6.2.1. Such an election causes the individual shareholder to be taxed currently on GILTI under the rules and at the rates that would apply to domestic corporations. Thus, the individual can claim the Section 250 deduction for the GILTI. In addition, the individual can claim the Section 960 indirect foreign tax credit for 80% of CFC-level income taxes attributable to the GILTI inclusion, resulting in the individual paying a residual US corporate tax amount in the year of inclusion. When earnings are distributed by the CFC to the individual shareholder (in the year of inclusion or subsequently), they would be included in the individual's

21. Sec. 904(d)(1)(A).
22. Treas. Reg. Sec. 1.904-4(o) and 1.904-6(e).
23. Sec. 951A(f). Allocation of the included GILTI amounts is also necessary to determine previously taxed earnings and profits (PTEP). *See* Chapter 6 section 6.3.4.1 for a discussion of previously taxed earnings and profits.
24. Treas. Reg. Sec. 1.951A-5(b)(2). Tested income is discussed in Chapter 6 section 6.4.2.
25. Sec. 954(b)(4); Treas. Reg. Sec. 1.951A-2(c)(7).
26. Sec. 904(b)(4).

income under usual rules for taxing dividends, except the individual is permitted deduction for the US tax paid on the deemed corporate inclusion.[27]

10.2.2 The Foreign Branch Category

The foreign branch category consists of income attributable to foreign branches of a US person, whether the branch activity is conducted directly or through a disregarded entity, and income from pass-through entities attributable to foreign branches, in each case excluding any passive category income.[28] A foreign branch generally is a qualified business unit ("QBU") (described in Chapter 13 section 13.2) that conducts a trade or business outside the United States, including a permanent establishment under a treaty and activities of a partnership carried on outside the United States that would be a QBU. Income is attributable to the QBU based on its separate books and records, subject to certain adjustments. In order to mitigate the possibility of substantial disparities between the branch tax base under US and foreign tax law, regulations address the issue of payments between a foreign branch that is a disregarded entity and the foreign branch owner that are recognized for foreign tax law purposes and are disregarded for US tax purposes. This design decision parallels the decision made to identify foreign income taxes according to income determined under foreign law and assign them to the category in which items of gross income determined under US tax law correspond to the foreign income.[29]

Generally, where the disregarded payment if regarded would be a deduction allocable to income of the branch, the branch income is adjusted downward for the allocable amount and the foreign branch owner's income is adjusted upward. If the disregarded payment is from the foreign branch owner to the foreign branch, the same adjustment is made in reverse, the foreign branch owner's income is decreased and the branch income is increased.[30] The adjustment is to the attribution of gross income and does not change the total amount, source, or character of the US person's gross income or the income in any category other than those of the branch or general category.

10.2.3 Carryback and Carryover of Excess Credits

Allowable foreign tax credits in any of the separate baskets in excess of those creditable in the current year may be carried back one year and forward ten years, except that

27. The law is unclear regarding the extent to which the later distribution is deemed to come from the notional domestic corporation (and be domestic source income) or from the actual CFC (in which case the dividend generally would be foreign source income). In *Smith v. Commissioner*, 151 T.C. 41 (2018), the Tax Court denied qualified dividend income treatment for a dividend from a non-treaty country CFC with respect to which the taxpayer had elected the application of Section 962 to subpart F income in a pre-2017 Tax Act year on the ground that the earnings came from a CFC whose distributions were not eligible for qualified dividend income. This case supports the view that the amounts actually distributed should be treated as distributed by the CFC.
28. Sec. 904(d)(2)(J); Treas. Reg. Sec. 1.904-4(f)(1).
29. Treas. Reg. Secs. 1.904-6 and 1.861-20(c) and (d). Special rules apply where there is no corresponding US income due to nonrecognition rules and for situations including base differences, foreign law inclusion regimes and distributions.
30. Treas. Reg. Sec. 1.904-4(f)(3)(vi).

foreign taxes in the GILTI basket are not allowed any carryover.[31] The credits can only be used in the basket from which they originated and then only to the extent there is "excess" limitation in that basket in the year to which they are carried. The lack of any carryover for GILTI may be a reason behind the elective regulatory relief for high-taxed GILTI, described in Chapter 6 section 6.3.4.1, which shifts the income to earnings eligible for the 100% foreign DRD (discussed in Chapter 6 section 6.5.2).

10.2.4 Income that Would Previously Have Been Placed in a Different Basket

The creation of two new baskets for non-passive foreign branch income and GILTI in the 2017 Tax Act causes income that otherwise would be in the general basket to instead be in the foreign branch basket or the GILTI basket. The more difficult issue is the carryover of foreign tax credits from the pre-effective date general basket. For carryover taxes from a pre-2018 general limitation category to a post-2017 foreign branch category, the regulations provide an elective safe harbor based on the ratio of foreign taxes paid by foreign branches for the year from which the taxes carryover to all creditable foreign taxes for that year.[32] Otherwise, the carryover foreign taxes must be assigned based on a reconstruction of foreign branch income under current law principles and identify foreign taxes on that income for the prior year.

10.3 THE LOOK-THROUGH RULES

10.3.1 Dividends, Interest, Rents, and Royalties from Controlled Foreign Corporations

Dividends, interest, rents, and royalties from a CFC are not placed in a separate basket and would thus generally fall within the passive basket. However, a special regime applies to a US taxpayer that owns 10% of the stock of a CFC. If the US taxpayer receives dividends, interest, rents, or royalties from the CFC, the taxpayer determines the proper basket for the income by "looking through" to the character of the underlying income in the hands of the foreign corporation out of which the payment was made.[33]

Dividends received from a CFC are treated as passive basket income in the ratio of the CFC's passive category earnings and profits to its entire earnings and profits. For example, assume US Corp received a USD 100 dividend from CFC Y, a wholly owned subsidiary incorporated in and operating exclusively in Country A. CFC Y has earnings and profits of USD 1,000 of which USD 800 (80%) is from its manufacturing operations in Country A and USD 200 (20%) is passive dividend income received by CFC Y from

31. Sec. 904(c).
32. Treas. Reg. Sec. 1.904-2(j)(1)(iii)(B).
33. In the case of a corporate US shareholder, dividends will be offset by the 100% foreign DRD in which case the look-through rules for foreign tax credit limitation are not relevant. They remain relevant, however, for other categories of US shareholders.

corporations in Country A. Eighty percent of the dividend to US Corp, USD 80, is placed in its general limitation income basket and 20%, USD 20, is placed in its passive income basket.

A different method of allocating income from a CFC to the appropriate basket applies to interest, rents, and royalties. Rents and royalties generally are directly allocated to income the expenditure generates (e.g., rent paid by the CFC for a building leased from a US affiliate would be allocable to income realized from leasing the building). In general, asset-based methods are employed similar to those discussed at Chapter 4 section 4.4.3 with respect to the allocation of interest when incurred as an expense. Interest payments, however, must first be allocated to the passive income basket to the extent of the CFC's passive income before the formula is applied.[34]

10.3.2 Dividends from Noncontrolled Section 902 Corporations

If a US shareholder owns less than 10% of the stock of a foreign corporation, dividends from that corporation are placed in the passive income basket. If, however, a US corporate shareholder owns 10% or more of the stock of a foreign corporation, but the foreign corporation is not a CFC and the dividends are not eligible for the Section 245A 100% foreign DRD, dividends from such a "noncontrolled Section 902 corporation" derived from earnings of the foreign corporation are subject to a look-through rule similar to that described in section 10.3.1. As a result, dividends are placed in the passive basket to the extent of the ratable share of earnings and profits that generated the dividend would be passive category earnings.[35]

10.4 THE TREATMENT OF LOSSES

10.4.1 Foreign Losses

A US corporation may incur an overall net foreign loss in a taxable year but in a subsequent year realize foreign source income. Section 904(f)(1) provides that the prior loss, which has previously offset US source income, must be "recaptured" by treating as US source income that portion of the taxpayer's subsequent foreign source income equal to the lesser of: (1) the amount of the prior foreign loss, or (2) 50% (or a larger percentage if the taxpayer so chooses) of the taxpayer's foreign source income.

The problem addressed by Section 904(f)(1) arises when a US corporation experiences current net losses (referred to as "overall foreign losses")[36] in its foreign operations and uses those losses to reduce US tax on its US source income. In later years, if income is earned in a foreign country (which does not allow loss carryover or is different from where the loss was incurred), a foreign tax would be due. Under normal principles, a foreign tax credit would be available for those taxes. However, this

34. The complex allocation rules are set forth in Treas. Reg. Sec. 1.904-5(c)(2) and (3).
35. Treas. Reg. Sec. 1.904-5(c)(4)(iii).
36. Sec. 904(f)(2).

result ignores the fact that the prior foreign losses had been used to reduce US taxable income so that a full crediting of the subsequent foreign taxes would give the US taxpayer a double benefit, i.e., a reduction of US taxes in earlier years and a foreign tax credit in later years.[37]

The operation of Section 904(f)(1) may be illustrated by the following example: Assume US Corp has overall foreign losses in year 1 of USD 500,000 (i.e., net losses from foreign sources) to reduce US taxable income. In year 2, it realizes foreign source taxable income of USD 1 million. Under the special source rule in Section 904(f)(1), USD 500,000 of US Corp's foreign income would be treated as US source income. As a result, the numerator of the Section 904(a) fraction would be reduced and so would the amount of creditable foreign taxes. In the above example, assume that US Corp had USD 1 million of US source taxable income in each of the two years. The deduction in year 1 produced a tax saving of approximately USD 105,000 (21% of USD 500,000). In year 2, the tentative US tax would have been USD 420,000 against which, absent the special rule, a maximum foreign tax credit of USD 210,000 (USD 420,000 × USD 1,000,000/USD 2,000,000) would have been available. Under the special rule in Section 904(f)(1) the maximum foreign tax credit in year 2 is reduced to USD 105,000 (USD 420,000 × USD 500,000/USD 2,000,000). Thus, the tax benefit granted by the US in year 1 is "recaptured" in year 2.[38]

Under Section 904(f)(3), previously deducted losses will be recaptured if property used outside the US is disposed of at a gain, regardless of whether the gain on the disposition would be taxed. Thus, if a taxpayer disposes of such property in a tax-free transaction, an amount of previously deducted losses equal to the full amount of the gain realized (but not recognized) in the transaction must be recaptured in the year of the disposition.

Section 904(f)(1) was adequate so long as the number of baskets was kept to a minimum. The introduction of numerous baskets of income for foreign tax credit limitation purposes made it necessary to provide more detailed rules as to how foreign losses were to be treated for Section 904(a) purposes as between the baskets. Although the reduction to two baskets as of 2007 made the intra-basket recharacterization rules in Section 904(f) less important, the addition of the foreign branch basket in after 2017 restores their relative importance.

37. The same problem could arise if income was subsequently earned in the same country in which the loss was incurred and the country did not allow a carryover of the prior loss. In that case, a foreign income tax would be paid, and, under normal principles, a foreign tax credit could be claimed.

38. In this example, the year 2 foreign tax credit limit of USD 105,000 is the US tax on the USD 500,000 of foreign income left after the initial USD 1,000,000 of foreign income is reduced by the USD 500,000 reclassified as US income under Section 904(f)(1). It is important to note that the entire overall foreign loss will often not be recaptured in a single year. Section 904(f)(1) limits the amount of foreign income that will be recharacterized as US source in any given year to the lesser of the amount of the overall foreign loss or 50% (unless the taxpayer elects to apply a higher percentage) of the taxpayer's foreign source income for that year. Any remaining overall foreign loss not recaptured currently is recaptured in future years, with the amount that may be recaptured in each succeeding year again subject to the same 50% limitation. The example in the text resulted in the entire overall foreign loss being recaptured in the current year because the overall foreign loss equaled 50% of the foreign income for that year.

The intra-basket recharacterization rules are contained in Section 904(f)(5). The general rule is that foreign losses in one basket must first be used to reduce proportionately foreign income in any other basket. Only after this allocation may the excess of the foreign loss be used to reduce US source income. Subsequently, when foreign income is realized in the basket that generated the loss, that income must be recharacterized so that it offsets the losses previously taken in the other basket. This recharacterization rule in Section 904(f)(5) applies in addition to, not in lieu of, the recapture rule in Section 904(f)(1), described above.

The operation of the foreign loss rules in Section 904(f) can best be understood by considering the following examples:

> Example (1): US Corp has a USD 100 foreign source loss in year 1 that is entirely within the general limitation income basket; it has no income in any other basket. US Corp can deduct the USD 100 against its US source income in year 1. When US Corp realizes USD 100 foreign source general limitation income in year 2, only the recapture rule of Section 904(f)(1) is operative since no recharacterization of the income is required. That rule treats 50% (or more if the taxpayer so elects) of the income as US source.
>
> Example (2): Assume the same facts as in Example (1), except that in year 1, US Corp. also had USD 75 in its passive income basket. The USD 100 general limitation loss would first reduce the USD 75 of passive limitation income and the USD 25 balance would offset US income. In year 2, USD 25 of the USD 100 of general limitation income would first be resourced as US income under the Section 904(f)(1) recapture rule and the balance of USD 75 would be allocated to the passive income basket under the Section 904(f)(5) recharacterization rule.

The recharacterization rules in Section 904(f) mitigate the effects of rigid year-by-year adherence to the foreign loss rules. For example, losses from a taxpayer's (low-tax) passive income basket might be required to be used to offset income in its general limitation income basket that is subject to a high rate of tax, thus creating an excess foreign tax credit situation. Conversely, if losses from a high-tax basket reduce income in the passive basket, the US Treasury loses its residual tax on the low-tax income. Recharacterization in this situation permits the Treasury to recover all or part of that tax.

10.4.2 US Losses

If a US taxpayer has a US source net loss, that loss is allocated between, and thus reduces, the income in the foreign income baskets proportionately to the income in each basket. Before a US loss is so allocated, a loss in any foreign income basket must first be allocated between the baskets.[39]

Prior to 2007, there was no recharacterization rule applicable to US source income earned in a subsequent year. Thus, for foreign tax credit limitation purposes, the effect of allocation of US losses was permanent. The failure to recharacterize US losses, at least to the extent they represented real economic losses, arguably was

39. Sec. 904(f)(5)(D).

inappropriate and presumably was adopted because of revenue considerations. However, beginning in 2007, Section 904(g) adopted the reverse of the rule in Section 904(f)(1). Suppose a taxpayer has an overall US loss in 2020, but realizes US source taxable income in 2021. That income is resourced to foreign source income to the extent of the lesser of: (i) the amount of the loss, or (ii) 50% of the taxpayer's US source taxable income in 2021. Thus, the effect of the US loss that had been allocated to baskets of foreign income in year 2020 (thereby reducing the allowable foreign tax credit) is reversed and foreign source income is increased for foreign tax credit purposes in 2021.

10.5 SPECIAL LIMITATIONS ON THE FOREIGN TAX CREDIT

In addition to the limitations on the foreign tax credit discussed in section 10.3, the amount of the credit may also be reduced by certain other limitations that are applicable to the natural resources industry[40] or that are intended to further nontax objectives of the US.[41] In addition, as discussed at section 10.7, where a credit is allowed by reason of a treaty alone the income is assigned a separate limitation.[42]

10.6 RELIEF FOR SMALL INVESTORS

In 1997, Congress took an initial step to relieve small individual investors from the burden of complying with the full panoply of the Section 904 limitations. Under Section 904(j), individuals who incur not more than USD 300 (USD 600 in the case of joint returns) of foreign taxes imposed on their passive income from foreign sources are not subject to the rules of Section 904. Instead, such individuals may elect to take the credit up to the specified amounts without being concerned with which basket their foreign investment income should be placed. As a corollary, for individuals who elect to have Section 904(j) apply, no foreign tax credits may be carried from or to the taxable year.

10.7 FOREIGN TAX CREDITS AND TREATIES

Although domestic law provides a comprehensive system of relief from double taxation, US tax treaties also address the subject. The US Model Treaty Article 23 provides for relief "in accordance with the provisions and subject to the limitations of the law of the United States." However, in some cases the treaty provisions for double

40. *See* Secs. 901(e), (f), and 907.
41. *See* Sec. 901(j) (denying a foreign tax credit for any taxes paid to a country whose government supports terrorism, does not have diplomatic relations with the US, or is not recognized by the US unless the President waives the application of the provision upon making a determination that such an action is in the US national interest and will expand US trade and investment opportunities in the country; foreign taxes disallowed under Section 901(j) are, however, deductible); Secs. 908 and 999 (foreign tax credit must be reduced to the extent that the credit is attributable to income derived by the taxpayer from participating in or cooperating with an international boycott; amount of disallowed direct (but not indirect) credit is deductible).
42. *See, e.g.*, US-Canada Treaty, Art. XXIV(3); Sec. 904(d)(6) and 904(h)(10).

tax relief may be more favorable to the taxpayer. For example, a treaty may list certain foreign taxes as being creditable even though they would not otherwise meet the requirements of Section 901 for creditability. Additionally, treaties may include special source rules that classify certain items of income as foreign source, even though they would constitute US source income under domestic law.[43] In that case, the statutory limitations in Section 904 require that if an item of income that would be classified as US source under domestic law, but is treated as foreign source under the applicable treaty, then that item shall be treated separately (i.e., its own basket) for purposes of Sections 902, 904, 907, and 960.[44]

Certain positions taken on a tax return based on treaty authority must be disclosed by the taxpayer. For example, disclosure is required when a taxpayer relies on a treaty to alter the source of an item of income of deduction,[45] or to claim a credit for a foreign tax that would not otherwise be creditable under the Code.[46]

10.8 SUMMARY PERSPECTIVES ON THE FOREIGN TAX CREDIT MECHANISM

After examining the "baskets" system of separate and overall limitations and the special limitations involved in determining the allowable credit for foreign taxes paid or incurred, one can reasonably ask whether there is anything left of the fairly straightforward principle that was asserted in Chapter 9, section 9.1 to undergird the foreign tax credit system. If a country adopts the foreign tax credit as its fundamental mechanism for adjusting international tax burdens, why are all the limitations required? An identification of the broad problems to which the varied limitations are addressed may shed some light on this question.

Any limitation on a foreign tax credit itself represents a deviation from the principle of pure locational neutrality that is one object of the credit mechanism. But some limitation is required for several reasons, as indicated in section 10.1. First, a limitation is necessary to protect the revenues of the US Government. A pure credit mechanism would provide for full crediting of foreign taxes whatever the rate of foreign tax and refunds by the US Government where foreign taxes exceeded US taxes (including US taxes on US income). This, of course, would put the US Treasury at the disposal of all foreign tax systems, a situation which neither the United States nor any other government has been willing to accept.

Hence, some limitation is required, and the question is what form the limitation should take. A single overall limitation has the advantage of administrative simplicity and eliminates the necessity that foreign taxes be traced to specific items of foreign

43. *See, e.g.*, US-Canada Treaty, Art. XXIV(3).
44. Sec. 904(d)(6), added in 2010. *See also* Section 904(h)(10), which similarly requires that Sections 904, 907, and 960 be separately applied to income received from a US-owned foreign corporation that would be US source income under domestic law, but would be foreign under the treaty, and the taxpayer has chosen the treaty.
45. Treas. Reg. Sec. 301.6114-1(b)(6).
46. Treas. Reg. Sec. 301.6114-1(b)(7).

income, a requirement which would impose record-keeping burdens on taxpayers and would be difficult to administer effectively by fiscal authorities.

However, an overall limitation in turn inherently involves an averaging of high and low-tax rates on foreign income. After the US reduced its top corporate rate to 34% in the 1986 Act, a general overall limitation could no longer be employed. The low US corporate rate would mean that most US multinational corporations would find themselves in an excess foreign tax credit situation. The concern then was that excessive pressure would be placed on the credit mechanism as US corporations sought to manipulate the source of income and deductions so that the averaging effects of the overall limitation would reduce or eliminate excess credit positions. The adoption of the system based on various "baskets" of income was intended to prevent manipulation for averaging purposes that Congress considered excessive. Averaging for "normal" business income was, however, still permitted.

The subsequent shift from a system of nine baskets to a system of two and now four principal baskets reflects reduced concern about averaging high and low-tax rates given the convergence of global corporate tax rates to a point closer to the US rate (or below). It was thought no longer necessary to carry the significant administrative burden that had been associated with nine baskets.

While the limitation on the foreign tax credit and the alternative forms it may take are reasonably understandable based on the considerations just reviewed, the rationale for restrictions on the allowance of foreign income taxes as credits added in the 2017 Tax Act are opaque. The 20% haircut on taxes attributable to GILTI reduces the incentive of foreign governments to increase their income tax to the effective US tax rate on GILTI. It also rewards US investment in zero foreign tax haven countries and in relative terms penalizes investment in foreign countries imposing positive rates of tax. While the objective may have been to limit revenue loss and to align with the effective US tax rate on export income benefitting from the foreign derived intangible income deduction, the GILTI haircut on creditable foreign income tax adds substantial complexity.

The second restriction on foreign tax credits added by the 2017 Tax Act is the denial of any carryover of foreign tax credits in the GILTI basket. The inability to carryover excess foreign tax credits also limits revenue loss. The provision may have been designed, however, to prevent foreign taxes associated with the GILTI inclusion in the portion of that is offset by the 50% deduction from being allowed as a credit.[47] The limit on GILTI carryovers, along with denial of credits for foreign taxes on foreign dividends eligible for the 100% DRD, provides a further incentive for a CFC to minimize foreign taxes on non-subpart F income. The combined effect of having three categories of CFC earnings, each subject to a different US effective tax rate for a 10% corporate US shareholder, and four categories of foreign tax credit limitations, results in a staggeringly complex regime for taxing foreign income. The following

47. The Section 250 deduction offsets the Section 78 dividend associated with the taxes on GILTI but does not reduce the taxes deemed paid that relate to that portion of the Section 78 dividend. If they were permitted to be used as foreign tax credits, there would be a double benefit. The statutory mechanism to prevent that is to eliminate the possibility of a carryover.

table captures just some of these complexities for a 10% corporate US shareholder in a CFC:

Variations in Foreign Tax Credit Limits for 10% US Corporate Shareholder

Category of Foreign Income	*US Tax*	*Percentage of Foreign Taxes Creditable*	*Separate Limit (SL) or Cross-Credit (CC)*	*Carryover (Back/ Forward)*
Exempt dividends (DRD)	0%	0%	NA	NA (None)
GILTI	10.50%	80%	SL	None
Passive (w/high-tax kick-out)	21%	100%	SL	1 and 10
Foreign branch	21%	100%	SL	1 and 10
General: subpart F and other foreign income	21%	100%	CC	1 and 10

To add to the complexity, the following chapter discusses the foreign derived intangible income (FDII) deduction allowed to a US corporation in relation to exported goods, intangible rights, and services. The FDII regime provides yet another effective rate on income earned from sales to foreign customers. Moreover, foreign source FDII also is in the general category and foreign taxes on that income may be cross-credited against US tax on other income in the same basket.

The taxation of an individual on foreign income also is complex. Before taking account of the option to elect Section 962 is considered, the following is a table of foreign tax credit limits comparable to the preceding table:

Variations in Foreign Tax Credit Limits for 10% US Individual Shareholder

Category of Foreign Income	*US Tax*	*Percent of Foreign Taxes Creditable; Corp. Level / Direct Tax*	*Separate Limit (SL) or Cross-Credit (CC)*	*Carryover (Back/ Forward)*
Foreign corp. dividends (no DRD)	37%	0%/100%	General; CC	1 and 10
GILTI	37%	0%/100%	SL	None
Passive (w/high-tax kick-out)	37%	0%/100%	SL	1 and 10
Foreign branch	37%	100%	SL	1 and 10
General: subpart F and other foreign income	37%	0%/100%	CC	1 and 10

CHAPTER 11
Special Treatment of Foreign Income

11.1 GENERAL

Generally, under US tax principles considered so far, no special treatment is provided for foreign income earned directly by US taxpayers because of the type of income involved, the activity that generates it, the geographical source of the income, or the personal circumstances of an individual income earner. If, under the source rules discussed in Chapter 4, the directly earned income is foreign source and attracts a foreign tax, the foreign tax credit mechanism is available; if it is US source income, it is simply subject to US tax. However, we saw in Chapter 6, that very different rules apply to income earned indirectly through controlled foreign corporation due to the 100% DRD in Section 245A and the Section 250 deduction for GILTI, both of which were adopted in the 2017 Tax Act.[1]

In some situations, however, the US has adopted preferential treatment for income earned directly by a US person from sales to foreign persons or from working abroad to further non-ax policy objectives: (1) to provide incentives for increased exports of US-produced goods and services; and (2) to encourage US citizens to accept employment abroad and encourage US trade.

11.2 INCENTIVES TO INCREASE US EXPORTS

11.2.1 Background

In 1971, concern over the level of US exports led Congress to adopt a tax subsidy for export income.[2] It enacted the Domestic International Sales Corporation (DISC)

1. *See* Chapter 6 sections 6.2 and 6.4.
2. The DISC was designed to address a balance of payments deficit by encouraging US investment and reducing the US trade deficit. By the end of 1971, however, the United States had delinked the US dollar from gold and by the end of 1973 had a free-floating currency. Under flexible exchange

provisions to provide a tax incentive for US companies to engage in export activities. The subsidy took the form of a deferral of US tax on a portion of export income channeled through a DISC, in effect an interest-free loan from the Treasury to US exporters. In 1976, however, a GATT panel found that the DISC rules violated the GATT provisions on export subsidies and that the DISC rules also appeared to constitute prohibited "export subsidies" under the agreements reached in the Tokyo Round of Multilateral Trade Negotiations.

In the face of pressure from its GATT trading partners to repeal DISC, Congress in 1984 adopted a new type of tax-preferred corporation, a Foreign Sales Corporation (FSC), which was designed to encourage exports and to try to eliminate the aspects of DISC that had caused it to be a prohibited export subsidy.[3] The DISC provisions were retained for small exporters but an interest charge equal to the US Treasury borrowing rate was imposed on the tax deferral.

The European Union challenged the FSC regime under World Trade Organization procedures. The FSC regime likewise was held to constitute a prohibited trade subsidy and thus was a violation of the WTO agreement. Congress tried again in 2000 by enacting the FSC Repeal and Exclusion of Extraterritorial Income Act of 2000 (ETI), which purported to adopt a (WTO compliant) territorial system (the new ETI regime), but which, in fact, continued the special treatment of export-related income. The EU again challenged the new law and again the WTO ruled that the new provisions were in violation of WTO rules.[4] In 2004 Congress repealed the ETI provisions for transactions after 2004, but included generous transition rules through 2006 (and even beyond, in some cases).

The 2004 Tax Act that eliminated the ETI regime also introduced its replacement: the Section 199 domestic manufacturing incentive.[5] This domestic production incentive remedied the WTO problems of prior provisions by applying the benefit regardless of the market destination of the sale (domestic or export). Under Section 199, taxpayers received a deduction equal to the lower of 9% of their "qualified production activities income" for the tax year or their taxable income, subject to the additional limitation that the deduction could not exceed 50% of the W-2 wages paid by the taxpayer during the year.[6] The 2017 Tax Act repealed Section 199.

---

rates, the effects of an export subsidy are reduced to the extent that increased exports also increased demand for dollars and the dollar exchange rate rose as a result. David L. Brumbaugh, *A History of the Extraterritorial Income (ETI) and Foreign Sales Corporation (FSC) Export Tax-Benefit Controversy*, 4 (2006); Paul R. McDaniel, *Trade Agreements and Income Taxation: Interactions, Conflicts, and Resolutions*, 57 TAX L. REV. 275, 296-297 (2004). Since 1973, US policymakers have regularly ignored these basic economic realities.

3. The FSC's substitution of a foreign for a domestic corporation was intended to mimic a foreign dividend exemption system used by certain US trading partners, but it employed the same artificial transfer pricing rules as used in the DISC and so was transparent in its effort to avoid WTO rules.
4. The WTO decisions are discussed and analyzed in McDaniel, *Trade Agreements*, *supra* note 2.
5. P.L. 108-357, § 102(A), American Jobs Creation Act of 2004.
6. Prior Section 199(a)(1) and (b). A taxpayer's "qualified production activities income" was the excess of its "domestic production gross receipts" over its cost of goods sold allocable to those receipts, plus its other expenses, losses, or deductions allocable to those receipts. Sec. 199(c). The deduction, which effectively lowered the income tax rate on income from production activities,

11.2.2 A New Export Subsidy: The Deduction for Foreign Derived Intangible Income (FDII)

11.2.2.1 Background

As described in Chapter 6, Congress made substantial changes in the 2017 Tax Act to the rules for taxing foreign income earned through a CFC, including exempting non-subpart F amounts up to a 10% return on a CFC's qualified business asset investment (QBAI). While the corporate tax rate also was reduced from 35% to 21%, Congress was concerned that this shift to a partial territorial system would encourage US businesses to earn income abroad rather than in the US. In response, Congress also added provisions that were meant to reduce the incentives for locating real activity and profits offshore, including the Base Erosion and Anti-Abuse Tax discussed at Chapter 5 section 5.10, current inclusion of GILTI subject to a 50% deduction, and, continuing the US tradition of subsidizing exporters, the deduction for the so-called Foreign Derived Intangible Income (FDII).[7]

11.2.2.2 The FDII Deduction

FDII is extremely complicated, but its mission is relatively simple. Effectively, it reduces the tax rate from 21% to 13.125% on the foreign portion of a US corporation's income in excess of a 10% return on tangible assets. In effect, the FDII regime is assuming that profits in excess of 10% of a US corporation's tangible property are attributable to intangible property.[8] The reduced tax on profits in excess of 10% of tangible assets is intended to encourage US corporations to not transfer intangible property (including intellectual property rights) overseas, but instead to keep it in the US. Note the parallels between GILTI and FDII. As discussed in Chapter 6 sections 6.1, 6.2.1 and 6.4.2, the GILTI regime taxes a CFC's profits in excess of 10% of its tangible assets under the assumption that the CFC's excess return is attributable to intangibles. In a very rough sense, GILTI attempts to discourage the transfer of intangibles to CFCs, while FDII attempts to encourage the retention of intangibles by US corporations.[9]

---

was available to corporations (including S corporations), partnerships, estates, trusts, and individuals engaging in production activities through a sole proprietorship.

7. Tim Dowd and Paul Landefeld, *The Business Cycle and the Deduction for Foreign Derived Intangible Income: A Historical Perspective*, 71 NAT. TAX J. 729, 730 (2018).
8. This explains the rational for the name, "Foreign Derived Intangible Income."
9. We say "in a rough sense" because the GILTI tax rate on profits in excess of 10% of tangible assets is 10.5%, while the reduced FDII tax rate is 13.125%. Even when the 80% limit on GILTI foreign tax credits is taken into account, there still may be a tax incentive to transfer intangible assets overseas if the foreign effective tax rate is sufficiently below 13.125%. This incentive may in some cases be offset by the reduction of the foreign tax credit for GILTI to 80% of the taxed imposed on GILTI by a foreign country and by the inability to carryover excess credits arising from GILTI.

Under Section 250(a)(1), a domestic corporate taxpayer is allowed a deduction for 37.5% of the corporation's FDII for the year.[10] This deduction in effect reduces the tax rate on the FDII to 13.125% (21% - (37.5% X 21%). The process for calculating FDII under Section 250 can be illustrated in the following formula:

> FDII = Deemed Intangible Income x (Foreign Derived Deduction Eligible Income / Deduction Eligible Income)[11]

The process begins by first calculating the US corporation's "Deduction Eligible Income." Deduction Eligible Income is a US corporation's gross income less certain exclusions and less the deductions allocable to the remaining gross income. The items excluded from gross income in calculating Deduction Eligible Income are income from a CFC (whether a dividend, an inclusion under subpart F or GILTI), any financial services income (domestic or foreign), domestic oil or gas extraction income, and any foreign branch income, less deductions allocable to the gross income (Section 250(b)(3)). Excluding foreign branch and CFC income from "deduction eligible income" has the general effect of restricting the foreign income portion of deduction eligible income to income earned directly by the domestic corporation. Thus, a US corporation would have an incentive to retain its intangibles in the US and license them from there rather than, for example, transferring them to a foreign subsidiary or branch.

Once Deduction Eligible Income is calculated, it is then further modified to calculate "Foreign-Derived Deduction Eligible Income" by eliminating all income other than the income derived by the US corporation from sales or licenses of goods, services, and rights to intangible property to foreign buyers for foreign use.[12] Note that the result is that the formula's fraction, Foreign Derived Deduction Eligible Income / Deduction Eligible Income, represents the portion of the US corporation's income that arises from the sale or license of goods, services, and intangible property to foreign buyers for foreign use.[13]

---

10. The deduction will be reduced to 21.875% for years beginning from December 31, 2025. Sec. 250(a)(3)(A). This reduction parallels the reduction of the GILTI Section 250 deduction to 37.5% for the same years.
11. The statute tells us that FDII bears the same portion to "deemed intangible income" as "foreign derived deduction eligible income" bears to "deduction eligible income." Sec. 250(b)(1). Placing this into a formula yields:

    FDII / Deemed Intangible Income = Foreign Derived Deduction Eligible Income / Deduction Eligible Income

    Solving this equation for FDII by multiplying both sides by "Deemed Intangible Income" in turn yields:

    FDII = Deemed Intangible Income x (Foreign Derived Deduction Eligible Income / Deduction Eligible Income)
12. Sec. 250(b)(4). A final piece of the statutory magic is to define the words sold, sells or sale to include any lease, license, exchange, or other disposition, thereby bringing foreign royalties within the reach of the subsidy.
13. The regulations under Section 250 refer to this fraction as foreign-derived ratio. Treas. Reg. Sec. 1.250(b)-1(b) and -1(c)(13).

The final determination is "Deemed Intangible Income," which is defined as the excess of Deduction Eligible Income over the "Deemed Tangible Income Return."[14] Deemed Tangible Income Return equals a return of 10% of the US corporation's qualified business asset investment (QBAI)[15], i.e., its tangible assets. As a result, Deemed Intangible Income represents the amount of the US corporation's Deduction Eligible Income in excess of 10% of its QBAI.

An example may help illustrate this mind-numbing calculation. Suppose US Corp sells Product A, which is made in the United States, to a foreign customer for USD 200. US Corp also licenses certain of its intangible rights to a foreign licensee for USD 20. US Corp sells USD 100 of Product A to US customers. Assume that the deduction eligible gross income is USD 320 (USD 200 plus USD 20 plus USD 100), deductions (allocable pro rata to all gross income) are USD 145, and QBAI is USD 200.

Start with the formula:

FDII = Deemed Intangible Income x (Foreign Derived Deduction Eligible Income / Deduction Eligible Income)

We first calculate the Deduction Eligible Income to be USD 175 (USD 320 income from sales and licenses - USD 145 of allocable expenses). The Foreign Derived Deduction Eligible Income is USD 120 (220/320 x 175 = 120). The Deemed Tangible Income Return is USD 20 (10% x 200 of QBAI) so the Deemed Intangible Income is USD 155 (USD 175 of Deduction Eligible Income - USD 20 of Deemed Income Tangible Return). Thus, filling in the formula, yields:

FDII = USD 155 x (USD 120 / USD 175)
FDII = USD 106

Under Section 250(a)(1)(A), the FDII deduction is USD 40, calculated as 37.5% of the USD 106 of FDII. At a US corporate tax rate of 21%, the effective tax rate on the FDII is 13.125% (21% x (1-37.5%)).

A concern with respect to any export sales subsidy is to restrict its benefits to sales to foreign customers, as well as to not reward "round trip" sales back to the United States. The regulations provide rules for determining place of use and substantiation requirements. The substantiation requirements are relaxed for taxpayers with aggregate sales under USD 25 million.[16] A taxpayer is also entitled to the benefit in the absence of substantiation if it knows or has "reason to know" the sale is to a foreign customer for foreign use.[17]

The different treatment of the deemed tangible investment return and the different effective rates for FDII and GILTI, as well as the FDII and GILTI foreign tax credits and

14. Sec. 250(b)(2).
15. Sec. 250(b)(2). The same definition for QBAI is used as is used in GILTI, discussed in Chapter 6 section 6.4.2.
16. Treas. Reg. Sec. 1.250-3, -4, and -5.
17. Treas. Reg. Sec. 1.250-3(f)(3).

limitations, add considerable complexity to an already complex area of tax law. Taxpayers are continuously evaluating how to optimize their tax position in light of the interactions of these rules and their evolution as regulations are finalized and amended. In addition, consideration has to be given to the future changes in statutory deduction rates, as well as reasonable expectations of future rate changes, in light of budget challenges resulting from the COVID-19 pandemic and changing political dynamics.

11.2.2.3 FDII and Treaties

In light of the history of trade-based challenges to previous US export provisions, it may seem surprising that there has not been more discussion of their compliance with trade standards. The discussion that has occurred has been inconclusive.[18] What does seem clear, however, is that denial of a FDII deduction to a US branch of a foreign corporation eligible for the benefits of a double taxation treaty would be inconsistent with the nondiscrimination article. Under Article 24(2) of the US Model, which is found in most treaties, the taxation of a permanent establishment may not be less favorable than the taxation of enterprises of the United States carrying on the same activities. In light of such a stark conflict, the issue falls into that of when legislation overrides a treaty discussed in Chapter 14.

11.2.3 Treatment of Income Earned Abroad

Another special provision related to exports allows US citizens or residents who work abroad to exclude a certain amount of earned income from gross income. This preferential provision is defended on the ground that it helps increase US exports by increasing the likelihood that foreign companies—controlled or uncontrolled—will acquire their products or services from US companies.

11.2.3.1 General

For many years, a US citizen who works in and is a resident of a foreign country has been granted preferential tax treatment for foreign source earned income in the form of an exclusion from tax of a specific amount of such income. The exclusion has been the subject of much controversy and numerous legislative changes, but in recent years has remained stable. Note that, if claimed, the exclusion replaces the foreign tax credit with

18. Rebecca M. Kysar, *Critiquing (and Repairing) the New International Tax Regime*, 128 YALE LAW J. FORUM 339 (2018) (FDII "likely violates WTO obligations because it is an export subsidy on goods"); Chris William Sanchirico, *The New U.S. Tax Preference for "Foreign Derived Intangible Income,"* 71 TAX LAW REV. 625, 645-649 (2018) (questioning whether revenue is forgone under the WTO standards depending on the baseline chosen for comparison); David Kamin, David Gamage, Ari Glogower, Rebecca Kysar, Darien Shanske, Reuven Avi-Yonah, Lily Batchelder, J. Clifton Fleming, Daniel Hemel, Mitchell Kane, David Miller, Daniel Shaviro and Manoj Viswanathan, *The Games They Will Play: Tax Games, Roadblocks, and Glitches Under the 2017 Tax Legislation*; 103 MINN. L. REV. 1439, 1499-1503 (2019) (summarizing issues).

respect to the earned income, which would otherwise be available to provide relief to US individual taxpayers earning income abroad that is subject to foreign income tax. Of course, an exclusion of foreign source income is not identical to a foreign tax credit. If the income bears little or no foreign income tax, then under a credit regime the income would essentially face full US income tax. However, under Section 911 any qualifying income escapes US income taxation entirely, regardless of the amount of foreign income tax paid.

While the tax preference is granted to individuals, its financial benefits may be captured in whole or in part by employers of the individuals in the form of lower salaries than they would have been required to pay in the absence of the exclusion. The employers defend the special tax benefit on the ground that it enables them to employ US citizens in the foreign operation rather than lower-paid foreign nationals; the US citizens will be more likely to purchase needed goods and services from US providers than would non-US employees; therefore, it is asserted, the exclusion helps ensure higher levels of US exports. The validity of this argument is contested by opponents who argue that the subsidy either provides a windfall to US multinationals for doing what they would have done in the absence of the tax subsidy or is an inefficient mechanism by which to attempt to achieve greater US exports when compared with more targeted subsidies. The frequent legislative changes in the exclusion reflect the ebb and flow of views in Congress regarding export subsidies and revenue needs.

In general, Section 911(a) permits a qualified US citizen or resident who works abroad to elect to exclude from US gross income the foreign-earned income up to an annually indexed amount (for 2021, that maximum is USD 108,700) plus a portion of the employer-provided housing costs (an alternative deduction is available if the individual's employer does not provide or pay for the housing).[19]

11.2.3.2 Eligibility for the Exclusion

An individual can qualify for the exclusion if the individual's "tax home" is in a foreign country and one of the two additional conditions is satisfied: (1) A US *citizen* establishes that he or she has been a bona fide resident of the foreign country for the entire taxable year; or (2) a US *citizen* or *resident* is physically present in the foreign country for 330 full days out of any twelve consecutive months period.[20] The maximum exclusion (plus alternative deduction) may not exceed the individual's foreign earned income for the year.[21]

While the rules generally are straightforward, they can be arbitrary at the margins. A series of Tax Court cases denied the ability to exclude labor income under

19. A separate exclusion is provided in Section 119(c) for the value of meals and lodging provided by an employer in a "camp" located in a foreign country. A "camp" is "lodging" which is: (1) provided by the employer for the employer's convenience because the place of work is in a remote area where satisfactory housing is unavailable, (2) located as near as practicable to the place of work, and (3) a common living area, not open to the public, accommodating ten or more employees. The definition is designed to benefit primarily construction firms and oil companies.
20. Sec. 911(d)(1).
21. Sec. 911(d)(7).

Section 911 on the grounds that labor income generated in Antarctica is not "foreign source."[22] Another case involved a determination that wages paid to a US citizen flight attendant for travel over international waters was not foreign source income and thus not eligible for exclusion under Section 911.[23]

The "tax home" of an individual is determined under the principles established by the Internal Revenue Service and the courts under Section 162(a)(2). That section permits deductions for travel expenses only when an individual is "away from home." Hence to establish deductibility of travel expenses, it is necessary to determine the taxpayer's "home" so that expenses incurred while "away" from that home may be identified.[24] The resolution of the issue is essentially a factual one although in very general terms a taxpayer's "tax home" is located at his principal place of business.[25]

11.2.3.3 The Foreign Earned Income Component

The "earned income" that may qualify for the exclusion (if from a foreign source as determined under the rules discussed in Chapter 4) is defined in Section 911(d)(2)(A) to include wages, salaries, professional fees, or other amounts received as compensation for personal services actually rendered. Certain items are, however, excluded from the definition of "foreign earned income," including pensions, annuities, payments from the US Government, or any amount received more than one year after the year in which the services were rendered.[26] Thus, assume a US employee in foreign country Y,

22. *See, e.g., Arnett v. Commissioner*, 126 TC 89 (2006), aff'd, 473 F.3d 790 (7th Cir. 2007) (Antarctica is not a foreign country for purposes of Section 911); *Howard v. Commissioner*, TC Memo. 2007-313 (Oct. 15, 2007) (same); *Brown v. Commissioner*, TC Summ. Op. 2007-166 (Sept. 24, 2007)(same); *Gober v. Commissioner*, TC Memo 2008-110 (Apr. 22, 2008) (same).
23. *LeTourneau v. Commissioner*, TC Memo. 2012-45 (Feb. 21, 2013). *See also Rogers v. Commissioner*, TC Memo. 2013-77 (Mar. 13, 2013).
24. In *Daly v. Commissioner*, TC Memo. 2013-147 (June 6, 2013), the Tax Court concluded that the taxpayer's "tax home" was in the US, because the taxpayer (husband) lived on US Air Force bases while in Iraq and Afghanistan and was not permitted to leave the bases. He also "maintained strong ties to his home in Utah" and "[h]is family did not go with him, and he did not travel. He did not open a bank account in Iraq or Afghanistan." In *Haskins v. Commissioner, aff'g per curiam* TC Memo 2019-87, the 11th Circuit agreed with the Tax Court that taxpayer's abode was in the United States and her connections to Afghanistan were transitory or limited to military bases.
25. Treas. Reg. Sec. 1.911-2(b). The leading case in the area is *Commissioner v. Flowers*, 326 US 465 (1946), in which the Supreme Court articulated a three-part test for deductibility of travel expenses under Section 162(a)(2): (1) The travel expenses must be reasonable and necessary; (2) the expenses must be incurred while away from home; and (3) the expenses must be incurred in pursuit of (i.e., directly connected to) business. The deductibility of travel expenses under Section 162(a)(2) is a frequently litigated issue and, accordingly, reference to that section is in fact a reference to a mass of confusing and often conflicting body of case law and administrative pronouncements. For a summary of the issues under Section 162(a)(2), *see* SIMMONS, MCMAHON, BORDEN, AND WELLS, FEDERAL INCOME TAXATION, 666-685 (8th ed., 2020). The statute also requires that the taxpayer not have his "abode" in the US although the exact content of this term is unclear. *See* Treas. Reg. Sec. 1.911-2(b) (maintenance of dwelling in US does not "necessarily" establish an "abode" in the US).
26. Sec. 911(b)(1)(B). The rules for determining foreign earned income and the exclusions therefrom are set forth in detail in Treas. Reg. Sec. 1.911-3.

who otherwise satisfies the conditions of Section 911, enters into a deferred compensation agreement pursuant to which payments are to begin five years after retirement. None of the payments will qualify for the Section 911 exclusion.

The amount excluded under Section 911 may reduce the taxpayer's tax on other nonqualified income; there is no provision for "exemption with progression."

11.2.3.4 The Housing Cost Component

In addition to the exclusion of foreign earned income, a qualifying individual may also exclude a portion of the value of employer-provided housing or housing costs reimbursed by the employer.[27] The "housing cost amount" that may be excluded under Section 911 is the excess of the individual's housing expenses (employer-provided)[28] for the year over 16% of the earned income exclusion amount under Section 911(b)(2)(D), as adjusted for inflation and the number of days the taxpayer is qualified during the year.[29] Under Section 911, the amount of individual's housing expenses that can be included in the formula is capped at 30% of the maximum earned income exclusion for that year.[30] For example, assume a US citizen employed in a foreign country incurs (and is reimbursed by her employer for) USD 25,000 of housing expenses during 2021. The maximum annual earned income exclusion for 2021 is USD 108,700. Thus, the employee could exclude USD 7,608 (USD 25,000[31] minus USD 17,392 (16% × USD 108,700)) as a housing cost amount under Section 911.[32]

If the employee's housing costs are not covered by the employer, the taxpayer-employee can still secure a housing tax benefit under Section 911. To the extent the employee incurs housing costs not covered by the employer, the employee may deduct those costs (subject to a limitation) in computing adjusted gross income. The amount of this deduction is limited to the excess the employee's foreign earned income for the year over the amount of foreign earned income excluded under Section 911(a) for the taxable year.[33] Any housing costs exceeding this limit (and thus not deductible in the current year) can be carried over one year (only) and deducted, subject again to the same earned income limitation in Section 911(c)(4)(B).[34]

27. Sec. 911(c)(1); Treas. Reg. Sec. 1.911-4.
28. Housing expenses must be "reasonable," not "lavish or extravagant." Sec. 911(c)(3)(A).
29. The theory of the provision is that costs in excess of the base amount reflect higher living expenses abroad. Note that the calculation of the housing exclusion was modified in 2006, and is now based on 16% of the earned income exclusion and *not* a specified government pay grade level as it was under the earlier version of the statute. Sec. 911(c)(1)(B). Additionally, the amount of housing expenses that can be used in the calculation under Section 911(c) to determine the actual exclusion is now capped by Section 911(c)(2)(A) at 30% of the earned income exclusion amount for the year as determined under Section 911(b)(2)(D).
30. Sec. 911(c)(1)(A) and 911(c)(2)(A).
31. The full USD 25,000 can be used in the formula because it does not exceed the Section 911(c)(2)(A) cap, which for 2021 would be calculated as 30% × USD 108,700, or USD 32,610.
32. The maximum possible housing exclusion for 2021 would be equal to (30% × USD 108,700) – (16% × USD 108,700) or USD 15,218.
33. Sec. 911(c)(4). Thus, the deduction is available to self-employed individuals.
34. If the deduction exceeds the limit, the excess may be carried over only to the next taxable year.

11.2.3.5 Election of Section 911 Benefits

The taxpayer must make an election to utilize the benefits under Section 911. The election is valid until revoked. If the taxpayer revokes an election without the consent of the Internal Revenue Service, generally no new election can be made until five years have elapsed after the year of revocation.[35]

A taxpayer who makes the Section 911 exclusion is denied any deduction, exclusion, or tax credit, including a foreign tax credit, to the extent allocable to the amount excluded from gross income.[36] Accordingly, a taxpayer who qualifies for the Section 911 exclusion and is deciding whether to make the election must first determine his US tax liability by including all foreign earned income in gross income, taking all appropriate deductions, and reducing US tax liability by the foreign tax credit. Then he must determine his US tax liability by excluding the Section 911 amount from income and reducing deductions and the foreign tax credit to the extent allocable to the income excluded. Since there is a five-year waiting period after a Section 911 election is revoked before it can be re-elected, careful projections are also required in deciding which of the alternative tax paths to follow.[37]

35. Sec. 911(e); Treas. Reg. Sec. 1.911-7; Rev. Rul. 90-77, 1990-2 C.B. 183.
36. Sec. 911(d)(6). Treas. Reg. Section 1.911-6 details the rules for allocating deductions, exclusions, and credits to the income excluded under Section 911(a).
37. Other tax considerations must be considered by a US taxpayer moving abroad, e.g., the special rules on deductible moving expenses where foreign moves are involved (Sec. 217(h)). Many of these other items, such as Section 2017(h) will be treated as "miscellaneous itemized deductions," which are not deductible through the year 2025. Sec. 67(b) and (g). *See* Chapter 2 section 2.3.2.4.

CHAPTER 12

Transfer Pricing

12.1 BACKGROUND

Section 482 authorizes the fiscal authorities to allocate gross income, deductions, and credits between related taxpayers to the extent necessary to prevent evasion of taxes or clearly to reflect the income of the taxpayers.[1] The section has a very broad scope. It applies to domestic as well as international transactions and does not require a finding of a tax avoidance purpose on the part of the parties involved for a reallocation of income to be undertaken. Detailed regulations have been issued under the section.[2]

1. A version of the first sentence of Section 482 has appeared in the United States Internal Revenue provisions since 1921. The second sentence was added in 1986 and the third sentence in 2017.
2. The Regulations were first issued in their present detailed form in 1968. In 1988, pursuant to Congressional instructions, the Internal Revenue Service prepared a comprehensive study of intercompany pricing rules and in particular the rules dealing with the transfer of intangibles. The study contains an extensive discussion of the history of Section 482 and its application to various types of transactions. Treasury Department and Internal Revenue Service, *Study of Intercompany Pricing* (Oct. 18, 1988). The "White Paper" study was followed by proposed and temporary regulations in 1992 and 1993, which followed some aspects of the method of analysis used in the White Paper, particularly the "comparative profits" approach. Final regulations were issued in 1994 that strongly influenced the OECD 1995 Transfer Pricing Guidelines. These two sets of highly influential guidance are broadly consistent. The OECD regularly revises its transfer pricing guidelines, as do the Treasury and the Service on a somewhat more episodic basis.

   In 2009, revised final regulations were issued governing the treatment of related party services. These Regulations, discussed below at section 12.4.3, sought to align the treatment of services with the more sophisticated rules applicable to sales of goods and transfers of intangibles. Treas. Reg. Sec. 1.492-9. In 2011, revised cost sharing regulations were finalized (*see* section 12.4.2.2 below) detailing how a cost sharing arrangement among related parties (i.e., an agreement to share the costs of developing an intangible that will be jointly owned by the parties to the agreement) will be treated for tax purposes. Treas. Reg. Sec. 1.482-7.

   In 1998, the Service released proposed regulations governing the pricing of related party "global dealing" transactions. 63 Fed. Reg. 11177 (Mar. 6, 1998). These proposed regulations were developed in part through the Service's experience in the Advance Pricing Agreement program with financial services and global dealing taxpayers under Notice 94-40, 1994-1 C.B. 351 (1994). The proposed regulations have never been finalized and the global dealing rules have

The Regulations are based in general on the principle that transactions between related parties should take place on an arm's length basis.[3]

The section performs two related but distinct functions in the US tax system. In the first place, it prevents a shifting of income or deductions among related taxpayers in order to take advantage of differentials in rate brackets, whether in the domestic or international context. In the international setting, however, the section plays an additional role. Even if intercompany transactions result in no overall reduction in tax burden on the controlled group when US and foreign taxes are taken into account, it is still necessary that the US protect its appropriate share of tax revenues in international transactions. Thus, the arm's length standard of Section 482 is invoked to allocate income to the US even where there has been no reduction in overall tax burden on the group because of the non-arm's length intercompany pricing practices in the group.

The following discussion views the operation of Section 482 primarily from the perspective of transactions between a US parent and its foreign subsidiary. But it must be kept in mind that the section is equally applicable to transactions between a foreign

---

been reserved in the services regulations. Treas. Reg. Sec. 1.482-9(m)(6).

3. The arm's length standard is not contained in the statute itself, which speaks only of the need clearly to reflect the income of related parties. The Regulations interpret the statutory requirement that income be "clearly reflected" in terms of the necessity of arm's length dealings between related parties. Treas. Reg. Sec. 1.482-1(b)(1). The standard is articulated as a counter-factual test:

> In determining the true taxable income of a controlled taxpayer, the standard to be applied in every case is that of a taxpayer dealing at arm's length with an uncontrolled taxpayer. A controlled transaction meets the arm's length standard if the results of the transaction are consistent with the results that *would have been realized if uncontrolled taxpayers had engaged in the same transaction under the same circumstances* (arm's length result). (emphasis added)

The counter-factual aspect of the arm's length standard in the regulations is a frequent point of disagreement and some argue that the only relevant consideration is what occurs in transactions between third parties irrespective of whether the circumstances are sufficiently similar. This was the principal point of disagreement in *Altera* regarding whether costs of compensatory stock options should be included in costs to be shared in a cost sharing arrangement in the face of evidence that cost sharing between unrelated parties would not take account of stock-based compensation (SBC). *Altera* dealt with a related party situation where the publicly traded stock was in the same parent company, and the Ninth Circuit Court of Appeals upheld IRS Regulations requiring that the SBC costs be taken into account. *Altera Corporation & Subsidiaries v. Commissioner*, 926 F.3d 1061 (9th Cir. 2019), *rehearing denied*, 941 F.3d 1200 (9th Cir. 2019), *cert. denied* (June 22, 2020).

Regulations treat use of profit split and comparable profits methods as consistent with the arm's length standard, notwithstanding that these methods move in the direction of a more formulary approach to transfer pricing. In addition, the Regulations contain a number of "safe harbor" rules. Although the OECD previously had not supported the use of safe harbors in transfer pricing, the OECD guidelines were revised (May 16, 2013) to provide guidance on the use of safe harbors. The OECD's most recent transfer pricing guidelines reflect the BEPS work including Actions 8-10 (Intangibles, Risks & Capital, and High-Risk Transactions) and Action 13 (Transfer Pricing Documentation and Country-by-Country Reporting). OECD, Transfer Pricing Guidelines for Multinational Enterprises and Tax Administrations (2017) ("OECD Guidelines"), https://doi.org/10.1787/tpg-2017-en.

parent and its US subsidiary and between commonly controlled "brother-sister" companies.[4]

12.2 SCOPE OF COVERAGE

The power to allocate income and deductions under Section 482 is only available to the fiscal authorities; the section may not be invoked by the taxpayer.[5] The section applies in any case where two taxpayers are "owned or controlled directly or indirectly by the same interests." The Regulations interpret the "controlled" requirement quite broadly and look to the realities of the situation and not to the presence of formal legal control or greater than 50% ownership.[6]

There was initially some question whether the section could be used to allocate income not in the taxpayers' records or in the contractual relations between the related parties. But the court decisions in general have upheld the authority of the Commissioner of Internal Revenue to allocate such unidentified income as well as allowing a corresponding adjustment to the related party. (Correlative adjustments are discussed at section 12.5.2.) For example, in the case of interest-free loans between parent and subsidiary, the Commissioner has successfully imposed an arm's length interest charge under Section 482 (and corresponding interest expense to the subsidiary).[7] Additionally, it is permissible under Section 482 for one related party to report income even though the overall group transaction was not profitable.[8]

---

4. Transactions between two foreign subsidiaries of a US parent corporation may be relevant to the United States. Although the US is not taxing the foreign subsidiaries directly (to the extent they do not earn income in the US and are not US resident taxpayers), the placement of income and deductions within the multinational group between the two subsidiaries may impact US taxes. For example, the location of such items may affect application of anti-deferral rules such as subpart F to the US parent (*see* Chapter 6) as well as associated foreign tax credits (*see* Chapters 9 and 10).
5. Treas. Reg. Sec. 1.482-1(a)(3). The taxpayer may report (on timely filed returns) income based on prices other than those actually charged in order to reflect true income. However, the inability of taxpayers to amend a tax return to adjust prices on related party transactions has generated increasing controversy. This question of whether a taxpayer can ever initiate a change in price (after the first timely return is filed) was addressed by the US Court of Federal Claims, which concluded that the regulations do not permit an adjustment by the taxpayer on an amended or an untimely return. *See Intersport Fashions West, Inc. v. U.S.*, 103 Fed. Cl. 396 (2012).

   A transfer pricing consistency constraint applies with respect to imported goods. Under Section 1059A(a), the costs on which the income determination is based may not exceed the amount used in customs valuation. In practical terms, this means that the "purchase price" paid by the US related party importer for Section 482 purposes cannot exceed the customs valuation. This rule is expected to curb tax planning because taxpayers typically seek low US customs valuations but high prices deemed paid under Section 482 by the US related party importer.
6. Treas. Reg. Sec. 1.482-1(i)(4).
7. *B. Forman Co. v. Commissioner*, 453 F.2d 1144 (2d Cir. 1972); *Kahler Corp. v. Commissioner*, 486 F.2d 1 (8th Cir. 1973); *Fitzgerald Motor Co. v. Commissioner*, 508 F.2d 1096 (5th Cir. 1975); *Likins-Foster Honolulu Corp. v. Commissioner*, 417 F.2d 285 (9th Cir. 1988). Section 7872 now specifically deals with the treatment of such interest-free loans. *See also Central de Gas de Chihuahua, S.A. v. Commissioner*, 102 TC 515 (1994) (rent imputed on equipment used with no charge).
8. For example, if a foreign parent manufactures cars and sells them to its US distributor for sale in the US, it is possible for the US distributor to report a tax profit even though the group overall

12.3 GENERAL APPROACH

The Regulations provide specific methods (discussed in section 12.4 below) to be used to determine whether transactions between related parties conform to the arm's length standard. If different types of transactions are interrelated, a different method may be applied to each aspect of the transaction. In selecting the method to be used, the taxpayer is instructed to apply the "best method," that is, "the method that, under the facts and circumstances provides the most reliable measure of an arm's length result."[9] Thus, there is no specified hierarchy of methods and "no method will invariably be considered to be more reliable than others."[10] The US reliance on the best method rule marks an important difference with countries that either apply a strict priority of methods, or informally apply a priority of methods.[11] In selecting the "best method," the Regulations focus on the degree of comparability between the related party transaction in question and an uncontrolled transaction and the "quality of the data and assumptions used in the analysis."[12] Thus, for example, if there are relatively poor data with regard to a comparable uncontrolled price (CUP) but good data as to a comparable profit method, the latter would be the "best" method even though not based on the price in an uncontrolled transaction.[13]

12.3.1 Determining Comparability

The various methods all depend on establishing comparable prices or profits of third parties dealing at arm's length ("uncontrolled" transactions), and all factors which could influence prices or profits have to be taken into account in determining the relation between the related party transaction under analysis and the uncontrolled transaction.[14] This analysis requires a consideration of the functions being performed

---

experienced a total loss from the manufacture of cars in the parent country and their final sale to customers in the US. This issue has created some conflict with US trading partners who are not inclined to allow the US distributor to report a profit while the foreign parent reports a large loss on the manufacture of the cars and their sale to the US distributor.

9. Treas. Reg. Sec. 1.482-1(c)(1).
10. *Id.* This was an important change from the 1968 Regulations, which prescribed an order of priority among the methods. Thus, if a party met its evidentiary burden to justify pricing using a higher priority method it would prevail over an evidentiarily supported lower method.
11. Similar to the 1968 Regulations, the 2017 OECD Guidelines use a "most appropriate method" standard, but provide that when "a traditional transaction method and a transactional profit method can be applied in an equally reliable manner, the traditional transaction method is preferable to the transactional profit method," and the CUP method is preferred over other traditional methods. 2017 OECD GUIDELINES, ¶¶ 2.2-2.3, 2.14-2.26.
12. Treas. Reg. Sec. 1.482-1(c)(2).
13. The application of the best method rule in the US regulations, along with the US views on what constitutes a "comparable" transaction, can lead the US tax authorities to disagree with other jurisdictions on the proper pricing of a transaction. *See* section 12.4.1.1 below.
14. Care needs to be taken to avoid relying on data that incorporates results of controlled transactions. For example, databases may include unconsolidated results of a subsidiary or a branch of a parent in a different country that engage in more than de minimis transactions with affiliates and be unreliable as a result. *See* Platform for Collaboration on Tax, *A Toolkit for Addressing Difficulties in Accessing Comparables Data for Transfer Pricing Analyses*, ¶3.3 and

by the parties, the terms and conditions of contractual arrangements, the risks being borne by each party, and the general economic conditions under which the transactions have taken place.[15] For example, if a CUP is being determined in a different geographical market from that in which the related party transaction took place, adjustments must be made to account for the differences in the two markets. "Market share strategy" involving temporarily reduced prices to increase market share can be used to justify a lower related party price. The taxpayer must show, however, that an uncontrolled taxpayer had engaged in a similar strategy and that the reduced prices are only used for a "reasonable" period of time.[16]

Similarly, the extent to which a party assumes a market or financial risk is a factor that will affect the determination of the degree of comparability of related and controlled transactions. For example, the price charged to a distributor by a manufacturer will be affected by the allocation of the risk of product liability for product defects. However, for the allocation of risk between related parties to be respected, the party bearing the risk must have sufficient financial capacity to absorb the loss should it occur.[17]

Volume differences can also affect comparability. A third-party transaction might not be considered a very strong comparable if that transaction constitutes only 10% of the taxpayer's business, whereas the related party transaction represents 90% of the taxpayer's business.[18]

The Service will impute contractual terms to a related party transaction based on the economic substance of the transaction. This practice reflects the reality that the absence of adversarial interest between related parties, unlike between unrelated parties, means related parties have much less incentive to document (or thoroughly

Annex 7 (International Monetary Fund, Organisation for Economic Co-operation and Development, United Nations, and World Bank Group (June 22, 2017), available at https://www.tax-platform.org/sites/pct/files/publications/116573-REVISED-PUBLIC-toolkit-on-comparability-and-mineral-pricing.pdf.

15. Treas. Reg. Sec. 1.482-1(d). The Regulations provide an extensive analysis of the factors to be considered and the adjustments needed to arrive at comparability.
16. Treas. Reg. Sec. 1.482-1(d)(4)(i).
17. Treas. Reg. Sec. 1.482-(d)(3)(iii).
18. Treas. Reg. Sec. 1.482-1(d)(3)(ii)(C) Ex. 1 (where taxpayer provided transportation for a third-party customer and for a related party customer, the fact that the third party constituted only 10% of the taxpayer's transportation business and the related party was 90% of the business was a difference in volume that "must be taken into account if such difference would have a material effect on the price charged."). The example is based on the facts of *U.S. Steel Corp. v. Commissioner*, 617 F.2d 942 (2d Cir. 1980), rev'g TC Memo 1977-140, which was criticized in the Joint Committee Explanation of the 1986 Act for treating uncontrolled transactions effectively as a safe harbor without taking account of differences in volume and risk. *See* Staff of Joint Committee on Taxation, *General Explanation of the Tax Reform Act of 1986*, 1014 (JCS-10-87). Consistent with that criticism, the Regulation's example would come to a different conclusion from that of the Second Circuit. If a material difference is identified between the related party transaction at issue and a potential comparable, the comparable should be adjusted to reflect that difference. For example, if the comparable is a sale of goods without delivery but the related party sale includes delivery, then the potential comparable should be adjusted (e.g., price increased) to account for delivery. But it is certainly possible that there will be material differences for which no adjustment is possible because inadequate data is available (e.g., sale of the same product with and without a brand name attached).

document) their transactions. Thus, in determining what exactly constitutes the terms of the related party transaction, the Service may need to look beyond any written terms to the actual conduct.[19]

12.3.2 Arm's Length Ranges

The Regulations recognize that the application of a method may not produce a single "correct" arm's length amount. Accordingly, the taxpayer is authorized to establish a "range" of results derived by applying the selected method to more than one set of adjusted comparable uncontrolled transactions. Statistical methods are used to improve the reliability of the range, with the results at both ends of the range being excluded. If the result shown in the related party transaction falls within the resulting "arm's length range," no adjustment will be made. If the taxpayer reported a result that falls outside the range, the Internal Revenue Service adjustment can be based on any value within the range.[20] It is important to note that while creation of a range is an option for the taxpayer, it is not required for the Service to make an allocation under Section 482. The Service can make an adjustment on the basis of a single comparable.[21] Relatedly, the Service does not consider a large number of low-quality comparables to be preferable to a few (or even one) very good comparable.

12.3.3 Determining "the Transaction"

In principle, the "true taxable income" from the related party transactions should be determined on the basis of the data involved in each individual transaction. However, the Regulations allow the taxpayer to apply the pricing methods to product lines or similar groups of products and to use sampling and other statistical techniques. In addition, interrelated transactions may be aggregated and data may be based on multiple years to reduce the effects of short-term variations that might distort prices or

19. For example, consider a foreign parent manufacturer that distributes its goods in the US through its US subsidiary. The parent's trade name for the goods is not known in the US so the US subsidiary undertakes a marketing campaign to build brand awareness. In assessing the Section 482 implications of the transactions between the foreign parent and the US subsidiary, the Service will consider the substance of the transactions. In particular, the fact that the US subsidiary spent its own funds to develop brand awareness in the US for the trade name will likely influence the Service's assessment of: (1) whether it is appropriate to impute a long-term distribution contract between the parties, and (2) whether it is appropriate to view the US subsidiary as owner (in part or full) of the US developed trade name even though there is no written contract addressing these questions. *See generally* Treas. Reg. Sec. 1.482-1(d)(3)(ii)(C) Exs. 3, 4, 5, and 6.
20. Treas. Reg. Sec. 1.482-1(e)(3). Selection of comparables is crucial in establishing the size of the range. In particular, the comparables that ultimately create the top or bottom end of the range can be very important and thus a subject of debate between the taxpayer and the Service. The wider the range the more likely that the taxpayer's own related party transactions will be within the range and not subject to adjustment. Challenges to the comparables at the top or bottom of the range can result in shrinking the size of the range and increasing the likelihood that the taxpayer's results are outside the range and will be adjusted (often to the median of all results). Treas. Reg. Sec. 1.482-1(e)(3).
21. Treas. Reg. Sec. 1.482-1(e)(4).

profits.[22] In recent years, the reliance on aggregation of transactions involving intangible property, in particular, has been the subject of litigation,[23] regulation,[24] and finally, statutory revision in Section 482 in 2017[25] at which time the following language was added to the end of the statute:

> For purposes of this section, the Secretary shall require the valuation of transfers of intangible property (including intangible property transferred with other property or services) on an aggregate basis or the valuation of such a transfer on the basis of the realistic alternatives to such a transfer, if the Secretary determines that such basis is the most reliable means of valuation of such transfers.

A related debate (*see* section 12.4.2), particularly in the context of cost sharing arrangements, has surrounded the meaning of the term "intangible" and the types of intellectual property for which a subsidiary might be required to compensate its US parent (in the case of US parent—foreign subsidiary transaction).

12.4 SPECIFIC TRANSACTIONS

12.4.1 Sales of Goods

The Regulations set forth six pricing methods to be used in determining the income from the sale of tangible property between related parties. They are: (1) the CUP method, (2) the resale price method, (3) the cost plus method, the comparable profits method, (4) the profit split method, and (5) the unspecified method.[26] The comparable

22. Treas. Reg. Sec. 1.482-1(f)(2).
23. *See, e.g., Amazon, Inc. v. Commissioner*, 934 F.3d 976 (9th Cir. 2019) (affirming Tax Court decision, which rejected the scope and application of the aggregation concept employed by the IRS in evaluating the taxpayer's cost sharing arrangement with its Luxembourg subsidiary).
24. Treas. Reg. Sec. 1.482-7(g)(2)(iv) (providing, in the context of cost sharing agreements (*see* section 12.4.2.2), that "it may be that the multiple transactions are reasonably anticipated ... to be so interrelated that the method that provides the most reliable measure of an arm's length charge is a method under this section applied on an aggregate basis."). A temporary regulation issued in 2015 that expired in 2018, further emphasized the role of aggregation of multiple transactions in order to determine an arm's length result, providing: "consideration of the combined effect of two or more transactions may be appropriate to determine whether the overall compensation in the transactions is consistent with the value provided, including any synergies among items and services provided." Treas. Reg. Sec. 1.482-1T(f)(2)(i)(B).
25. The *Amazon, Inc.* case referred to in *supra* note 23, involved taxable years prior to the 2017 amendment to Section 482. Congress intended that the new language added in 2017 would reject the holding in *Amazon, Inc.* H. REP. NO. 115-409, TAX CUT AND JOBS ACT p. 389 n. 650 (115th Cong. 1st Sess. 2017).
26. Treas. Reg. Sec. 1.482-3(a). The Regulations confirm that use of an unspecified method should be grounded in the principle that "uncontrolled taxpayers evaluate the terms of a transaction by considering the realistic alternatives to that transaction." Treas. Reg. Sec. 1.482-3(e)(1). Additionally, use of an unspecified method is bound by the same constraints of "best method" and "comparability" that apply to a specified method. If taxpayers rely on internal data rather than third-party data to support their analysis, the reliability of the analysis and the results will be reduced. Treas. Reg. Sec. 1.482-3(e)(1). Note that of the six methods only the profit split method takes account of both sides of the related party transaction. *See* Bret Wells and Cym Lowell, *Tax Base Erosion: Reformation of Section 482's Arm's Length Standard*, 15 FLA. TAX REV. 737, 248-765 (2014). Taxpayers may want to consider the use of more than one method to

profits method and the profit split method are also used in connection with intangibles, discussed in section 12.4.2. As indicated, there is no order of preference and the various methods are subject to the "best method" rule discussed in section 12.3.

12.4.1.1 Comparable Uncontrolled Price Method

Under the "CUP" method, the price is determined on the basis of "uncontrolled sales" made to buyers that are not members of the same controlled group. Such comparable sales include sales made by a member of the group to an unrelated party and sales of the same product made between parties that are not members of the controlled group and are unrelated. In determining the basis for comparability, differences in the properties of the product sold and the circumstances surrounding the sale are taken into account under the principles discussed in section 12.3.1. In determining comparability, the most important factor is the similarity of the products.[27] Where trademarked goods are involved, for example, the effect of the trademark on price must be taken into account and may prevent an uncontrolled price from being appropriately adjusted, thus requiring the use of some other method under the "best method" rule.[28]

12.4.1.2 Resale Price Method

The resale price method bases the determination of arm's length price on the gross profit margin of sales in uncontrolled transactions. That margin is subtracted from the resale price involved in the related party transaction to establish the transfer price on the related party sale.[29] Assume, for example, that property is manufactured by the parent corporation, sold to a distribution subsidiary, and then is sold outside the group by the distributor subsidiary in an uncontrolled sale for a price of USD 100. An examination of comparable uncontrolled sales establishes a gross profit margin of 20%. The arm's length price for the sale within the group from the manufacturing parent to the distributor subsidiary would thus be USD 80 (100 minus (20% × USD 100)). Comparability is determined principally on functions performed and risks borne

support their transfer pricing decisions (e.g., a primary method plus a second method used to demonstrate the soundness of the primary method). This approach has the added advantage of helping a taxpayer effectively manage its transfer pricing reporting and documentation for two jurisdictions where those jurisdictions have differing views on what methods are appropriate.

27. Treas. Reg. Sec. 1.482-3(b)(2)(i). Despite the "best method" approach, the regulations state that "generally" the results from applying the CUP method will be the most direct and reliable measure of an arm's length price. Treas. Reg. Sec. 1.482-1(c)(2)(i). *See also Compaq Computer Corp. v. Commissioner*, T.C.M. 1999-220, for a case in which the court made adjustments in the various factors to determine the taxpayer's use of the CUP method. But despite this regulatory language (which might be read to suggest that the Service will generally find and prefer use of the CUP method), tax practitioners generally consider the US tax authorities less likely to accept a CUP than other jurisdictions. The Service is viewed as imposing a higher standard of comparability and as less likely to accept taxpayer efforts to adjust for differences between their related party transaction and the proffered comparable.
28. Treas. Reg. Sec. 1.482-3(b)(4) Ex. 1.
29. Treas. Reg. Sec. 1.482-3(c).

by the distributor in the controlled sale compared with the uncontrolled distributors in the comparable uncontrolled sales.[30]

The resale price method can be available in circumstances in which the CUP method is not because the goods being sold are not similar enough to qualify for use of the CUP method. That is, although the goods being sold in the uncontrolled sale should be sufficiently similar to the goods being sold in the controlled sale such that the distribution functions in each case are comparable, they need not be as similar as required under application of CUP.[31] The resale price method is generally appropriate when the reseller does not add substantial value to the product and is functioning primarily as a distributor.[32]

12.4.1.3 Cost Plus Method

Under the cost plus method, the cost of goods sold of the company selling to the related party is determined under normal accounting principles and then an appropriate "gross profit markup" derived from an analysis of uncontrolled transactions is applied. Assume as in the prior example that property is manufactured by the parent corporation at a cost of USD 64, the property is sold to a distribution subsidiary, which then sells the property outside the group in an uncontrolled sale for a price of USD 100. An examination of comparable uncontrolled sales establishes a gross profit markup on manufacturing costs of 25%. The arm's length price for the sale within the group from the manufacturing parent to the distributor subsidiary would thus be USD 80 (64 + (25% × USD 64)).

The cost plus method is usually used in situations involving the production or manufacture of products that are then sold to related parties.[33] Cost plus is essentially the companion method to resale price, where cost plus is applied to the manufacturer's costs and resale price is used to determine the distributor's resale price margin. Just as with resale price, a close physical similarity of goods between the controlled sale and the uncontrolled sale is less critical for the cost plus method than it is in the use of the CUP method.[34] In deciding whether resale price or cost plus may be a more appropriate method the taxpayer must determine: (1) if the related party manufacturer and/or the related party distributor performed just their stated functions (i.e., manufacturing or

30. Treas. Reg. Sec. 1.482-3(c)(3)(ii).
31. Treas. Reg. Sec. 1.482-3(c)(3)(ii)(B) (comparability under resale price is less dependent on "close physical similarity" of goods than the CUP method).
32. Often a taxpayer's best comparable under the resale price method may be its own distribution activities on behalf of other (unrelated) manufacturers. For example, if the parent manufactures chairs and sells them to its subsidiary for sale outside the group, good data for the resale price method may be derived from the subsidiary's distribution of other goods. If the subsidiary distributes stools on behalf of an unrelated manufacturer, the subsidiary's gross profit margin on the sale of stools might be the best comparable. The taxpayer would have all of the information necessary to compare the two transactions, and it is likely that the subsidiary's function as distributor would be similar in the two cases.
33. Treas. Reg. Sec. 1.482-3(d)(1).
34. Treas. Reg. Sec. 1.482-3(d)(3(ii)(B).

distribution), or instead added additional value to the transaction, and (2) if it has better uncontrolled data on manufacturing transactions or on distribution transactions.

12.4.1.4 Comparable Profits Method

The most radical change in the 1994 Regulations was the introduction of the comparable profits method ("CPM"). Rather than looking at prices or gross profit margins in uncontrolled transactions, the CPM looks at the profit level indicators of uncontrolled parties and in effect adjusts the related party transfer prices so that the controlled party makes an equivalent profit.[35] CPM is roughly the equivalent of the "transactional net margin method" provided in the OECD transfer pricing guidelines.

12.4.1.4.1 Profit Level Indicators

The first step in applying the CPM is to establish appropriate measures of profitability, "profit level indicators," based on data of uncontrolled parties. Profit level indicators are ratios that measure the relation between expenditures and profits or rates of return. Thus, the rate of return on operating assets, the ratio of operating profits to sales, and the ratio of gross profit to operating expenses are all given as examples of profit level indicators.[36] As with all the methods, the comparability of the external data is a key factor in the CPM though the Regulations give little guidance beyond a reference to general factors such as the lines of business, asset composition, size and scope of operations, and the stage in a business or product cycle.[37] Profit level indicators must be established for several years to measure reasonably the returns being realized by third parties in comparable activities.

12.4.1.4.2 Calculating Operating Profit

After the profit level indicators have been established, they are applied to the financial data of the "tested" related party. This is generally the related party that has the least complex business and for which it would be most possible to isolate the relevant

35. Initially, when the comparable profits method was introduced in 1994, there seemed to be some tendency to restrict the role of CPM, in part perhaps to allay taxpayer fears of indiscriminate use of CPM by Internal Revenue Service agents on audit. Thus, the Treasury Decision announcing the 1994 Regulations stated that, given the general availability of data on price and margins, CPM "generally would be considered a method of last resort"—despite the introduction of the "best method rule" in those same 1994 Regulations. T.D. 8852, 1994-2 C.B. 93. However, in the intervening two decades, CPM has become a very common method. For example, the annual report on the US Advance Pricing Agreement Program released in March 2021 noted that for the calendar year 2020, the dominant transfer pricing method used in APAs was CPM. Internal Revenue Service, "Announcement and Report Concerning Advance Pricing Agreements," Announcement 2021-6, IRB 2021-15 at 1011 (Mar. 23, 2021) (84% of APAs executed for the transfer of tangible goods and intangible in 2020 relied on the CPM/TNMM).
36. Treas. Reg. Sec. 1.482-5(b)(4). Other measures can also be used as long as they are based on "objective" data.
37. Treas. Reg. Sec. 1.482-5(c)(2).

business activities. The "comparable operating profit" calculated in this manner is then compared to the reported operating profit to determine if the related parties have been dealing at arm's length.

Assume, for example, that US parent company M manufactures a consumer product that it sells through a foreign distributor subsidiary FD. M has no sales to uncontrolled parties, there are no CUPs of similar products, and reliable data is not available for gross profit markups on costs or for resale price margins. Thus, CPM would generally be the "best method" for establishing arm's length results. FD would be the tested party because it is engaged in less complex activities than M. Based on data from independent distributors in the same industry segment, the average ratio of operating profits to sales is 3%. FD's sales for the relevant period were USD 10,000 and its reported operating profit USD 350. Under the CPM, its profits would be decreased to USD 300 and a corresponding increase would be made to the income of M to reflect the results of the CPM analysis.

In some cases, neither related party is an appropriate candidate to be the "tested party." This would be the case, for example, if both parties used valuable intangibles in their functions (e.g., the manufacturer M had a valuable patent involved in the production of the consumer product, and the foreign distributor FD used a valuable brand name it developed in distributing the goods). In that case, CPM would not be a best method, and the taxpayer would need to consider another alternative, typically, profit split, as described below in section 12.4.1.5.

12.4.1.5 Profit Split

The "profit split" method, though not formally recognized in the 1968 version of the Regulations, was followed in a number of court cases[38] and became one of the accepted methods in the 1994 Regulations. The profit split method examines the "combined operating profit or loss" in a related party transaction and allocates that amount based on the relative value of the contributions to the generation of the profit made by each member of the related party group.[39] Under the profit split method, the profit allocated to one member is not limited to the combined operating profit of the group. In a given year one member may have a profit while another has a loss.[40] As a technical matter, the Regulations provide for two types of profit splits, a "comparable profit split" and a "residual profit split." The comparable profit split is very rarely used. Five years after formal introduction of the comparable profit split into the regulations, the IRS Advance Pricing Agreement Study guide stated in 1999 that the comparable profit split method had only been used once in an APA.[41] During 2014, the IRS reported that 8% of APAs

38. *See, e.g., Eli Lilly & Co. v. Commissioner,* 856 F.2d 855 (7th Cir. 1988).
39. Treas. Reg. Sec. 1.482-6(a).
40. Treas. Reg. Sec. 1.482-6(b).
41. *See* Internal Revenue Service, "APA Study Guide," (1999) at 62, available at http://www.irs.gov/pub/irs-apa/apa_study_guide_.pdf.

used the *residual* profit split method that year.[42] Subsequent APA reports provide more limited details.[43] In a comparable profit split, the split is determined by looking at the division of operating profits among uncontrolled taxpayers performing similar activities under similar circumstances. The contractual allocation of risks and functions in the uncontrolled situation are particularly important in determining comparability. The residual profit split method attributes normal market returns to the routine contributions made by each party. Then any residual profits are allocated to the intangibles owned by each of the related parties, based on the fair market values of those intangibles if those can be determined, or on some estimated value based on the capitalized costs of developing the intangibles.[44] These are obviously daunting valuation issues but in appropriate circumstances the residual profit split will nonetheless be the "best method."[45]

12.4.2 Intangibles

Developing appropriate transfer pricing methods to deal with intangibles is one of the most difficult tasks in the transfer pricing area. Many intangibles are unique, and it is impossible to find a comparable transaction in order to establish an arm's length price or royalty. The 1968 Regulations simply listed various factors to be taken into account but gave no indication of the weight each factor was to be given. In response to these difficulties, Congress in 1986 amended Section 482 as it applies to intangibles by specifically providing that in the case of a transfer or license of an intangible "the income with respect to such transfer or license shall be commensurate with the income attributable to the intangible." This amendment had two functions. In the first place, it required periodic reviews of the relation between the consideration paid for the intangible and the income that the intangible in fact generated. Under the "commensurate with income" standard it would not be possible to license an intangible at a low royalty rate when the possible success of the intangible was unknown and then keep that rate if in fact it turned out that the intangible was successful. The royalty would have to be adjusted periodically to reflect the success of the intangible.[46] Introduction of the commensurate with income standard in 1986 generated controversy with some US trading partners who considered the provision a departure from the arm's length

---

42. Internal Revenue Service, "Announcement and Report Concerning Advance Pricing Agreements," (Mar. 27, 2015), available at https://www.irs.gov/pub/irs-utl/2014%20APMA%20Statutory%20Report.pdf.
43. Providing very little information, the 2021 APA report observes only that 84% of tangible and intangible property transfer APAs used the comparable profits method in 2020. Note that the comparable profits methods (CPM) is *not* the same as the comparable profit split method.
44. Treas. Reg. Sec. 1.482-6(c)(3)(i)(B).
45. *See* Treas. Reg. Sec. 1.482-8(b) Exs. 8 and 12 for the conditions necessary to apply the residual profit split as the "best method."
46. Treas. Reg. Sec. 1.482-4(f)(2). Adjustment is required regardless of the form that the consideration for the transfer takes. Thus, if the transfer involves a lump sum payment, the payment is converted into a series of payments over the life of the agreement based on present value principles and the amount of that deemed payment is compared with the subsequently determined arm's length amount in future years. Treas. Reg. Sec. 1.482-4(f)(6).

standard around which an international consensus had developed, although this concern reflected a narrow understanding of the standard. In considering this argument it is useful to recall that the statute (Section 482) sought to "clearly reflect income" and regulations, in the absence of comparable transactions, evaluated what unrelated parties would have done in the same circumstances. The Treasury's White Paper justified periodic adjustments as consistent with the arm's length standard on the ground that unrelated parties would take account of actual profit experience and not enter into long-term contracts fixing the rate of return without opportunity for renegotiations.[47] The second function performed by the 1986 addition of the "commensurate with income" requirement was to shift the inquiry in the intangibles area more directly to profits-based methods such as the profit split method and comparable profits method[48] (*see* sections 12.4.1.5 and 12.4.1.4).

Further amendment of Section 482 was undertaken in the 2017 Tax Act to address challenges in establishing the value of intangibles transferred between related parties. Although existing regulations authorized reliance on both aggregation and realistic alternatives in evaluating transfers, the IRS often faced challenges from taxpayers when it applied these approaches. As noted above in section 12.3.3, a new sentence was added at the end of Section 482 calling for valuation of the transfers of intangibles (including mixed transfers of intangible property, tangible property, and services) *on an aggregate basis*, or *on the basis of "realistic alternatives"* to the transfer where those approaches are likely to produce the most reliable valuation.

Finally, in 2018, the statutory language in Section 482 was updated to cross-reference new Section 367(d)(4) for a definition of intangible property. As a result of disputes[49] over the scope of the term "intangible property," Congress sought to employ a more comprehensive definition for purposes of Section 482. Post amendment, the definition now includes as its final catch-all category after a list of specific intangibles: "any … other item the value or potential value of which is not attributable to tangible property or the services of any individual."[50] This more sweeping language replaces the prior, narrower residual category: "any similar item."[51]

12.4.2.1 Comparable Uncontrolled Transaction

The Regulations provide four methods for the determination of an arm's length result in the case of intangibles: (1) the "comparable uncontrolled transaction" ("CUT")

47. *See* Notice 88-123, 1988-2 C.B. 458, 477; Treas. Reg. Sec. 1.482-4(f)(2)(ii)(B)(2). The taxpayer is not required to make a periodic adjustment if it can establish a comparable uncontrolled agreement that does not call for readjustment. The Regulations provide several different versions of this exception to applying the commensurate with income standard. Treas. Reg. Sec. 1.482-4(f)(2)(ii)(A), (B), (C), (D), and (E).
48. The Section 482 White Paper discussed in *supra* note 2 of section 12.1 contains an extensive analysis of the issues involved in developing the commensurate with income standard and many of the positions taken there were ultimately adopted in the current Regulations, especially as concerns profit-based methods.
49. *See, e.g., Veritas Software Corp. v. Commissioner*, 133 T.C. 297 (2009), nonacq., 2010-49 IRB (2010); *Amazon.com v. Commissioner*, 934 F.3d 976 (9th Cir. 2019), aff'g 148 T.C. No. 8 (2017).
50. Sec. 367(d)(4) (cross-referenced by Sec. 482).
51. Repealed Sec. 936(h)(3)(B).

method, (2) the comparable profits method, (3) the profit split method, and (4) the unspecified method.[52] Only the "CUT" method is unique to the transfer of intangibles, but in reality it is the intangibles version of the CUP method. Like the corresponding CUP method for tangible property, the CUT method attempts to establish the arm's length charge for the transfer or license of an intangible based on comparable uncontrolled transfers of the same or very similar intangible.[53] Substantial guidance is given with respect to the factors to be taken into account in determining comparability of uncontrolled transactions involving intangibles. The intangibles must be used in connection with similar products in the same general industry, they must have the same "profit potential" expressed in terms of the net present value of the anticipated returns, and the transfer must be made in similar circumstances, including the extent of the rights granted and the duration of the license.[54] Under the "best method" rule, the CUT method will only be applied when the data and assumptions used for that method are superior to the other methods.[55] Thus, it is likely that in most situations involving intangibles, the CUT method will not be available and CPM or the profit split method will be applicable (*see* sections 12.4.1.4 and 12.4.1.5).

12.4.2.2 Cost Sharing Agreements

US multinationals holding valuable intellectual property have regularly sought to transfer that property to a low-tax foreign subsidiary with the goal of keeping the profits generated by that intangible outside the US taxing reach. Historically this planning effort has been constrained by application of transfer pricing provisions. For example, a simple sale of a valuable intangible to a foreign subsidiary would be subject to Section 482 which would require adequate compensation to the US parent that developed the intangible. Payment of that appropriate compensation in the year of transfer would negate the value of the underlying tax strategy. Reporting significant US income now on the sale of the intangible at an arm's length price to avoid reporting future income generated by the intangible makes little sense. Strategies to underprice the transfer from the US parent to the foreign subsidiary (by for example making an "early" transfer when the property's value was "unproven") are blocked by the 1986 introduction of the commensurate with income rule which would require compensation be paid to the US parent in this example should the intangible prove valuable in subsequent years. Alternative efforts to move the intangible to the foreign subsidiary in a "tax-free" transfer are also limited. If the US parent established a foreign subsidiary, basic corporate tax rules (Section 351) would allow the US parent to contribute property tax free to the subsidiary. However, given the abuse potential in allowing valuable, highly

52. Treas. Reg. Sec. 1.482-4(a).
53. Treas. Reg. Sec. 1.482-4(c)(1).
54. Treas. Reg. Sec. 1.482-4(c)(2)(iii).
55. For example, the CUT method might meet the best method rule if the taxpayer licenses a drug patent to an unrelated manufacturer and also to a related manufacturer under similar terms and circumstances. To the extent that this business model is not common in many intangible intensive businesses where multinational businesses tend to be vertical integrated, CPM or profit split will be the likely best method.

appreciated property to shift to a foreign entity, Section 367 overrides Section 351 (and other nonrecognition provisions) for offshore transfers.[56] Thus, intangibles cannot be moved readily to foreign subsidiaries in tax-free transactions.

How then can the US parent achieve its goal of having intangibles held by its foreign subsidiary? Taxpayers have pursued a strategy that focuses on the foreign subsidiary becoming a "creator" and thus part owner of the new intangible. If the foreign subsidiary is an owner from the outset there is no need to transfer the intangible and face the challenges of Section 482, commensurate with income, or Section 367. Such "part owner" strategies are often structured as "cost sharing arrangements" pursuant to which two or more related parties will enter into an agreement to share the costs of developing a new intangible and share the ownership of the intangible (typically on a geographic basis).[57] Two important issues in cost sharing agreements are: (1) whether they will be respected, and (2) whether there are any Section 482 issues within the cost sharing arrangement.

New final costs sharing regulations were released in December 2011.[58] Under the Regulations, a cost sharing arrangement ("CSA") is one in which the "controlled participants share the costs and risks of developing cost shared intangibles in proportion to their RAB shares [reasonably anticipated benefits]."[59] That is, the costs of developing the new intangible are allocated among the participants in the CSA in proportion to the reasonably expected benefits assigned to each of them under the agreement.[60]

When such cost sharing arrangements are present, no charge need be made between related parties for intangible property developed under the agreement. Thus, for example, assume a US parent company and its foreign subsidiary enter into a cost sharing agreement to develop an intangible that the parent company will exploit in the US market and the subsidiary will exploit in the rest of the world. The costs would be allocated on the basis of the anticipated sales in the relevant markets, with reimbursements required where one party incurs more than its share of costs. In this case, adjustments would be required under Section 482 only to the extent necessary to insure that each party bears its appropriate share of the costs. Once the intangible has been developed each party will be an owner of the intangible and no additional charge or royalty need be paid to exploit the property.[61]

56. For a more extensive discussion of Section 367, *see* Chapter 7 section 7.2. The reach of Section 367, in requiring gain recognition on outbound asset transfers, was expanded further in the 2017 tax reform.
57. For example, the US parent might receive the US rights to the intangible, and the foreign subsidiary would receive the rights to license and use the intangible throughout the rest of the world.
58. Treas. Reg. Sec. 1.482-7.
59. Treas. Reg. Sec. 1.482-7(b). More specifically, an arrangement must satisfy four requirements to qualify as a CSA: (1) substantive requirements, (2) administrative requirements, (3) proper treatment of platform contribution transactions (PCTs), and (4) requirements governing the division of interests in the cost shared intangibles. Treas. Reg. Sec. 1.482-7(b)(1), (2), (3), and (4).
60. Treas. Reg. Sec. 1.482-7(b).
61. Treas. Reg. Sec. 1.482-7(e)(2)(ii)(E) Ex. 6.

If, in the context of a cost sharing agreement, one of the participants makes available existing intangibles that it owns to the other participant, there must be a payment that reflects an arm's length charge for the use of those intangibles.[62] Historically, this payment had been known as the buy-in payment. However, the final 2011 Regulations following the 2009 temporary regulations broadened the scope of intangibles for which compensation may be required and labeled the provision of these intangibles as a "platform contribution transaction," or PCT. Compensation made for use of these intangibles in the cost sharing venture is now referred to as the PCT payment. Classic examples of the kind of intangible that would be covered by a PCT payment might include an earlier generation of the intangible being developed.[63] The regulatory definition of a PCT, for which compensation may be needed, includes "any resource, capability, or right that a controlled participant has developed, maintained, or acquired externally to the intangible development activity ... that is reasonably anticipated to contribute to developing cost shared intangibles."[64] In addition to providing a comprehensive definition of PCTs, the Regulations provide a detailed set of methods for determining the appropriate PCT payment to be made.[65] Given the circumstances in which many CSAs arise (e.g., next generation products, related lines of products), it is likely that one party will be bringing valuable existing intangibles to the CSA. Thus, PCT payments will be necessary. The Regulations generated strong reactions, and as cases arise under the definitions and under the methods for pricing PCT payments, such controversy likely will continue.[66]

One issue of longstanding in cost sharing arrangements is whether the compensation costs of stock-based compensation (SBC) should be included in the pool of costs to be shared. The IRS initially took the position that these costs should be shared under 1995 Regulations that did not specify a rule for SBC, but lost the issue in the Tax Court and on appeal to the Ninth Circuit based in part on taxpayer arguments that unrelated

62. Treas. Reg. Sec. 1.482-7(b)((1)(ii) and -7(c).
63. For example, in software development, new products are frequently developed based on a prior platform. The owner of that existing software would require compensation (e.g., royalty, or lump sum payment) for use of that intangible to create a next generation product. Treas. Reg. Sec. 1.482-7(c)(4)(ii) Ex. 2; *see generally*, Treas. Reg. Sec. 1.482-7(b)(5)(iii) Ex. 1.
64. Treas. Reg. Sec. 1.482-7(c)(1). The examples provide concrete applications for this broad definition. *See, e.g.*, Treas. Reg. Sec. 1.482-7(c)(5) Ex. 2 ("the expertise and existing integration of the research team [provided by one participant in the CSA] is a unique resource or capability ... which is reasonably anticipated to contribute to the development of the [new intangible]" thus provision of this team to the CSA project constitutes a PCT for which payment from the other parties to the CSA is required).
65. Treas. Reg. Sec. 1.482-7(g)(1).
66. *See, e.g.*, *Veritas Software Corp. v. Commissioner*, 133 T.C. 297 (2009) nonacq., 2010-49 IRB (2010). Although *Veritas* arose under prior cost sharing regulations, the opinion, which referenced the new Regulations, has been viewed by some commentators as a preview of potential objections and reactions. Similarly, the 2019 case involving Amazon, which was governed by pre-2011 cost sharing regulations, highlights disagreements over the kinds of property for which compensation must be made and the appropriate reference points for making those pricing determinations. The Ninth Circuit in *Amazon.com* acknowledged, however, that it would reach a different decision under the 2009 temporary regulations expanded concept of platform contribution transaction (Temp. Treas. Reg. Sec. 1.482-7T(c) (2009)) and the 2017 Tax Act revision of the definition of intangible. *Amazon.com v. Commissioner*, 934 F.3d 976, 979 (*supra* note 1) (9th Cir. 2019). *See also* section 12.3.3.

parties did not share the costs.[67] The IRS issued final regulations in 2003 specifically requiring inclusion of SBC in costs to be shared and taxpayers immediately challenged the regulations on administrative law grounds. After taxpayers won again in the Tax Court, the IRS prevailed in its appeal as the Ninth Circuit upheld the position in the regulations.[68]

12.4.3 Services

In 2009, a new framework for taxing related party services was introduced.[69] This substantial change to the treatment of services under Section 482 reflected the government's view that: (1) services had become an increasingly central part of the economy, (2) the value of services provided was significant, (3) the line between services and intangibles in the contemporary economy was often narrow, and (4) the old regulations were inadequate to manage the new role of services in economy. The resulting Regulations issued in 2009 now provide a treatment for related party services that looks much more similar to the rules governing sales of goods and transfers of intangibles. Under the Regulations, related party services must be priced using one of seven methods:[70] (1) the services cost method ("SCM")—a limited safe harbor, (2) the comparable uncontrolled services price (CUSP—this is the services version of the CUP for goods and the CUT for intangibles), (3) gross services margin method,[71] (4) cost plus, (5) CPM,[72] (6) profit split, and (7) unspecified methods. As with the analysis of related party sales of goods and transfers of intangibles, the baseline rules of best method, comparability, and the use of ranges, continue to apply to pricing of related party services.

---

67. *Xilinx Inc. v. Commissioner*, 125 T.C. 37, (2005), aff'd, 598 F.3d 1191 (9th Cir. 2010).
68. *Altera Corporation & Subsidiaries v. Commissioner*, 926 F.3d 1061 (9th Cir. 2019), *rehearing denied*, 941 F.3d 1200 (9th Cir. 2019), *cert. denied* (June 22, 2020). One company, Alphabet (aka Google) reported a USD 4.4 billion tax effect from the Ninth Circuit decision. Alphabet, Inc., Form 10-K at 78 (Feb. 3, 2017). The potentially large impact of the issue helps explain why taxpayers will continue to pursue litigating the question in hopes of obtaining a different decision in another Circuit Court of Appeals and ultimate review by the Supreme Court.
69. Treas. Reg. Sec. 1.482-9.
70. Treas. Reg. Sec. 1.482-9(a).
71. The gross services margin method looks a bit like the resale price method, and is typically applied where a taxpayer serves as a commission agent for its related party. For example, consider US Parent with a foreign subsidiary X which engages in the manufacture of industrial equipment. US Parent acts as a commission agent for X by arranging for X to make direct sales of the equipment it manufactures to unrelated buyers in the US market. US Parent does not take title, but instead receives from X commissions that are determined as a specified percentage of the sales price of the equipment sold to the unrelated US buyer. Under the gross services margin method, the price US Parent charged is evaluated against the gross profit margin charged in uncontrolled transactions. Essentially, the question is what percentage, or "cut," of the sale price to the buyer would an uncontrolled commission agent charge in similar circumstances. *See* Treas. Reg. Sec. 1.482-9(d)(4) Exs. 1 and 2.
72. In the context of a related party services transaction, the most appropriate PLI, or profit level indicator (*see* section 12.4.1.4.1), to use in applying the CPM method would be Operating Profits (OP)/ Total Services Cost. Treas. Reg. Sec. 1.482-9(f)(2)(ii). In this context, "total services cost" is a defined term. Treas. Reg. Sec. 1.482-9(j).

The inclusion of the safe harbor method[73] (i.e., the SCM) is an acknowledgment that although the role of services in the economy has changed dramatically in the past twenty-five years, not all services are high value or important services. Under the SCM, if a transaction satisfies the test, then the arm's length charge is determined by looking at the "total services costs" as defined in the Regulations.[74] The test includes four requirements directed at establishing that the related party service being provided is a low margin, back-office function, and not the kind of service that contributes "significantly to key competitive advantages, core capabilities, or the fundamental risks of success or failure in one or more trades or businesses of the controlled group."[75]

A common question that arises in the context of related party services is whether any compensation is required at all. The general rule is that *if* the services do not provide a benefit to a recipient, and would not be *reasonably anticipated* to provide a benefit, then there is no transaction to price.[76] Relatedly, if a benefit is so indirect or remote that no recipient would pay an uncontrolled party, then there is also no transaction to price.[77] If the service provided by the related party duplicates activity performed (or reasonably anticipated to be performed) by the controlled recipient, then "the activity is generally not considered to provide a benefit to the recipient, unless the duplicate activity itself provides an additional benefit to the recipient."[78] But if duplication does provide a benefit to the recipient then an arm's length services charge is required.

12.4.4 Loans

Loans between related parties in general must be made at an arm's length interest rate. Interest is required on any extension of credit, not just formal loans, unless one of the specified exceptions applies.[79] Such interest must be charged beginning with the day after the indebtedness arises and continuing through the day the debt is satisfied.[80] In general, the interest rate prevailing at the situs of the lender or creditor is the

---

73. Treas. Reg. Sec. 1.482-9(b).
74. Treas. Reg. Sec. 1.482-9(j).
75. Treas. Reg. Sec. 1.482-9(b)(5). Services that meet the tests for the SCM are a significant exception to the definition of base erosion payment in the BEAT (discussed in Chapter 5 section 5.10).
76. Treas. Reg. Sec. 1.482-9(l)(3)(i).
77. Treas. Reg. Sec. 1.482-9(l)(3)(i) and (ii).
78. Treas. Reg. Sec. 1.482-9(l)(3)(iii). For example, imagine US Parent has a foreign subsidiary Z which is planning to enter into a complicated joint venture with a third party. Z has hired outside counsel to assess the intellectual property dimensions of the venture. Before Z commits to the deal, US Parent's in-house counsel reviews the documents and other aspects of the transaction and concurs in the advice given by Z's lawyers on the matter. In this case, the activities of US Parent substantially duplicate the services Z has already purchased (its outside counsel). But these duplicate services also reduce the commercial risks associated with the transaction, which is an additional benefit. Therefore, Z has benefitted from US Parent's services and must compensate US Parent accordingly. Treas. Reg. Sec. 1.482-9(l)(5) Ex. 6.
79. Treas. Reg. Sec. 1.482-2(a)(1)(i) and (ii).
80. Treas. Reg. Sec. 1.482-2(a)(1)(iii)(A). Certain exceptions apply to allow an interest-free period on qualifying intercompany trade receivables (i.e., debt arising in the ordinary course of

standard.[81] However, if the loan represents the proceeds of a borrowing by the lender undertaken at the situs of the related party-borrower, that rate may be used.[82]

The Regulations also provide a range of "safe haven" rates within which the actual rate of interest will not be challenged.[83] The safe haven rates are based on the so-called applicable Federal rate, i.e., the rate paid by the Federal Government on similar obligations at the time the related party loan is made. If the related party loan bears an interest rate that is at least 100% and not more than 130% of the applicable Federal rate, the safe haven test will be met and no adjustment will be made under Section 482. Thus, if the applicable Federal rate is 10% any interest rate between 10% and 13% would be acceptable. If less than 10% interest were charged, the interest rate would be adjusted up to 10% unless the taxpayer could establish that the lower rate was in fact an arm's length rate. Similarly, if the interest charged were above 13%, the rate would be adjusted down to 13%, again unless the taxpayer could establish a different arm's length rate.[84]

The Section 482 rules are coordinated with the rules governing original issue discount and shareholder-corporation below market or interest-free loans. In general terms, the latter rules apply first to establish the interest rate and that rate is then adjusted under the Section 482 rules.[85]

12.5 OTHER ASPECTS OF SECTION 482 ALLOCATIONS

12.5.1 Set Offs

The Regulations provide that in making allocations under Section 482, the fiscal authorities must consider the effect of any other non-arm's length transactions between the parties in the taxable year in question. For example, if one party performs services without an arm's length charge for a related party which in turn sells products to the first party at a discount, the value of the services received without charge would be set off against the allocation which otherwise would be made under Section 482 as to the discount.[86]

---

business from sales, leases, or services between related persons that is not evidenced by a written interest requiring payment of interest). Treas. Reg. Sec. 1.482-2(a)(1)(iii)(A), (B), (C), (D), and (E).

81. The appropriate interest rate is the rate of interest that would be charged at the time the debt arose, in transactions between unrelated parties, under similar circumstances. The factors relevant in determining "similar circumstances" include principal amount, duration, security provided, and credit standing of the borrower. Treas. Reg. Sec. 1.482-2(a)(2)(i).
82. Treas. Reg. Sec. 1.482-2(a)(2)(ii).
83. Treas. Reg. Sec. 1.482-2(a)(2)(iii)(A)(1).
84. Treas. Reg. Sec. 1.482-2(a)(2)(iii)(B). The safe haven rules only apply to loans made in US dollars. Treas. Reg. Sec. 1.482-2(a)(2)(iii)(E).
85. Treas. Reg. Sec. 1.482-2(a)(3).
86. Treas. Reg. Sec. 1.482-1(g)(4).

12.5.2 Correlative Adjustments

The Regulations require that where the fiscal authorities make an adjustment to the income of one member of a group under Section 482 a corresponding adjustment ("correlative adjustment") must be made in the income or deductions of the related party.[87] For example, in a situation in which inadequate interest is charged on a related party loan, imputation of interest income to the lending party results in a corresponding interest expense to the borrowing party. In a purely domestic context, this could result in a reduction of income tax liability for the related party or perhaps in an increased net operating loss carryover.

In the international context, where the related party is not subject to US tax jurisdiction, no such direct correlative adjustment can be made. However, if it later becomes necessary to determine the income of the related party, for example, in connection with the foreign tax credit, the earnings and profits of the related party will be computed as if the correlative adjustment had been made.

12.5.3 Adjustments of Accounts after Section 482 Allocation

When a Section 482 allocation has been made, the income of one of the related parties will be increased. However, the actual funds representing that allocation will still remain with the other party. If no special rules were applicable, when those funds were subsequently transferred to the related party, for example, as a dividend distribution by a subsidiary to its parent, an additional tax would be incurred. To solve this problem the Internal Revenue Service has issued administrative guidelines that deal with this situation.[88] A taxpayer to whom income is allocated under Section 482 may receive a corresponding dividend payment from the related party that it can exclude from its US income. Alternatively, a taxpayer may set up an interest-bearing account receivable on its books reflecting the amount of the Section 482 adjustment. The normal rules apply to payments on the receivable, including limitations on the deductibility of interest and the availability of a foreign tax credit for any foreign taxes imposed on the payments.[89] If the Internal Revenue Service initiated the primary adjustments, the relief provisions are available only if the penalty provisions of Section 6662(e) (*see* section 12.8) do not apply to the transactions. In the case of taxpayer-initiated adjustments, these relief

87. Treas. Reg. Sec. 1.482-1(g)(2).
88. Rev. Proc. 99-32, 1999-2 C.B. 296.
89. For an example of adjustments in the case of overpayments, imagine a US distributor "D" buys product from its foreign parent "F." The sale is reviewed by the IRS which determines that the arm's length price would have increased D's taxable income by USD 5 million. Thus, the IRS adjusts D's income to reflect its true taxable income. To conform its cash accounts and reporting to reflect the Section 482 allocation, the "extra" cash (USD 5 million) now sitting in F's accounts must be explained. It cannot constitute part of the purchase price because that number was adjusted downward by the Service on audit. The taxpayers would have the option of characterizing that USD 5 million as either a dividend from D to F (with all the tax implication that flow from that label), or alternatively, treat that USD 5 million as an account receivable from D to F on which F will owe arm's length interest to D. Treas. Reg. Sec. 1.482-1(g)(3)(i) and (ii).

procedures apply even if the Section 6662(e) penalties are applicable, but in no case do the relief provisions apply if fraud is involved.

12.6 INTERNATIONAL ASPECTS

12.6.1 Treaties

All comprehensive US income tax treaties contain an article that allows the US to determine the income of persons subject to its taxing jurisdiction on the basis of an arm's length principle in any situation in which arrangements or conditions in transactions between related parties do not conform to the arm's length standard.[90] In general, the tests applied under Section 482 are also relevant under the treaties. Under recent treaties, where a reallocation of income has been made by one country, the other country agrees to make corresponding adjustments to the extent that it agrees with the US redetermination of income. To the extent that the other country does not agree with the redetermination, the two countries endeavor to reach a compromise under the general mutual agreement procedures contained in the treaty.[91] If no such compromise can be reached, the taxpayer is faced with unrelieved international double taxation as a result of the countries' disagreement on the proper allocation of the income or deductions in question. In a few treaties (and the new 2016 US Model), competent authorities may be directed to mandatory arbitration to resolve an issue of double taxation.[92]

12.6.2 Foreign Tax Credit

Under the US foreign tax credit provision discussed in Chapter 10, the amount of foreign income tax allowed as a credit is determined in part by the US taxpayer's foreign source income. Thus, a Section 482 allocation that, coupled with the source rules, has the effect of increasing the US taxpayer's US source income and correspondingly decreasing the income of a foreign related party can have an effect on the available foreign tax credit. For example, suppose a US parent corporation reports GILTI inclusions from a CFC, and claims the deemed paid foreign tax credit under Section 960 for the foreign taxes paid by the subsidiary on that income. In a subsequent year, a Section 482 adjustment is made allocating income, which was reported initially by the foreign subsidiary (and formed some of the GILTI inclusion), to the US parent corporation. Under the correlative adjustment principle, the foreign subsidiary's income will be reduced correspondingly and the foreign tax credit calculation, which

90. *See, e.g.*, US Model Treaty, Art. 9. The only bilateral income tax treaty without an equivalent to Article 9 is the treaty with Bermuda which applies to insurance enterprises and allows domestic law transfer pricing rules to apply. US-Bermuda Insurance Income Tax Convention, Art. 4(5).
91. *See* Rev. Proc. 2015-40, 2015-35 IRB 236, for procedures to be used by taxpayers to obtain the assistance of the US competent authority with respect to tax treaty mutual agreement procedures.
92. *See* Chapter 14 section 14.12.2.

under Section 960 is based in part on the subsidiary's income in the year in question, will be changed. To claim the foreign tax credit for the foreign taxes imposed on the items of income allocated under Section 482 from a foreign subsidiary to the US parent, the taxpayer must establish that the foreign subsidiary has exhausted its administrative remedies under foreign law in seeking a refund of the foreign taxes paid on the income so reallocated. Otherwise, it is presumed that the foreign taxes paid were in fact a voluntary contribution to the foreign government not qualifying for the foreign tax credit. In addition, if the allocation under Section 482 made in connection with a foreign subsidiary in a country with which the US has an income tax treaty, the parent must demonstrate that it exhausted its rights under the competent authority provision of the treaty.[93]

Thus, the US insures that, if at all possible, the increase in revenue under the Section 482 allocation will not simply be offset by a larger than warranted foreign tax credit resulting from a failure to adjust the taxes paid in the foreign country to reflect the Section 482 adjustment and reduction in foreign subsidiary income.

12.6.3 Blocked Income

If a payment between related parties is prevented because of currency or other restrictions under the laws of a foreign country, but a Section 482 allocation is made, can the taxpayer defer the reporting of the Section 482 allocation under the general method for accounting for income subject to currency restrictions? Domestic parallels in the case law established the principle (the "blocked income rule") that a taxpayer could not be forced to report income under Section 482 that it was blocked from receiving under (domestic) law.[94] But the Service had taken the position in a 1992 case that a Section 482 allocation was proper where the law blocking receipt of income was a foreign law.[95] The Service lost the case, but issued new Section 482 Regulations in 1994 setting forth a number of conditions that must be fulfilled before the blocked income rule can be invoked by the taxpayer.[96] These requirements have the effect of limiting the taxpayer's ability to secure deferred accounting—effectively narrowing the scope of the taxpayer victory in the 1992 case. In March 2013, US multinational 3M Company filed in Tax Court challenging the validity of the blocked income requirements in the Section 482 Regulations.[97] As of 2021, this case remains pending, and its outcome will directly impact application of the blocked income rule in the cross-border context.[98]

---

93. *Id.*
94. The Supreme Court established the principle in *Commissioner v. First Security Bank of Utah*, 405 US 394 (1972).
95. *Proctor & Gamble Co v. Commissioner*, 95 TC 323, *aff'd*, 961 F.2d 1255 (6th Cir. 1992).
96. Treas. Reg. Sec. 1.482-1(h)(2).
97. *3M Company and Subsidiaries v. Commissioner of Internal Revenue*. Tax Court Docket No. 005816-13.
98. *See, e.g., The Coca Cola Company v. Commissioner*, 155 T.C. No. 10 (Nov. 18, 2020) ("As the parties have observed, the validity of section 1.482-1(h)(2), Income Tax Regs., has been challenged by the taxpayer in *3M Co. & Subs. V. Commissioner*, T.C. Dkt. No. 5816-13 (filed Mar.

12.7 ADVANCE PRICING AGREEMENTS

Beginning in 1990, the IRS established procedures which allow taxpayers to obtain "advance pricing agreements" ("APAs") with respect to proposed transactions involving intercompany pricing issues. The taxpayer submits a request for an advanced ruling with respect to the transfer pricing methodology it proposes to use in anticipated transactions. The request must be accompanied by the kind of data on comparability required by the Regulations for a particular method.[99] The taxpayer is expected to provide information regarding the industry generally[100] as well as broad financial and tax data for the past three years, detailed information on the search for comparables, and detailed financial data on selected comparables. Additionally, the taxpayer will provide data and analysis focusing on the functions, assets, costs, risks, and contractual terms for each party to the transactions to be covered by the APA. Finally, the taxpayer must show the application of its best method to the parties' tax and financial data on covered transactions for "each taxable year completed while the APA request is pending."[101] It is important to note that the focus of the APA discussion and analysis is on constructing a good transfer pricing *method* that can be applied across the years of the APA—not on achieving a particular numerical result. An important part of the analysis is the identification of "critical assumptions"—any fact, the continued existence of which is material to the taxpayer's transfer pricing methodology. Such critical assumptions may relate to the taxpayer, to third parties, or to the industry generally, and may involve a range of business or economic conditions. Examples of critical assumptions might include expected volume, or relative values of foreign exchanges. Any APA granted may need to be revised if and when any critical assumption fails.

The taxpayer will propose a term for the APA, typically at least five years (although it can be shorter where appropriate). For the calendar year 2020, the most common term for an APA was five years. It is possible to have an APA "roll-back" which allows the APA terms to cover prior years. In some cases, this possibility is a strong incentive for a taxpayer to enter into the APA process. Once signed, the APA agreement is a binding agreement that is limited to the taxpayer.[102] The taxpayer must

11, 2013). The Court has granted a motion to submit the *3M* case for decision without trial under Rule 122, and the case is still pending. We will accordingly reserve ruling on the parties' arguments concerning the blocked income regulation until an opinion in the 3M case has been issued.").

99. Rev. Proc. 2015-41, 2015-35 IRB 263, sets forth the procedures for obtaining an APA.
100. Typically, this will include an economic study of general industry pricing practices and economic functions performed within market and geographic areas covered by the APA request.
101. Rev. Proc. 2015-41, 2015-35 IRB 263, Sec. 3.10(3).
102. APAs can be revoked or cancelled where the taxpayer has engaged in misconduct or noncompliance regarding the APA or APA process. In a rare move, the Service cancelled Eaton Corporation's two APAs in December 2011. Eaton Corp. challenged the cancellation in Tax Court. In a June 2013 ruling, the Tax Court had rejected Eaton's argument that: (1) an APA is an enforceable contract, and (2) the Service must demonstrate breach of contract by the taxpayer *before* it can cancel an APA. Instead, the Tax Court ruled that an APA is an administrative determination and the taxpayer bore the burden to show that the Service's

file an annual report with the IRS noting its compliance with the agreement. A taxpayer may request that an APA be renewed, and to the extent that circumstances have not changed significantly, it may be possible to expedite the process.[103] In a November 2020 case involving Coca Cola, the Tax Court ruled that the taxpayer could not rely on an old APA to justify its related party pricing under Section 482 in subsequent years not covered by the terms of the APA.[104]

The Service strongly encourages taxpayers to pursue a bilateral APA where appropriate. A bilateral APA is an agreement negotiated with the taxpayer, the Service, and the tax authorities of the other jurisdiction involved in the transaction. Securing a bilateral APA assures the taxpayer that the same pricing methodology will be acceptable in the two (or more) countries involved in the transactions at issue.[105] A bilateral APA may not always be possible (the other jurisdiction must have a tax treaty with the US because the APA negotiations are conducted through the competent authorities) or a bilateral APA may not be necessary (where for example the other jurisdiction imposes little or no tax).[106]

Information submitted in connection with an APA request is confidential, and the agreement itself is not made public, not even in redacted form.[107] Under legislation enacted in 1999, the Internal Revenue Service is required to publish annually statutorily prescribed information with respect to the APA program.[108] After some initial reluctance on the part of taxpayers to participate in the APA program, the number of requests has increased substantially.

---

cancellation of the two APAs was improper. *Eaton Corp. v. Commissioner*, T.C., No. 5576-12, 140 T.C. No. 18 (June 26, 2013). In a 2017 ruling on whether the IRS cancellation of the APA was an abuse of discretion, the Tax Court concluded that the IRS did abuse its discretion and that an "APA is a binding agreement and it should be canceled only according to the terms of the revenue procedures." *Eaton Corp v. Commissioner*, TC Memo 2017-147 at 193.

103. Rev. Proc. 2015-41, 2015-35 IRB 263.
104. The *Coca-Cola Co. v. Commissioner*, 155 T.C. No. 10 (2020).
105. The first widely publicized international APA involved Apple Computer's activities in Australia.
106. During the calendar year 2020, of the total APAs applications filed (121), 103 were requests for a bilateral APA and 3 were requests for a multilateral APA. Internal Revenue Service, "Announcement and Report Concerning Advance Pricing Agreements," Announcement 2021-6, IRB 2021-15 at 1011 (Mar. 23, 2021) at Table 1.
107. The question of whether APAs should be disclosed in redacted form was the subject of litigation. *See BNA v. IRS*, D.C. No. 96-CV376 (Feb. 27, 1996). The parties agreed to dismiss the case when Congress intervened in 1999 and amended Section 6103(b) to prevent disclosure of APAs.
108. The Annual Report is to cover such matters as the operation of the APA program, data with respect to the numbers of applications made and agreements reached, and the types of taxpayers and transactions dealt with in the APAs. In addition, the report is to include any published model APA. The Service has issued a model dealing with global trading companies. Notice 94-40, 1994-1 C.B. 351 (note that the approach of the Notice would be modified substantially by Prop. Treas. Reg. Sec. 1.482-8 (1998)). The Annual APA report released in March 2021 includes two Model APAs: one based on Rev. Proc. 2006-09 and one based on Rev. Proc. 2015-41. Internal Revenue Service, "Announcement and Report Concerning Advance Pricing Agreements," Announcement 2021-6, IRB 2021-15 at 1011 (Mar. 23, 2021) (Appendices 1 & 2).

In 2012, the Service undertook a restructuring and moved the APA program from the Office of Chief Counsel and merged and integrated it into the Office of Transfer Pricing Operations, Large Business and International Division of the IRS (TPO). Within TPO the APA work was combined with the US Competent Authority staff that handles transfer pricing cases under the mutual agreement procedures of US tax treaties. That combined program is now known as the Advance Pricing and Mutual Agreement (APMA) Program. In 2018, APMA Program restructured its management and the organization of its teams, while remaining in TPO.

12.8 ACCURACY-RELATED PENALTIES

In addition to the "carrot" of the APA procedures and the wide range in choice of methods under the Regulations, Congress has also equipped the tax authorities with the "stick" of the accuracy-related penalties of Section 6662. These penalties, extended to transfer pricing cases in 1990 and further strengthened in 1993, impose a 20% or 40% penalty where the taxpayer's transfer pricing methodology resulted in reported income substantially less than that ultimately determined to be due. The 20% penalty is imposed if there is a "substantial valuation misstatement" in the amount reported by the taxpayer with respect to a related party transaction. A substantial valuation misstatement is present if the price reported is more than 200% higher or 50% lower than the amount determined to be correct under Section 482 (the "transactional" penalty). In addition, there is a substantial valuation misstatement if the total transfer pricing adjustment exceeds the lesser of USD 5,000,000 or 10% of the taxpayer's gross receipts (the "net adjustment" penalty).[109] The penalty is increased to 40% in the case of a "gross valuation misstatement" which applies if the transactional misstatement on prices is 400% too high or 25% too low or the total adjustment is the lesser of USD 20,000,000 or 20% of the taxpayer's gross receipts.[110] The penalties can be avoided if the taxpayer acted in "good faith" and had "reasonable cause" for the misstatement.[111] The Regulations spell out some of the factors relevant in establishing "reasonable cause" including when reliance on the advice of experts can be exculpatory.[112] In addition, the net adjustment penalty can be avoided if the taxpayer "reasonably" (though wrongly) used one of the stipulated methods and has contemporaneous documentation supporting the method chosen and why such method was reasonable.[113] The requirement of contemporaneous documentation is especially important

109. Sec. 6662(e)(1)(B).
110. Sec. 6662(h).
111. Sec. 6664(c).
112. Treas. Reg. Sec. 1.6664-4(c)(1).
113. Sec. 6662(e)(3)(B).

and the required documents are spelled out in detail and must be available at the time of the filing of the US return.[114]

114. Treas. Reg. Sec. 1.6662-6(d)(2)(iii). The emphasis on documentation is a result of the belief (or suspicion) by the Internal Revenue Service that taxpayers were "making it up as they went along" in many transfer pricing situations. On the other hand, some foreign taxpayers (and foreign governmental officials) view the documentation requirements and the Section 6662 penalties as an attempt by the US to insure that foreign taxpayers will bend over backwards to allocate income to the US to avoid any suggestion that the penalties would apply, all to the detriment of the foreign fisc. In recent years, so many jurisdictions are actively pursuing transfer pricing enforcement it seems less likely that the documentation requirements would have this effect. In fact, many other jurisdictions mandate transfer pricing documentation (rather than making it a condition to avoidance of penalties). Moreover, the widespread adoption of the OECD BEPS Action 13 Country-by-Country (CbC) reporting requirements for multinational corporations offers tax authorities assistance in identifying related party transactions warranting further scrutiny. *See, e.g.*, OECD, Guidance on the Implementation of CbC Reporting: BEPS Action 13 (December 2019), https://www.oecd.org/ctp/guidance-on-the-implementation-of-country-by-country-reporting-beps-action-13.pdf, *see also* section 12.1.

Independent of, and prior to, the new CbC reporting, the Service had found that initially (surprisingly) few taxpayers were preparing the documentation necessary to secure the benefits of Section 6662(e)(3)(B). Over time the Service witnessed increased "documentation" but has considered much of the documentation prepared to be insubstantial and essentially a pro forma effort to avoid penalties. More recently, the Service has become stricter in evaluating whether proffered documentation is of sufficient quality to provide the taxpayer penalty protection under Section 6662(e)(3)(B).

CHAPTER 13

Foreign Currency Issues

13.1 BACKGROUND

The importance of currency to taxation is easily overlooked if a taxpayer's transactions are all in a single currency. The currencies discussed in this chapter all are national currencies, meaning they are issued under the authority of a sovereign state, as opposed to the emerging phenomenon of virtual or crypto-currencies. A national currency serves at least three functions relevant to taxation, it is: (1) a medium of exchange, (2) a measure of value, and (3) a store of value. For purposes of US taxation, the US dollar has a constant value and serves as the measuring rod for changes in value of assets and of income and loss.[1]

Once a border is crossed, however, and economic activity or a transaction is conducted in a national currency other than the US dollar, tax rules are necessary to take into account the fact that a foreign currency has a value different from the dollar. It then becomes necessary to compute the taxpayer's tax liability from non-dollar economic activity and transactions.

Several different issues are involved. First, there must be some method of translating the income derived in the foreign currency into the currency utilized by the taxing system. In addition, transactions with foreign currency aspects can result in gain or loss because of the change in the relationship of the currencies involved, quite apart from the gain or loss on the underlying transaction. Finally, some taxpayers are actually conducting a business in a foreign currency, while others have only occasional foreign currency transactions, and different rules are necessary for these two classes of taxpayers.[2]

1. Since the early days of the income tax, taxes have had to be paid in US dollars. *See* O.D. 419, 2 Cum. Bull. 60 (1920).
2. A few basic examples of taxpayers engaged in transactions and activities involving foreign currency can provide a sense of the scope of issues involved:

Prior to 1986, the US tax rules applicable to foreign currency transactions were quite undeveloped. Some limited administrative pronouncements dealt with the possible methods of translation for income of foreign branches. Court cases had come to conflicting conclusions as to the appropriate treatment of foreign currency gain or loss, though generally foreign currency was treated as property.[3] To date, crypto or virtual currencies have been treated as property and taxed on that basis (as foreign currencies were under pre-1986 law).[4] In this chapter, we turn to the rules for national currencies.

The 1986 Act introduced a comprehensive set of rules dealing with foreign exchange issues in a new Subpart J of Subchapter N of the Code, that has been augmented, mostly by regulation, over the subsequent years. We briefly preview the approach taken by Subchapter J to foreign currency issues.

The basic approach is to identify when a taxpayer (through a branch) or a foreign corporation engages in sufficient activity in a foreign currency environment to warrant determining income or loss for a taxable period in the foreign currency and only translate the results into dollars at the end. The mechanism used to identify these cases is to determine when a branch or foreign corporation has a non-US "functional currency."[5] The concept of a functional currency and the determination of when a "qualified business unit" (QBU) of a US person or a foreign corporation uses a non-dollar functional currency is discussed in section 13.2.1.[6]

The next issue addressed is when and how the foreign income or loss earned primarily in a functional currency should be translated into dollars and at what

---

(1) A US corporation sells goods through its UK branch's London store which keeps its receipts and expenses in the British pound.
(2) A US corporation has a Mexican subsidiary that paid MXN 1.2 million in income taxes to Mexico. The US parent may seek to credit these taxes under Sections 901 and 960 if an inclusion under GILTI or subpart F is required.
(3) A US corporation has a South Korean branch that has borrowed 5 million won on Jan. 1, 2021 when the exchange rate was KRW 1000 = USD 1. Repayment was made on Sept. 1, 2021, when the exchange rate was KRW 1000 = USD 0.75.
(4) A US corporation purchases JPY 800,000 on Mar. 15, 2021 for USD 8,000. On Oct. 1, 2021, the corporation sold all of the yen for USD 7,000.
(5) A US corporation enters into a forward contract on Jan. 1, 2021 to acquire 400,000 gallons of a key chemical used in its manufacturing operations for JPY 5 million yen on June 1, 2021. At the time the contract is entered into, JPY 100 = USD 1. On June 1, when the contract is due JPY 100 = USD 0.75. Effectively, the US corporation will have to pay out fewer dollars (converted to yen) to acquire the chemicals than it anticipated at the time it entered into the forward contract.

These examples are drawn from Reuven S. Avi-Yonah, Diane M. Ring & Yariv Brauner, U.S. International Taxation: Cases and Materials, 535 (Foundation Press, 4th ed. 2019).

3. For a comprehensive review of the tax law governing the taxation of foreign currency prior to the 1986 Act, *see* Donald R. Ravenscroft, Taxation and Foreign Currency (Harvard International Tax Program 1973).
4. *See* Notice 2014-21, 2014-16 IRB 938; Rev. Rul. 2019-24, 2019-44 IRB 1004.
5. In 1981, the Financial Accounting Standards Board (FASB) adopted Statement No. 52, which implemented the functional currency concept into financial accounting rules that were the model for the use of the functional currency concept in the 1986 Act.
6. A QBU is colloquially referred to as a branch though it can encompass certain investment, as well as trade or business activity. *See* section 13.2.1.

exchange rate. For income or loss of a QBU involving a taxable period such as a year, the average exchange rate for the period is used, but sometimes a special rule is required. For a foreign corporation, the issue is at what rate to translate earnings included in the income of a US shareholder. The translation rules for a QBU or foreign corporation are discussed in section 13.2.2.

The final set of issues addressed in Subchapter J is to identify three groups of circumstances in which a transaction by a US taxpayer involving a foreign currency warrants the measurement of the foreign currency gain or loss realized in the transaction and, in some cases, its taxation separate from the income or loss realized. These cases generally involve an obligation in foreign currency over a period of time such that some portion of the gain or loss reasonably could be traced to currency gain or loss. A foreign currency lending or borrowing transaction is within the scope of the rules, but the gain or loss on an equity holding in a company operating in an exclusively foreign currency environment is not. In the latter case, it would not be feasible to identify with reasonable certainty what portion of a gain or loss on the equity is attributable to changes in currency value between the US dollar and the foreign currency in which the company operates. The foreign currency rules for transactions in a nonfunctional currency are discussed at section 13.3.

13.2 BASIC CONCEPTS

13.2.1 Functional Currency and Qualified Business Unit

Section 985(a) provides that income determinations are initially to be made in the taxpayer's "functional currency." The functional currency is the currency used to measure the taxpayer's income and expenses for tax purposes.

In general, Section 985 establishes the US dollar as the functional currency, and all relevant computations are in dollars.[7] However, in the case of a taxpayer's "qualified business unit," ("QBU") the functional currency is the currency of the economic environment in which the unit conducts its activities and in which it keeps its books and records.[8] Detailed regulations define a "QBU" as a "separate and clearly identified unit" of the taxpayer's trade or business for which separate books and records are maintained.[9] For example, the foreign sales branch of a domestic manufacturing company that has separate books and records would be a QBU.

A US QBU generally has the US dollar as its functional currency.[10] In contrast, a QBU conducting its business outside the US normally has a functional currency that is

7. Sec. 985(b)(1)(A). As a result, for most US taxpayers, transactions with foreign currency aspects (except for those specified in Section 988 discussed at section 13.3.1) do not have any independent foreign exchange implications. The necessary calculations are simply made in dollars and there is no separate treatment of foreign currency gain or loss. *See* section 13.3.3.
8. Sec. 985(b)(1)(B).
9. Treas. Reg. Sec. 1.989(a)-1(b)(2). An individual's investment activities can constitute a "trade or business" for these purposes. Treas. Reg. Sec. 1.989(a)-1(c).
10. Treas. Reg. Sec. 1.985-1(b)(1)(iii). An exception is permitted to the extent "provided by ruling or administrative pronouncement." For an example of one such ruling, *see* Letter Ruling

the foreign currency used to conduct its business and keep its books.[11] Thus, for example, if a US bank has a branch in France, the functional currency for computing the income of the branch would be the Euro.[12]

The same taxpayer can have several QBUs, each of which may have a different functional currency. Thus, if a US corporation has a branch operation in Switzerland and a second branch operation in Sweden, the functional currency of each branch may be the local currency while the functional currency of the head office would be the dollar.[13] Similarly, if a Swiss corporation has a branch operation in the US, the functional currency of the US branch would be the dollar.

Taxpayers in hyperinflationary economies are generally required to use the dollar as their functional currency in recognition of the special problem of unrealized foreign exchange losses in such economies.[14] Treasury Reg. Section 1.985-3 requires such taxpayers to use an accounting method called the "US dollar approximate separate transaction method" ("DASTM"). The DASTM, in effect, allows taxpayers in hyperinflationary environments to account for exchange rate losses currently.[15]

The IRS generally will not rule on whether a currency is a functional currency of a QBU (Section 985), or whether a unit of a taxpayer's business is a QBU (Section 989(a)).[16]

13.2.2 Translation of Foreign Currency Income and Foreign Taxes into Dollars

13.2.2.1 Translation of Branch Operations

If, under the rules discussed in section 13.2.1, the taxpayer (or a part of its activities constituting a QBU) has established a foreign currency as its functional currency, it will calculate its income in that foreign currency. It must then use some method to translate the income, as determined in that foreign functional currency, into dollars to establish its US tax liability.

200901026 (taxpayer's exchange traded funds which were treated as separate US corporations for federal tax purposes could, under the facts described, have a currency other than the US dollar as their functional currency).

11. Treas. Reg. Sec. 1.985-1(c)(1). The currency allowed for US financial accounting purposes generally will be accepted for tax purposes. Treas. Reg. Sec. 1.985-1(c)(5).
12. A US QBU will generally have the US dollar as its functional currency except "as otherwise provided by ruling or administrative pronouncement … ." Treas. Reg. Sec. 1.985-1(b)(1)(iii).
13. Treas. Reg. Sec. 1.985-1(f) Ex. 8.
14. Treas. Reg. Sec. 1.985-1(b)(2)(ii)(A). There are two exceptions to the requirement that the dollar be the functional currency. First, a QBU of a foreign corporation is not required to use the dollar as its functional currency, but may instead use the currency of the foreign corporation so long as that currency is not hyperinflationary. Second, a foreign corporation (or its QBU branch), which is not a controlled foreign corporation, is also not required to use the dollar as its functional currency. Treas. Reg. Sec. 1.985-1(b)(2)(ii)(B)(1) and (2).
15. *See* Treas. Sec. Reg. 1.985-1(b) and (c). DASTM is especially important for banks that have branch operations in countries with high rates of inflation and in which substantial amounts of capital are at risk.
16. Rev. Proc. 2020-7, 2020-1 IRB 281.

Section 987 states that the income measured in the functional currency is converted into dollars using the "appropriate exchange rate." In the case of branch operations, the appropriate exchange rate is the "average exchange rate," which is defined as the simple average of the daily exchange rates for the taxable year.[17]

In 2006, the Treasury and IRS released new proposed regulations detailing the application and implementation of Section 987 for QBUs. These regulations replaced the 1991 proposed regulations, which were withdrawn. The Treasury issued a slightly revised version of the 2006 proposed regulations as "final" regulations in 2016. We insert quotation marks around "final" because the IRS and Treasury have continuously postponed the effective date of the 2016 regulations, stating that they "are considering changes to the final regulations that would allow taxpayers to elect to apply alternative rules for transitioning to the final regulations and alternative rules for determining section 987 gain or loss ... ."[18] In the meantime, taxpayers may elect to apply the 2016 regulations or the 2006 proposed regulations so long as they apply the regulations consistently to all QBUs.[19]

The concern that prompted the withdrawal of the 1991 proposed regulations and the issuance of the 2006 proposed regulations and the 2016 "final" regulations was the ability of taxpayers to trigger recognition of non-economic exchange gain or loss (especially with the introduction of the "check-the-box" regime in 1996).[20] The Preamble to the 2006 proposed regulations explains:

> The IRS has faced many cases in which taxpayers have claimed substantial non-economic exchange losses largely on the basis of the 1991 proposed regulations. An example may be instructive. Assume that a domestic corporation (US Corp) with the dollar as its functional currency forms a foreign corporation in Country X and then elects under the check the box regulations to treat that corporation as a DE ["Disregarded Entity"]. The DE conducts mineral extraction in Country X and owns all the necessary equipment. The equipment owned by the DE was contributed by US Corp. The DE has no employees; it contracts with a subsidiary of US Corp for the employees needed in the business of extraction. US Corp, as the entity's sole owner, claims that the DE is a QBU for purposes of section 987. The DE has minimal financial assets and conducts no activities other than mineral extraction. US Corp claims that the DE's functional currency is Country X currency. A decline in the value of Country X currency relative to the dollar does not produce any economic loss for US Corp because the assets of the DE are not financial assets subject to currency fluctuation. Nevertheless, US Corp claims under the 1991 proposed regulations that the equity of the DE, which consists almost exclusively of equipment, gives rise to a substantial non-economic exchange loss and that terminating the DE (for example, by another check the box election) triggers recognition of such loss. Taxpayers have claimed similar results under other fact patterns.

17. Sec. 987(2) and 989(b)(4); Treas. Reg. Sec. 1.989(b)-1.
18. Notice 2019-65, 2019-52 IRB 1507.
19. *Id.*
20. The exchange gain or loss is referred to as "non-economic" because the realization of gain or loss was linked to a tax-based trigger and not to removal of the asset from use in a foreign functional currency environment. Typically, the recognition event involved the termination of the foreign QBU without changing the operation of the business and use of the assets in the foreign country.

The 2016 "final" regulations address the concern regarding DE's equipment in the above-quoted Preamble by requiring that the exchange rate applied to "historic" assets, such as the DE's equipment, be the historic exchange rate existing at the time DE acquired the equipment, not the average exchange rate for the current year. That would eliminate US Corp's exchange loss in the Preamble's example because any declines in the exchange rate occurring after DE's acquisition of the equipment are not considered.

The 2016 "final" regulations adopt a multi-step approach to determine a QBU's US tax items. This approach, called the "foreign exchange exposure pool method," proceeds in three stages[21]:

(1) Step 1: Identify the QBU's assets, liabilities, and items of income, gain, deduction, and loss that are reflected on the QBU's separate records and books and adjust such items to conform to US income tax principles.[22]
(2) Step 2: Using the items identified in step 1, determine each item of income, gain, deduction, or loss of the QBU for US income tax purposes using the QBU's functional currency.[23]
(3) Step 3: Convert the items of income, gain, deduction, and loss determined in step 2 in the QBU's functional currency into the *QBU owner's* functional currency. In general, this conversion occurs using the yearly average exchange rate.[24] Any tax calculation that involves a recovery of basis (such as from a sale or depreciation) for an historic asset, however, must use the historic exchange rate, not the yearly average exchange rate.[25] In general, historic assets are assets other than financial instruments and include equipment and inventory.[26] The historic exchange rate in general is the average exchange rate for the year that the QBU acquired the asset.[27]

21. *See* JOSEPH ISENBERGH, 900-2ND T.M., FOUNDATIONS OF U.S. INTERNATIONAL TAXATION, Sec. III.T.3.a (2020).
22. Treas. Reg. Sec. 1.987-2(b)(1). Non-portfolio stock, partnership interests, and certain types of acquisition indebtedness are excluded from this process. Treas. Reg. Sec. 1.897-2(b)(2).
23. Treas. Reg. Sec. 1.987-3(b)(1).
24. Treas. Reg. Sec. 1.987-3(c)(1).
25. Treas. Reg. Sec. 1.987-3(c)(2). The use of a historic exchange rate effectively eliminates currency gain or loss on the historic assets consistent with the view that the recognition triggering event is not an appropriate event for currency gain or loss recognition.
26. The definition of "historic assets" is found by following a regulatory path that is torturous even by international tax standards. Treas. Reg. Section 1.987-3(c)(2)(i) refers to Treas. Reg. Section 1.987-1(e) for the definition of "historic asset." Treas. Reg. Section 1.987-1(e) in turn defines historic asset as an item that is not a "marked item," which is defined in Treas. Reg. Section 1.987-1(d). Treas. Reg. Section 1.987-1(d) in turn defines a "marked item" as an item that would be a "section 988 transaction" if held by the QBU's owner. Finally, Section 988(c)(1), in general, defines a "section 988 transaction" as the acquisition of debt instruments, forward contracts, futures contracts, options, "or similar financial instruments" and the accrual of accounts receivable and payable.
27. Treas. Reg. Sec. 1.897-1(c)(3).

The gains and losses calculated under Section 987 are treated as ordinary, not capital, gains or losses.[28] Moreover, the source of such gains and losses is determined by reference to the assets generating the income—specifically, by using the method for allocating and apportioning interest expense under Section 861 (*see* Chapter 4, section 4.4.3.1).[29]

13.2.2.2 Translation of Corporate Earnings and Profits

If a foreign corporation using a foreign functional currency makes a distribution to a US shareholder, the earnings and profits of the corporation are first computed in the corporation's functional currency to determine whether the distribution will be treated as "out of earnings and profits" and hence a dividend for tax purposes (*see* Chapter 2, section 2.2.5).[30] The amount treated as a dividend is then translated to dollars at the spot exchange rate in effect at the time the dividend and is included in income by the shareholder.[31] This has the effect of treating the exchange rate gain or loss in the period between the time the income is earned and the time it is distributed as an increase or decrease in earnings and profits. The earnings and profits, which were calculated in the functional currency, are reduced by the functional currency amount of the dividend distribution.

In the case of the inclusion of the undistributed earnings of a foreign corporation by a US shareholder of subpart F income or GILTI, the foreign corporation's earnings, as calculated in the functional currency, are translated into dollars at the average exchange rate for the taxable year.[32] The actual distribution of previously taxed income, which is translated using the spot exchange rate, can give rise to exchange rate gain or loss measured by any change in exchange rates between the date of inclusion and the date of distribution.[33] For example, suppose a US shareholder is required to include USD 100 of income under the applicable average exchange rate and subsequently the foreign income is distributed at a time when the dollar has weakened so that the foreign currency dividend is worth USD 125. The additional USD 25 is includible at the time of distribution as ordinary income with a foreign source.[34]

28. Sec. 987(a)(1)(A).
29. Sec. 987(a)(3)(B); Treas. Reg. Sec. 1.987-6(a) and (b).
30. Sec. 986(b)(1).
31. Secs. 986(b)(2) and 989(b)(1). The amount included in income may qualify for the DRD of Section 245A if the requirements of that section are satisfied.
32. Sec. 989(b)(3); Treas. Reg. Sec. 1.951A-1(d)(1)(penultimate sentence).
33. Sec. 986(c)(1).
34. Sec. 986(c)(1). The distributing foreign corporation would not recognize any additional income under Section 311 (*see* Chapter 2, section 2.2.5) since it is distributing its functional currency which, in its hands, should not be treated as appreciated property. The US taxpayer would increase its basis in the CFC shares by USD 100 at the time of the initial income inclusion and reduce it by the same amount at the time of actual distribution. The USD 25 currency gain does not affect the basis of the CFC shares.

13.2.2.3 Translation of Foreign Taxes

In general, for foreign tax credit purposes, an accrual method taxpayer translates foreign taxes at the average exchange rate for the taxable year in which the taxes are accrued.[35] If there is a difference between the dollar amount accrued and the amount actually paid, the foreign tax credit is adjusted appropriately.[36] A cash method taxpayer translates foreign taxes using the spot exchange rate existing at the time the taxes were paid.[37]

13.3 TRANSACTIONS IN A NONFUNCTIONAL CURRENCY

In the situations considered so far, the foreign exchange rate issues have principally involved translating gains and losses when two different functional currencies were involved for one taxpayer or related taxpayers, for example, a US company with a foreign branch or a foreign corporation with a US shareholder. However, if the taxpayer, having one currency as its functional currency, engages in particular transactions that involve another currency (a "nonfunctional currency") a new set of issues arise. In addition to the income or loss on the underlying transaction expressed in terms of the nonfunctional currency, the taxpayer may also have foreign currency gain or loss because of the change in exchange rates between the functional and nonfunctional currency. From the perspective of the functional currency, the nonfunctional currency is a commodity that can independently generate gains and losses. For example, suppose a US taxpayer with the dollar as its functional currency purchases an asset in a nonfunctional currency (NF) for NF 1,000 when USD 100 = NF 100. Later, when the exchange rate has changed to USD 100 = NF 80, it sells the asset for NF 1,000. Economically, the taxpayer has engaged in two transactions: the purchase of an asset that did not change in intrinsic value and the sale of which produces no gain or loss and a foreign currency transaction on which, viewed from the perspective of the dollar as the functional currency, the taxpayer has a foreign currency gain of USD 250.[38] To consider another example, suppose the taxpayer borrows NF 1,000 when the

35. Sec. 986(a)(1)(A). Exceptions apply if the foreign income taxes: (a) are paid for more than two years after the close of the taxable year of accrual, (b) are paid before the taxable year of accrual, or (c) are denominated in an inflationary currency. Sec. 986(a)(1)(B) and (C). Where the exceptions apply, the foreign taxes are translated using the exchange rate existing at the time the foreign taxes are paid. Sec. 986(a)(2). In addition, a taxpayer may elect to use the exchange rate existing at the time the foreign taxes are paid, so long as the foreign taxes are denominated in a nonfunctional currency. Sec. 986(a)(1)(D). This election will, in practice, apply primarily to withholding taxes. In the case of deemed paid foreign taxes, the translation rules for taxes changed the pre-1986 result under the *Bon Ami Co.*, 39 B.T.A. 825 (1939), which translated deemed paid foreign taxes at the spot rate for the date of a dividend even if the taxes were paid many years earlier when exchange rates were different. The general effect of the 1986 Act change was to protect the US fisc from currency exchange risk with respect to the value of foreign tax after it was paid or accrued.
36. Sec. 905(c).
37. Sec. 986(a)(2).
38. That is, the NF 1,000 that the taxpayer receives back at the end of the transaction is worth USD 250 more than the initial dollar investment despite the fact that the value of the investment in terms of NF has not changed.

exchange rate is USD 100 = NF 100 and repays the loan later when the rate is USD 100 = NF 200. Viewed from the perspective of the dollar, the taxpayer has USD 500 of gain attributable solely to the change in exchange rates.

Section 988 provides the framework for dealing with these issues.

13.3.1 "Section 988 Transactions"

Section 988 defines certain transactions as "Section 988 transactions." In general terms, Section 988 covers three types of transactions: (1) borrowing or lending a nonfunctional currency or acquiring a nonfunctional currency debt obligation, (2) accruing for tax purposes an item of expense or income expressed in a nonfunctional currency, and (3) acquiring and disposing of nonfunctional currency directly.[39] Any foreign currency gain or loss attributable to Section 988 transactions is taxed as ordinary income or loss.[40] The source of such ordinary gain or loss is generally sourced to the residence of the taxpayer, or in the case of a QBU, to the QBU's principal place of business.[41]

To identify the foreign currency gain or loss attributable to a Section 988 transaction involving debt instruments, it is necessary in effect to isolate gain or loss attributable to the underlying transaction from the gain or loss arising from foreign currency fluctuations. For example, suppose a US taxpayer invests NF 250 in a bond when the exchange rate is USD 100 = NF 100. Taxpayer later sells the bond for NF 300 when the exchange rate is USD 100 = NF 125. (In other words when NF is only worth 80% (100/125) of what it was worth at the time of the bond purchase.) Economically, the taxpayer has a gain of USD 40 (NF 50 × 0.80 = USD 40) on the investment in the bond but an exchange loss of USD 50 (NF 250 invested = USD 250; NF 250 received on disposition = USD 200) for an overall loss on the Section 988 transaction of USD 10.

After the amounts of gain or loss on the foreign currency and underlying transactions are determined, the two types of gain or loss are netted.[42] If the foreign currency gain or loss exceeds the gain or loss on the underlying transaction, the excess is treated as attributable to a Section 988 transaction and taxed as ordinary income or loss.[43] It is sourced at the residence of the taxpayer or the location of the QBU with which it is associated.[44] In the above example, the investment gain of USD 40 is netted against the currency loss of USD 50. The net loss of USD 10 is a foreign currency loss taxable as an ordinary loss. The loss would be US source unless it arose in a foreign QBU, in which case it would be foreign source.[45]

39. Forward contracts and the like involving foreign currency are discussed below at section 13.3.2.
40. Sec. 988(a)(1)(A).
41. Sec. 988(a)(3).
42. Sec. 988(a)(1)(A), 988(b)(1) and (2), 988(c)(1); Treas. Reg. Sec. 1.988-2(b)(8). *See also* H.R. Conf. Rep. No. 841, 99th Cong., 2d Sess. at II-664 (1986) (stating that "foreign currency gain or loss is recognized only to the extent of the total gain or loss, taking into account gain or loss on an underlying transaction").
43. Sec. 988(a)(1)(A).
44. Sec. 988(a)(3).
45. Sec. 988(a)(1)(A) and 988(a)(3). Sourcing foreign currency gain or loss at the residence of the taxpayer in the absence of a foreign qualified business unit means that the gain or loss will not

Continuing the example, if the bond had been sold for NF 400, the investment gain would have been USD 120 (NF 150 × 0.8 = USD 120), the exchange loss would have been USD 50, and the overall gain USD 70. In this case, the source and character of the overall gain would be determined under normal rules; no foreign exchange gain or loss is involved after the netting process because the investment gain exceeds the currency loss.

Similar principles apply to accounts payable or receivable denominated in a nonfunctional currency. The amount of foreign exchange gain or loss is calculated by subtracting: (a) the product of the receivable (or payable) multiplied by the spot currency exchange rate on the date it is booked from, (b) the product of the receivable (or payable) multiplied by the spot currency exchange rate on the date it is paid.[46] Suppose a taxpayer with the dollar as its functional currency sends a bill for NF 1,000 for services performed abroad when the exchange rate is USD 100 = NF 100. When the bill is later collected, the exchange rate is USD 100 = NF 80. Under Section 988, the taxpayer would have USD 1000 of foreign source services income and USD 250 ((NF 1000 × 1.25) – (NF 1000 × 1)) of US source foreign currency gain.

13.3.2 Foreign Exchange Futures Contracts, Hedges, and Other Financial Transactions

Section 988 and the corresponding regulations provide extremely complex rules dealing with foreign exchange forward contracts, futures contracts, options, and similar financial instruments that are often used by taxpayers both to trade in a foreign currency and to hedge against exposure to fluctuating exchange rates. In general, entering into such contracts constitutes a "Section 988 transaction," and thus the gains or losses on the contracts will be subject to the source and character rules of Section 988. Section 988 also applies to "notional principal contracts" if the payments under the contract are determined with reference to a nonfunctional currency.[47] If a currency swap contract is disposed of, the resulting gain or loss is subject to Section 988.[48]

Section 988(d) has a special rule for fully hedged transactions where the taxpayer has in effect completely eliminated the risk of currency fluctuation and insured itself a cash flow or expense in its functional currency. In such cases, the foreign currency aspects of the transaction are ignored. For example, a fully hedged foreign currency borrowing, which locks in a dollar cost, is treated as a dollar borrowing with dollar interest payments. Consider a US taxpayer whose functional currency is the dollar and

affect the numerator of the foreign tax credit fraction. *See* Chapter 10 section 10.1. This is the appropriate result since this gain or loss will not be subject to tax by the foreign jurisdiction. From that country's perspective, there has been no gain or loss on the transaction and hence no question of double or under-taxation arises. Allowing any gain to be treated as foreign source would artificially inflate the foreign tax credit limitation.

46. Treas. Reg. Sec. 1.988-2(c)(2).
47. Treas. Reg. Sec. 1.988-1(a)(2)(iii)(B)(1). The definition of "notional principal contracts" includes swaps, caps, collars, and the like where payments are determined with reference to a notional principal amount calculated with reference to a particular index. Treas. Reg. Sec. 1.988-1(a)(2)(iii)(B)(2).
48. Treas. Reg. Sec. 1.988-2(e)(2).

who borrows Euros. The taxpayer immediately hedges the currency risk of having to make payments with more expensive Euros (in dollar terms) by entering into forward contracts to purchase the Euros it will need to pay its Euro-based obligations. If the taxpayer properly identifies the transaction as a hedge, the hedge transaction will be integrated with the borrowing as a "synthetic debt instrument" denominated in the currency to be paid under the hedge. In this example, that approach results in a dollar denominated borrowing because the forward contract to purchase Euros was paid in US dollars and no exchange rate gain or loss is generated because the dollar is the taxpayer's functional currency.[49]

13.3.3 Other Transactions

Section 988 deals only with certain specifically enumerated transactions. For all other transactions, gain or loss is determined with reference to the taxpayer's functional currency and there is no separate computation of foreign currency gain or loss. Thus, with respect to tangible property and financial assets not covered by Section 988, foreign currency gain or loss is treated as part of the gain or loss on the underlying transaction. For example, if a dollar-based US taxpayer invests NF 1,000 in the stock of a foreign company when the exchange rate is USD 100 = NF 100 and sells the stock for NF 1,000 when the exchange rate is USD 100 = NF 80, the USD 250 of gain calculated in dollars is treated as attributable to the stock investment and the source and character of the gain are not affected by Section 988.

Section 988 also generally does not apply to personal, noncommercial transactions, such as purchasing foreign currency for travel and exchanging remaining amounts for dollars after the trip. Instead, general tax principles will apply to currency gains and losses. Section 988 does contain a provision, however, that excludes currency gains of up to USD 200 on personal transactions from income.[50] The result is that gains in excess of USD 200 are taxable, while losses are not deductible since the US does not generally allow deductions for personal losses.[51]

49. Treas. Reg. Sec. 1.988-5(a)(9)(ii).
50. Sec. 988(e).
51. *See Quijano v. United States*, 93 F.3d 26 (1st Cir. 1996), where the taxpayer borrowed in a foreign currency to purchase a residence that was later sold at a gain. The taxpayer used the exchange rate at the time the property was purchased to calculate tax basis and the exchange rate at the time of the sale to calculate the amount realized. Due to changes in the exchange rate, the taxpayer realized a loss on the repayment of the mortgage. The exchange loss on the mortgage was not deductible as a Section 988 transaction since it involved a personal transaction and the court refused to integrate the lending and purchasing transactions to net the gain and loss.

CHAPTER 14
Income Tax Treaties

14.1 BACKGROUND

The US has entered into numerous bilateral income tax conventions[1] and a few estate and gift tax conventions.[2] The following material will focus on the extent to which the tax treaty provisions modify the otherwise applicable US tax rules discussed in the preceding chapters. Two points must be kept in mind at the outset, however. First, each of the individual treaties represents a separate and independent source of law. Hence, a particular question may be resolved one way in Treaty A, another way in Treaty B, and not dealt with at all in Treaty C. Second, since the treaties are not uniform, it is sometimes difficult to use the interpretation of one treaty as precedent in a case arising under another treaty. Nonetheless, the treaties show common patterns and are all based, to a greater or lesser degree, on the pioneering Organization for Economic Cooperation and Development Model Convention. There is also a Model US Convention, most recently revised and updated in 2016, which has many features in common with the OECD model.[3] Thus in many areas there is a kind of treaty "common law" that is reflected in the pattern of individual treaties.

---

1. The United States had sixty-six bilateral income tax treaties in force as of June 30, 2020. *See* IRS Tax Treaty Tables, Table 3 List of Tax Treaties (as of June 30, 2020) (not including the insurance income treaty with Bermuda, and also treating the nine CIS (Commonwealth of Independent States) treaties as separate from the treaty with Russia). While the international agreements here considered are technically conventions, following common usage, they will also be referred to as tax treaties or simply treaties. The United States has not signed the Multilateral Convention to Implement Tax Treaty Related Measures to Prevent Base Erosion and Profit Shifting ("MLI"), an agreement intended to facilitate countries' reconciliation of their existing bilateral treaties to certain commitments in the OECD BEPS project.
2. The United States has thirteen in force estate and gift tax treaties with Australia (1953), Austria (1982), France (1978), Finland (1952), Germany (1980), Greece (1950), Ireland (1949), Italy (1955), Japan (1954), the Netherlands (1969), South Africa (1947), Switzerland (1951), and United Kingdom (1978).
3. The 2016 United States Model Convention (the "US Model") superseded the 2006 Model (which itself superseded the 1996 Model). Although no Technical Explanation accompanied the release

14.2 TREATY OBJECTIVES AND TECHNIQUES

US tax treaties, like those of all countries, deal basically with the problems of double taxation that result when two countries assert taxing jurisdiction over the same persons or transactions. This problem is dealt with unilaterally by most countries either by granting a foreign tax credit or by exempting foreign source income. What then do the treaties add? The treaties, by and large, operate to refine and adapt these unilateral methods for avoiding international double taxation to the specifics of the tax relationships between the two countries involved. Additionally, treaties provide a process for resolution of conflicts under the treaty, including in some cases, the prospect of binding arbitration. To fully appreciate the impact of treaties, it is important to note that the unilateral measures adopted by virtually all states reflect the international "norm" that the residence country should yield to the source country and allow the source country to be the one to impose tax.[4] International tax norms are currently (spring 2021) being debated in the context of the OECD's Pillar 1 and Pillar 2 blueprints which were drafted to respond to two sets of concerns voiced by some countries: (1) Digitalization: given increased digitalization of the economy, existing tax rules do not allocate an appropriate portion of an MNE's revenue to market jurisdictions (not a previously recognized basis for allocating revenue under income tax) (Pillar 1); and (2) Base Erosion: cross-border base erosion continues to undermine the income tax, which can be strengthened through measures including adoption of a minimum tax (Pillar 2).[5]

---

of the 2016 Model, the 2006 Model was accompanied by a very helpful Technical Explanation ("US Technical Explanation") outlining the US understanding of the positions taken in the US Model. That 2006 Technical Explanation remains valuable with respect to treaty provisions that were unchanged in 2016. For a useful examination of the 2006 US Model, *see* New York State Bar Association Tax Section, "Report on the Model Income Tax Convention Released by the Treasury on November 15, 2006" (Apr. 11, 2007). The OECD Model Convention is available on the OECD website and is updated periodically to reflect changes to the Articles and the Commentary on the Convention.

4. Identifying this practice as a norm captures both its widespread force and its more informal nature. Given that there is no overarching international tax law that constrains states' behavior, the far-reaching acceptance of this "solution" (i.e., that the residence country should be the one to solve the problem and give up tax dollars through either a credit or exemption) can appropriately be referred to as a norm. Two of the four minimums standards to which BEPS associates commit upon joining the Inclusive Framework directly involve treaties (BEPS Action 6—treaty abuse; BEPS Action 14—improved dispute resolution). (The Inclusive Framework released a second peer review of BEPS Action 6 (treaty abuse, treaty shopping in January 2020. OECD/G20 Base Erosion and Profit Shifting Project, Inclusive Framework on BEPS: Action 6, *Prevention of Treaty Abuse—Second Peer Review on Treaty Shopping* (Jan. 30, 2020), abuse http://www.oecd.org/tax/beps/prevention-of-treaty-abuse-second-peer-review-report-on-treaty-shopping.htm. An earlier peer review, evaluated work on BEPS Action 14, dispute resolution. OECD, *BEPS Action 14 on More Effective Dispute Resolution Mechanisms: Peer Review Documents* (October 2016), http://www.oecd.org/tax/beps/beps-action-14-on-more-effective-dispute-resolution-peer-review-documents.pdf; *see also* OECD.org, *Action 14 Mutual Agreement Procedure*, http://www.oecd.org/tax/beps/beps-action/action14.
5. *See* OECD, Tax and digital: *OECD/G20 Inclusive Framework on BEPS invites public input on the Pillar One and Pillar Two Blueprints* (Oct. 12, 2020), https://www.oecd.org/tax/beps/oecd-g20-inclusive-framework-on-beps-invites-public-input-on-the-reports-on-pillar-one-and-pillar-two-blueprints.htm.

Perhaps most importantly in terms of double taxation, most US tax treaties (and those of other countries) result in each country reducing or surrendering its source-based jurisdiction on certain income. Thus, the US negotiates on a reciprocal basis with its treaty partners for each of them to either reduce or eliminate certain source-based withholding tax that they would otherwise impose on treaty partner residents. This negotiation involves the country of source ceding taxing jurisdiction in whole or in part to the country of residence. The provisions are generally reciprocal, thus the net effect of this treaty modification to the underlying international tax norm is not significant where the treaty partners have comparable cross-border flows of direct and portfolio investment and resulting income received with respect to the investment. But where there is a notable imbalance between countries, the "mutual" surrender of source jurisdiction may not be neutral in effect. This, for example, may be pronounced in a treaty between the US and a developing economy. Unless the treaty partner has significant investment flows into the US, the treaty benefit of reduced or eliminated US source taxation for treaty partner residents does not match the revenue lost when the treaty partner surrenders its source-based jurisdiction over income earned by US residents.

Treaties also alter the premise that "residence should yield to source" through the treaty article on permanent establishments. The role of the permanent establishment provision in a treaty (including US treaties) is to establish a threshold level of presence in the source country below which nonresidents should not be taxed at source. That is, although the source jurisdiction would have authority to tax under the international norms (because source would be a basis for taxation and because residence countries should solve the double taxation problem) by agreeing to a permanent establishment provision in a treaty, a country is surrendering its source taxing rights to the extent taxpayer activity falls below that threshold. Although there are valid reasons to implement a permanent establishment provision in a treaty, if the investment flows are not balanced, the loss of taxing power will pose a greater risk for developing countries. The impact of treaties (and of the more traditional permanent establishment provision) on developing countries continues to be a subject of examination. For example, in October 2020, the UN Committee of Experts on tax matters introduced a draft for a proposed new Article 12B for automated digital services that would permit the jurisdiction from which payment originates to impose tax on certain digital services income regardless of the taxpayer's presence in the country.[6] The UN draft language reflects an effort to address the issue of digital services from a developing country perspective.

As negotiated agreements, bilateral tax treaties represent a bargain struck between two countries at a specific moment in time, and with a certain assessment of the net effects of the deal based on each other's domestic tax laws. Consistent with this reality, the 2016 US Model introduces a new provision that enables a partial termination of the treaty where the domestic law of the treaty partner has changed. New Article

6. Co-Coordinators' Report, Committee of Experts on International Cooperation in Tax Matters: Tax Consequences of the Digitalized Economy—Issues of Relevance for Developing Countries, E/C.18/2020/CRP.41 (Oct. 11, 2020).

28, "Subsequent Changes in Tax Law," outlines the specific kinds of domestic tax law changes that grant the other Contracting State the right to pursue partial termination of the treaty (in particular, the articles offering special taxation of dividends, interest, royalties, and other income). At present, no US bilateral treaties include such a provision.[7]

Because treaties do not eliminate source-based taxation, the foreign tax credit remains very important. The treaties attempt to clarify and modify the otherwise applicable principles involved in the implementation of the US foreign tax credit to ensure that, to the extent possible, the provision achieves its objective of eliminating tax barriers to foreign investment by US residents.[8] In addition, the treaty partner obligates itself to grant to its residents some form of relief from double taxation (foreign tax credit or exemption) on investment in the US by its taxpayers. This provision removes double tax barriers to investment in the US by treaty country residents.

In addition to tackling issues most directly related to double taxation, US treaties also coordinate definitions, specify "tiebreaker rules," and manage the administration of the treaty. Treaties call for the identification of the "competent authority" for each country which is the individual or body that will work with its treaty partner counterpart in implementing the treaty and resolving disputes. Treaty provisions outline the procedures by which dispute and other issues under the treaty can be resolved. Finally, treaties include an exchange of information article (*see* section 14.12.3) which details what tax related information must be shared with a treaty partner and under what conditions.

More generally, the Preamble to the 2016 US Model introduces a shift in treaty focus that mirrors themes of the OECD BEPS project regarding tax base erosion. Whereas the 2006 Model identified its purpose as the "avoidance of double taxation and the prevention of fiscal evasion" the 2016 Models explains its purposes as the "elimination of double taxation … without creating the opportunities for non-taxation or reduced taxation through tax evasion or avoidance (including through treaty-shopping arrangements aimed at obtaining reliefs provided in this Convention for the indirect benefit of residents of third states)."[9] Concrete changes and additions to the 2016 US Model move the treaty in a direction reflective of these anti-evasion and avoidance goals, including revisions to the limitation on benefits provision (curbing treaty shopping, section 14.4.4), and a new rule denying treaty benefits for certain payments (e.g., interest, royalties, guarantee fees) if a related party is the beneficial owner of the payment *and* benefits from a special tax regime (section 14.4.5). At present, no US tax treaties have been negotiated on the basis of the new 2016 US Model.

7. The 2016 US Model was published as discussions were underway in the G20/OECD Inclusive Framework group regarding provisions to be included in the Multilateral Convention to Implement Tax Treaty Related Measures to Prevent Base Erosion and Profit Shifting (MLI) and appeared to be in part an effort to influence those discussions. Unlike prior US Models, it is less certain that novel provisions in the 2016 Model such as new Article 28 represent the US negotiating position.
8. As discussed in Chapter 10, section 10.7, the United States has included guardrails in the Code around favorable treaty foreign tax credits by subjecting these credits to a separate foreign tax credit limitation.
9. This change anticipated the provision in the MLI at Art. 6(1).

14.3 STATUS OF TREATIES

Under Article VI, Clause 2 of the US Constitution, international treaties and legislative enactments are of equal force. As a result, where treaties and legislative provisions conflict, the later in time prevails.[10] This means that, in principle, the US through subsequently enacted legislation can override an inconsistent treaty provision. In so acting, of course, it is breaching the international law obligation which it undertook to its treaty partner. Historically, there were very few instances of the legislative override of treaties. Beginning in the 1980s, however, Congress showed a greater inclination to override treaties through legislative enactments, despite the violation of international law which such action entails.

Because the legislative override of treaty obligations can have foreign policy implications, the courts have been reluctant to hold that treaty obligations have been legislatively abrogated in the absence of a clear Congressional expression of that intent.[11] In the context of tax treaties, this principle has been interpreted by the IRS to require that there be some indication in the legislative history of the overriding statutory enactment that Congress intends that the later legislative pronouncement should control over prior inconsistent treaty obligations.[12] In light of shifting standards of interpretation, the standard for evidence of an intent to override a treaty in legislative history is unclear.

The question of the relation between treaties and legislation was expressly addressed in 1988 legislation, though the exact effect of that enactment on prior practice is not entirely clear. Section 7852(d)(1) provides: "For purposes of determining the relationship between a provision of a treaty and any law of the US affecting revenue, neither the treaty nor the law shall have preferential status by reason of its being a treaty or law." In addition, Section 894(a), which previously stated expressly that any income exempted by treaty remained exempt despite any Code provision to the contrary, was amended to state only that Code provisions should be applied with "due regard" to US treaty obligations. The legislative history of these two provisions indicates that their purpose was to give to treaties "[t]hat regard which [they] are due under the ordinary rules of interpreting the interactions of statutes and treaties."[13] The

10. *See, e.g., Reid v. Covert,* 354 U.S. 1 (1957) (constitution renders treaties and statutes of equal standing); *Whitney v. Robertson,* 124 U.S. 190, 194 (1888) ("By the Constitution a treaty is placed on the same footing, and made of like obligation, with an act of legislation. Both are declared by that instrument to be the supreme law of the land, and no superior efficacy is given to either over the other. ... If the two are inconsistent, the one last in date will control the other. ... ").
11. *See Cook v. United States,* 288 US 102 (1933). There the Supreme Court stated: "A treaty will not be deemed to be abrogated or modified by a later statute unless such purpose on the part of Congress has clearly been expressed." 288 US at 120. *See also* Restatement (Fourth) of Foreign Relations Law of the United States Section 309.
12. *See, e.g.,* Rev. Rul. 80-223, 1980-2 C.B. 217.
13. H. Rep. 100-1104, 100th Cong., 2d Sess. 16 (1988). The House of Representatives version of the legislation contained a "residual" override provision that would have given the 1986 Act precedence over any conflicting treaty obligation even if the conflict had not been specifically identified. The House Report took the position that *Cook v. United States, supra* note 11, did not require as a general matter that Congress specifically advert to treaty conflicts for the subsequent legislation to override treaty obligations. H. Rep. 100-795, 100th Cong., 2d Sess. 305 (1988). The

extent to which these legislative changes will, in fact, affect the relation between treaties and statutes remains for the courts to decide in the context of particular situations of conflict that may arise in the future.

In addition to dealing with the general question of the relation between treaties and the Code, the 1988 legislation expressly provided that some treaty obligations were intended to be overridden by provisions of the Tax Reform Act of 1986.[14] The 2017 Tax Act prompted debates as to whether any of the new provisions, in particular the BEAT rules (Base Erosion Anti-Abuse Tax, Section 59A, *see* Chapter 5, section 5.10), constitute a treaty override, although Congress identified none of them as intended treaty overrides.

14.4 QUALIFICATION FOR TREATY BENEFITS

14.4.1 Persons Covered

The various benefits contained in US tax treaties are generally provided to "residents," both natural and juridical, of the countries involved. Residence is typically defined in terms of a person or entity being liable to taxation on the basis of a personal connection with the taxing jurisdiction.[15] Some treaties provide a more detailed definition of residence for treaty purposes, dealing with special situations such as tax-exempt organizations, pension funds, and the like. In the absence of a special definition, reference is initially made to the law of the country involved to determine whether the particular individual or organization claiming treaty benefits qualifies as a resident.[16]

14.4.1.1 "Tiebreaker" Clause

The Model Treaty, Article 4, provides for a "tiebreaker" that establishes a single residence for treaty purposes if, under the definitional article, the taxpayer would be a resident of both countries. The details of the tiebreaker provision, which is contained

---

Conference Committee Report reference to the "ordinary rules" of interpretation may be viewed as reaffirming the *Cook* approach requiring a clear expression of Congressional intent.

14. 1988 Act Sec. 1012(aa)(2)(B). The 1986 Act changes in the foreign tax credit are to prevail over conflicting treaty rules. On the other hand, treaty rules prevail over the changes in the source of income rules in Section 865(e)(2) 1988 Act. Section 1012(aa)(3)(A)(ii) (*see* Chapter 4 section 4.2.6 for a discussion of Section 865(e)(2)). Other examples of treaty overrides in recent decades include the Foreign Investment in Real Property Tax Act (Sections 897 and 1445) and the Branch Level Interest Tax (Section 884).
15. US Model, Art. 4. The fact that the US imposes worldwide taxation on the basis of citizenship raises some special problems in the definition of residence for treaty purposes. Some countries are reluctant to grant treaty benefits to persons who, while US citizens, have no significant connection with the US even though they are subject to worldwide US taxation and thus are in the same situation as residents generally. Some treaties exclude US citizens from resident status in these circumstances. *See, e.g.*, Sweden, Art. 4.1(b) (US treaties are cited by the name of the treaty partner).
16. For an unusual case denying tax residence under a treaty notwithstanding a treaty partner's administrative determination as to residence, *see Johansson v. United States*, 336 F.2d 809 (5th Cir. 1964).

in most modern treaties, differ in details from treaty to treaty. The general approach is to select and give priority to various personal connections between the taxpayer and the two countries in order to establish a single residence.[17]

In the case of corporations, a problem of dual residence often arises where the US determines corporate residence on the basis of the place of incorporation while the other jurisdiction applies a place of management test. The 2016 US Model Treaty, in a break with the 2006 Model, provides that if a company is considered resident in both treaty partner jurisdictions (dual resident corporations), then it will not be "treated as a resident of either ... for purposes of its claiming the benefits" of the treaty.[18] This approach to dual resident corporations was already seen in some existing US tax treaties.[19]

14.4.1.2 "Hybrid" Entities

"Hybrid entities" (like hybrid instruments)[20] often pose challenges for the tax system. Although sometimes these issues are entirely domestic, many of the most "attractive" uses of hybrids occur in the cross-border context, particularly with the application of treaties. Taxpayers could use hybrid entities to avoid having any tax (US or foreign) apply to income. For example, income earned by a US entity taxable as a partnership for US purposes might not be taxable because of favorable treaty provisions that would apply to foreign partners in the partnership. At the same time, if the entity were characterized as a corporation in the foreign partners' country, its income might not be taxable in that country because it is not a resident of that country.

The appropriate treatment of so-called hybrid entities has long been a vexing problem in determining qualification for treaty benefits. Statutorily the US has sought to resolve some treaty issues with hybrids through the application of Section 894(c) and the regulations thereunder. The regulations under Section 894(c) adopt different approaches that depend on whether the hybrid is a "domestic reverse hybrid" entity. A "domestic reverse hybrid" entity is a domestic (i.e., US) entity that is treated as not fiscally transparent for US tax purposes and as fiscally transparent under the laws applicable to a person holding an interest in the entity.[21] The regulations provide that for entities that are *not* "domestic reverse hybrid" entities, an item of income will be considered to be derived by a resident for tax treaty purposes if the resident country asserts taxing jurisdiction over that item.[22] Thus, the tax characterization by the

17. US Model, Art. 4.3.
18. US Model, Art. 4.4. Note that the effect of this approach is to divest the competent authorities of the ability to agree on a country of residence. This may be contrasted with the MLI, Art. 4(1) which provides that the competent authorities will endeavor to determine residence of such an entity, but if they cannot agree then residence status is denied.
19. *See, e.g.*, Australia, Art. 3.1(g) (entered into force in 1983).
20. In broad terms, hybrids (whether entities or instruments) are those that are classified one way by one jurisdiction, and differently by another. For example, in the case of entities, a typical example of a hybrid entity is one that is treated as a partnership by one jurisdiction and a corporation by another.
21. Treas. Reg. Sec. 1.894-1(d)(2)(i).
22. Treas. Reg. Sec. 1.894-1(d)(1).

resident country whether an item of income is derived by an entity that is not a "domestic reverse hybrid" entities will generally control for purposes of applying a treaty. In the example in the preceding paragraph, the entity is not a domestic reverse entity because it is fiscally transparent in the US. If the country of the foreign partner does not assert taxing jurisdiction (on the grounds that the entity is nontransparent and not a resident of that country), the US will not apply the reduced treaty rate.

The treatment of an entity that is a domestic reverse hybrid entity is more complex and depends on whether the domestic reverse hybrid entity is receiving or making a payment. With respect to payments received by a domestic reverse hybrid entity, the regulations state that a tax treaty cannot reduce the tax applied to such payments that are from a US source.[23] Thus, even though another country might tax a person holding an interest in the domestic reverse hybrid entity upon the *entity's* receipt of US source payments, the US will not apply the treaty rates to such person's share of the income received by the domestic reverse hybrid entity.[24] Payments from the domestic reverse hybrid entity will be characterized for treaty purposes as though paid by a nontransparent entity.[25] Consequently, if a domestic reverse hybrid entity makes a payment to one of its interest holders, it will be characterized as a payment from a nontransparent US entity (such as a dividend or an interest payment from a corporation) for purposes of applying the treaty's tax rates. Special rules apply to determine the character of the payment by the domestic hybrid entity to an interest holder if the payment consists of amounts the hybrid received as a tax-free dividend from a subsidiary. In that situation, the payment by the hybrid to an interest holder will be treated as a nondeductible dividend payment, regardless of whether it is in fact an interest payment.[26]

At the treaty level, the US also seeks to curb potential abuses through the use of hybrid entities. The US Model Treaty follows the approach of the OECD Model in dealing with entities which are treated differently in the two treaty jurisdictions. In case of entities which are fiscally transparent in either jurisdiction, the treaty determines treaty residence (and hence entitlement to benefits) with reference to the person who, under the laws of the treaty partner, is required to include the item in question in income.[27] This determination controls regardless of the treatment of the entity in the jurisdiction of the payer. Thus, for example, if a US corporation pays a dividend to a foreign entity which is treated as fiscally transparent in the other jurisdiction, the participants in that entity who are treaty country residents will be entitled to the benefits of this treaty even if, under US principles, the entity itself would have been the relevant taxpayer. Similarly, if a US payer makes a payment to an entity that the US treats as a fiscally transparent partnership but the other jurisdiction treats as a

23. Treas. Reg. Sec. 1.894-1(d)(2)(i). This is consistent with the reservation of US taxing rights with respect to US residents found in the savings clause of US Model Art. 1(4) discussed in section 14.4.1.3.
24. *See* Treas. Reg. Sec. 1.894-1(d)(2)(iii) Ex. 1 for an example applying this rule.
25. Treas. Reg. Sec. 1.894-1(d)(2)(ii).
26. Treas. Reg. Sec. 1.894-1(d)(2)(ii)(B).
27. US Model, Art. 1.6.

corporation, treaty relief will depend on whether the income is liable to tax in the treaty country in the hands of the entity.[28]

A new provision added to the 2016 Model reinforces the focus on curbing base erosion by addressing certain triangular permanent establishment scenarios. Under new Article 1.8, if a resident of one Contracting State derives income from the other Contracting State but that first Contracting State (residence) treats the income as earned by the a permanent establishment located in a third jurisdiction, then that income generally cannot secure treaty benefits if either: (1) the income bears a low aggregate effective tax rate in the third jurisdiction and the Contracting State of residence or (2) the third jurisdiction lacks a comprehensive tax treaty with Contracting State from which the income was derived.

14.4.1.3 *"Saving Clause"*

Most US treaties contain a so-called saving clause that in general allows the US to continue to tax its citizens and residents as if the treaty had not come into effect.[29] As a result, even though a particular treaty article may, by its terms, appear to assign exclusive taxing jurisdiction of a particular type of income to the country of source, the saving clause would operate to deny that benefit to a US citizen or resident.

However, the treaties generally provide that they may not operate to the detriment of the taxpayers covered by the treaty. Accordingly, in general, the benefits of a provision of the Internal Revenue Code cannot be limited by a more restrictive treaty provision. For example, if a treaty authorizes a withholding tax on interest but interest payments to nonresidents are exempt under the Code, the treaty will not operate to impose a tax. However, there are limitations on the taxpayer's ability to select the most favorable of Code or treaty rules. Where a treaty benefit is subject to limitations that are not present in the Code, the taxpayer cannot claim the treaty benefit and at the same time apply the more generous Code limitations.[30]

14.4.2 Disclosure Requirements

Section 6114 requires that any taxpayer taking the position that a treaty provision overrides or modifies a Code provision must disclose the position taken on its return. If no return otherwise would be required, regulations nevertheless require the taxpayer to file a return that includes its address and a statement that discloses its position,

28. Sec. 894(c); Treas. Reg. Sec. 1.894-1(d).
29. US Model, Art. 1.4. There are usually exceptions in the saving clauses which allow US citizens or residents to claim treaty benefits under the "relief from double taxation" article, the "nondiscrimination" article, the mutual agreement procedure article, and some other specialized articles. US Model, Art. 1.5. In addition, the article determining residence for treaty purposes is itself generally excepted from the savings clause. Thus, an alien who is a US resident under the Code definition of residence (*see* Chapter 5 section 5.5.2) but a resident only of the treaty country under the treaty tiebreaker rule would not be subject to the saving clause.
30. US Model, Art. 1.2; Rev. Rul. 84-17, 1984-1 C.B. 308. For a discussion of other aspects of this "cherry picking" problem, *see* 2006 US Technical Explanation, Art. 1, para. 2.

signed under penalties of perjury.[31] Section 6712 imposes fines for failure to comply with the disclosure requirements.

14.4.3 Limitation on Treaty Benefits

14.4.3.1 Background

All US treaties extend treaty benefits to corporations and other juridical persons that qualify as residents of the treaty partner. As a result, individuals or corporations from third countries could in principle obtain the benefits of a particular treaty by forming a corporation in the treaty country.[32] This course could be advantageous for the third-country investor if there were no treaty between the US and his country or if the third-country treaty had less favorable terms. The US has always had certain restrictions on the ability of third-country residents to "treaty shop" by using a corporation formed in a jurisdiction having a favorable treaty with the US.[33] The scope and importance of such limitations, however, have increased dramatically in recent years, and the insistence on an extensive limitation on benefits article is a hallmark of current US treaty policy.[34]

Historically, limitations on treaty benefits were usually imposed if the treaty corporation was subject to a special tax regime in its home country and, more generally, if the "principal purpose" of establishing the treaty corporation was to obtain treaty benefits.[35] However, an anti-treaty shopping policy was not actively pursued prior to the 1980s and, indeed, both the Treasury Department and the Internal Revenue Service in effect encouraged treaty shopping in some circumstances.[36]

31. Treas. Reg. Sec. 301.6114-1. There are important exceptions to this tax return disclosure requirement, including with respect to income subject to withholding which has been reported to the withholding agent by the withholding agent. *See* Treas. Reg. Sec. 301.6114-1(c).
32. The treaty benefits involved would typically be the reduction or elimination of US source-based taxation on outbound payments such as dividends, interest, and royalties. In addition, business income could escape US tax if the treaty country corporation was engaged in business in the US but did not have a US permanent establishment.
33. *See, e.g., Aiken Industries, Inc. v. Commissioner,* 56 TC 925 (1971) (interest income was not "received by" a treaty country corporation owned by non-treaty country residents where the corporation was obligated to pay out a corresponding amount in a back-to-back loan transaction; hence the interest did not qualify for treaty benefits). In addition, so-called anti-conduit regulations issued in 1995 give the Internal Revenue Service the authority to disregard the participation of an intermediate treaty-benefited participant in a financing transaction if the structure is part of a tax avoidance plan. The regulations would apply to a "classic" back-to-back loan through a treaty conduit as well as to more complex financial schemes. *See* Treas. Reg. Sec. 1.881-3. The US regards these rules as consistent with limitation on benefits principles and with tax treaties generally. Under the anti-conduit rules, the "real" taxpayer is identified; the limitation of benefits rules then determine if the taxpayer so identified is still entitled to treaty benefits. 2006 US Technical Explanation, Art. 22 para. 1.
34. 2006 US Technical Explanation, Art. 22 sets out the policy rationale for the limitation on benefits approach. The 1996 US Model Treaty Technical Explanation, Art. 22 provides additional discussion of the US policy perspective and rationale.
35. *See, e.g.,* Luxembourg, Art. 15 (terminated 1962 treaty).
36. Prior to the repeal of the withholding tax on portfolio interest, US corporate borrowers utilized the treaty with the Netherlands Antilles to avoid the US withholding tax on interest payments to

Beginning with the inclusion of a restrictive limitation on benefits article in the Model Treaty in 1981, the US has shown a much greater concern with treaty shopping issues in recent years. All of its post-1981 treaties have had substantial restrictions on treaty shopping and Congress has indicated that it will not approve a treaty that does not contain such provisions.[37] As noted above at section 14.2, the 2016 Model continues the trend of revising the limitation on benefits article with the introduction of two new tests (the derivative benefits plus base erosion test and the limited headquarters company test) along with a tightening of the existing treaty tests for qualifying for treaty benefits.

14.4.3.2 Structure of Limitation on Benefits Article

While the details of the limitation on benefits provisions vary substantially, they generally provide a "safe haven" test based on share ownership by treaty country residents coupled with restrictions to ensure that the corporation has not reduced its tax base in the residence country through deductible payments. If the treaty country corporation has substantial resident share ownership[38] and does not make extensive deductible payments to third-country residents who are not entitled to treaty benefits,[39] it is fair to assume that the corporation was not established in the treaty jurisdiction simply to obtain treaty benefits and that treaty shopping is not involved.

If the shareholder/base erosion test cannot be met, under most recent treaties the corporation can still qualify for treaty benefits if the corporation is engaged in an active trade or business in the residence country and derives income from the source state

nonresident lenders. The Treasury Department indirectly supported these treaty shopping activities because of balance of payments considerations and the Internal Revenue Service issued a number of favorable rulings involving the Netherlands Antilles finance companies. The partial termination of the Netherlands Antilles treaty (leaving its interest article in place) in 1988 put an end to such transactions (in effect allowing continued application of the prior provisions for outstanding financing arrangements).

37. In addition to anti-treaty shopping rules in the treaties, the 1986 Act imposed special statutory rules involving treaty shopping in connection with the branch profits tax. As discussed at section 14.11 below, in some cases the nondiscrimination articles of treaties can prohibit the imposition of the branch profits tax. However, Section 884(e) provides that the branch profits tax will nonetheless be applicable, despite treaty provisions to the contrary, unless the foreign corporation is a "qualified resident" of the treaty country. "Qualified resident" is defined in terms of share ownership and base erosion safe havens with a more generalized test based on the active conduct of a trade or business in the treaty country. Treas. Reg. Sec. 1.884-5. If a corporation qualifies under a treaty-based limitation on benefits test contained in a treaty entered into after Dec. 31, 1986, it will likewise be treated as a qualified resident under Section 884. Treas. Reg. Sec. 1.884-4(b)(8).
38. US Model, Art. 22.2(f) has an "at least 50%" test paired with a base erosion test.
39. US Model, Art. 22.2(f)(ii) requires that less than 50% of the gross income be paid out to nonqualified persons in deductible payments. This restriction is focused on "conduit" companies that receive treaty-benefited income and then pay it out in deductible payments that are not subject to treaty country withholding tax. The third-country recipients would indirectly get the benefit of the initial reduction in US source taxation and pay no offsetting tax in the treaty country of residence.

connected with that business.[40] The business presence in the source and residence states is deemed to insure that the treaty shopping is not present as long as the income in question arises as part of that business. Similarly, if the "principal class" of shares of a corporation (and any "disproportionate class of shares") is regularly traded on recognized stock exchanges *and* either: (1) the primary exchanges are in the Contracting State in which the corporation claims residence, or (2) the company's primary place of management and control is in that residence Contracting State, then again treaty shopping is assumed to be absent.[41] The 2016 US Model introduces a derivative benefits provision (with a companion base erosion test), although some existing US treaties have included a version of such a test.[42] Under the Model Treaty version of the test, even if a corporation resident in a Contracting State fails to be a qualified person under the treaty, it will still be entitled to benefits if "at least 95% of the aggregate vote and value of its shares ... is owned ... by seven or fewer persons" who are qualified to receive benefits under a comprehensive treaty with the Contracting State from which the benefit is sought—and a base erosion test is met.[43] A number of other specialized rules dealing with headquarters companies,[44] management companies, and internationally owned joint ventures are contained in various forms in some treaties.[45] Finally, if none of the explicit tests can be met, competent authority relief may be available.[46]

14.4.4 Overall Evaluation of Limitation on Benefits Provisions

Limitations on treaty benefits raise some difficult issues of tax treaty policy. The developments in the US undoubtedly have been influenced by the existence in the past of tax treaties with tax haven countries. These treaties provided treaty benefits to third-country investors having no real economic connection (and making no significant tax payments (!)) to the treaty country. It clearly is undesirable for the US to have a "treaty with the world" through a tax haven. Beyond this generalization, however, the question is how to define a "real" corporation in a treaty jurisdiction which should be entitled to treaty benefits. The present rules, with their various proxy tests to insure that treaty shopping is not involved, offer one approach to the problem. It must be noted that the US remains something of an "outlier" in this area because of its

40. US Model, Art. 22.3. For example, interest on short-term investment in working capital would qualify under this test, as would interest on trade receivables. *See* 2006 US Technical Explanation, Art. 22, para. 3.
41. US Model, Art. 22.2(c). Additionally, the US Model considers a corporation a "qualified person" if "at least 50% of the aggregate vote and value of the shares (and at least 50% of the aggregate vote and value of any disproportionate class of shares) in the company is owned directly or indirectly by five or fewer companies entitled to benefits" under Article 22.2(c), "provided that, in the case of indirect ownership, each intermediate owner is a resident of the Contracting State from which the benefit under this Convention is being sought or is a qualifying owner." US Model, Art. 22(d)(i). This indirect test for securing treaty benefits however, requires that the corporation also satisfy a base erosion test. US Model, Art. 22(d)(ii).
42. US Model, Art. 22.4.
43. US Model, Art. 22.4 and 22.7(e).
44. US Model, Art. 22.5.
45. *See, e.g.*, Switzerland, Art. 22.1(d), 22.3 and 22.4; Austria, Art. 16.1(f)-(h).
46. US Model, Art. 22.6.

insistence on a detailed limitations articles in all cases, even when a "serious" and high-tax country is the treaty partner and the possibility of treaty shopping would be highly unlikely.

The limitations on benefits articles also raise a number of practical problems of enforcement. The withholding agent is not usually in a position to determine if the payee is covered by the treaty shopping provision. The payee's status may change from year-to-year due to changes in share ownership and in income mix. As discussed in Chapter 5 section 5.9.2.1, a withholding agent may rely on certifications made by the payee on withholding forms. There are circumstances, however, where the taxpayer-payee will not have sufficient knowledge about its shareholders or members to be able to make such certifications, in which case the treaty benefit will not be allowed.

14.4.5 New "Special Tax Regime" Rule

The 2016 US Model introduces a new limit on taxpayers' ability to secure treaty benefits by denying certain benefits where the parties benefit from a special tax regime (STR). Article 3(1)(l) defines a special tax regime as any "statute, regulation or administrative practice in a Contracting State" that meets several conditions (regarding the kind of tax benefit, links to activity in the jurisdiction, the expected tax rate, and the type of taxpayers to whom the regime applies). The new rule aims to implement the Preamble's language about eliminating double taxation "without creating opportunities for non-taxation or reduced taxation through tax evasion or avoidance."

To qualify as an STR, a regime must:

(1) produce one or more of the following:
   (a) a preferential tax rate for interest, royalties, or guarantee fees—as compared to sales of goods or services;
   (b) permanent reduction in the tax base for interest, royalties, or guarantee fees (but not sales of goods or services) via an exclusion from gross receipts, or other base-reducing feature;
   (c) special rate or tax base reductions for substantially all of a company's income or substantially all of its foreign source income where the company does not engage in the active conduct of a trade or business in that jurisdiction;
(2) in the case of tax benefits for royalties, not condition the benefit on research and development activities in that jurisdiction;
(3) generally be expected to produce a tax rate of less than the lesser of 15% or 60% of the general statutory company tax rate in the other Contracting States;
(4) not primarily be applicable to pension funds, specially regulated investment vehicles for securities or real estate, or to organizations formed for religious, charitable, scientific, artistic, cultural, or education purposes.

Notice must first be given to the other Contracting State, identifying the STR as such, before being so treated under the treaty. The consequences of declaring an STR are found in Article 11(2)(c) (Interest), Article 12(2)(a) (Royalties), and Article 21(2)(a) (Other Income—guarantee fee). Each of these provisions grant taxing rights to the Contracting State in which the payment arose, contrary to the general treaty rule governing such payments.

14.4.6 Taxes Covered

The US treaties generally cover Federal income taxes but are not extended to US state and municipal levies.[47] Social security and unemployment taxes are expressly excluded in the Model Treaty.[48] In the past, a treaty partner sought to require its treaty with the US to include a provision that barred the states of the US from using a unitary or formulary approach to determining income allocation. The effort was unsuccessful because of the US view that such a provision would constitute an inappropriate intrusion into the sovereignty of the states in the context of the US federal system.[49]

14.5 TREATMENT OF BUSINESS INCOME

14.5.1 In General

As discussed in Chapter 5, a nonresident alien or foreign corporation is generally taxed on business income from US sources at the usual US tax rates. Technically, the tax is imposed on all income that is effectively connected with the foreign taxpayer's US trade or business. This Code treatment of business income is modified by US treaties. In general, the treaties provide that a foreign taxpayer will not be taxed on business income unless that income is attributable to a permanent establishment located in the US.[50] If no permanent establishment is present, business income that would otherwise be subject to US tax is exempt under the treaty.

Conversely, a US taxpayer who realizes business income in a foreign country with which the US has a treaty will be taxed in that country only if the income is attributable to a permanent establishment located there. While the foreign taxes attributable to the foreign business profits would generally qualify for the foreign tax credit, the exemption is nonetheless important to the US taxpayer. In the first place, it frees the US taxpayer from the burdens of filing and paying foreign taxes which it would then subsequently credit. More importantly, it allows the taxpayer to avoid any problems of the possible nonapplication of the foreign tax credit. For example, suppose the foreign country's concept of source of income differed from that of the US. Potentially, the income could be subject to foreign taxation but not qualify as foreign

47. In treaties with countries that also have federal systems, including those with Canada, Germany, and Switzerland, subnational taxes of the treaty partner are covered taxes. This nonreciprocal position reflects longstanding US Federal deference to state tax sovereignty.
48. US Model, Art. 2.3(b). Generally, the "nondiscrimination" articles of US treaties do extend to state taxes (*see* section 14.11). US Model, Art. 24.7.
49. *See, e.g.*, The Impact of the OECD and the UN Model Conventions on Bilateral Tax Treaties 1157 (Lang, Pistone, Schuch, & Staringer, eds. Cambridge 2012).
50. US Model, Art. 7.1.

source income for purposes of the foreign tax credit provisions. The exemption for business income absent a permanent establishment avoids such problems.

The introduction of the permanent establishment threshold was the second example of how treaties reduce source-based taxation relative to the background norms. As noted above, this reduction is meant to decrease the compliance burden on nonresident businesses with only minimal contacts with the source jurisdiction. But the "benefit" of the reduced compliance burden negotiated through the treaty is *mutually* beneficial *if* business investment flows are comparable. Otherwise, a country may consider that it has surrendered more in source jurisdiction than it has gained in administrative ease and prevention of double taxation for its own residents. That said, a country may nonetheless conclude, either unilaterally in its domestic law or through its negotiated treaty that a balance in the benefits is less important than being an attractive business destination that allows investors to "test the waters" before establishing a more significant business presence in the country. The precise terms and resulting thresholds of treaty permanent establishment provisions has become a significant topic of debate in many countries. This issue has been an ongoing factor in the negotiation of treaties as well as the policy work of the OECD and UN.[51] As of 2021, the debate over digital services taxes (including the work of the OECD in Pillar 1[52]), reflects the most current tensions about the threshold of business activity in a jurisdiction required to justify income taxation.

14.5.2 Permanent Establishment

The definitions of permanent establishment in the various US treaties are similar in outline but differ substantially in detail. In general, a permanent establishment may take the form of an office or other fixed place of business or a resident agent of the taxpayer with authority to enter into contractual relationships or who fills orders from a stock of goods located in the agent's country. However, an agent of "independent status" will not constitute a permanent establishment.[53] Beyond these general principles, many treaties enumerate in detail the types of activities that will or will not constitute a permanent establishment, reflecting to some extent the special circumstances of the economic relationships between the Contracting States. For example, the Norwegian treaty deals at some length with the treatment of offshore drilling operations.[54]

Most treaties provide that a domestic subsidiary corporation of the foreign taxpayer will not "of itself" be treated as a permanent establishment, though the

51. *See, e.g.*, OECD, *Revised OECD Model Tax Convention: Discussion Draft on the Definition of 'Permanent Establishment' (Article 5) of the OECD Model Convention* (Oct. 19, 2012).
52. *See* OECD/G20 Base Erosion and Profit Shifting Project, *Tax Challenges Arising from Digitalisation—Report on Pillar One Blueprint* (Oct. 14, 2020), http://www.oecd.org/tax/beps/tax-challenges-arising-from-digitalisation-report-on-pillar-one-blueprint-beba0634-en.htm.
53. *See Taisei Fire & Marine Ins. Co. v. Commissioner*, 104 TC 535 (1995) (US corporation that did reinsurance business for four unrelated Japanese insurance companies had independent status; the US company was legally and economically independent from the Japanese companies).
54. Norway, Art. 4A.

subsidiary's activities on behalf of the parent could cross the permanent establishment threshold. The permanent establishment of a partnership is attributed to the partners.[55]

A difficult issue in connection with permanent establishment definition is the treatment of "electronic commerce"—which, as discussed in section 14.4, has been reframed in recent years as taxation of the digital economy. In earlier iterations of these technology-driven debates about the scope of permanent establishments, a typical question considered whether a computer server located in a state constituted a permanent establishment and how to handle "e-commerce."[56] Now, taxation of the digital economy more generally has taken center stage in international discussions and debates over the taxation of business activity and income of foreign businesses.[57]

The OECD BEPS project included some recommendations to prevent inappropriate taxpayer avoidance of a permanent establishment under the treaties. For example, BEPS Action 7[58] introduces a new anti-fragmentation rule, in paragraph 4.1 to Article 5, that seeks to prevent a business from dividing up its business activities in a jurisdiction among related parties so that each one individually falls below the treaty threshold for triggering permanent establishment status. Although the US has not embraced most of these BEPS changes in its 2016 Model,[59] it did adopt the BEPS Action 7 recommendation designed to prevent businesses from avoiding permanent establishment status for building sites, and construction/installation projects. Typically, treaties consider such activities to meet the permanent establishment threshold only if they last more than twelve months. Taxpayers have relied on efforts to divide up work among different contracts individually lasting under twelve months to avoid this rule. BEPS Action 7 proposed recommendations and aggregation rule for Article 5 to curtail these strategies. The 2016 US Model does include this anti-abuse rule in Article 5.3.

55. *Donroy, Ltd. v. United States*, 301 F.2d 200 (9th Cir. 1962).

56. *See, e.g.*, Commentary on the Articles of the 2017 OECD Model Income and Capital Tax Convention Article 5, paras. 122-131; Interpretation and Application of Article 5 (Permanent Establishment) of the OECD Model Tax Convention, public discussion draft (2012), available at http://www.oecd.org/tax/taxtreaties/48836726.pdf; U.N. Economic and Social Council, Committee of Experts on International Cooperation in Tax Matters, *Definition of Permanent Establishment: Finalized Amendments to Current Commentary on Article 5—Permanent Establishment*, at 47 (Oct. 20-24, 2008) (E/C.18/2008/CRP.10); Commentary on the Articles of the 2008 OECD Model Income and Capital Tax Convention Article 5, paras. 42.1-42.10; US Treas. Dep't White paper on Tax Policy Implications of Global Electronic Commerce (November 1996); OECD, *Report of the Business Profits Technical Advisory Group on the Current Treaty Rules for Taxing E-Commerce* (2003).

57. *See* OECD/G20 Base Erosion and Profit Shifting Project, *Tax Challenges Arising from Digitalisation—Report on Pillar One Blueprint* (Oct. 14, 2020), http://www.oecd.org/tax/beps/tax-challenges-arising-from-digitalisation-report-on-pillar-one-blueprint-beba0634-en.htm.

58. *See* OECD/G20 Base Erosion and Profit Shifting Project, *Preventing the Artificial Avoidance of Permanent Establishment- Action 7- 2015 Final Report* (Oct. 5, 2015), https://www.oecd.org/tax/beps/preventing-the-artificial-avoidance-of-permanent-establishment-status-action-7-2015-final-report-9789264241220-en.htm.

59. For example, Treasury explicitly decided not to adopt BEPS permanent establishment recommendations regarding changes to the treatment of dependent and independent agents, as well as the exemption for preparatory and auxiliary activities. US Treasury, *Preamble to the 2016 U.S. Model Income Tax Convention* (Feb. 17, 2016) at 9, https://home.treasury.gov/system/files/131/Treaty-US-Model-Preamble-2016.pdf.

14.5.3 Business Profits

The permanent establishment exemption applies in general only to the business income of the foreign taxpayer. Older US treaties use the expression "industrial or commercial profits" but the US Model and more modern treaties refer to "business profits."[60] The terms are defined with various degrees of specificity in the treaties.

14.5.4 "Attributable To"

The business profits which may be taxed because of the presence of a permanent establishment are generally limited to those which are "attributable to" the permanent establishment. In reality, although jurisdictions and taxpayers regularly debate the appropriate definition and scope of permanent establishments in Article 5, the resolution of that question still leaves unresolved the critical question of precisely what income is attributed to the permanent establishment and thus subject to tax in the jurisdiction of the permanent establishment.

In general, US treaties by their terms treat the permanent establishment as if it were an independent entity engaged in arm's length dealings with third parties and the home office, rather than allocating the worldwide income of the enterprise on some formula basis.[61] Thus, in general, dealings between the permanent establishment and head office will be based on arm's length principles (*see* Chapter 12 section 12.3). However, the 2006 US Model treaty (as compared to its 1996 predecessor)[62] moved more in this direction consistent with the "authorized OECD approach"[63] (known as the AOA).[64] The US support for the AOA and stronger reliance on transfer pricing principals to determine the profits of the permanent establishment was reflected not only in the 2006 US Model Treaty but also in more recently negotiated US treaties.[65] For example, the 2006 Model noted that "the principles of the OECD Transfer Pricing

60. US Model, Art. 7.1.
61. US Model, Art. 7.2.
62. Under the 1996 US Model and earlier negotiated treaties the US took the position that in determining the deductions allowed to a permanent establishment, US allocation rules applied for treaty purposes despite the general acceptance of the "independence" of the permanent establishment. Thus, in practice, the US did not really apply a transfer pricing model in determining the business profits of a permanent establishment. *See, e.g.*, New York State Bar Association Tax Section, *Report on the Model Income Tax Convention Released by the Treasury on November 15, 2006*, at 31 (Apr. 11, 2007).
63. OECD, *2010 Report on the Attribution of Profits to Permanent Establishments* (July 22, 2010), available at http://www.oecd.org/ctp/transfer-pricing/45689524.pdf.
64. *See* 2006 US Technical Explanation, Art. 7, paras. 2 and 3.
65. For example, in 2012 the US and Canada announced a competent authority agreement "regarding application of principles set forth in the [OECD] Report on the Attribution of Profits to Permanent Establishments" to Article VII (Business Profits) in the US-Canada Treaty. The competent authority agreement provided that: "Article VII of [their] Convention is to be interpreted in a manner entirely consistent with the full AOA as set out in the Report. All other provisions of the Convention that require a determination of whether an asset or amount is effectively connected or attributable to a permanent establishment are also to be interpreted in a manner entirely consistent with the full AOA as set out in the Report." Announcement 2012-31, 2012-2 C.B. 315.

Guidelines will apply for purposes of determining the profits attributable to a permanent establishment, taking into account the different economic and legal circumstances of a single entity."[66] The 2016 Model makes several modifications to Article 7, although it appears to maintain the 2006 move towards the AOA.

The determination of interest expense allocable to a permanent establishment in the US has been a subject of some debate over the past fifteen years. Under domestic law, the deduction for interest expense is determined under Section 882 allocation principles and not on the basis of the interest expense actually booked and paid by the branch. The application of Section 882 was challenged by a UK taxpayer and held to be inconsistent with the then-in force UK treaty because the Section 882 Regulations did not treat the US branch of the UK bank as a separate entity.[67] The 2006 Technical Explanation to the 2006 US Model sought to respond to the issue of interest expense allocation and provide a treaty-based approach that departs from Section 882 and is more consistent with principles of Article 7.[68]

Additionally, the Treaty between the US and Poland (signed Feb. 13, 2013 but pending as of March 2021) incorporates the new OECD approach for attribution of profits to a permanent establishment. However, many current US treaties do not incorporate the new OECD AOA, and thus those treaties would require revision to adopt and incorporate the AOA. *See* Official US Treasury Statement (released June 7, 2007); *see also* 2006 Protocol to the German Treaty (modifying the existing treaty to reflect the AOA for attributing profits to permanent establishments).

66. 2006 US Model Treaty, Art. 7, footnote (1).
67. Treas. Reg. Sec. 1.882-5(a)(3). The court in *National Westminster Bank v. US*, 44 Fed. Cl. 129 (Ct. Fed. Cl. 1999), held that the Regulation was inconsistent with Art. 7(2) of the then applicable UK treaty because the Regulation did not treat the US branch of a UK bank as a separate entity as the court believed was required by the treaty. The exchange of diplomatic notes that accompanied the current (2001) UK treaty stated that the OECD Transfer Pricing Guidelines would be applied by analogy in determining profits of a branch under the separate entity approach, including the formulary profits methods (*see* Chapter 12 sections 12.4.1.4 and 12.4.1.5). A subsequent decision by the same court rejected the Internal Revenue Service methodology for computing the US branch profits because it also was inconsistent with Art. 7 of the applicable UK treaty. *National Westminster Bank v. US*, 58 Fed. Cl. 491 (Ct. Fed. Cl. 2003).
68. *See* 2006 Technical Explanation, Art. 7, para. 3: "The method prescribed by U.S. domestic law for making this attribution is found in Treas. Reg. Section 1.882-5. Both Treas. Reg. Section 1.882-5 and the method prescribed in the notes start from the premise that all of the capital of the enterprise supports all of the assets and risks of the enterprise, and therefore the entire capital of the enterprise must be allocated to its various businesses and offices. However, section 1.882-5 does not take into account the fact that some assets create more risk for the enterprise than do other assets. An independent enterprise would need less capital to support a perfectly-hedged U.S. Treasury security than it would need to support an equity security or other asset with significant market and/or credit risk. Accordingly, in some cases section 1.882-5 would require a taxpayer to allocate more capital to the United States, and therefore would reduce the taxpayer's interest deduction more, than is appropriate. To address these cases, the notes allow a taxpayer to apply a more flexible approach that takes into account the relative risk of its assets in the various jurisdictions in which it does business. In particular, in the case of financial institutions other than insurance companies, the amount of capital attributable to a permanent establishment is determined by allocating the institution's total equity between its various offices on the basis of the proportion of the financial institution's risk-weighted assets attributable to each of them. This recognizes the fact that financial institutions are in many cases required to risk-weight their assets for regulatory purposes and, in other cases, will do so for business reasons even if not required to do so by regulators."

14.6 TREATMENT OF INVESTMENT INCOME

14.6.1 In General

As discussed in Chapter 5, investment-type income of a foreign taxpayer from US sources is generally taxed at a flat 30% rate on the gross amount of the income. If the income is effectively connected with a US trade or business, it is treated as business income and subject to tax on net basis at the normally applicable rates.

US treaties generally modify the rules for investment-type income that is not attributable to a permanent establishment in the US by providing for a reciprocal reduction of rates (often to zero) for investment-type income. Typically, the rates on dividends are reduced to 15%, with a 5% rate applicable in the case of dividends paid by a subsidiary to a parent company.[69] Interest income is generally exempt (in the US Model) or subject to a 15% rate. Royalties of various types also usually are exempt.

Where investment-type income is attributable to a permanent establishment, it is taxed typically under the business profits article.[70]

The 2016 US Model introduces anti-inversion provisions in the articles that otherwise grant reduced source taxation for dividends, interest, and royalties.[71] When applicable, these rules apply for ten years from the inversion.

14.6.2 Classification Issues

The basic "schedular" approach of the treaties in classifying income in categories in order to apply the treaty rules raises some special issues. Thus, for example, while the line between business profits (to which the permanent establishment rule applies) and investment income (taxable at reduced rates) is generally clear, there are some difficult borderline situations. Consider, for example, the case of a commercial bank. Its income consists principally of interest that normally is treated as investment income. However, interest in the hands of a bank clearly represents business income. A similar problem exists with respect to leasing and rental activities. The banking situation is solved in the US Model by providing a zero rate on interest. Thus, if a foreign bank receives interest which is not connected with a US permanent establishment, there is no US tax as would be the case for business profits of a commercial business. If the interest is connected to a US permanent establishment, it would be taxed on a net basis.

An important current classification issue involves the treatment of computer software. Depending on the circumstances, a transfer of software can involve a sale of

69. The US Model requires a 10% level of shareholding for the reduced 5% rate to apply. US Model, Art. 10.2(a). In the U.K. treaty, however, the withholding rate on dividends was reduced to zero in the case of dividends paid by an 80% controlled subsidiary. UK Treaty, Art. 10.3. An anti-abuse rule was included to prevent third country taxpayer efforts to take advantage of the new provision. Similar reductions in the dividend withholding rate to zero were included in treaties with Australia, Belgium, Denmark, Finland, France, Germany, Japan, Mexico, Netherlands, New Zealand, Spain, and Sweden.
70. *See* US Model, Art. 10.8.
71. US Model, Arts. 10(5), 11(2)(d), and 12(2)(b).

goods (despite the formal structure of the transfer as a license), a royalty, or the provision of services. Regulations offer guidance on the treatment of some commonly recurring fact patterns.[72]

A similar classification issue can arise where the two treaty jurisdictions treat the same payment differently. In *Boulez v. Commissioner*, 83 TC 584 (1984), the taxpayer received a payment which the US treated as referable to personal services performed in the US which, under the terms of the US-Germany treaty, the US as the source country had the right to tax. Germany classified the payment as a royalty that was exempt from source country taxation but taxable in Germany as the country of residence. The competent authorities of the two countries were unable to agree on the classification issue and the item of income was subject to tax in both jurisdictions with no double tax relief.

14.7 REAL PROPERTY

Income from real property may be taxed without treaty limitation by the source state. An election to have such income taxed on a net basis is provided.[73] Taxation extends to gain on the disposition of directly held real estate and, in addition, all modern treaties allow the source country to tax gain on the disposition of the stock of a corporation whose assets consist principally of real property located in the source country.[74]

14.8 GAINS FROM THE DISPOSITION OF PROPERTY

US treaties generally exempt from source taxation gains on the disposition of assets. However, gains from the disposition of property that are attributable to a permanent establishment or fixed base may be taxed by the source country.[75]

14.9 TREATMENT OF PERSONAL SERVICES INCOME

14.9.1 Employees

Under the Code, a nonresident alien employee of a foreign employer not engaged in a US trade or business is not subject to US tax on compensation for labor or personal services performed in the US if the nonresident is not present within the US for more than ninety days in the taxable year, the compensation does not exceed USD 3,000 and the service is for a foreign employer that does not have a trade or business or for a foreign business of a US person. This exemption is liberalized in a number of US

72. Treas. Reg. Sec. 1.861-18.
73. US Model, Art. 6(5). The treaty net election may be made annually, which is more favorable than the one-time election allowed under the Code, discussed at Chapter 5 section 5.2.2.
74. US Model, Arts. 6 and 13.
75. US Model, Art. 13.

treaties. For example, in the US Model the time limit is extended to 183 days, and there is no dollar limitation on the compensation that can be received without tax. Similar to the Code rule, the compensation must be paid by a foreign employer and not "borne by" the foreign employer's permanent establishment within the US. Thus, the exempted income will not have figured as a deduction in the accounts of the permanent establishment.[76]

Most treaties also contain special rules dealing with the taxation of students, professors, government service, and others in special employment categories.[77]

14.9.2 Independent Personal Services

If a nonresident alien individual performs independent personal services in the US (e.g., as a lawyer), under normally applicable Code principles she would be engaged in a US trade or business and would be subject to tax at normal rates. However, a number of treaties exempt such income from US taxation under varying conditions. The 1996 US Model had a provision explicitly addressing the treatment of independent services. The 2006 US Model instead expanded the concept of "business"[78] to cover such services and thus tax the resulting income pursuant to Article 7.[79] The 2016 US Model follows this inclusion of independent services under business income. Under Article 7, independent services income earned by a nonresident alien will be subject to tax if the income is attributable to a permanent establishment.[80] Services of athletes and entertainers, however, continue to be taxed even if not connected with a permanent establishment under Article 16 if the amount received for performing activities in the source state exceeds USD 30,000.[81] A special rule prevents entertainers and athletes from avoiding Article 16 by utilizing an interposed company (a "rent-a-star" company), to argue that Article 7 governs and, therefore, that there is no source country tax because there is no permanent establishment.[82] Pursuant to Article 16, the corporate

---

76. US Model, Art. 14.
77. US Model, Arts. 15 (Directors' Fees), 16 (Entertainers and Sportsmen), 19 (Government Service) and 20 (Students and Trainees).
78. US Model, Art. 3.1(e) (defining the term "business" to include "performance of professional services and of other activities of an independent character").
79. The change in 2006 to the treatment of independent services in the US model tracked the OECD Model which already had eliminated the special article on independent services and shifted to treating such activities under the permanent establishment and business profits articles.
80. US Model, Art. 7. Thus, by moving independent services to Art. 7 the source-based taxation of this income is dependent on the finding of a permanent establishment. In the past, under old Art. 14 (1996 Model), the source-based taxation of these services depended on the finding of a fixed place of business. As had been previously observed, there is an obvious parallel between "fixed base" and the "permanent establishment" concept in connection with business profits. The two concepts have been labeled "similar, but not identical." 1996 US Model Technical Explanation, Art. 14, para. 1. Revenue Ruling 2004-3, 2004-1 C.B. 486, held that a nonresident partner in a German service partnership that had a fixed base in the US was subject to US tax on the partner's share of partnership income under Art. 14 of the German treaty. The ruling applies to all treaties with similar independent personal services articles.
81. US Model, Art. 16.
82. US Model, Art. 16.2. The personal services income of the entertainer or athlete channeled through the corporation is *not* subject to Art. 16 taxation if the "contract pursuant to which the

income of the "rent-a-star" company can be taxed by the source country despite the lack of a permanent establishment.

14.10 FOREIGN TAX CREDIT ASPECTS

In accordance with the overall purpose of tax treaties to reduce international double taxation, the US in its treaties commits itself, with varying degrees of specificity, to grant its citizens and residents a foreign tax credit for the foreign income taxes paid to treaty countries. Correspondingly, the US insists that its treaty partners likewise provide some mechanism to their nationals for the relief of double taxation, by either granting a credit for US taxes or exempting income from US sources.

In addition, some US treaties clarify the operation of the foreign tax credit with respect to the taxes of the treaty partner. For example, Article 10 of the French treaty (in effect prior to the French elimination of the avoir fiscal in 2004 and 2005 and the new protocol to the US-French treaty in 2009) had set out specific rules for dealing with the France's "integrated" corporation tax and its treatment for foreign tax credit purposes.[83] Some treaties expressly give a credit for a foreign tax that arguably would not be creditable under the Code definition of an income tax.[84]

Sometimes the treaties modify source rules that would otherwise prevent the crediting of foreign taxes on items of income because, under normal US concepts, the income would be deemed to be from US sources.[85] Some treaties, including the US Model, contain a general rule that any income that may be taxed by the source country under the treaty will be deemed to have its source in that country for purposes of the

personal activities are performed allows that other person [e.g. the corporation] to designate the individual who is to perform the personal activities." US Model, Art. 16.2. The purpose of this additional rule is to limit the source country taxation only to those cases in which the performer is being engaged *specifically* to perform and the corporation is used to avoid taxation. It does not seek to tax those cases in which the corporation has been engaged to perform the services (as in the case of a symphony or band engaged to perform a concert).

83. For some interpretative difficulties with such an article, *see Xerox Corp. v. US*, 41 F.3d 647 (Fed. Cir. 1994) (addressing the treatment of the UK's imputation credit under Art. 10, Dividends).
84. *See, e.g.*, United Kingdom, Art. 2.3(b)(iv) (petroleum revenue tax (PRT)). In *Exxon v. Commissioner*, 113 T.C. 338 (1999), the court held that the PRT, which was creditable under the treaty, was also a creditable tax under US domestic law (*see* Chapter 9 section 9.4.1.2). Effective 2008, Mexico introduced a new tax, the "impuesto emprasarial a tasa unica" (IETU), whose creditability under US domestic foreign tax credit rules was in doubt. The IETU's limited tax base, including the exclusion of certain kinds of deductions, led many tax observers to wonder whether the tax failed to qualify as an income tax as required for creditability under US domestic law. In response to this uncertainty, the IRS issued Notice 2008-3, 2008-1 C.B. 253 which stated that the IRS would study the IETU to determine whether it is creditable, and in the interim would treat the IETU as "an income tax that is eligible for a credit under Article 24 of the Treaty." Effective 2014, Mexico repealed the IETU without the IRS ever announcing a conclusion regarding its study of the status of the IETU.
85. *See, e.g.*, Japan, Art. 23.2 (flush language); Rev. Rul. 79-28, 1979-1 C.B. 457 (for purposes of the direct foreign tax credit, income of a US citizen residing in Japan from services performed within the US as a flight attendant on international flights of a Japanese airline was considered foreign source income under the source rules of the treaty; the source rules of the Treaty take precedence over the usual source rules of the Internal Revenue Code).

treaty credit article.[86] US treaties generally subject the obligation of the United States to provide a credit to "the limitations of the law of the United States (as it may be amended from time to time without changing the general principle hereof)."[87] Under this provision, the Code requires that the income item be in a separate category for purposes of the foreign tax credit limitation.[88]

Most modern treaty foreign tax credit articles take into account the fact that the US citizens who are resident in a treaty country (under the residence tiebreaker rule discussed in section 14.4.1.1) are potentially subject to worldwide taxation in both countries. In effect, the US limits its primary tax claim to the amount it could have collected as a source jurisdiction if the recipient had not been a US citizen and the US allows the US citizen a foreign tax credit for any foreign tax imposed by the resident country (up to the amount of the US tax) even if the income arises in the US. The treaty partner agrees to credit the "notional" US source tax. In effect, source jurisdiction is recognized as primary, residence-based personal jurisdiction as secondary, and citizenship-based personal jurisdiction as tertiary.[89]

14.11 NONDISCRIMINATION

US treaties typically contain a "nondiscrimination" article, albeit of varying scope. For example, Article 24.1 of the US Model provides:

> Nationals of a Contracting State shall not be subjected in the other Contracting State to any taxation or any requirement connected therewith that is more burdensome than the taxation and connected requirements to which nationals of that other Contracting State in the same circumstances, in particular with respect to residence, are or may be subjected.

The qualifying language with respect to "residence" in effect gives the US wide latitude in the taxation of nonresident aliens since they are, by definition, not subject to worldwide tax and thus are not in "similar circumstances" to US citizens and residents who are so taxed.

In addition, the US permanent establishment of an enterprise of the treaty partner may not be subjected to "less favorable" taxation than a US enterprise engaged in the same activity. Finally, US enterprises that are owned by residents of the treaty partner

86. *See, e.g.*, US Model, Art. 23.3. The 1996 US Model did not include a general re-sourcing provision; it was introduced in the 2006 US Model. Many US treaties do not currently contain a re-sourcing provision, such as the US-Australia Treaty. *But see* Belgium, Art. 22(3) (providing a re-sourcing rule).
87. US Model, Art. 23(2).
88. Sec. 904(d)(6).
89. *See* US Model, Art. 23.4. For example, suppose a US citizen resident in a treaty country receives USD 100 of dividend income from US sources. If the US tax rate is 35% and the foreign rate 25%, the US would be entitled to a "notional" 15% withholding tax under the treaty, thus collecting the first USD 15 of tax. The treaty partner would allow a credit for the notional USD 15 of tax against its USD 25 of tax otherwise due. The US would then credit the USD 10 of additional foreign tax due (despite the fact that it is imposed on US source income) and collect a residual tax of USD 10, reflecting the fact that the US rate exceeds the foreign rate. 2006 US Technical Explanation, Art. 23, para. 4.

may not be subject to "more burdensome" taxation than that applicable to similar US-owned enterprises.[90] The nondiscrimination clause applies to state and municipal taxes as well as to Federal taxes.[91]

Some interpretative questions have arisen under the nondiscrimination article. Under the generally applicable Code rules, a US subsidiary that is liquidated into its parent corporation is not required to recognize gain on the distribution of appreciated assets in the liquidation.[92] However, a special rule requires the recognition of gain where the liquidating distribution is made to a foreign parent corporation.[93] The Internal Revenue Service initially took the position that the special rule requiring gain recognition where a foreign parent corporation was involved violated the treaty nondiscrimination provisions which prohibit "more burdensome" treatment of foreign-owned US corporations. Subsequently, however, the Service reversed itself and held that no treaty violation was involved based on the argument that a foreign-owned US subsidiary was not "similar" to a US-owned US subsidiary. The liquidating distribution to a foreign parent could remove the appreciated assets from the reach of the US taxing jurisdiction, while in the US-owned situation the assets in the hands of the US parent would remain potentially subject to US tax. This difference in circumstances justified differing treatment for the two situations without any prohibited discrimination.[94]

A nondiscrimination issue is also involved in the application of the branch profits tax (*see* Chapter 5 section 5.6.5.3), which imposes a second "layer" of tax on the profits of the US branch of a foreign corporation. This additional tax can be viewed as "more burdensome" taxation imposed on the permanent establishment of a treaty corporation since a US corporation engaged in similar activity would not be subject to the tax.[95] Section 884(e)(1)(A) specifically recognized that the tax might conflict with treaty obligations and Regulations provided a list of the treaties that prohibit the imposition of the tax.[96] However, treaty protection is only available to foreign corporations that are not treaty shopping (*see* section 14.4.3.1).

The US has a number of Treaties of Friendship, Commerce and Navigation ("FCN" treaties) containing nondiscrimination clauses which in the past have had application in the tax area.[97] The 1996 US Model Article 1.3 went to great length to

---

90. US Model, Art. 24.5.
91. US Model, Art. 24.7.
92. Sec. 337.
93. Sec. 367(e)(2).
94. Notice 87-5, 1987-1 C.B. 416, revoked in part by Notice 87-66, 1987-2 C.B. 376. This view is confirmed by the 2006 US Technical Explanation, Art. 24, para. 5.
95. The branch profits tax replaced the "second level" withholding tax on dividends distributed by a foreign corporation with US source income to its foreign shareholders. Since that tax was technically imposed on the shareholders, no treaty nondiscrimination issues were involved. Though the branch profits tax is in effect a substitute for the second level dividend tax, it is imposed on the foreign corporation itself and hence arguably involves a nondiscrimination question.
96. Treas. Reg. Sec. 1.884-1(g)(3).
97. *See* Notice 88-1, 1988-1 C.B. 471, dealing with the nondiscrimination clause of the US-Netherlands FCN treaty as it applies to foreign corporations making the election to be treated as US corporations for purposes of Section 897.

make it clear that the Model Treaty was the exclusive source of relief for discrimination complaints in the matters that it covered, except for the General Agreement on Tariffs and Trade (GATT).[98] Both the 2006 and 2016 US Models, in contrast to the 1996 Model, generally do not aim to override nondiscrimination provisions in other agreements." They only override Article XVII (National Treatment) of the General Agreement on Trade in Services ("GATS").[99]

14.12 ADMINISTRATIVE PROVISIONS

14.12.1 Competent Authority Provisions

US treaties contain a so-called competent authority provision which provides a mechanism whereby the taxpayer can insure that its rights under the treaty are respected by the countries involved. In order to invoke the competent authority provision, the taxpayer must in general establish that an action of one or both of the tax authorities of the Contracting States has resulted or will result in taxation contrary to the provisions of the treaty. In such a case, if the state agrees that the claim is worthy of consideration, the competent authority of the state attempts to deal with the problem unilaterally and if that is not possible, endeavors to reach some agreement with the other country in order to avoid double taxation. However, there is no requirement that the two states reach an agreement, only that they "endeavor to resolve" the issue. In case of disagreement, the taxpayer is faced with the possibility of unrelieved double taxation.

The most important function of the competent authority provision is to deal with the allocation of income between related taxpayers. The Internal Revenue Service has issued detailed guidelines as to how US taxpayers can invoke the competent authority procedure in such cases, including the question of the relation between the competent authority and any ongoing audit or litigation proceedings.[100]

98. *See* 1996 US Model Technical Explanation, Art. 1, paras. 14-16. This approach from the 1996 Model would seem to displace FCN treaties as well as trade agreements, at which the provision is presumably aimed, from providing a basis for nondiscrimination claims under subsequent treaties based on the US Model.

99. 2016 US Model, Art. 1(3)(a); 2006 US Model, Art. 1(3)(a). Joint Committee on Taxation, "Comparison of the United States Model Income Tax Convention of September 20, 1996 with the United States Model Income Tax Convention of November 15, 2006," JCX-27-07 (May 8, 2007) at 2. The reference to GATT in the 1996 US Model was eliminated in the 2006 and 2016 US Models.

100. 2015-2 C.B. 236. For a situation in which the taxpayer tried unsuccessfully to force a competent authority procedure prior to litigation of issues involved in the Tax Court, *see Yamaha Motor Corp v. United States*, 779 F. Supp. 610 (D.D.C. 1991).

14.12.2 Mandatory Arbitration

The 2016 US Model includes a provision implementing mandatory arbitration, as does the OECD Model Treaty.[101] In the US Model, the arbitration decision process is structured according to what is colloquially referred to as "baseball arbitration": the arbitration panel must select one of the two States' positions as its decision on the issue.[102] The US has a number of treaties that already include a mandatory arbitration clause, including its treaties with Belgium, Germany, Canada, and France.[103] There are some variations among the provisions. For example, the 2009 Protocol to the US-France treaty allows the taxpayer to submit a position paper to the arbitration panel.[104] Generally, though, the US mandatory treaty provisions follow the "baseball arbitration" approach.[105]

14.12.3 Exchange of Information

US treaties have included exchange of information provisions for decades, and the 2016 (and 2006) US Model provision on this subject is essentially unchanged from the 1996 US Model.[106] However, following the banking scandals that began to unfold in 2008,[107] the US has devoted increased attention to its exchange of information treaty provisions. In cases where the US does not have a bilateral income tax treaty with another country, it has negotiated Tax Information Exchange Agreements (as have many other jurisdictions).[108] For other countries with which the US has an existing bilateral tax treaty but a less than effective exchange of information provision, the US has begun to seek revision of the treaty provision.[109]

Several new directions in exchange of information practices have emerged. The first was triggered primarily by the US introduction of a domestic law regime, the Foreign Account Tax Compliance Act ("FATCA").[110] In brief, the FATCA regime (which took effect in 2014) imposes certain tax burdens on foreign financial institutions that fail to provide designated information on US taxpayers with accounts at those

101. US Model, Art. 25.6; 2017 OECD Model Treaty, Art. 25.5. The UN Model Treaty offers two versions of the Mutual Agreement Procedure Article, one with mandatory arbitration and on without. 2017 UN Model Treaty, Art. 25B.
102. US Model, Art. 25.9(j).
103. Belgium, Art. 24.7; Germany, Art. 25.5; Canada, Art. XXVI (6); France, Art. 26.5.
104. 2009 Protocol to the US-France Treaty, Memorandum of Understanding, clause (h).
105. *See, e.g.*, Germany, 2006 Protocol, Art. XVI, para. 22(h).
106. 2016 US Model, Art. 26; Joint Committee on Taxation, *Comparison of the United States Model Income Tax Convention of September 20, 1996 with the United States Model Income Tax Convention of November 15, 2006*, JCX-27-07 (May 8, 2007) at 20.
107. *See, e.g.*, US Dept. of Justice Press Release Announcing Federal Judge Approves IRS Summons for UBS Swiss Bank Account Records, available at http://www.justice.gov/opa/pr/2008/July/08-tax-584.html; Lynnely Browning, *UBS Executive Indicted in U.S. Inquiry*, N.Y. Times, Nov. 13, 2008, at Sec. B9.
108. *See, e.g.*, 2009 US-Monaco TIEA; 2010 US-Panama TIEA (effective 2011); 2008 US-Liechtenstein TIEA (effective 2009).
109. *See, e.g.*, Switzerland 2009 Protocol (entered into force 2019).
110. *See* Secs. 1471-1474.

financial institutions. Given difficulties that foreign financial institutions could face in complying with the FATCA regime's information requirements, a number of jurisdictions entered into agreements with the US to provide a special (and presumably more feasible) way for their own resident financial institution to comply with the US domestic regime. These agreements are referred to as Intergovernmental Agreements (IGAs). Following the introduction of this US-based regime, EU states began jointly developing their own agreement to share financial account information in 2013, prompted by the experience with the US FATCA legislation and the resulting IGAs.[111]

The second major trend emerged from the OECD BEPS Action 13, which introduced Country-by-Country (CbC) reporting requirements for multinational corporations. The US has issued regulations ensuring that US multinationals report in compliance with the CbC rules (which require parents of multinational corporations to file a report with their home jurisdiction that can then be exchanged by that home jurisdiction with other countries in which the multinational operates).[112] Although most countries are exchanging CbC reports pursuant to the Multilateral Competent Authority Agreement (which enables exchanges under the Multilateral Convention for Mutual Administrative Assistance on Tax Matters), the US has opted to exchange CbC reports pursuant to its bilateral tax treaties and TIEAs.[113]

All tax professionals and states should be aware of the increasing array of international agreements and domestic legislation that may require third parties to provide information, especially financial information on an automatic basis.[114]

111. *See* Letter from the UK, France, Germany, Italy and Spain to EU Commissioner Algirdas Šemeta, (Apr. 9, 2013) available at https://www.gov.uk/government/uploads/system/uploads/attachment_data/file/208068/g5_letter_to_european_commission_090413.pdf.

112. Treas. Reg. Sec. 1.6038-4.

113. *See, e.g.*, Arrangement Between the Competent Authority of the United States of America and the Competent Authority of the Republic of Singapore on the Exchange of Country-by-Country Reports (Oct. 6, 2020), based on the 2018 US-Singapore TIEA.

114. In addition to its many bilateral treaties with exchange of information, its TIEAs, and its participation in the new CbC regime, the US also ratified the OECD's Convention on Assistance in Tax Matters (which includes exchange of information).

CHAPTER 15

Wealth Transfer Taxation

15.1 THE US WEALTH TRANSFER TAX SYSTEM: GENERAL DESCRIPTION

15.1.1 Background

The US imposes a gift tax[1] on transfers during lifetime and an estate tax[2] on transfers at death. A unified rate structure applies the same rates to gifts and transfers at death.

Although the estate and gift taxes have a unified progressive tax rate structure, a very generous exemption (USD 11.7 million in 2021)[3] results in all taxable gifts and estates being taxed at the maximum marginal rate of 40%. The USD 11.7 million exemption is implemented in the form of a tax credit, called the "unified credit."[4]

The US also has a third wealth transfer tax, the generation-skipping tax. Its purpose is to ensure that property transferred to someone more than one generation below the transferor will be subject to a transfer tax that approximates the taxes that would have been paid had the property not skipped over the generation immediately below the transferor.[5]

---

1. Sec. 2501.
2. Sec. 2001.
3. Sec. 2010. The 2017 Tax Act nominally increased the exemption amount from its prior level of USD 5 million to USD 10 million. The 2017 Tax Act required, however, that the USD 10 million exemption amount be adjusted for inflation occurring after 2010. The result of the inflation adjustments dating back to 2010 was that the exemption amount in 2018, the first year in which the increased exemption became effective, was USD 11.18 million. As stated in the text, the exemption amount for 2021 is USD 11.7 million.
4. Secs. 2505(c) and 2010(c).
5. Since the generation-skipping transfer tax seeks only to replicate the tax that would have been paid had the property not skipped over the generation immediately below the transferor, it is possible to skip over several generations and pay only one generation-skipping tax. For example, if transferor gives property to her great grandchild, only a single generation-skipping tax will be due event though the transfer skipped over two generations (her child and her grandchild).

The future of wealth transfer taxation in the US has been a hotly debated topic. Proponents of a wealth transfer tax have been concerned about the impact of wealth accumulation on democracy and economic growth.[6] Opponents have been concerned about the impact of the wealth transfer tax on capital formation.[7] After a period of significant uncertainty, in which the estate tax was repealed and then retroactively revived, the wealth transfer taxes seem to be on a more stable foundation. The very high exemption of USD 11.7 million, however, results in very few taxpayers currently being subject to the taxes.

15.1.2 The Estate Tax on US Citizens and Residents

Section 2001 imposes an estate tax on the "taxable estate" of every citizen or resident of the US.[8] The taxable estate is equal to the "gross estate" less certain allowable deductions. The gross estate includes the value of all property interests owned by the decedent at the date of death. Most typical of these are such items as bank accounts, real estate, and securities. The gross estate is not limited, however, to the value of assets that are physically in the decedent's actual or constructive possession. It includes the value of any interest in property that the decedent had at the time of death, such as a general power of appointment. In addition, there also is included in the gross estate the value of transfers made by the decedent during his lifetime that, under the Code, are treated as substitutes for testamentary dispositions (e.g., a transfer to a revocable trust or a transfer with a retained income interest). The gross estate, therefore, may exceed greatly the actual wealth that the decedent had in physical possession immediately before death.[9]

The permissible deductions from the gross estate include funeral and administration expenses, claims against the estate, and uncompensated casualty losses arising during the settlement of the estate.[10] A few special deductions from the gross estate are provided for nontax policy reasons. Among these are deductions for transfers to or for charitable organizations.[11]

Generally, the transfer of property by a decedent to the surviving spouse is not taxed at the time of death by virtue of a "marital deduction." Instead, estate taxation is deferred until the death of the surviving spouse, at which time the then fair market value of all the property of the marital unit is subject to estate tax.[12] In effect, spouses are generally treated as a single tax unit for estate tax purposes.

The marital deduction is not available to a decedent's estate if the surviving spouse is not a US citizen.[13] This rule applies even if the surviving spouse is a US

6. *See, e.g.*, James R. Repetti, *Democracy, Taxes and Wealth*, 761 NYU L. Rev. 825 (2001).
7. *See* David Joufaian, The Federal Estate Tax: History, Law and Economics 101-121 (2019) (reviewing studies of whether the estate tax affects savings).
8. Sec. 2001(c)(2)(c). The maximum rate is 40%.
9. Items included in the gross estate are defined in Sections 2033-2044.
10. Secs. 2053-2054.
11. Sec. 2055.
12. Secs. 2056 and 2044.
13. Sec. 2056(d).

resident. However, the surviving spouse's estate is allowed a tax credit for the tax previously paid by the estate of her deceased spouse on property that passed to her.[14] The credit is not refundable and, thus, can do no more than reduce her estate tax liabilities to zero.

The harshness of the deduction denial is mitigated somewhat if the property passing to the non-US citizen surviving spouse is placed in a "qualified domestic trust" (often called a "QDOT").[15] The deceased spouse's estate is permitted to claim a full marital deduction for property transferred to the QDOT. Any distribution of principal from the QDOT during the life of the surviving spouse, however, triggers an estate tax (unless the distribution is made on account of hardship of the surviving spouse), and the balance in the QDOT is subject to estate tax upon the death of the surviving spouse.[16] The tax is imposed on the trustee, but is "treated as" a tax paid with respect to the estate of the first deceased spouse. The amount of the tax is the amount that the first deceased spouse would have paid had the property been subject to tax.[17] The estate of the surviving spouse is entitled to a credit for the tax paid by the QDOT.[18]

After the taxable estate has been thus determined, a tentative estate tax is computed in a two-step process. First, the wealth transfer tax rates existing at the time of the decedent's death are applied to the sum of the taxable estate plus the "adjusted taxable gifts" (i.e., taxable gifts made by the decedent after December 31, 1976 less any gifts that are included in the estate of the decedent). Second, this "tentative" tax is then reduced by a hypothetical tax calculated by applying the wealth transfer tax rates existing at the time of death to taxable gifts that decedent made after 1976.[19] Ultimately, the decedent's taxable gifts are not subject to actual taxation in the estate tax calculation. Rather the purpose of the two-step process is to determine a tax base that includes both the taxable gifts and the estate, and then in effect to "stack" the estate on top. Prior to the very generous current USD 11.7 million exemption (*see* section 15.1.1), this would ensure that the estate would be taxed at the higher rates in the progressive tax rate structure. As discussed above in section 15.1.1, however, the generous exemption means that an estate that exceeds the exemption will always be taxed at the maximum progressive rate of 40%.

---

14. Secs. 2056(d)(3) and 2056A(b)(7); Treas. Reg. Sec. 20-2056A-7.
15. Secs. 2056(d)(2) and 2056A(a). A "QDOT" is a trust: (1) that has at least one trustee who is either a US citizen or domestic corporation and who is personally liable for any tax imposed), (2) that complies with such regulations as may be promulgated, and (3) for which the executor of the estate of the decedent spouse irrevocably elects to be treated as a QDOT. Sec. 2056A(a). The regulations that apply to QDOTs are in Treas. Reg. Sections 20.2056A-O to 20.2056A-13.
16. Sec. 2056A(b).
17. Sec. 2056A(b)(2).
18. The purpose of the provision is to prevent a US decedent from transferring property to the surviving spouse free of US tax and then have the surviving spouse expatriate and remove the property from US taxing jurisdiction so that the property can be transferred free of US tax at his or her death. The QDOT approach adopted in Section 2056A, however, produces different, and not readily defensible, patterns among spouses whose nationality, residence, and reasons for transferring property from the US vary. The US may modify the QDOT rules by treaty. *See, e.g.*, Art. XXIXB of the US-Canada Income Tax Treaty. Even though Section 2107 discussed at section 15.6, deals directly with the expatriation situation, Section 2056(d) was retained when Congress expanded the reach of Section 2107.
19. Sec. 2001(b).

The final estate tax payable is then determined by subtracting from the tentative estate tax the credits against tax. These credits include: (1) the unified credit against the estate tax, which results in an exemption from tax of USD 11.7 million in 2021; (2) a credit for certain state death taxes with respect to decedents who died prior to 2005; (3) a credit for foreign death taxes; (4) a credit for certain transfer taxes paid on prior transfers of property; and (5) a credit for gift taxes paid with respect to property transferred prior to 1977 and included in the gross estate.[20] The subtraction of these tax credits from the tentative estate tax constitutes the final step in the determination of the estate tax payable.

15.1.3 The Gift Tax on US Citizens and Residents

The tax on any gift made by a donor is determined by adding the amount of the taxable gift to prior taxable gifts and imposing the same progressive tax rates as those applicable to transfers at death under the estate tax. As discussed above in section 15.1.1, however, the large exemption (USD 11.7 million in 2021) has the effect of applying a flat 40% tax rate to taxable gifts that exceed the exemption.

The tax base for the gift tax is "taxable gifts." This term means the total gifts made during the calendar year minus allowable exclusions and deductions. The allocable exclusions and deductions include: (1) a USD 10,000 per donee annual exclusion adjusted for inflation after 1998 (USD 15,000 in 2021);[21] (2) a deduction for charitable contributions;[22] (3) an unlimited marital deduction for gifts to spouses who are US citizens.

The gift tax is computed by applying the progressive tax rates to the taxable gifts. The unified credit then is applied to the gift tax due. To the extent the unified transfer tax credit is utilized by a donor during lifetime, it is reduced for purposes of computing the estate tax and subsequent gift taxes.[23]

For example, suppose that a taxpayer, who has made no prior taxable gifts, makes USD 11.7 million of taxable gifts in 2021. The unified credit will exempt her gifts from the gift tax. However, she will have used her entire unified credit. If she dies at the end of 2021 with assets included in her taxable estate, those assets will be fully taxed at a 40% rate because she used her entire unified credit to shelter her gifts.

20. Secs. 2010, 2012, 2013, 2014, 2015, 2016, and former Sec. 2011. The estates of decedents dying after 2004 are permitted a deduction for state estate taxes instead of a credit. Section 2058(a).
21. Sec. 2503(b). Section 2513 allows spouses to treat a gift made by one of them as made by both in order that they may apply both of their USD 10,000 (USD 15,000 adjusted for inflation) annual exclusions to the gift.
22. Sec. 2522.
23. Sec. 2505(a). *See* Paul R. McDaniel, James R. Repetti and Paul L. Caron, Federal Wealth Transfer Taxation 76 (2015) (describing method in which the unified credit is adjusted for prior gifts).

15.1.4 The Generation-Skipping Tax

The generation-skipping tax tries to ensure that property transferred to someone more than one generation below the transferor will be subject to a transfer tax that approximates the taxes that would have been paid had the property not skipped over the generation immediately below the transferor.[24] For example, suppose that A, has a child, B, and a grandchild, C. If A makes a gift to her grandchild C, two things will happen. First, for gift tax purposes, A will have made a taxable gift to C. Second, the generation-skipping tax will also apply to the A's transfer to C.

The generation-skipping tax rate is a flat rate equal to the highest marginal unified tax rate of 40%. The amount of tax approximates the amount which would have been payable had A transferred the property to B, who then transferred it to C.

In very general terms, the generation-skipping tax is imposed on any "generation-skipping transfer." A generation-skipping transfer is, in general, the transfer of property or a present interest in property to a "skip person." A skip person is an individual who is in a generation that is two or more generations below that of the transferor.[25] Technically, a generation-skipping transfer occurs in three forms: a "taxable distribution," a "taxable termination," or a "direct skip." A *taxable distribution* occurs when property is distributed from a trust to a skip person.[26] A *taxable termination* occurs at the time a beneficiary's interest in a trust terminates and all the remaining interests are held by skip persons.[27] A *direct skip* is a transfer directly to a skip person or to a trust in which all the beneficiaries are skip persons.[28] The transfer, above, from A to C is a direct skip because A transferred the property directly to C, a skip person.

The following examples illustrate the various types of generation-skipping transfers:

(1) *Example 1: Taxable Distributions*: A transfers property in trust to B (his child) for life, with the power in the trustee to make discretionary distributions of income and principal to any of A's grandchildren. A's grandchildren are skip persons since they are in a generation that is two or more generations below A. Taxable distributions occur upon any distribution of income or principal to A's grandchildren. As a result, the generation-skipping tax is imposed on each distribution and the distributee is obligated to pay the tax.

(2) *Example 2: Taxable Terminations*: Upon the death of B in Example 1, a taxable termination will occur because B's interest in the trust will have terminated and the only person having an interest in the trust is C, a skip

24. As a result, it is possible to avoid the generation-skipping tax if more than one generation is skipped. For example, if transferor gives property to her great grandchild, only a single generation-skipping tax will be due event though the transfer skipped over two generations (her child and her grandchild).
25. Sec. 2613(a).
26. Sec. 2612(a).
27. Sec. 2612(b).
28. Sec. 2612(c).

person. A generation-skipping tax will be imposed when the trust terminates and the trust's property is transferred to A's grandchildren. The tax is assessed on the value of the property in the trust and the trustee must pay the tax.

(3) *Example 3: Direct Skips:* A transfers property outright to C (A's grandchild) and also transfers property to a trust for the benefit of C (A's grandchild). Both transfers are direct skips. C, A's grandchild, is a skip person, and the trust is also a skip person because all the beneficial interests in the trust are held by a skip person, C. A generation-skipping tax is imposed on the value of the property transferred in trust and outright to C. The tax is payable by A.

It should be kept in mind that in each of the above examples A also incurred a gift or an estate tax at the time of A's transfer; the generation-skipping tax is in addition to those transfer taxes.

A generation-skipping tax exemption equal to the unified credit exemption (USD 11.7 million in 2021) is allowed for each transferor. The transferor has discretion to allocate the exemption among her transfers as she wishes.[29] For example, if A makes a generation-skipping transfer of USD 21.7 million in 2021 and allocates her USD 11.7 million exemption to the transfer, only the USD 10 million amount in excess of the USD 11.7 million exemption will be taxed and a generation-skipping tax of USD 4 million (40% x USD 10 million) is due.[30] Had none of the exemption been allocated to the transfer, a generation-skipping tax of USD 8.68 million (40% × USD 21.7 million) would have been incurred.

15.2 JURISDICTIONAL PRINCIPLES

As in the case of the income tax, the US tax jurisdiction with respect to transfers at death or by gift is global in reach for its citizens and residents. The term "resident" is defined differently for purposes of the wealth transfer taxes than for income tax purposes. An individual generally is treated as a US resident if her "domicile" is in the US.[31] The determination of domicile is a factual one, depending in part on whether the decedent had an intention to remain in the US.[32]

Since the transfer taxes are global for US citizens and residents, the value of the gross estate is determined by including the value of all property owned by the decedent

29. Sec. 2631.
30. The statutes adopt a more complex method to calculate the tax. The maximum Federal estate tax rate is multiplied by the "inclusion ratio," which is equal to one minus a fraction, the numerator of which is the amount of the exemption allocated to the transfer and the denominator of which is the value of the property transferred. In the text example, the fraction is one-half (USD 11 million allocated exemption divided by the USD 22 million transfer), the inclusion ratio is also one-half (1 minus the fraction of one-half). A 20% tax rate (half times 40%) is thus applied to the USD 22 million transfer, resulting in a generation-skipping tax of USD 4.4 million. Secs. 2602, 2641, and 2642.
31. Treas. Reg. Secs. 20.0-1(b)(1), (2), and 1.2501-1(b).
32. *See, e.g.*, Rev. Rul. 80-209, 1980-2 C.B. 248.

"wherever situated."[33] Likewise, the gift tax applies to all lifetime donative transfers by US citizens or residents regardless of where the property is located.[34] The same is true of the generation-skipping tax. International double taxation is alleviated through the mechanism of the foreign tax credit and/or by death tax conventions.

Special rules are provided for nonresident aliens. As in the case of the income tax, the scope of the US jurisdiction is determined on a geographical basis. Thus, the estate tax, the gift tax, and the generation-skipping tax in general apply to nonresident aliens only with respect to property that is "situated within the United States."[35] The same rates of tax are imposed on transfers by nonresidents as are applied to estates of US decedents.

The US has also entered into a relatively few bilateral tax treaties governing wealth transfer taxation. And, as with the income tax, certain special provisions are included to prevent avoidance of US wealth transfer taxes.

15.3 ESTATE TAX: INTERNATIONAL ASPECTS

15.3.1 Situs Rules

The US applies an estate tax to the property of a nonresident that is "situated" in the US.[36] The "situs" rules developed to apply the estate tax perform a function similar to the "source of income" rules in the income tax (discussed in Chapter 4). US citizens and resident aliens may claim a foreign tax credit for income sourced outside the US, and nonresidents may be taxed on income sourced in the US. The estate tax statutory provisions and regulations follow a similar approach. US citizens and residents may claim a credit for estate taxes paid on property situated outside the US and nonresidents are subject to the estate tax on property situated in the US. The situs rules may be modified by treaty.

15.3.1.1 Property Situated Within the United States

The following property is considered situated within the US:

(1) real estate located in the US;[37]
(2) tangible personal property located in the US[38] (except for certain works of art as noted in section 15.3.1.2);
(3) shares of stock issued by a corporation organized under the laws of the US;[39]

33. Sec. 2031(a).
34. Secs. 2501(a) and 2511.
35. Secs. 2103 and 2511(a).
36. Sec. 2103.
37. Treas. Reg. Sec. 20.2104-1(a)(1).
38. Treas. Reg. Sec. 20.2104-1(a)(2).
39. Sec. 2104(a). As a result of this rule, foreign portfolio investors usually employ a foreign corporation as their investment vehicle. Separately, a special look-through rule, which is no longer available, had allowed decedents who died before Jan. 1, 2012 to exclude from their gross

(4) property situated in the US either at the time of transfer or at decedent's death if decedent retained certain interests in, or powers over, the transferred property;[40]
(5) debt obligations issued by a US "person"[41] or by the US government or a state or local government (except as noted in section 15.3.1.2);[42] and
(6) certain deposits with a US branch of a foreign corporation if the branch is engaged in the commercial banking business.[43]

15.3.1.2 Property Situated Outside the United States

The following property is considered situated outside the US:

(1) real estate located outside the US;[44]
(2) tangible personal property located outside the US;[45]
(3) works of art owned by a nonresident alien that are at the time of death on loan or exhibition in the US;[46]
(4) shares of stock in a corporation organized and incorporated under the laws of a foreign country;[47]
(5) proceeds of insurance on the life of a nonresident alien;[48]
(6) debt obligations issued by a US corporation and deposits with a US bank if the interest thereon was exempt from tax under Section 871(h) or (i) (Chapter 5 section 5.5.5);[49]
(7) deposits with a foreign branch of a US commercial bank.[50]

---

estate a proportion of stocks they held in RICs (Chapter 2, section 2.7.1.) equal to the proportion of stock owned by the RIC that the decedent could have excluded had he owned such stock directly. Sec. 2105(d).

40. Secs. 2104(b), 2036, 2037, and 2038. The retained interests and powers that trigger this rule include retained income interests in the transferred property and retained powers to revoke the transfer. *See, e.g., Estate of Swan v. Commissioner*, 247 F.2d 144 (2d Cir. 1957) (property in a revocable *inter vivos* trust was situated within the US where cash and securities were deposited with New York trust companies).

    Property is also treated as situated in the US if the decedent: (1) transferred property, (2) retained an interest in or power over that property, (3) revoked such interest or power within three years of death, and (4) the property was either located in the US at the time of transfer or the time of death. Secs. 2104(b) and 2035.
41. A "person" includes an individual, a trust, estate, partnership, association, company, or corporation. Sec. 7701(a)(1).
42. Sec. 2104(c).
43. Sec. 2104(c).
44. Treas. Reg. Sec. 20.2105-1(a)(1).
45. Treas. Reg. Sec. 20.2105-1(a)(2).
46. Sec. 2105(c).
47. Treas. Reg. Sec. 20.2105-1(f).
48. Sec. 2105(a).
49. Secs. 2104(c), 2105(b)(1), and (3).
50. Sec. 2105(b)(2).

15.3.2 US Taxation of Citizens and Resident Aliens: The Foreign Tax Credit

US citizens and resident aliens who die owning property situated in another country are subject to full US estate taxation under the rules described in section 15.1.2.

The estates of US citizens and resident aliens are allowed a foreign tax credit for "estate, inheritance, legacy, or succession" taxes actually paid to a foreign country with respect to the property situated within that country.[51] The rules discussed in section 15.3.1 are applied to determine the country in which the property is situated. Thus, for example, stock of a corporation is situated only in the foreign country in which the corporation is incorporated.[52]

As in the case of the income tax, the allowable foreign tax credit for estate tax purposes is subject to limitations. The maximum credit is the smaller of:

(1) the foreign country's death taxes actually imposed on property in the foreign country that is included in the decedent's US computed gross estate (the so-called first limitation); and
(2) the portion of the US estate tax attributable to property that is located in the foreign country, subject to death taxes therein, and included in the decedent's US computed gross estate (the so-called second limitation).[53]

The limitations operate to provide a full credit for foreign death taxes where the effective foreign tax rate is lower than that imposed by the US, but the allowable credit cannot exceed the tax that the US would have imposed on the foreign property.

The "first limitation" is computed by applying a fraction to the foreign country's wealth transfer taxes imposed at death. The numerator of the fraction is the value of the property that is subject to the foreign country's death taxes and that is included in the decedent's US computed gross estate. The denominator of the fraction is the value of all the decedent's property subject to the foreign country's death taxes. "Value" is determined under the foreign country's tax rules and then converted to US dollars.[54]

The "second limitation" is computed by applying a fraction to the US federal estate tax liability of the decedent. The numerator of the fraction is the "adjusted value" of the decedent's property that is situated within a foreign country, subject to death taxes therein, and included in the decedent's US computed gross estate. The denominator of the fraction is the value of the decedent's entire gross estate minus any allowable charitable contributions deduction and marital deduction. The term "adjusted value" refers to the value of the decedent's gross estate minus any charitable

51. Sec. 2014(a). The foreign tax must be a "wealth transfer tax." Thus, the Canadian tax imposed on transfers of appreciated property at death is part of Canada's income tax and would not be creditable under Section 2014. *Estate of Ballard v. Commissioner*, 85 TC 300 (1985). Art. XXIXB of the Canada treaty, however, provides a credit against US wealth transfer taxes for the Canadian income tax.
52. Treas. Reg. Sec. 20.2014-1(a)(3).
53. Sec. 2014(b).
54. Treas. Reg. Sec. 20.2014-2.

contributions deduction or marital deduction allowable with respect to, and allocated to, the foreign property.[55]

As in the case of the income tax, the foreign tax credit is in general allowed to resident aliens.[56]

15.3.3 Estate Taxation of Nonresident Aliens

The US estate tax imposed on the transfer of property by a nonresident alien begins with a determination of the value of that part of the decedent's gross estate[57] that is situated in the US under the rules described in section 15.3.1 at the time of death.[58]

From the gross estate situated within the US are subtracted the portion of debts, expenses of administration, claims against the estate, mortgages, funeral expenses, state death taxes, and losses suffered by the estate that is allocable to the US.[59] A deduction for transfers to qualifying charitable organizations is also allowed.[60] The estate of a nonresident alien is allowed a full marital deduction to the extent property situated in the US passes to a surviving spouse *who is a US citizen.*[61] The result of the subtraction of these items from the gross estate is the taxable estate.

The wealth transfer tax rates applicable to US decedents are then applied to the sum of the taxable estate and the "adjusted taxable gifts" (i.e., taxable gifts made by the decedent after December 31, 1976 other than gifts that are included in the gross estate).[62] This "tentative" tax is then reduced by a hypothetical tax calculated by applying the wealth transfer tax rates existing at the time of death to the taxable gifts decedent made after 1976. In effect, the amounts subject to tax in the estate are treated as coming "on top of" the taxable gifts for purposes of applying the progressive tax rates. The tax thus determined is then reduced by two credits against tax:

(1) the credit for gift taxes paid on gifts made prior to 1977 that were included in the decedent's gross estate; and
(2) the credit for estate tax paid by another transferor with respect to property included in the decedent's estate where the prior transferor died within ten years before or two years after the decedent.[63]

---

55. Treas. Reg. Sec. 20.2014-3.
56. *See* Sec. 2014(h).
57. Under Section 2031, the gross estate includes the value of "all property, real or personal, tangible or intangible, wherever situated."
58. Sec. 2103.
59. Sec. 2106(a)(1) and (4). In general, the deductions are allowed in the proportion that the US assets bear to the decedent's worldwide assets. The deductions are available only if the US estate tax return discloses the portion of the decedent's gross estate that is located outside the US. Sec. 2106(b).
60. Sec. 2106(a)(2). In general, a deduction is granted only for contributions to charitable organizations that are organized and operated in the US for prescribed charitable purposes such as education, religion, and scientific research.
61. Sec. 2106(a)(3).
62. Sec. 2101(b).
63. Secs. 2012 and 2013.

Finally, the estate is allowed a wealth transfer tax credit in the amount of USD 13,000. When the graduated tax rates are applied, this credit has the effect of exempting USD 60,000 from the estate tax.[64]

15.4 GIFT TAX: INTERNATIONAL ASPECTS

15.4.1 Gift Taxation of US Citizens and Resident Aliens

The US gift tax is a cumulative tax imposed annually on all transfers "in trust or otherwise, whether the gift is direct or indirect, and whether the property is real or personal, tangible or intangible."[65] For US citizens and resident aliens, the tax is imposed on all transfers wherever the property is situated under the rules described in section 15.3.1. No marital deduction is allowed for a gift to a spouse who is not a US citizen. But a USD 100,000 annual exclusion (adjusted for inflation and USD 159,000 in 2021) for gifts of present interests is available for gifts to such spouses.[66] No statutory foreign tax credit is allowed for transfers of property located abroad even though the transfers are subject to gift tax by a foreign country.

15.4.2 Gift Taxation of Nonresident Aliens

The US imposes a gift tax on transfers by nonresidents who are not US citizens only if the subject of the gift is real property or tangible personal property physically situated in the US; gifts of intangible property are therefore not subject to US gift tax.[67] If a taxable gift is made, the generally applicable US wealth transfer tax rates apply. Gifts by nonresident aliens qualify for the USD 10,000 annual per donee exclusion (adjusted for inflation and USD 15,000 in 2021) but not for the marital deduction or the wealth transfer unified tax credit.[68] A deduction for charitable contributions is available if, in general, the transfer is to a US organization that will use the gifted funds in the US.[69]

The above rules apply irrespective of whether the donor is engaged in business in the US.

15.5 THE GENERATION-SKIPPING TAX: INTERNATIONAL ASPECTS

As discussed in section 15.1.4, the US imposes a tax on certain generation-skipping transfers. Treasury Regulations apply the generation-skipping tax to nonresident aliens

64. Sec. 2102(b)(1). When required by treaty, the estate of a nonresident alien is allowed the full US wealth transfer credit under Section 2010 multiplied by the proportion of the decedent's worldwide estate that is situated in the US. Sec. 2102(c)(3). *See* Art. XXIXB of the Canada Tax Treaty. In addition, the Treaty with Canada exempts from US transfer taxes, US estates of Canadian residents that have a value of USD 1.2 million or less to the extent that gain from the sale of such US estate would not have been subject to US income tax. *Id.*
65. Treas. Reg. Sec. 25.2511-1.
66. Secs. 2501(a)(1), 2511(a), and 2523(i).
67. Sec. 2501(a)(2); Treas. Reg. Sec. 25.2511-3(a)(1) and (b)(1).
68. Secs. 2503(b), 2523(a), and 2505.
69. Sec. 2522(b).

only if a US gift or estate tax also applies to the transfer.[70] For example, if a nonresident grandparent makes a gift of US real estate to a nonresident grandchild, the property is subject to both US gift and generation-skipping transfers. But if the property transferred were cash or securities, no US gift tax would be incurred and hence no generation-skipping tax either.[71]

15.6 EXPATRIATION TO AVOID TRANSFER TAXES

The treatment of bequests and gifts by former US citizens and residents depends on when the taxpayer expatriated. A special set of estate and gift tax rules, described in sections 15.6.1 and 15.6.2 below, applies to former US citizens and residents who expatriated before June 17, 2008. In contrast, the regular estate and gift tax rules applicable to nonresident aliens apply to taxpayers who expatriated on or after June 17, 2008. In addition, however, as discussed in section 15.6.3, gifts and bequests from taxpayers who expatriated on or after June 17, 2008 are now subject to an inheritance tax.

15.6.1 Estate Tax for Taxpayers Who Expatriated Before June 17, 2008

Special rules apply to a taxpayer who expatriated from the US prior to June 17, 2008 and died while subject to Section 877.[72] If the taxpayer dies in a year in which she is in the US for more than thirty days, Section 877(g) requires that the US estate tax apply to all her property, wherever situated.

If the decedent, who expatriated from the US prior to June 17, 2008 and is subject to Section 877,[73] was not present in the US for more than thirty days in the year she died, then the estate tax in general applies only to her US-situs property. A wealth transfer tax credit of USD 13,000 is allowed against the tax so computed (the equivalent of a USD 60,000 exemption).[74] A special rule requires the inclusion in the gross estate of a portion of the value of the stock owned by the decedent in a foreign corporation if: (1) the decedent owned directly 10% or more of the voting power of all classes of stock of the foreign corporation, and (2) the decedent owned directly and by attribution more than 50% of the voting power of all classes of stock of the foreign corporation. The amount includible in the decedent's US gross estate is determined by applying to the fair market value of the stock owned outright by the decedent a fraction, the numerator of which is the fair market value of the corporation's assets in the US and the

70. Treas. Reg. Sec. 26.2663-2.
71. Sec. 2663(2); Treas. Reg. Sec. 26.2663-2.
72. A taxpayer is subject to Section 877 for ten years after he or she repatriates if at the time of repatriation: (1) his or her average tax liability for the five preceding years exceeds USD 124,000 (adjusted for inflation), (2) his or her net worth exceeds USD 2 million, or (3) the individual fails to certify that he or she has complied with all US income tax obligations for the preceding five years. Sec. 877(a) and (e).
73. For rules determining whether a taxpayer is subject to Section 877, *see* the immediately preceding footnote.
74. Sec. 2107(a) and (c)(1).

denominator of which is the total fair market value of the corporation's entire assets.[75] A proportionate foreign tax credit is then granted if another country also imposes a tax on the property included in the US gross estate by reason of the foregoing rules.[76]

15.6.2 Gift Tax for Taxpayers Who Expatriated Before June 17, 2008

If a nonresident alien who expatriated before June 17, 2008 and who is subject to Section 877[77] makes a gift in a year in which she was in the US for more than thirty days, the US gift tax applies under Section 877(g) regardless of where the transferred property is located and regardless of the nature of the property.

Special rules also apply to gifts by a nonresident alien expatriating before June 17, 2008 who is subject to Section 877 but was not in the US for more than thirty days. The US gift tax applies to transfers by such person of intangible property situated in the US, as well as transfers of tangible property in the US.[78] Contrary to the normal US rule, a foreign tax credit is allowed for any foreign taxes imposed on such gifts.[79] The following property is considered situated in the US and hence subject to gift tax:

(1) shares of stock in a US corporation;
(2) debt obligations of a US person, including bank deposits;
(3) debt obligations of the US or a state or local government;
(4) intangible property of any type issued by or enforceable against a US resident or corporation.

These special rules apply regardless of where the stock or written evidence of the property or obligation is located.[80] A rule similar to that applicable to the estate tax with respect to transfers of stock in certain foreign corporations (section 15.6.1) is also applicable in the gift tax context.[81]

15.6.3 Estate and Gift Tax for Taxpayers Who Expatriated on or after June 17, 2008

The regular estate and gift tax rules applicable to nonresident aliens apply to taxpayers who expatriated on or after June 17, 2008 (sections 15.3.3 and 15.4.2). In addition,

75. Sec. 2107(b). In determining the value of the stock of the foreign corporation, no reduction is allowed for corporate liabilities. Treas. Reg. Sec. 20.2107-1(b)(1)(ii)(a). The rules of Section 957, discussed in Chapter 6 section 6.3.3, are applied to determine if the requisite "voting power" exists.
76. Sec. 2107(c)(2).
77. A taxpayer is subject to Section 877 for ten years after he or she repatriates if at the time of repatriation (1) his or her average tax liability for the five preceding years exceeds USD 124,000 (adjusted for inflation), (2) his or her net worth exceeds USD 2 million, or (3) the individual fails to certify that he or she has complied with all US income tax obligations for the preceding five years. Sec. 877(a) and (e).
78. Secs. 2501(a)(3)(A) and 2511(a).
79. Sec. 2501(a)(3).
80. Sec. 2511(b); Treas. Reg. Sec. 25.2511-3(b).
81. Sec. 2501(a)(5).

however, US citizens and residents receiving gifts and bequests from "covered expatriates" (Chapter 5 sections 5.5.7.1 and 5.5.7.2) who expatriated on or after June 17, 2008 are subject to a special inheritance tax.[82] A tax is imposed at the highest transfer tax rate (40% in 2021) on the gift or bequest and is reduced by any foreign gift or estate tax paid with respect to the transfer.[83]

15.7 WEALTH TRANSFER TAX TREATIES

15.7.1 Background

The US network of wealth transfer treaties is substantially smaller than its income tax treaty network. Double taxation in the estate tax area can arise either because both countries claim the decedent as a domiciliary, and thus taxable on his worldwide estate, or because the decedent was domiciled in one country while holding property with a situs in the second country. The US estate tax treaties in general deal with these problems by agreeing on rules to determine a single domicile, by providing rules with respect to which country may tax transfers of particular types of property, and by granting a credit for foreign death taxes paid in certain situations. Since the US unilaterally grants a foreign tax credit for death taxes paid by those estates subject to its worldwide estate tax jurisdiction, the primary function of the estate tax treaties for these taxpayers is to ensure that the credit mechanism functions properly. For other taxpayers, the change in the domiciliary or situs rules may either eliminate assets from the reach of US estate taxation or may qualify the US tax paid on those assets for a credit in the foreign country. In any event, both classes of taxpayers are generally protected by an article that provides that the provisions of the treaty shall not be construed so as to increase the tax imposed by either country.[84]

US treaties generally apply only to the federal estate tax and do not cover state inheritance taxes. The US gift and generation-skipping taxes are covered only by a limited number of treaties.[85]

The estate tax treaties contain provisions for nondiscrimination, competent authority procedures, and exchange of information that are parallel to those found in the income tax treaties.[86]

15.7.2 Domicile

Under the US Model Treaty, domicile is determined as an initial matter under the domestic law of each country. An individual is domiciled in the US if he is a citizen or

82. Sec. 2801(a) and (e).
83. Sec. 2801(d).
84. *See, e.g.*, the US Model Estate, Gift and Generation-Skipping Tax Convention of Nov. 20, 1980 ("US Model Treaty"), Art. 1.1. Since the Model Treaty forms the basis of US tax treaty negotiations, the following discussion is in general based on that Treaty.
85. *See, e.g.*, Denmark Estate Gift and Tax Treaty.
86. *See* US Model Treaty, Arts. 10-12.

"resident" of the US.[87] The Model Treaty then employs a "tiebreaker" rule to establish a single residence for wealth transfer tax purposes.[88] An overriding proviso is, however, included: A citizen of one country who is domiciled in both countries by reason of residence is ultimately treated as domiciled in the country of citizenship if he had been resident in the other country for less than seven of the preceding ten years.[89] Under the "savings clause," the US retains the right to tax its citizens on a worldwide basis, although special rules apply to avoid double taxation (*see* section 15.7.5).

15.7.3 Rules for Taxation

In the older US estate and gift tax treaties, specific rules were adopted as to the situs of particular types of property. In the US Model Treaty and newer US tax treaties, situs provisions are replaced by rules for determining which of the treaty countries has primary or exclusive jurisdiction to tax the transfer of particular types of property.

15.7.3.1 Real Property

Under Article 5 of the US Model Treaty, the transfer by a domiciliary of one country (for simplicity, hereinafter referred to as the US) of real property located in the other country may be taxed in that other country (for simplicity, hereinafter referred to as Country X). Thus, Country X may tax the transfer by a US citizen of real property located in Country X. The US will also tax the transfer, but give a credit for the Country X tax.[90]

15.7.3.2 Business Property

Under Article 6 of the US Model Treaty, a transfer by a US citizen of assets forming part of the business property of a permanent establishment situated in Country X may be taxed in Country X. Again, Country X has a primary but not exclusive right to tax the transfer. A similar rule applies to transfers of assets pertaining to a fixed base used for the performance of independent personal services.[91]

15.7.3.3 Other Property

Transfer by a US domiciliary of other property may be taxed *only* by the US, regardless of the nature or location of the property. Exclusive taxing jurisdiction is likewise given

87. US Model Treaty, Art. 4.1.
88. US Model Treaty, Art. 4.2.
89. *Id.*, Art. 4.3. This provision prevents temporary moves by citizens of one country from creating unlimited wealth transfer tax liability in the country of temporary residence.
90. US Model Treaty, Arts. 5.1 and 9.
91. *Id.*, Art. 6.1. The term "permanent establishment" is defined in a manner similar to the definition in the US Model Income Tax Treaty. *See* Chapter 14 section 14.5.2. There is no definition of "fixed base."

to Country X as to its domiciliaries.[92] This provision, for example, surrenders the right of the US to tax transfers of stock in US corporations by a domiciliary of Country X. Special rules are provided for transfers of interests in partnerships and trusts.[93]

15.7.4 Deductions and Exemptions

Article 8 of the US Model Treaty provides a deduction for the "debts"[94] of an estate in a ratio of the value of the property subject to tax in the taxing country to the total value of all property of the decedent wherever situated. Provision is also made for a charitable contributions deduction.[95]

The provisions in the 1980 US Model Treaty regarding the marital deduction and the unified transfer tax credit have been superseded by subsequent legislation.

15.7.5 Relief from Double Taxation

Article 9 of the US Model Treaty establishes reciprocal obligations on the treaty partners to avoid double taxation by means of a foreign tax credit where one of the countries has a primary but not exclusive right to tax a transfer under Article 5 or 6 of the Treaty.

Article 9.6 of the US Model Treaty limits the credit allowed to the portion of the tax imposed on the property with respect to which the credit is allowable. This allocation prevents the credit for one country's tax from offsetting the other country's tax on property as to which the other country has sole taxing jurisdiction under the Treaty. Thus, suppose a US citizen who is a Country X domiciliary transfers US real estate (Article 5) plus other business assets not associated with a US permanent establishment (Article 7). While the US will initially assert jurisdiction to tax all assets on the basis of citizenship, it must allow a credit for the Country X tax on the other business assets; Country X must allow a credit for the portion of its tax attributable to the transfer of the US real estate.

Treasury Regulations specifically state that where the credit for foreign death taxes provided under an estate tax treaty is more favorable than the Code credit under Section 2014, the estate may elect to apply the treaty credit.[96]

---

92. *Id.*, Art. 7.1. The US still retains the right to tax its citizens, although domiciled in another jurisdiction, on a worldwide basis but gives a foreign tax credit for the tax imposed by the treaty partner on all assets except those with respect to which the US retains primary taxing jurisdiction. US Model Treaty, Art. 9.1(b). This provision allows a credit for tax imposed on assets that under the Code rules would be situated in the US. *See* section 15.3.1.
93. *Id.*, Art. 7.2.
94. The US interprets the term "debts" to include all items deductible under Sections 2053-2054 of the Internal Revenue Code. Accordingly, the Treaty provision simply conforms to US domestic law.
95. By virtue of the override provision in the US Model Treaty, Art. 1.3, the provision is relevant only when the US is taxing on a situs basis.
96. Treas. Reg. Sec. 20.2014-4(a)(1).

Index

A

Accounting
  Annual Accounting concept, 31
  Foreign currency transactions, *see* Foreign currency
  Installment sales, 31
  Methods of accounting, 30–31
  Original issue discount, 31
Accumulated earnings tax
  Domestic corporations, 17, 88–89
  Foreign corporations, 88
  Foreign shareholders, 89
Allocation of deductions, 50
  General rules, 50–52
  Interest, 52–56
  Other expenses, 58–59
  Research and experimentation expenses, 56–58
  Worldwide allocation of interest, 53–54
    Alternative minimum tax (AMT), 26
    AMT and Foreign Investment in Real Property Tax Act, 73
    AMT Taxable Income, 26
    AMT Taxable Excess, 26
    AMT Rates, 26
    Final tax liability, 26

B

Base Erosion Anti-Abuse Tax (BEAT), 95, 97–98
Basis
  Definition, 8
  Formation of corporation, 14
  Liquidation, 15
  Reorganization, 15–16
Branch profits tax, 84–86
Branch interest tax, 87–88

C

Capital gains and losses
  Capital assets defined, 12
  Capital losses, 12–13
  Fixed or Determinable Annual or Periodic (FDAP) Income, 61
  Nonresident aliens, 81
  Rates
    Corporations, 7
    Individuals, 18–19
    Foreign investment in US real property, 73
  Source of gain, *see* Source of income
Consolidated returns, 16
Controlled foreign corporations (CFC)
  Boycotts, bribes, etc., 118
  Definition of a CFC, 111
  Disposition of stock in a CFC: Section 1248
    Background, 119
    Calculation of tax, 120
    Scope of coverage, 119–120
  Distributions and adjustments to basis, 118

Foreign personal holding company income, 113–114
Foreign tax credit, 118
Subpart F
Basic structure, 109–110
Income, 112–115
Earnings invested in US property, 116–117
Tax treatment of US shareholder, 110–111
Corporation income tax
Accumulated earnings tax, *see* Accumulated earnings tax
Capital gains and losses, 12–13
Credits against tax, 13
Dividends received deduction, 10
Foreign corporations, *see* Foreign corporations
Personal holding company tax, *see* Personal holding companies
Tax base
Deductible expenditures, 8–10
Expenditures not deductible, 10–11
Gross income, 7–8
Interest deduction limitation, 11
Net operating loss, 11–12
Tax shelter loss limitation, 11
Tax rates, 7
Transactions between corporations and shareholders, *see* Corporations and shareholders
Corporations and shareholders
Controlled foreign corporations, *see* Controlled foreign corporations (CFC)
Corporate inversions, 142–144
Dividends 14
Corporate shareholders, 14
Earnings and profits, 14
Foreign dividends received deduction, *see* Foreign dividend exemption
Individual shareholders, 14, 15
Stock dividends, 15
Tax rate, 19
Formation of corporation
Domestic, 14
Foreign, 130
Inversions, *see* Inversions
Liquidations, *see* Liquidations
Redemption of stock, 15
Reorganizations
Domestic corporations, 130–132
Foreign corporations, 132–140
Treatment of distributing corporation, 14–15
Credits against tax, 13, 26
Foreign taxes, *see* Foreign tax credit
General business credit, 13
Individuals receiving dividends, 19
Covered Expatriates, 81–83

D

Deductions
Capital expenditures, 8–10
Capital losses, *see* Capital gains and losses
Costs of producing income, 8
Depreciation, *see* Depreciation
Foreign taxes, *see* Foreign tax credit
Losses, *see* Losses
Miscellaneous Itemized deductions, 21
Mixed business-personal expenditures, 21, 25
Nondeductible expenditures
Corporations, 10–11
Individuals, 21
Personal, 18
Personal exemptions, 18
Production of income, 20
Source rules, *see* Allocation of deductions
Standard deduction, 25
Deemed Repatriation Tax on Deferred Earnings, 120–122
Depreciation
Accelerated, 9
Real estate, 10, 20
Recapture, 12

Tangible personal property, 9–10
Digital services, 239, 251
Digitalization, 238
Dividends
see also Corporations and shareholders
Consolidated groups, 16
Dividend repatriation, 138–141
Dividends received deduction (DRD), 10, 14, 44, 107, 115, 116, 120, 125–126, 130, 162, 178–182, 187, 189
Foreign dividends received deduction, *see* Foreign dividend exemption
Qualified dividends, 19, 107, 125, 144
Source rules, *see* Source of income
Tax treaties, 244, 255
Domestic International Sales Corporation (DISC), 174, 189
Domestic reverse hybrid, 243–244

E

Earned income
Exclusion for income earned abroad, 194–198
Estate tax, *see* Wealth transfer taxation
Expatriates
Covered Expatriates, 82, 83, 278

F

Fixed or Determinable Annual or Periodic (FDAP) Income, 61–63, 67, 69, 70, 78, 83, 91, 95, 97
Foreign Account Tax Compliance Act (FATCA), 32, 95, 98–99
Foreign corporations
Accumulated earnings tax, *see* Accumulated earnings tax
Alternative minimum tax, *see* Corporation income tax
Branch interest tax
General, 87–88
Treaty aspects, 88
Branch Profits tax, 84
Structure, 84–85
Treaty aspects, 86
Classification of foreign entities
Foreign corporations, 6
Foreign trusts, 91–92
Comparison of branch and subsidiary operations, 89–90
Exempt US source income, 79–81
Formation, reorganization and liquidation, *see* Section 367
Foreign corporations controlled by US persons, *see* Controlled foreign corporations (CFC)
Foreign tax credit, 161
Income 'effectively connected' with US trade or business, *see* Income 'effectively connected' with US trade or business
Income taxed at 30 percent rate, 78–79
Personal holding company tax, *see* Personal holding companies
Previously taxed earnings and profits (PTEP), 113, 125, 161–164
Return and disclosure requirements, 94–95
US 'trade or business', *see* US 'trade or business'
Withholding at source, *see* Withholding at source
Foreign currency
Functional currency, 227–228
Qualified business unit (QBU), 227–228
Transactions in nonfunctional currency, 232–235
Translations into US dollars, 227–228
Foreign derived intangible income (FDII)
Deduction eligible income, 192–193
Deemed tangible investment return, 193–194

Foreign derived deduction eligible income, 192, 193
Foreign dividend exemption
Foreign dividend received deduction, 125–127
Hybrid dividend, 126
Foreign Investment in Real Property Tax Act (FIRPTA)
Capital gains, 73
Effectively Connected, 73
Foreign sales corporations 190
Foreign tax credit
Anti-abuse rules, 165–169
Baskets, 171–180
Carryback and carryover of excess credits, 180–181
Controlled foreign corporations, 181–182
Direct foreign tax credit
In lieu of taxes, 160
Nonresident aliens and foreign corporations, 161
Persons eligible for tax credit, 157
Taxes eligible for tax credit, 157–160
Foreign taxes, treatment of in general, 153–154
High-Tax Kick-Out, 178
Indirect foreign tax credit, 161–165
Limitations on the foreign tax credit
Background, 171–178
De minimis rule and foreign passive income, 185
Dividends from non-controlled Section 902 corporation, 182
Financial services income basket (prior law), 174
Foreign branch category, 180
Foreign losses, 182–184
General limitation income basket, 171–175
GILTI category, 179–180
High withholding tax interest basket (prior law), 174
Passive income basket, 175–178
US losses, 184–185
Objectives of the foreign tax credit, 154–156
Perspective on the foreign tax credit mechanism, 186–188
Relief for small investors, 185
Special limitations on the foreign tax credit, 185

G

Global intangible low-taxed income (GILTI)
Foreign Tax Credit, 161–164
Foreign Tax Credit Limitation Basket for GILTI, 179–180
GILTI high-tax election, 115, 122, 125, 126
Net CFC tested income, 123
Net CFC tested loss, 123
Net deemed tangible investment return, 124
Qualified business asset investment (QBAI), 124, 145
Section 250 GILTI deduction, 124–125, 164, 179, 189
Tested income, 115, 123–124, 163
Gift tax, *see* Wealth transfer taxation
Generation-skipping tax, *see* Wealth transfer taxation

H

Hybrid, 6, 90, 166, 243–245

I

Income
Capital gains, *see* Capital gains and losses
Effectively connected income, *see* Income 'effectively connected' with US trade or business
FDII, *see* Foreign derived intangible income

Gains from disposition of US real property, 46
GILTI, *see* Global intangible low-taxed income (GILTI)
Gross income, 18–19
International boycott income, 118
Nonresident aliens, *see* Nonresident aliens
Qualified business asset investment return, *see* Global intangible low-taxed income (GILTI)
Source rules, *see* Source of income
Subpart F income, 112–115
Taxable income, 7, 18
Income 'effectively connected' with US trade or business
'Asset use' test, 69–70
'Business-activities' test, 70
Capital gains and fixed or determinable income, 69–73
Foreign source income effectively connected with a US business, 71–73
Gains from the disposition of US real property interests, 73–75
Individual income tax, 18
Alternative minimum tax, 26
Credits against tax, 26, *see also* Credits against tax
Tax base
Capital gains and losses, 19–20
Deductible expenditures
Business and investment, 20–21
Personal, 25
Expenditures not deductible, 21
Expatriation, 81–83
Former citizens, 81–83
Former residents, 81–83
Gross income, 18–19
Limitation on deductions
Amount at risk, 21–22
Interest expense, 22–24
Passive activity losses, 24–25
Trusts and estates, *see* Trusts and estates
Intercompany pricing rules, see Transfer Pricing
Accuracy related penalties, 223–224
Advance pricing agreements, 221–223
Blocked income, 220
Correlative adjustments, 218
Determining comparable prices, 202–204
Foreign tax credit, 219–220
Intangible property, 210–215
Loans, 216–217
Sale of goods, 205–210
Services, 215–216
Set-offs, 217
Treaties, 219
Interest income
Foreign tax credit, 160, 165, 177, 181–182, 255
Source rules, *see* Source of income
Tax treaties, 249–250, 255–256
Inversions, 142–144
Tax Treaties, 255

J

Jurisdictional principles
Controlled foreign corporations, 37
Estate tax, 270–271
Foreign trusts and estates, 35, 91–93
Gift tax, 270–271
Nonresident aliens, *see* Nonresident aliens
Treaties, *see* Tax treaties
US citizens, 35–36
US corporations, 36
US residents, 35–36

L

Liquidations
Basis, 15
Domestic corporation, 15
Foreign corporation, 132, 138–140

Losses
  Capital losses, *see* Capital gains and losses
  Foreign tax credit, 182–185
  Net operating loss carryforward and carryback, 11–12

M

Miscellaneous itemized deductions, 21, 25

N

Nonresident aliens
  Determination of status as resident or nonresident, 75
    183-day test, 76
    Permanent residence test, 76
  Exempt income, 79
    Bank deposits, 80
    Capital gains, 81
    Dividends from foreign business income, 80
    Portfolio interest, 80–81
  Income taxed at 30 per cent rate, 78–79
  Income taxed at full US tax rates, 79
  Return and disclosure requirement, 94–95
  Treaties, 81
  US 'trade or business', *see* US 'trade or business'
  Withholding at source, *see* Withholding at source

O

OECD
  BEPS, 39, 240, 252, 263
  Pillar One, 238, 251, 252
  Pillar Two, 238

P

Partnerships
  Classification issues, 6
  Foreign partners in a US or foreign partnership, 90–91, 243
  Foreign partnerships, 90, 95, 152
  Source of interest paid by, 43
  Withholding on foreign partners, *see* Withholding at source
Passive foreign investment company (PFIC)
  Definition, 146–147
  Qualified electing funds, 148–149
Personal holding companies
  Domestic corporations
    Calculation of tax, 17–18
    Shareholding requirement, 17–18
  Foreign corporations, 89
  Foreign shareholders, 89

Q

Qualified Business Asset Investment (QBAI), 124, 191, 193
Qualified Domestic Trust (QDOT), 267
Qualified Business Unit (QBU), 180, 226–230, 233

R

Rates of tax
  Alternative Minimum Tax, 26,
  Corporations, 7, 83–84
  Effectively Connected Income, 61
  Fixed or determinable annual or periodic (FDAP) income, 61
  Individuals, 18, 79
  Treaties, Impact on Rates Applicable to Investment Income, 255
Real estate investment trust (REIT), 30, 74
Real estate mortgage investment conduit (REMIC), 30
Redemption of stock, *see* Corporations and shareholders
Regulated investment company (RIC), 29–30

Residence
Permanent Residence Test, 76
Substantial Presence Test, 76–77

S

S corporations, 29
Sales or exchanges
Reorganizations, *see* Corporations and shareholders
Tax-free exchanges, 13, 75
Transfers of appreciated property to foreign organizations, 132–133
Section 367, 129–143
Branch loss recapture, 133–135
Formation, 138–140
Inbound transactions, 138–140
Intangibles, 135–136
Liquidation, 130, 132, 138–140
Reorganization, 129–133, 135–138
Outbound transfers, 132–133, 135–138, 140–141
Source of income
Cloud computing, 46
Computer program, 46
Deductions, *see* Allocation of deductions
Dividends, 44
Gains from disposition of real property, 46
Gains from sale of personal property, 46–48
Guarantee fees, 49
Income partly from US sources and partly from foreign sources, 47
Insurance Income, 48
Interest, 43–44
Inventory, 47–48
Natural resources, 49
Personal services income, 44–45
Rents and royalties, 45–46
Sale of a partnership interest, 56
Scholarship, 49
Site license, 46
Software, 45
Statute of limitations and penalties, 32–33
Subpart F. *see* Controlled foreign corporations (CFC)

T

Tax returns, 16, 18, 27, 31, 32, 77, 94, 95, 102, 152, 245–246
Tax treaties
Income tax treaties
Arbitration, 262
Disclosure on tax return, 245–246
Capital gains, 81
Competent authority provisions, 261
Exchange of information, 262–263
Foreign tax credit, 258–259
Industrial or commercial profits, 253
Investment income, 255–256
Limitation on benefits, 246–249
Nondiscrimination provisions, 259–261
Objectives, 238–240
Permanent establishment, 251–252
Personal services income
Employees, 256–257
Independent contractors, 257–258
Persons covered, 242–245
Real property, 256
Special Tax Regime "STR", 249–250
Status, 241–242
Taxes covered, 250
Tie breaker, 242–243
Treaty shopping, 246–249
Wealth transfer tax treaties
Business property, 279
Domicile, 278–279
Exemptions and deductions, 280
Relief from double taxation, 280
Objectives, 278
Other property, 279–280
Real property, 279
Rules for taxation, 279

Trade or Business
  Defined, 63
  Effectively Connected, 67–73
  Existence, 63–65
  Location, 65–66
  Real Estate, 65
  Significance, 62–63
Transfer Pricing, 199–201
  Accuracy related penalties, 223–224
  Adjustments, 218–219
  Advanced Pricing Agreements, 221–223
  Arm's length range, 204
  Best method, 202
  Blocked income, 220
  Comparability, 208–209
  Control, 201
  Correlative adjustments, 218
  Cost sharing, 212–215
  Foreign tax credit, 219–220
  General approach, 202–205
  Intangibles, 210–215
  Loans, 216–217
  Methods
    Cost plus, 207–208
    CUP, 206
    CUT, 211–212
    Comparable profits method, 208–209
    Profit split, 209–210
    Resale price, 206–207
  Penalties, 223–224
  Platform Contribution Transaction, 214
  Scope, 201
  Sale of goods, 205–210
  Services, 215–216
  Setoffs, 217
  Treaties, 219
Trusts and estates
  Foreign grantor trusts 93–94
  Foreign trusts
    Classification issues, 91–92
    Taxation of foreign trusts, 92–93
  Taxation of foreign beneficiaries, 93

U

US 'trade or business'
  Existence of a trade or business, 63–65
  Location of a trade or business in the US, 65–66
  Transactions on the Internet, 65

W

Wealth transfer taxation
  Estate tax
    Adjusted taxable gifts, 267
    Deductions, 266–267
    Expatriation to avoid tax, 276–278
    Foreign tax credit, 273–274
    Gross estate, 266
    Jurisdictional principles, 270–271
    Nonresident aliens, 274–275
    Rates, 267
    Resident aliens, 273–274
    Situs rules, 271–272
    Taxable estate, 266–268, 274
    Tentative estate tax, 267, 268
    Treaties, *see* Tax treaties
    Unified transfer tax credit, 268
  Generation-skipping tax, 269–270, 275–276
  Gift tax
    Deductions, 268
    Expatriation to avoid tax, 277–278
    Nonresident aliens, 275
    Rates of tax, 268
    Resident aliens, 275
    Situs rules, 271–272
    Taxable gifts, 265, 268
    Treaties, *see* Tax treaties
    Unified transfer tax credit, 268
Withholding at source
  Disposition of US real property interests, 96–97
  Fixed or determinable income, 95–96
  Foreign Account Tax Compliance Act (FATCA), 98–99
Withholding on foreign partners, 97